THE LIMITS OF ORTHODOX THEOLOGY

THE LITTMAN LIBRARY OF
JEWISH CIVILIZATION

Dedicated to the memory of
LOUIS THOMAS SIDNEY LITTMAN
*who founded the Littman Library for the love of God
and as an act of charity in memory of his father*
JOSEPH AARON LITTMAN
and to the memory of
ROBERT JOSEPH LITTMAN
who continued what his father Louis had begun
יהא זכרם ברוך

*'Get wisdom, get understanding:
Forsake her not and she shall preserve thee'*
PROV. 4:5

The Littman Library of Jewish Civilization is a registered UK charity
Registered charity no. 1000784

The Limits of Orthodox Theology

&

Maimonides' Thirteen Principles Reappraised

&

MARC B. SHAPIRO

London

The Littman Library of Jewish Civilization

in association with Liverpool University Press

The Littman Library of Jewish Civilization
Registered office: 4th floor, 7–10 Chandos Street, London WIG 9DQ

in association with Liverpool University Press
4 Cambridge Street, Liverpool L69 7ZU, UK
www.liverpooluniversitypress.co.uk/littman

Managing Editor: Connie Webber

Distributed in North America by
Oxford University Press Inc., 198 Madison Avenue
New York, NY 10016, USA

First published 2004
Reprinted, with corrections, 2005
First published in paperback, with corrections, 2011
Paperback reprinted 2015

Catalogue records for this book are available from the
British Library and the Library of Congress

ISBN 978-1-906764-23-4

Publishing co-ordinator: Janet Moth
Copy-editing: Lindsey Taylor-Guthartz
Proof-reading: Philippa Claiden
Index: Peter Andrews
Designed by Pete Russell, Faringdon, Oxon.

Printed and bound in Great Britain by
CPI Group (UK) Ltd., Croydon, CR0 4YY

To Lauren

❧

'*Set me as a seal upon thy heart*'
SONG OF SONGS 8: 6

❧

Preface

A s will be explained in the introduction in Chapter 1, this book grew from an article I wrote some years ago. In the intervening period, many people were kind enough to share their comments with me, for which I thank them all. In particular, I would like to thank Yisrael Dubitsky and Zalman Alpert, librarians at the Jewish Theological Seminary of America and Yeshiva University, who were most helpful throughout the writing of this book. I must also thank Professor Zev Harvey, who very patiently answered my numerous queries about the most arcane points of Maimonidean philosophy. Finally, I must express my appreciation to an outstanding scholar who wishes to remain anonymous and who was always generous with his time and knowledge. For financial support, I thank the Lucius N. Littauer Foundation and the University of Scranton.

My parents and in-laws have been incredibly supportive throughout the writing of this book. The same is true for my wife, Lauren. While actively pursuing her own successful career and taking care of our family, she has selflessly enabled me to devote myself to scholarly pursuits. I could not have wished for a better partner in life. My children, Aliza, Yael, Danielle, and Joshua continually bring joy to my life. My greatest pride remains watching them grow up.

Contents

🔊

Note on Transliteration and Conventions Used in the Text

ॐ

THE transliteration of Hebrew in this book reflects consideration of the type of book it is, in terms of its content, purpose, and readership. The system adopted therefore reflects a broad approach to transcription, rather than the narrower approaches found in the *Encyclopaedia Judaica* or other systems developed for text-based or linguistic studies. The aim has been to reflect the pronunciation prescribed for modern Hebrew, rather than the spelling or Hebrew word structure, and to do so using conventions that are generally familiar to the English-speaking Jewish reader.

In accordance with this approach, no attempt is made to indicate the distinctions between *alef* and *ayin*, *tet* and *taf*, *kaf* and *kuf*, *sin* and *samekh*, since these are not relevant to pronunciation; likewise, the *dagesh* is not indicated except where it affects pronunciation. Following the principle of using conventions familiar to the majority of readers, however, transcriptions that are well established have been retained even when they are not fully consistent with the transliteration system adopted. On similar grounds, the *tsadi* is rendered by 'tz' in such familiar words as barmitzvah, mitzvot, and so on. Likewise, the distinction between *ḥet* and *khaf* has been retained, using *ḥ* for the former and *kh* for the latter; the associated forms are generally familiar to readers, even if the distinction is not actually borne out in pronunciation, and for the same reason the final *heh* is indicated too. As in Hebrew, no capital letters are used, except that an initial capital has been retained in transliterating titles of published works (for example, *Shulḥan arukh*).

Since no distinction is made between *alef* and *ayin*, they are indicated by an apostrophe only in intervocalic positions where a failure to do so could lead an English-speaking reader to pronounce the vowel-cluster as a diphthong—as, for example, in *ha'ir*—or otherwise mispronounce the word.

The *sheva na* is indicated by an *e*—*perikat ol*, *reshut*—except, again, when established convention dictates otherwise.

The *yod* is represented by *i* when it occurs as a vowel (*bereshit*), by *y* when it occurs as a consonant (*yesodot*), and by *yi* when it occurs as both (*yisra'el*).

Names have generally been left in their familiar forms, even when this is inconsistent with the overall system.

Thanks are due to Jonathan Webber of Birmingham University for his help in elucidating the principles to be adopted.

ॐ

The abbreviation R. (for 'Rabbi') before a name is used to designate those scholars whom I regard as traditional authority figures, who are the focus of this book. When dealing with pre-modern scholars about whom we have no information other than their works, I have placed an R. before the name, as there is no reason to assume that they were not part of the traditional community.

References to Maimonides' *Guide* and to other classic works (such as *Emunot vede'ot*, *Kuzari*, *Sefer ha'ikarim*, *Pardes rimonim*) are to volume and chapter.

Although I have made use of the standard translations (especially Pines' translation of the *Guide*), I have not hesitated to make changes where it appeared they were warranted.

Abbreviations

CCAR   Central Conference of American Rabbis
EJ   Encyclopaedia Judaica
HTR   Harvard Theological Review
HUCA   Hebrew Union College Annual
JJS   Journal of Jewish Studies
JQR   Jewish Quarterly Review
JSQ   Jewish Studies Quarterly
MGWJ   Monatsschrift für Geschichte und Wissenschaft des Judentums
PAAJR   Proceedings of the American Academy of Jewish Research
REJ   Revue des Études Juives
TUMJ   Torah u-Madda Journal

ONE

Introduction

☙

I FIRST BEGAN exploring the subject of this book a number of years ago after reading an article by R. Yehudah Parnes in the *Torah u-Madda Journal*, published by Yeshiva University. In this article Parnes argued that as far as Orthodox Judaism is concerned, heresy is defined by the Thirteen Principles of Maimonides (Moses ben Maimon, 1138–1204), which appear in his *Commentary on the Mishnah* (*Sanhedrin*, introduction to chapter 10). Parnes further asserted that one is forbidden to study anything that disagrees with these Principles, since it is *ipso facto* heresy.[1]

Although I had never before read such a sharp formulation of the issue, Parnes' point made logical sense. If it is true—and most people seem to think so—that Maimonides' Thirteen Principles are the Orthodox catechism, then Parnes is correct in saying that any writer disagreeing with the Principles would be advocating a heretical position. The second stage of his argument relies on the notion, widely accepted in the Orthodox world, that one is forbidden to study heresy. Thus, the equation is complete:

A   (anything in dispute with Maimonides' Principles is heresy)

+

B   (it is forbidden to study heresy)

=

C   (it is forbidden to study anything that does not conform to
     Maimonides' Principles)

However, despite its apparent logical structure, Parnes' argument was without historical precedent, since it would mean that much of Jewish literature of the most traditional variety, including portions of the Talmud, Zohar, *rishonim* (early authorities), and *aḥaronim* (later authorities) were forbidden reading, since they disagreed with aspects of Maimonides' theological formulations in the Principles.[2] Although the majority of traditional scholars, including the most right-wing among them, would certainly not go as far as Parnes, the underlying assumption that the Thirteen Principles are the

---

[1] Parnes, 'Torah u-Madda'.

[2] After I called attention to this fact in a short letter to the editor, Parnes reaffirmed his view. See *TUMJ* 3 (1991–2), 155–6.

bedrock of Orthodoxy has never been openly challenged in modern times by those who identify with Orthodoxy. Indeed, the most influential assault on the veracity of the Thirteen Principles is Louis Jacobs's *Principles of the Jewish Faith*,[3] and this book was written in part as an explanation of why he could no longer regard himself as Orthodox. That is, for Jacobs, Orthodoxy is essentially viewed as identical with the Thirteen Principles. This is so despite the fact that many post-Maimonidean scholars, continuing into modern times and including those with impeccable 'Orthodox' credentials, have never felt entirely bound by the Principles.

It was this realization which led me to explore the history of the acceptance of Maimonides' Principles, and the first fruits of this research, an article entitled 'Maimonides' Thirteen Principles: The Last Word in Jewish Theology?', appeared in the same journal that had published Parnes' earlier piece.[4] This article, written under the pressure of time constraints, accomplished its purpose which, as indicated by its title, was to show that traditional Jewish theology has allowed for much more latitude than found in the Thirteen Principles. As a result, many outstanding sages did not regard the Thirteen Principles as the last word in Jewish theology. Indeed, there is a history of opposition to Maimonides' Principles among the ranks of traditional, or as it is called in modern times, Orthodox Judaism.

What is fascinating is that this opposition exists together with widespread assertions that the Thirteen Principles are the defining features of Judaism. As a method of shorthand, the Principles are indeed a very good way of expressing the fundamentals of Judaism as understood by most Jews until the rise of the Reform movement. However, as with most shorthand formulations, while correct in many essentials, they are not correct in their entirety. A good parallel to this is the popular expression that a righteous person observes all 613 (*taryag*) commandments, an expression also mentioned by Maimonides.[5] This catchphrase is even used with reference to the patriarch Jacob, who lived long before the giving of the Torah.[6] Of course, as everyone is well aware, it is impossible for any individual to observe 'all *taryag mitsvot*', but this does not take away from the power of the idea behind the phrase.

The nature of this subject is such that by the time the original article appeared, I had already assembled enough information to enlarge it signifi -

---

[3] New York, 1964.   [4] *TUMJ* 4 (1993), 187–242.

[5] See *Letters*, ed. Shailat, i. 53; *Letters*, ed. Kafih, 118 n. 85.

[6] Genesis 32: 5 reads: עם לבן גרתי, 'I have lodged with Laban.' Playing upon the letters of the word גרתי, there is an *agadah* that puts the following into Jacob's mouth: 'Though I have lodged (גרתי) with Laban, I have observed the 613 (תרי"ג) commandments.' See Rashi ad loc. For the textual issues concerning this comment of Rashi, which actually appears to be a later interpolation, see M. Kasher, *Torah shelemah*, *ad loc.* and the Ariel edition of Rashi (Jerusalem, 1988), ad loc.

cantly. Since then the material has continued to accumulate, until I felt it was time to put it all into book form. Hardly a week goes by without my coming across more sources that bolster the book's conclusion, leading to the realization that a delay in publication would have produced an even more complete book. However, since such a concern would have prevented the book from ever seeing the light of day, I thought it was better to adopt Hillel's maxim, 'If not now, when?' (Mishnah *Avot* 1: 14). I realize that some readers of this book might be put off by its somewhat encyclopedic nature, but no other approach seemed to be capable of proving my point. I also recognize that the numerous sources I have gathered will become a reference tool for many, although I hope that the interpretations I have offered will also be given due regard.

Anyone thinking about Maimonides' Thirteen Principles should be struck by the irony of it all, in that just as Maimonides' halakhic masterpiece, the *Mishneh torah*, did not put an end to traditional talmudic dialectics and confusion about the law but instead led to even more disputes, so too Maimonides' formulation of the Principles did not put an end to discussion regarding the fundamentals of Judaism, but rather propelled later thinkers into new discussions on the very topic which Maimonides thought he had closed. However, in spite of all the discussions and disagreements with Maimonides, the rhetorical acceptance of the Principles could not be avoided. This acceptance is illustrated by the popularity of the *Yigdal* hymn and the *Ani ma'amin* catechism. To be sure, these popularizations carry on the spirit of Maimonides' ideas, yet they also vulgarize, and at times distort, a philosophically sophisticated text. It was this vulgarization which received widespread rhetorical acceptance. As Menachem Kellner has noted, 'Not only were Maimonides' principles accepted without the theological substrate which gave them coherence and which made of them something more than an elegant literary device for teaching Jewish ideas; they were not even accepted in the form in which Maimonides presented them, but, rather, in a simplified, even debased fashion.'[7]

Maimonides and Dogma

Kellner, in his justly praised *Dogma in Medieval Jewish Thought*,[8] has already demonstrated the all-pervasive influence of Maimonides' Thirteen Principles in late medieval times. Maimonides' formulation assumed such significance that all the post-Maimonidean dogmatists were forced to confront it. Kellner

---

[7] *Must a Jew Believe Anything?*, 69.   [8] Oxford, 1986.

also points out the interesting fact that the Principles, and dogma as a whole, were not given extended treatment in the two centuries after Maimonides, and that it was only in the fifteenth century that scholars began to concentrate on issues of dogma. It was then, in response to Christian polemics, that thinkers first commented in detail on Maimonides' formulation. Before Kellner, Louis Jacobs wrote his now classic *Principles of the Jewish Faith*, which provides a valuable elucidation of the text itself, in addition to examining the Principles from a modern philosophical and scholarly outlook.

My goal is not to continue Kellner's treatment into more modern times, nor to expand Jacobs' discussion. Rather, I will concentrate on those aspects of the Principles which did not receive unqualified acceptance, and, in doing so, will probe the outer limits of Orthodox theology. Although Jacobs dealt with this topic to some extent, and I freely acknowledge my debt to him in this regard, it still demands a systematic and comprehensive treatment, which I attempt to offer in this book. To be sure, there are times when I depart from these narrow confines and elucidate aspects of the Principles themselves. I do so when the context requires it and when I believe that I can offer an original contribution. However, throughout the book I assume that the reader already has an understanding of the Principles. Those who do not are well advised to study the books of Kellner and Jacobs before tackling this one.

The Thirteen Principles are a very conservative document, yet the sources discussed by Kellner focus overwhelmingly on disagreements with Maimonides over whether certain Principles are actually 'roots' of Judaism—an entirely semantic issue—rather than with the correctness of Maimonides' fundamental theological views. As Kellner puts it, 'the plethora of competing systems reflects not conflicting views of the nature of Judaism, but a dispute concerning the nature of dogmas or principles of faith.'[9] For the scholars on whom Kellner concentrates, Maimonides' thirteen tenets are correct, even if many of them do not qualify as 'principles'—that is, as theological positions upon which Judaism stands or falls. My concern, in contrast, is with those scholars who thought that Maimonides' Principles were wrong, pure and simple.

With regard to the question of how far back Jewish dogmatics can be traced, Kellner has argued that Maimonides was rabbinic Judaism's first true dogmatist.[10] However, this is incorrect, for R. Sa'adiah Gaon (882–942), rabbinic Judaism's first great philosopher, had himself posited principles of faith. Nevertheless, this list of principles had no influence on subsequent

---

[9] *Dogma*, 1.

[10] Kellner (ibid.) calls attention to the principles of biblical faith of Philo, but as he notes, Philo did not operate within the context of rabbinic Judaism.

generations, and indeed was unknown until modern times, presumably because it was written in Arabic and did not appear in R. Sa'adiah's *magnum opus, Emunot vede'ot*.[11]

Kellner himself notes that R. Hananel ben Hushiel of Kairouan (c.975–1057) anticipated Maimonides in saying that certain beliefs are necessary to merit the world to come.[12] However, as Kellner points out, Maimonides goes further than R. Hananel, and R. Sa'adiah as well, by saying that acceptance of his Principles are also a *sufficient* condition for attaining paradise.[13] That is, Maimonides holds that one can commit every possible sin, but as long as the sinner accepts the Principles and his sins are not part of a rebellion against God, he will receive a share in the world to come. Such a man is regarded as a 'sinner in Israel', and one must love him and show him compassion.[14] By the same token, Maimonides states that not only one who denies, but even one who harbours so much as a doubt about any of the Principles is a heretic who has removed himself from the Jewish people. Other Jews are in turn obligated to hate and destroy him.[15] The fact that this 'heretic' may be a punctilious observer of *mitsvot* is irrelevant according to Maimonides.[16] Contrary to Kellner, these latter points need not be included in a definition of dogma, and there is thus no question that R. Hananel should also be regarded as a dogmatist. As with R. Sa'adiah, R. Hananel's dogmas had no influence on subsequent thinkers and were not even published until the nineteenth century.

[11] See his *Commentary on Psalms*, 82 n.; Ben-Shamai, 'Sa'adiah', 11–26. As Ben-Shamai shows, principles of faith are also found in R. Sa'adiah's other works, including *Emunot vede'ot*, but they are not numbered or listed together as a catechism.   [12] *Commentary*, 28.   [13] *Dogma*, 8.

[14] Since Abarbanel, *Rosh amanah*, ch. 23, S. Luria, 'Hanhagat maharshal', 326, and a number of modern scholars (see Kellner, *Dogma*, 35) have argued that Maimonides was influenced in his approach to dogma by early Islamic theologians, it is worth noting the similarity of his position to that of al-Ghazali, who also argued that 'not a single one of the faithful will abide eternally in the fire of hell. One who has in one's heart the weight of a single grain of faith will be brought out of it.' See the excerpt published in Williams, *Word*, 162–3. Although the Kharijites and Mutazilites disagreed, this was the Orthodox Muslim position. See Wensinck, *Muslim Creed*, 45–9, 61–2, 103–4, 125, 130, 180–2, 192.

[15] See R. Samuel David Luzzatto's criticism of Maimonides in this regard, in id., *Letters*, iv. 599. Lamm, 'Loving', 150 ff., argues that in his later works Maimonides somewhat softened his harsh stance towards heretics: 'At the very least, there is enough material in his halakhic code to support the contention that he was no longer as certain then that heresy leads to exclusion from the Jewish people as he was when he wrote the *Commentary to the Mishnah*' (pp. 156–7).

[16] *Commentary on the Mishnah*, iv, *San.* 10: 1, p. 145 (all future references will be to this edition). See also *Mishneh torah*, 'Hilkhot rotse'aḥ' 13: 14. R. Joseph Albo, *Sefer ha'ikarim*, i. 1, understands Maimonides to be saying that one who does not consider his Principles to be just that, namely basic principles of the faith, is also a heretic. In *Sefer ha'ikarim*, i. 1–2 Albo proceeds to refute this position, while concluding nonetheless that such a person is a sinner. In truth, Maimonides says nothing of the kind attributed to him by Albo. What is important for Maimonides is whether or not one accepts his Principles. In his view, one who accepts them but nevertheless believes that they are not basic to Judaism is neither a heretic nor a sinner.

Thus, even though Maimonides can no longer be regarded as the first Jewish dogmatist, he is certainly the first dogmatist of any lasting influence.

As noted above, Maimonides' Thirteen Principles appeared in his first major work, his *Commentary on the Mishnah*, which was designed to be a popular work and was written in Arabic. Nevertheless, it is significant that Maimonides himself in his later years, even in his 'exoteric' works, did not feel bound to them in the way that later became the norm in Jewish history. From what is known of the subsequent history of the Thirteen Principles, one would have expected Maimonides to put great emphasis on them, quoting them in his later works and letters—but this is hardly the case. Although Maimonides revised the text of the Principles later in life, as he indeed revised his entire *Commentary on the Mishnah*, he refers only once to the Principles as fundamentals of Jewish faith.[17] Even here the Thirteen Principles are not set apart as being fundamentally more significant than the rest of the *Commentary on the Mishnah* or the *Mishneh torah*. He writes:

When I learned of these exceedingly deficient folk and their doubts, who, although they consider themselves sages in Israel, are in fact the most ignorant, and more seriously astray than beasts. . . . I concluded that it was necessary that I clearly elucidate religious fundamentals in my works on law . . . I therefore published principles that need to be acknowledged in the introduction to the *Commentary on the Mishnah* regarding prophecy and the roots of tradition and what every Rabbanite had to believe concerning the Oral Law. In chapter 10 of *Sanhedrin* I expounded fundamentals connected with the beginning and the end, i.e. what pertains to God's unity and the world to come and the other tenets of the Torah. I acted the same way in my major work, which I called *Mishneh Torah*.[18]

On the other occasions on which Maimonides makes reference to the Principles, it is only with regard to specific points discussed there. For example, in *Guide* ii. 35 Maimonides notes that he explained the nature of Moses' prophecy in the *Commentary on the Mishnah* (where the Principles appear). Another example is found in a responsum where he refers to his discussion of the Eighth Principle, concerning the equal sanctity of all parts of the Pentateuch.[19] Certainly, had Maimonides continued to regard the Thirteen Principles as the essence of Judaism one would expect more than this.[20]

In his great code of Jewish law, the *Mishneh torah*, which also defines heresy and what Jews are obligated to believe, Maimonides does not list the Thirteen Principles as a unit. To be sure, all of the Principles, with the

---

[17] *Essay on Resurrection*, in *Letters*, ed. Shailat, i. 320 (Arabic), 342 (Hebrew).

[18] Translation in Halkin and Hartman, *Crisis*, 212–13.   [19] *Responsa*, ii, no. 263.

[20] As Kellner, *Dogma*, 236 n. 181, points out, in one of his medical works he makes reference to a composition on the 'principles of religion', but this could just as easily refer to the *Guide*. Kellner also refers to the almost certainly apocryphal *Ma'amar hayihud* as making reference to the Principles.

addition of some others, are to be found in this work, scattered in a few different places.[21] Yet if he had regarded the Thirteen Principles as his final statement on the fundamentals of Jewish faith, one would have expected them to be listed at the very beginning of his code, in the section entitled 'Hilkhot yesodei hatorah' (Laws of the Foundations of the Torah). Furthermore, not all of the *details* of the Thirteen Principles are repeated in the *Mishneh torah*. Presumably, Maimonides would be surprised that in seeking to define the essentials of Judaism, later generations of Jews, both scholars and masses, had latched onto his earlier work rather than his more detailed formulation in the *Mishneh torah*.

Finally, remembering that Maimonides stated that belief in the Thirteen Principles is essential to being a Jew, one must wonder why there is no mention of the Principles in his discussion of what a future convert should be taught about the religion. While it is common today for prospective Orthodox converts to be instructed in the Principles, all that Maimonides himself writes about theology and converts is the following: 'He should then be made acquainted with the principles of the faith, which are the oneness of God and the prohibition of idolatry.'[22] This limited theological instruction is itself significant, since the Talmud has nothing of the kind, mentioning only that a convert is instructed in 'some of the less weighty and some of the more weighty commandments'.[23] As Maimonides was adding to the talmudic prescription, why did he not add the other Principles, especially the Third Principle, that of divine incorporeality?

In the *Guide* there is also no listing of the Principles. Seeking to explain this omission, R. Isaac Abarbanel (1437–1508) writes: 'He postulated the Principles for the masses, and for beginners in the study of Mishnah, but not for those individuals who plumbed the knowledge of truth, for whom he wrote the *Guide*.'[24] In Abarbanel's mind, only limited attention should therefore be paid to Maimonides' early formulation of dogma, and it would certainly be improper to make conclusions about his theological views on the basis of a text designed for beginners.

Even if one does not accept Abarbanel's understanding of Maimonides' purpose in writing the Principles, the question still remains: why is there no place in the *Mishneh torah* and the *Guide* where all the Principles are listed? It certainly seems that Maimonides was not as closely tied to his youthful

---

[21] See ibid. 228 n. 60.   [22] *Mishneh torah*, 'Hilkhot isurei biah', 14: 2.

[23] BT *Yev.* 47a. See Twersky, *Introduction*, 474–5.

[24] *Rosh amanah*, ch. 23. See also ibid., ch. 9. See the similar formulation of R. Gedaliah b. Solomon Lipschuetz in his commentary on Albo's *Sefer ha'ikarim*, i. 3: 'He enumerated them [the Principles] for the benefit of the masses in order to strengthen their belief in the Torah.' See also ibid. iii. 18. However, the conclusion R. Gedaliah draws from this is quite different from that of Abarbanel.

formulation of the Principles as is often assumed. This would make the Principles one of a number of examples where one finds different emphases, if not outright contradictions, between what Maimonides writes in his *Commentary on the Mishnah* and what appears in his later works. In fact, this very suggestion has already been proposed by two rabbinic scholars, R. Joseph Schwartz (1804–65)[25] and R. Shelomoh Goren (1917–96),[26] both of whom called attention to the fact that Maimonides did not include the Principles in his later works, in particular in the *Mishneh torah*, where he presents his various categories of heresy. To their minds this indicates that he abandoned his earlier system of Thirteen Principles.

As far as Maimonides' *Mishneh torah* is concerned, it is also important to note that the definition of a heretic in this work differs from that in the *Commentary on the Mishnah*. In the section 'Hilkhot yesodei hatorah' Maimonides does indeed discuss most of the Principles as part of his overall exposition of Jewish theology. If all we had was 'Hilkhot yesodei hatorah' we would probably assume that the *Mishneh torah* shares the perspective of the *Commentary on the Mishnah*, and that lack of belief in any of the Principles makes one a heretic. However, when it is time to define the parameters of heresy for which one loses one's share in the world to come, Maimonides' formulation in the *Mishneh torah* reads: 'Five individuals are described as *minim*: 1. One who *says* there is no God or ruler of the world; 2. One who *says* that there is a ruler but that there are two or more', and so forth ('Hilkhot teshuvah' 3: 7–8). Maimonides also follows this model in defining an *epikoros* and a *kofer batorah* (two other types of heretic).[27] In other words, according to this text it is essential that one's heresy be stated publicly. Apparently, one who has heretical thoughts but conducts himself as a good Jew does not lose his share in the world to come.[28]

To be sure, in the *Mishneh torah* Maimonides warns people to keep away from heretical thoughts, which can lead to spiritual destruction. Citing

---

[25] *Divrei yosef*, iii–iv, no. 57.

[26] *Torat hashabat*, 570. Goren even suggests that Maimonides retreated from his Thirteen Principles in favour of a conception of Jewish theology later advocated by Abarbanel. As we shall see, Abarbanel argued that one cannot distinguish between so-called principles of Judaism and other aspects of the religion, since all must be regarded as equal.

[27] For his own conceptual reasons, which have no talmudic basis, Maimonides distinguishes between the *epikoros*, the *min*, and the *kofer batorah*. This is only a technical differentiation since all of these people are guilty of a form of heresy and lose their share in the world to come. See *Mishneh torah*, 'Hilkhot teshuvah', 3: 6–8, and Rabinovitch, *Yad peshutah*, ad loc. At times, the distinctions between the terms break down and they can be seen as synonymous. For example, in 'Hilkhot teshuvah', 3: 8 Maimonides defines a *kofer batorah* as one who says that the Torah is not from Heaven. However, in his *Responsa*, ii, no. 263 (based on BT *Berakhot* 12*a*), he refers to this person as a *min*. See Kellner, *Dogma*, 20–1; Shailat's note in *Letters*, i. 37–9; Shloush, *Ḥemdah genuzah*, ii. 115.

[28] Cf. Nissim b. Moses, *Ma'aseh nisim*, 159–60.

Numbers 15: 39, he even regards this as a negative commandment. Yet although he comes close in this halakhic formulation, he never actually states that entertaining the thought *alone* makes one a heretic with no share in the world to come.[29] Similarly, Maimonides writes: 'Whoever permits the thought to enter his mind that there is another deity besides this God violates a prohibition, as it is said, *You shall have no other gods before Me* (Exod. 20: 3, Deut. 5: 7), and denies the essence of religion—this doctrine being the great principle on which everything depends.'[30] However, once again, Maimonides does not say that such a person is a heretic. He has violated a commandment and has, *in his mind*, denied the essence of Judaism, but as long as his heresy is not publicly voiced he apparently remains a (sinning) Jew in good standing.

R. Hayim Hirschensohn (1857–1935), a liberal halakhist of the last century, particularly stressed this point, expanding upon it in a way that goes beyond anything Maimonides wrote in the *Mishneh torah*.[31] According to Hirschensohn, someone who merely thinks heretical thoughts is absolutely blameless, for one does not have control over one's thoughts. In support of this assumption, he cites R. Asher ben Jehiel (*c*.1250–1327),[32] who put forth an innovative understanding of the talmudic statement that, in contrast to other sins, when it comes to idolatry there is punishment for mere intention.[33] According to R. Asher, all this means is that, if you worship an idol, God combines your intention before the act together with the act itself. However, if you do not worship the idol, then your thoughts remain no more than thoughts. According to Hirschensohn, this is a proof that simply having a heretical thought, in this case that idols have power, does not make you a heretic unless you actually concretize this heresy in the real world.

Hirschensohn also offers his own distinction between publicly voicing one's heresy and attempting to influence others to follow in one's path. According to him, it is only the latter which causes one to lose one's share in the world to come, as well as to be punished by an earthly court. The lone heretic, even if his heresy is publicly voiced, is left to God, who can punish him as He sees fit. However, such a person does not lose his share in the world to come. Hirschensohn thus denies Jewish courts the role of inquisitor, except when the innocent population is put at spiritual risk.

[29] 'Hilkhot avodah zarah', 2: 3.
[30] 'Hilkhot yesodei hatorah', 1: 6. See also 'Hilkhot melakhim', 11: 1, 'Hilkhot ishut', 8:5, and *Sefer hamitsvot*, Negative Commandments, nos. 1 and 47.
[31] See his comments in *Hamisderonah*, 1 (1885), 188–9, 233, 240–3; id., *Malki bakodesh*, ii. 168, 170. See similarly S. D. Luzzatto, *Yesodei hatorah*, 70–9.
[32] *RH* 1: 6 (36*b* in the Vilna edition). For Maimonides' view of this passage, see 'Hilkhot ishut', 8: 5.
[33] BT *Kid.* 40*a*.

Hirschensohn himself notes that his point about humans being unable to control their thoughts was also the opinion of a leading medieval philosopher, R. Hasdai Crescas (died *c*.1412). Crescas was adamant that beliefs are always involuntary, as one cannot force oneself to disbelieve that which one believes. Contrary to Maimonides, according to Crescas there can thus be no reward or punishment for belief. If someone, for whatever reason, does not believe in one of Maimonides' dogmas, he cannot be held culpable for this disbelief. What, then, does Crescas do with the notion, found throughout rabbinic literature, that a heretic is punished in the afterlife? In very original fashion, Crescas argues that, while one is not punished for disbelief, he is punished for the joy he feels through this disbelief as well as for the lack of effort made to discover the truth. Similarly, and again contrary to Maimonides, 'one is not rewarded for belief, but for the effort [*hishtadlut*] to apprehend the truth of the belief',[34] and for the joy that accompanies this.[35]

To return to the Thirteen Principles: not only does Maimonides require one to affirm them without any doubt, but he also leaves no room for honest error, a point concerning which there was a good deal of debate in medieval times, with R. Simeon ben Tsemah Duran (1361–1444)[36] and R. Joseph Albo (fifteenth century)[37] emerging as Maimonides' great critics.[38] According to them, even one who disagrees with a basic Jewish doctrine is not regarded as a heretic, if his error arose as a result of well-intentioned study. R. David ibn Zimra (1479–1573) goes so far as to include in this category one who thinks it reflects positively on Moses that some of the ancients thought he was God.[39] These opponents of Maimonides thus made it very difficult to condemn someone as a heretic, as long as the person in question was known to be a committed Jew who erred unintentionally.

Approaching matters from a different angle, R. Abraham Isaac Kook (1865–1935) also differed with Maimonides. While, as noted above, Maimonides does not leave any room for the honest doubter, Kook specifically excludes such a person from being categorized as a heretic. In a passage that deserves to be quoted at length, Kook writes:

Know that, as far as the halakhah is concerned, it is absolutely forbidden and a festering sore for one even to cast a doubt concerning the truth of the content of our

---

[34] W. Z. Harvey, *Physics*, 145–6.

[35] See Crescas, *Or hashem*, ii. 5: 5. According to Harvey, the upshot of Crescas' view is that 'it is better to be a spiritually tormented infidel than an apathetic, passionless believer' (*Physics*, 146). R. Obadiah Sforno also claims that one does not have control over one's thoughts, and that therefore there are no biblical commands 'to believe'. See Sforno, *Kitvei*, 411–12, 418.

[36] *Ohev mishpat*, 15a. Duran excludes from his defence one who rejects the 'roots' of the religion, for instance by believing in two gods.   [37] *Sefer ha'ikarim*, i. 2.

[38] See Kellner, 'What is Heresy?', 55–70; id., 'Inadvertent Heresy', 393–403; id., 'Heresy'.

[39] *She'elot uteshuvot haradbaz*, no. 1258.

perfect faith. However, we do not find our Sages deeming such individuals heretics. Only one who definitely denies, that is, who decides that the very opposite of our faith is true, is included in this category. A categorical denial cannot possibly be found in Israel except in one who is completely wicked and an intentional liar, for the greatest wickedness can only sow doubt in the minds of the weak. One who is brazen enough to say that he is a complete denier is thus certainly wicked . . . and he cannot claim that he has no control over his thoughts. If the heresy in our generation was honest it would always be in a position of doubt, and its doubts could be easily clarified. However, it intentionally falsifies and claims certainty in its denial, even though those weakest in faith can only arrive at a level of doubt.[40]

Kook's recognition that doubt is part of the religious struggle, and his consequent refusal to label the doubter a heretic, is in direct contradiction to Maimonides. He does not stand alone in this view, however. R. Nahman of Bratslav (1772–1810) stated: 'It is entirely proper that objections can be found to God. It is right and suitable that this should be so because of God's greatness and exaltedness. Since in His exaltedness He is so far above our minds there are bound to be objections to Him.'[41] Concluding a wide-ranging analysis on the subject of doubt in the religious experience, the contemporary Modern Orthodox leader R. Norman Lamm wrote: 'We found that there is place for doubt within the confines of cognitive faith; it must not be allowed to interfere with normative halakhic practice, which is the expression of functional faith.'[42] In this regard, it is also worth quoting the following story, immortalized by Martin Buber.

Once when Rabbi Noah [of Lekhovitz] was in his room, he heard how one of his disciples began to recite the Principles of Faith in the House of Study next door, but stopping immediately after the words 'I believe with perfect faith,' whispered to himself: 'I don't understand that!' and then once more: 'I don't understand that.' The zaddik left his room and went to the House of Study.

'What is it you do not understand?' he asked.

'I don't understand what it's all about,' said the man. 'I say "I believe." If I really do believe, then how can I possibly sin? But if I do not really believe, why am I telling lies?'

'It means', answered the rabbi, 'that the words "I believe" are a prayer, meaning "Oh, that I may believe!"' Then the hasid was suffused with a glow from within. 'That is right!' he cried. 'That is right! Oh, that I may believe, Lord of the world, oh, that I may believe!'[43]

Maimonides, however, had a very different view. According to him, one who does not believe in his Principles, or even doubts one of them, is a

[40] *Igerot hare'iyah*, i. 20–1.

[41] *Likutei moharan*, 2nd ser., no. 52, trans. in Jacobs, *Beyond Reasonable Doubt*, 24.

[42] *Faith and Doubt*, 30.   [43] *Tales*, ii. 158.

heretic, and it makes no difference if the heretic knows no better (e.g. if he has been taught to think in this way from his youth). It is true that in his later works Maimonides counsels tolerance when dealing with Karaites who do not realize that they are heretics,[44] but there he is only concerned with how Jews are supposed to relate to them. That is, rather than hating them and hoping for their destruction, which is normally the case with regard to heretics, one should treat them with friendship and respect and attempt to convince them to abandon their errant ways. From a theological perspective, however, a heretic is doomed to eternal perdition and cannot be exculpated on the basis of the argument that he did not know any better.[45]

To be sure, Maimonides' position has found its modern defenders, and in a famous rhetorical flourish R. Hayim Soloveitchik (1853–1918) proclaimed that a 'heretic, *nebich*, is still a heretic'.[46] That is, it is unfortunate that he is a heretic and condemned to hell, but what can one do—this is the way of the world. Yet Orthodoxy as a whole, both ultra-Orthodox and Modern Orthodox, has not accepted Maimonides' judgement in this regard. One must search long and hard to find a contemporary Orthodox writer who asserts that a non-religious Jew who doesn't know any better is damned.

Why did Maimonides adopt this uncompromising view that unintentional heresy prevents one from attaining the world to come? The answer is found in his understanding of how one attains immortality, which for him is not a 'reward' bestowed by God. Rather, as with prophecy, it is a natural process that depends on the perfection of one's intellect so that one can apprehend the Creator and the various intelligibles. It is this knowledge which gives one immortality. If one were to hold a heretical opinion,[47] for whatever reason, this acts as a block on the intellect's move towards perfection.[48] In trying to

[44] Maimonides' later edition of his commentary on Mishnah *Ḥulin* 1: 2 (see J. Kafiḥ's edition, ad loc., n. 33); *Mishneh torah*, 'Hilkhot mamrim', 3: 3; *Responsa*, no. 449.

[45] See R. Isaac Ze'ev Soloveitchik, quoted in Sternbuch, *Teshuvot vehanhagot*, 452.

[46] Wasserman, *Kovets ma'amarim*, 19; Gerlits (ed.), *Hagadah*, 175. For elaboration of Soloveitchik's view, see Schulzinger, *Mishmar halevi: Ḥagigah*, unpaginated letter at the end of the book (called to my attention by Rabbi Chaim Rapoport).

[47] According to his formulation in the Thirteen Principles, denial, or even doubt, about any of the Principles causes one to lose his share in the world to come. However, from a Maimonidean philosophical perspective, it is only denial of one of the first five Principles that causes one to be excluded from the world to come. Denial of the other eight only leads to exclusion from the community of Israel. See Kellner, *Dogma*, 34–49; id., *Must a Jew Believe Anything?*, 83–6. See also Hyman, 'Maimonides' "Thirteen Principles"', 141–2.

[48] According to Alexander Altmann's last essay on the topic, this perfection is not conjunction with the Active Intellect, but merely the achievement of similarity to it. In Altmann's words, 'Similarity, not identity, is the only realistic goal of accomplishment.' See his *Aufklärung*, 85. A development in Altmann's views is apparent here. In his essay 'Verhältnis', 305, he spoke of conjunction without any hesitation. In his later article, 'Beatitude', he wrote, with less certainty, that Maimonides 'seems to refer to conjunction' with the Active Intellect.

make this medieval idea more palatable, Rabbi J. David Bleich suggests: 'The situation is crudely analogous to that of the student who fails to master algebra through no fault of his own and must then be refused permission to enroll in a calculus course. Such denial is not by way of punishment, but an assessment of the fact that one who has not mastered the rudiments of a subject cannot profit from advanced instruction in that discipline.'[49] For the opponents of Maimonides, on the other hand, immortality is a reward bestowed by God through a supernatural act. He can therefore forgive heretical opinions arrived at unintentionally. He is the Almighty, after all.

Once Maimonides' conception of immortality is properly understood, we are confronted with how, in his discussion of heresy in 'Hilkhot teshuvah', he could state that the heretic must publicly voice his heresy for him to be condemned to perdition. In the *Mishneh torah* Maimonides writes as if God has some role in this affair, and can choose to give someone a share in the afterlife if the person is prudent enough not to voice his heretical opinions. However, according to Maimonides, an anthropomorphist or an idolater is by definition unable to achieve the intellectual perfection required for immortality. Whether this heresy is stated or only believed is thus of no significance in Maimonides' theology. Any assertion to the contrary, as was attempted by Harry A. Wolfson,[50] is directly contradicted by Maimonides' words in *Guide* i. 36: 'I do not consider as an infidel one who cannot demonstrate that the corporeality of God should be negated. But I do consider as an infidel one who does not *believe* in its negation.'[51] It is also obvious, according to Maimonides, that one who voices a heretical opinion without believing it is not denied a share in the world to come. As Maimonides states in *Guide* i. 50: 'Belief is not the notion that is uttered, but the notion that is represented in the soul when it has been averred of it that it is in fact just as it has been represented.'[52]

We must therefore conclude that Maimonides' use of the words 'one who *says*' in describing a heretic are only in imitation of Mishnah *Sanhedrin* 10: 1, where the same formulation is found, and not too much should be read into this. One who believes in a corporeal God or in the existence of many gods, even without saying so publicly, is indeed a heretic as far as Maimonidean theology is concerned. Such a person will not face any penalties from an earthly court, but he is certainly denied a share in the world to come.

---

[49] *With Perfect Faith*, 180.   [50] *Studies*, ii. 443 ff.

[51] See also Maimonides' introduction to Mishnah *Avot*, ch. 2: 'I maintain that observance and transgression may also originate in the rational faculty, in so far as one believes a true or a false doctrine, though no action which may be designated as an observance or a transgression results therefrom.'

[52] See the commentaries of Narboni, Efodi, and Abarbanel ad. loc.; *Mishneh torah*, *Sefer hamada*, ed. Kafih, 608 n. 31; H. A. Wolfson, *Studies*, ii. 163–4.

Returning to the Thirteen Principles, the characteristic that gave them their afterlife and caused them to become *the* formulation of the Jewish creed is precisely their outer form, that is, the fact that they were formulated as a catechism with all the Principles listed together. Had Maimonides listed a different number of Principles in the *Mishneh torah* (e.g. twelve or fourteen), these would have become the principles of Judaism. But he did not, and thus the Thirteen Principles stuck.

Had Maimonides never drawn up his Principles, issues of Jewish belief in the popular mind would have developed very differently. In fact, the widespread acceptance of Maimonides' creed is not so much a function of scholarly approval but rather of popular acceptance. Although later authors tried to offer competing creeds,[53] none could displace that of Maimonides, both because of his supreme authority and because popular piety prefers more dogmatic statements rather than fewer.[54] That is, thirteen principles are more appealing than three, as were offered by Duran and Albo.[55]

In addition, the masses could never be expected to latch on to any of the competing systems of dogma, with their subtle distinctions between principles of faith without which the religion is inconceivable, and other equally true and required beliefs which are less significant in a structural sense, though not in any essential way. Since popular piety is attracted to a creed, something which people can hold on to and look towards as their document of faith, it is not surprising that Abarbanel's approach, in which there are no special beliefs but rather all aspects of the Torah are equal, was never able to win widespread acceptance.

I have mentioned above that in the *Guide* Maimonides did not record the Thirteen Principles as the fundamental beliefs of Judaism. Indeed, as we shall see, there is at least one Principle that is explicitly contradicted by the *Guide*, and if read as an esoteric work it is clear that the theology of the *Guide* is not

---

[53] Even in our day new principles of faith continue to be formulated: see e.g. Peli, 'Attempt'. Peli does not reject any of the Maimonidean Principles; he only wishes to add some more.

[54] Petuchowski, *Theology*, 25, attributes the Orthodox acceptance of Maimonides' Principles to the popularity of *Yigdal*, 'which has found its way into all synagogues'. This merely begs the question, why did *Yigdal* find its way into synagogues, and further, why were poetic compositions of Maimonides' Principles, of which *Yigdal* is only the most famous, composed? Obviously, widespread acceptance of the Principles pre-dates the poetic versions, not the other way around. As for *Yigdal* finding its way 'into all synagogues', this too is incorrect, as will be documented below.

[55] I should call attention to a significant philosophical and halakhic point which appears to have gone unnoticed. The Vilna Gaon (R. Elijah b. Solomon Zalman, 1720–97) apparently believed that the First and Second Principles are the only true principles in Judaism. According to him, one who believes in God's existence and unity, despite his other sins, is regarded as a Jew in good standing and he is thus able to be included in a *minyan* (quorum for public prayer). None of the numerous discussions regarding whether a Sabbath violator may be included in a *minyan* seems to have taken note of the Gaon's comment, which appears in his commentary on *Tikunei zohar*, 42a. See also the interesting approach of R. Jacob Moelin, *She'elot uteshuvot maharil*, no. 194.

the theology of the Thirteen Principles. This latter point will not concern me greatly, however, since my focus is primarily the rabbinic scholars who were, almost without exception, oblivious to the radical possibilities inherent in Maimonidean philosophy as expressed in the *Guide*.

It is certainly one of the great ironies of Jewish history that the Thirteen Principles became the standard by which orthodoxy was judged, for, as is well known, Maimonides himself was attacked for supposedly holding heretical views, at odds with his very own Principles. Where else, in Judaism or any other religion, do we have a parallel example in which an authority's doctrinal formulations, dependent in large measure on his religious standing, are regarded as binding but the authority himself is condemned for insufficient orthodoxy?

Quite apart from the debate over the esoteric meaning of the *Guide*, some of Maimonides' openly proclaimed views were also attacked mercilessly, even by scholars who at other times were great defenders of Maimonides. For example, he argued that certain stories recorded in the Torah only occurred in dreams. Concerning this view, Nahmanides (1194–1270) writes: 'Such words contradict Scripture. It is forbidden to listen to them, all the more to believe in them.'[56] R. Yom Tov Ishbili (Ritva, *c.*1250–1330) defended Maimonides in the face of this attack,[57] but on another occasion, in discussing the latter's view of biblical exegesis,[58] was just as unrelenting as Nahmanides had been, referring to Maimonides' view as 'heretical' (*da'at minut*).[59] In the *Igeret hakodesh*, which for a long time was mistakenly attributed to Nahmanides and which Charles Mopsik has most recently argued was written by R. Joseph Gikatilla (1248–*c.*1325),[60] Maimonides' view, in agreement with Aristotle,[61] that the sense of touch is a 'disgrace to us',[62] is characterized as having a 'taint

---

[56] Commentary on Gen. 18: 1. R. Abraham Hayim Viterbo uses almost identical language when referring to this view of Maimonides; see his *Emunat hakhamim*, 33a–b.

[57] See his *Sefer hazikaron*, 55–62.

[58] See the introduction to Maimonides, *Commentary on the Mishnah*, i. 10, where Maimonides argues that *asmakhta* (a type of scriptural support for a law) is only a mnemonic provided by the rabbis to connect the law to Scripture, but that in reality the law is entirely independent of any scriptural proof. See Schimmel, *Oral Law*, 55–6; Kooperman, *Peshuto*, ch. 9.

[59] Commentary on BT *RH* 16a. Ritva does not mention Maimonides by name, leading M. Roth, *Kol mevaser*, ii, nos. 21–2, to argue that he had Ibn Ezra in mind, and that had he known that Maimonides held the same view he would not have used such harsh language. See Ibn Ezra's commentary on Exod. 21: 8 (long and short versions), 25: 18, Lev. 21: 2, 22: 7. This shared position of Ibn Ezra and Maimonides was overlooked by my late teacher, Professor Isadore Twersky, 'Did Ibn Ezra Influence Maimonides?'. See also Judah Halevi, *Kuzari*, iii. 73, who appears to be the first to suggest the explanation later offered by Ibn Ezra and Maimonides.

[60] *Lettre*, 13 ff.   [61] *Nicomachean Ethics* iii. 10.

[62] *Guide* ii. 36, 40, iii. 8, 49. In *Guide* iii. 51 Maimonides states that Moses' intellect 'attained such strength that all the gross faculties in the body ceased to function; I refer to the various kinds of the sense of touch'. Strauss, *Persecution*, 75–6, argues that Maimonides' esoteric opinion is somewhat less ascetic than this.

of heresy' (*shemets minut*).[63] As is well known, Maimonides believed that only humans can receive individual providence and that the animal and plant kingdoms receive a general providence. Individual animals, plants, and inanimate objects are thus subject to the vagaries of chance.[64] Yet two hasidic leaders, R. Simhah Bunem of Przysucha (*c.*1765–1827)[65] and R. Hayim Eleazar Shapira (1872–1937),[66] both claimed that this view is heresy. R. Simhah Bunem was not merely satisfied with asserting that the view itself is heresy, but even stated that the one who holds this view is a heretic!

Some kabbalists taught that as a punishment for what Maimonides wrote in his philosophical writings he was condemned to be reincarnated as a worm.[67] The kabbalist and rabbinic scholar R. Joseph Ashkenazi (1525–77), known as the '*tana* of Safed', publicly denounced Maimonides as a heretic.[68] R. Gedaliah ibn Yahya (1515–87) reports that opponents of Maimonides defaced his tombstone, writing on it 'excommunicated' and 'heretic'.[69] In more recent times, R. Nahman of Bratslav is also known to have held a very negative view of Maimonides, reportedly even saying, 'There are certain philosophers generally considered great, particularly Maimonides, but in the future it will be known that he was a heretic and an unbeliever.'[70] It is a testa-

---

[63] Although R. Israel b. Joseph al-Nakawa incorporated the entire *Igeret hakodesh* into his own *Menorat hamaor*, he was careful to omit the criticism of Maimonides. See *Menorat hamaor*, iv. 90. An almost identical formulation to that which appears in *Igeret hakodesh*, and clearly adapted from it, is offered by the kabbalist R. Abraham Saba; again Maimonides is not mentioned. See id., *Tseror hamor*, on Gen. 4: 1. R. Jacob Emden, whose own sexuality was quite complex, also spares Maimonides. See his *Mor uketsiah*, no. 240: גם חכמי אר"ה אומרים חוש המישוש חרפה היא לנו (אם אמנם אין זו זו דעת התורה (…. האלהית); id., *Amudei shamayim*, 352b: ומ"ש הפלוסופים חוש המשוש חרפה היא לנו בנפשם דברו. R. Moses Sofer writes almost identically: see id., *She'elot uteshuvot*, 'Even ha'ezer', 2, no. 40. Elsewhere Emden takes great glee in recounting how Aristotle himself succumbed to physical lusts: see id., *Migdal oz*, 49a ('Neveh ḥakham: Ḥalon tsuri', no. 64); id., *Mitpaḥat sefarim*, 154. Regarding this legend, see Shmuel Ashkenazi, *Alfa*, 234–6. For the many scholars who agreed with Maimonides' negative view of the physical, see Kaufmann, *Sinne*, 188–9; Malter, 'Shem Tob', 480; Saperstein, *Decoding the Rabbis*, 93.

[64] *Guide* iii. 17. This view is shared by many others. D. M. Halperin, *Ḥemdah genuzah*, 1, provides references to Nahmanides, *Sefer haḥinukh*, R. David Kimhi, R. Bahya b. Asher, Gersonides (R. Levi b. Gershom), R. Obadiah Sforno, R. Moses Cordovero, R. Moses Hayim Luzzatto, and R. Joseph Ergas.

[65] *Simḥat yisra'el*, 'Ma'amrei simḥah', no. 32. See also R. Pinhas Shapiro of Korets, *Imrei pinḥas*, vi, no. 95, that one is obligated to believe that God's providence extends to everything.

[66] *Minḥat ele'azar*, i, no. 50. Shapira writes that it is forbidden to read such a view, which I assume means that he regards it as heretical.

[67] R. Joseph Karo—or rather the *magid* or heavenly guide who appeared to him—claimed that although this was indeed Heaven's decree, Maimonides' Torah learning and good deeds protected him so that he was not forced to become a worm, although he did have to go through one reincarnation before reaching heaven. This passage appears in an expurgated version in *Magid meisharim*, 'Vayakhel' (*batra*). See Werblowsky, *Karo*, 31, 170 n. 2. For kabbalists, belief in the doctrine of metempsychosis (*gilgul*) is itself one of the fundamental principles of Judaism, and, in the words of R. Levi b. Habib, 'we are all obligated to believe in it without any hesitations or doubts': id., *She'elot uteshuvot ralbaḥ*, no. 8. [68] See the text published by Bloch, 'Streit', 264.

[69] *Shalshelet hakabalah*, 101. [70] Green, *Tormented Master*, 331 n. 8.

ment to Maimonides' towering stature that, despite such assaults on his orthodoxy, his doctrinal formulation retained its authority.

To return to the point already mentioned above, if there is one thing Orthodox Jews the world over acknowledge, it is that Maimonides' Thirteen Principles are the fundamentals of Jewish faith. The common knee-jerk reaction is that there is room for debate in matters of faith, as long as one does not contradict any of these Principles. In line with this conception, R. Abraham Isaiah Karelitz (the Hazon Ish, 1878–1953), one of the last century's preeminent non-hasidic scholars, stated that he ordered his life on the basis of complete faith in the Thirteen Principles.[71] Among hasidic luminaries, R. Hayim Eleazar Shapira stated: 'We are believers, sons of believers, in the Thirteen Principles in accordance with their simple meaning, in accordance with their innermost truth.'[72] Another hasidic leader, R. Pinhas Shapiro of Korets (1726–91), recommended daily recital of the Principles.[73] Similarly, the non-hasidic and saintly R. Israel Meir Hakohen (the Hafets Hayim, 1839–1933) wrote that it is a *mitsvah* to recite the Principles every day.[74] Going even further, R. Aaron (Arele) Roth (1894–1944) wrote that it is praiseworthy to repeat the Thirteen Principles upon waking, before going to sleep, and at other times during the day.[75] It seems that there is even halakhic significance to the Principles, as seen in the fact that R. Israel Meir Hakohen records that one who denies the divinity of the Torah, reward and punishment, the future redemption, and the resurrection cannot serve as a prayer leader.[76] Had Maimonides not included these Principles in his list, it is unlikely that denial of the last two, which are not necessarily of prime importance to a religious life, would disqualify one in this way.

Earlier I noted Kellner's observation that Maimonides' Principles were not the subject of scholarly discussion in the first two centuries after their appearance, though this did not stop them from achieving a great measure of popularity even then. This can be seen from the early date of the hymn *Yigdal*,

---

[71] *Kovets igerot*, ii. 41, 111. Interestingly enough, it was actually Karelitz who softened Maimonides' harsh judgement about the status of a heretic and 'redeemed' him. He argued that all the harsh things said about heretics, not least of which was that they should be killed, were only stated with reference to an era in which one could properly rebuke sinners and in which God's providence was manifest; however neither of these apply in contemporary times. See id., *Ḥazon ish*, 2: 16, 28. However, while rebuke was certainly more of a possibility in Maimonides' day than in Karelitz's (since more Jews in medieval times accepted the authority of the Torah), divine providence was hardly more manifest in the twelfth century than in the twentieth. Concerning this point, Karelitz should be regarded as disputing with Maimonides, not interpreting him.

[72] *Divrei torah*, iii, no. 96.   [73] *Midrash pinḥas*, 119.   [74] *Mikhtevei ḥafets ḥayim*, no. 18.

[75] *Shomer emunim*, i. 232b. See also R. Abraham Isaac Hakohen (the leader of the conservative hasidic sect of Toldot Aharon), *Zekhor le'avraham*, 124, and Magid, 'Modernity'.

[76] *Mishnah berurah*, 126: 2. In the section 'Sha'ar hatsiyun', n. 3, he claims that this formulation is taken from Orenstein's *Yeshuot ya'akov*, but I have been unable to find the reference.

which summarizes the Principles and was composed by either Daniel ben Judah Dayan of Rome (*c*.1300) or, less likely, by Immanuel of Rome (*c*.1261–after 1328), who is the author of a very similar poem.[77] *Yigdal* is known to have entered the daily Ashkenazi liturgy in the fifteenth century,[78] and is mentioned in this regard by R. Yom-Tov Lipmann Heller (1579–1654).[79] R. Joseph Yuzpa Hahn (*c*.1730–1803) recorded that it was the practice in Germany to recite *Yigdal* after every prayer, which apparently means three times a day. He also recommended studying it carefully and saying it with *kavanah*.[80]

In another illustration of how popular the Principles became, we know of almost a hundred different poetic versions of them, of which *Yigdal* is only the most famous. These originated in a variety of countries, beginning in the early fourteenth century.[81] Today *Yigdal* is a standard prayer, appearing in most prayer books. Yet there are different customs related to it, with some people reciting it every day and others saying it only on Friday night, when it is usually sung publicly. Many Moroccan Jews recite it on Sabbath morning before the *Barukh she'amar* prayer.[82] This custom is probably based on the notion that the Thirteen Principles are hinted at in *Barukh she'amar*, with each of the thirteen instances of the word *barukh* (blessed) in this prayer corresponding to a different Principle.[83] In Morocco and Gibraltar there was also a custom of reciting *Yigdal* at circumcisions, redemptions of the first-born, and burials.[84] There is even a Christian adaptation of *Yigdal* which to this day is sung in many Anglican as well as other Protestant churches in the

[77] See Elbogen, *Jewish Liturgy*, 77; I. Davidson, *Otsar hashirah*, ii. 266–7. R. Eliyahu Katz sees a hint of Daniel b. Judah's authorship in the first word of the song, יגדל. The first two letters allude to the Thirteen Principles and the last two letters allude to the author's name, Daniel. See his letter in D. Barda, *Revid hazahav*, 108. Surprisingly, R. J. S. Delmedigo, *Novelot ḥokhmah*, 92*b*, assumed that Solomon ibn Gabirol wrote *Yigdal*. R. Jacob Emden, who at times went so far as to deny Maimonides' authorship of the *Guide* (see Schacter, 'Iggeret', 442 n. 12), actually believed that Maimonides wrote *Yigdal*. See his *Amudei shamayim*, 176*b* (introduction to *Shir hayiḥud*, no. 3). Although Emden did not include *Yigdal* in his prayer book, it is found in the popular and oft-reprinted *Sidur beit ya'akov*, which, although attributed to Emden, is largely a product of the printer. In this *Sidur*, 95*a*, 'Emden' advised the God-fearing to recite the Thirteen Principles every day—words of advice which are not to be found in Emden's *Amudei shamayim*. Although he nowhere offered his own list of principles of faith, Emden claimed that a literal understanding of the kabbalistic notion of *tsimtsum* is a fundamental concept of Judaism: מהמושכלות הראשונות לבעל דתנו. See his *Mitpaḥat sefarim*, 117.

[78] See Davis, 'Philosophy', 215. In this article Davis argues that 'the belief in dogmas of Judaism entered Ashkenazic culture in the late Middle Ages'.

[79] See his introductory *derashah* to R. Asher b. Jehiel, *Orḥot ḥayim*, 10 (final numbering).

[80] *Yosif omets*, no. 60 (although the title of this work is often given as *Yosef omets*, this is incorrect; see Ben-David, *Shevet miyehudah*, no. 20).

[81] See Marx, 'List', 305–36; I. Davidson, *Otsar hashirah*, iv. 492.

[82] See Ovadiah, *Natan david*, 336; Azrad, *Torat imekha*, 101–2.

[83] See Auerbach, *Oraḥ ne'eman*, 'Oraḥ ḥayim', 51: 1.   [84] See Gaguine, *Keter shem tov*, i. 196.

English-speaking world.[85] In addition to *Yigdal*, most prayer books also contain the *Ani ma'amin*, and in years past some Sephardi communities would gather in the synagogue the day before Rosh Hodesh (New Moon) in order to recite this as well.[86]

The widespread popularity of *Yigdal* and similar compositions actually led to concern among some rabbinic authorities that this concentration on the Thirteen Principles would overshadow the rest of what Judaism has to say. R. Jacob Moelin (*c.*1360–1427) wrote:

The rhymes and poems that people write in Yiddish on the unity of God and the Thirteen Principles—would that they were not written! For most of the ignorant believe that all of the commandments depend on this, and they despair of various positive and negative commandments, such as *tsitsit* and *tefilin* and the study of Torah. And they believe that they fulfil their obligation by saying those rhymes with *kavanah*. And those rhymes do not mention a single one of the 613 commandments that Jews are commanded—only the fundamentals of Jewish belief.[87]

R. Solomon Luria (*c.*1510–74) expressed himself similarly to Moelin. He noted that there were people in his day who believed that they could commit all the sins in the world as long as they accepted the Thirteen Principles. Luria agreed with Abarbanel's suggestion that Maimonides' formulation was no more than a Jewish response to the medieval Islamic philosophers who put their own faith in the form of principles. Not surprisingly, he recited neither *Yigdal* nor the *Ani ma'amin*.[88]

---

[85] See Petuchowski, *Theology*, 25; Rothkoff, 'Yigdal'.

[86] See Gaon, 'Recitation', 39–41. Gaon refers to special Hebrew and Ladino publications of the Principles, designed to be recited at this time, printed in Venice, 1700 and Salonika, 1775. See also Isaac De Fes' Hebrew and Judaeo-Spanish *Hoda'at emunat yisra'el*. Strictly speaking, one cannot speak of *the Ani ma'amin*, for in addition to the Ashkenazi (standard) version there are at least two Sephardi versions. It is not known who composed any of the versions.

Both the standard *Ani ma'amin* and *Yigdal* formulations of the Thirteen Principles differ in a number of ways from what Maimonides actually wrote. Regarding this, as well as textual variations of *Yigdal*, see Gaguine, *Keter shem tov*, i. 198; Lamm, *Faith and Doubt*, 159 n. 31; Goren, *Torat hashabat*, 556, 572; Schueck, *She'elot uteshuvot rashban*, 'Orah hayim', no. 45; Hirschensohn, *Malki bakodesh*, ii. 238–42; E. M. Preil, *Hamaor*, 13–15; Waxman, 'Maimonides', 402–3; Pines, *History*, 16–20; id., 'Philosophic Purport, 3; Messas, *Mayim hayim*, 97; Berliner, *Writings*, i. 19–20, 122, ii. 230; Birnbaum, *Peletat soferim*, 83–4; Sparka, *Yesodei ha'emunah*, 63–8; Rosenberg, 'Biblical Research', 88; D. Cohen, *Masat kapai*, 92; David Yitshaki's comment in *Tsefunot*, 5 (Tishrei 5750 [Oct. 1989]), 107; Warhaftig, 'Notes', 18; Katan, 'I Believe', 41–4; Cosman, 'Maimonides' Thirteen Principles', 337–48 (some of these sources contain errors because they rely on the faulty translation of Maimonides' Mishnah commentary found in the standard editions of the Talmud).

[87] *Sefer maharil*, 626 (translation in Davis, 'Philosophy', 215). R. Joseph B. Soloveitchik is reported to have opposed the recitation of *Yigdal*, which he regarded as an imitation of the Christian practice of recitation of the catechism; see Schachter, *Nefesh harav*, 231.

[88] Abarbanel, *Rosh amanah*, ch. 23; S. Luria, 'Hanhagat maharshal', 326. As has already been noted, Abarbanel also argued that Maimonides' Principles were designed exclusively for the masses.

R. Isaac Luria (1534–72) is also known to have opposed recitation of *Yigdal*, but for a different reason entirely, which has nothing to do with the practical concerns expressed by Moelin. As his student R. Hayim Vital (1542–1620) explained, Luria did not recite any song or poetic composition that was not a product of the early luminaries such as R. Akiva, R. Ishmael, and R. Eleazar Kalir.[89] He believed that such early works were full of kabbalistic significance, unlike works composed by later authors, 'who do not know what they are saying'.[90] Luria's influence was so great that R. Isaac Safrin of Komarno (1806–74), an important hasidic teacher, was led to remark that those who do not remove *Yigdal* from the prayer book are showing their 'lack of faith'.[91] Taking Luria's words most seriously, hasidic prayer books are conspicuous in their exclusion of *Yigdal*.

Although in more recent centuries the Thirteen Principles have indeed become identified with the fundamentals of Judaism, there were also scholars in earlier times, such as R. Meir Aldabi (*c*.1310–*c*.1360),[92] R. David ben Yom Tov ibn Bilia (fourteenth century),[93] R. Simeon ben Samuel of Regensburg (fourteenth–fifteenth centuries),[94] and R. Moses ben Joseph Trani (1500–80),[95] who regarded the Thirteen Principles as *the* beliefs that defined Judaism. The outstanding medieval philosophers did not share this view, however. This was so even when they believed in the Principles, and even when they believed that denial of a Principle equalled heresy. Believing the Principles to be true, even obligatory, and regarding them as *the* fundamentals of Judaism were regarded by medieval philosophers as two separate things. It is because of this that they spent so much time dissecting Maimonides' method and categories and defending their alternative systems.[96]

[89] He believed Kalir to be a *tana*, as is stated in Tosafot, *Ḥagigah* 13*a*, s.v. *veraglei*; *Maḥzor vitri*, 362–4 (quoting Rabenu Tam); Asher b. Jehiel, *Berakhot* 5: 21; and see Langer, 'Kalir'. Some medieval scholars recognized that Kalir's dates were much later. See Tosafot, *Menaḥot* 35*b*, s.v. *vekamah* and *Ḥulin* 109*b*, s.v. *nidah*.

[90] Vital, *Peri ets ḥayim*, i. 15 (also recorded in the commentary on the *Shulḥan arukh* by Judah Ashkenazi, *Ba'er heitev*, 'Oraḥ ḥayim', 68: 3). The anonymous *Ḥemdat yamim*, 57*a*, claims that Luria's objection was to the first four stanzas, which are not in accord with kabbalistic truth. Therefore, *Ḥemdat yamim* concludes, there is no objection to reciting the rest of the poem. For a suggestion as to what, in particular, motivated Luria's kabbalistic objection, see R. Meir Mazuz's comment in Y. Barda, *Yitsḥak yeranen*, 113. Citing unnamed kabbalists, and calling attention to some problematic linguistic aspects in the poem, Emden also opposed recitation of *Yigdal*; see id., *Amudei shamayim*, 175*b*.

[91] *Shulḥan hataḥor*, 68: 3 (section 'Zer zahav'). On the other hand, the famed kabbalist R. Isaiah Horowitz, *Shenei luḥot haberit*, i. 94*a* ('Sha'ar ha'otiyot'), refers to *Yigdal* as an 'excellent hymn'. R. Shabetai Sofer was unaware of any kabbalistic opposition to *Yigdal*. After mentioning that other scholars, in particular Abarbanel, disputed with Maimonides as to the proper number of principles, he wrote: 'Perhaps it is due to this dispute that a small number of people refused to recite this hymn.' See id., *Sidur shabetai sofer*, ii. 2. [92] *Shevilei emunah*, Netiv 1.   [93] *Yesodot hamaskil*, 56.

[94] See Davis, 'Philosophy', 195–222.   [95] See Kellner, *Dogma*, 77, 198–9.

[96] See Kellner, *Dogma*, who discusses the different theoretical bases for the various dogmatic formulations.

The disputes of the medieval rabbis were soon forgotten, however, and as mentioned above, in more recent centuries there was general agreement among traditional Jews that the Thirteen Principles were indeed the fundamentals of Judaism. Denial of even one Principle was usually enough for one to be branded as a heretic. For the masses, and for many rabbis as well, this became unquestioned truth. In the seventeenth century, R. Saul Morteira (*c*.1596–1660) declared that 'all agree' with Maimonides' Principles, 'and whoever denies them has no share in the world to come'.[97] In the eighteenth century, Isaac Wetzlar (*c*.1685–1751), in his Yiddish *Libes briv*, urged that all children be taught the Principles.[98] Sharing Wetzlar's sentiments, Gedaliah ben Abraham Teikus published his *Emunat yisra'el* (Amsterdam, 1764), a Hebrew–Yiddish elaboration of the Principles designed for the common people. It was reprinted a number of times, thus illustrating its popularity. For those rabbis who were aware of many of the disputes we shall be discussing, appeal to the Principles still had religious and, just as important, rhetorical power, in particular when confronting religious dissenters. Many citations illustrating the centrality the Principles assumed could be given, and I offer here only some representative examples.

As part of his attempt to undermine traditional Judaism, Saul Berlin (1740–94), in his notorious forgery *Besamim rosh*, aimed his arrows at the Thirteen Principles. He inserted into the mouth of R. Asher ben Jehiel the notion that the Principles of Faith are not eternal but can be re-evaluated with the passage of time.[99] In his response to Berlin, R. Mordechai Banet (1753–1829) wrote, with reference to the Thirteen Principles: 'Our teacher Moses [Maimonides] did not add or subtract anything, and all his words are explicit in Scripture and in the writings of the Sages.'[100] In his polemic against the nascent Reform movement, R. Tsevi Hirsch Chajes (1805–55) noted that until the rise of this heretical movement all of Jewry was united around the Thirteen Principles.[101] In an anonymous, harshly worded letter to R. Esriel Hildesheimer (1820–99), while attempting to show that one of his students had departed from the proper path, the author wrote: 'I don't know if he believes in the Thirteen Principles.'[102] Moses Leib Lilienblum (1843–1910), discussing his path to heresy, wrote, 'When I rejected Maimonides' articles of faith, I did not rejoice.'[103] It was obvious to Lilienblum that since he had rejected the Thirteen Principles he was an unbeliever. When the Orthodox

[97] *Givat sha'ul*, 76*a* ('Tetsaveh').
[98] See Faierstein, *Libes Briv*, 96–7 (English), 50–1 (Yiddish).
[99] *Besamim rosh*, no. 251. Nahman Krochmal agreed with Berlin; see Krochmal, *Kitvei ranak*, 439.
[100] *Parashat mordekhai*, no. 5. See also Hayim Berlin, *Nishmat hayim*, no. 180 (beginning).
[101] *Kol sifrei*, ii. 979–80. See, similarly, Z. J. Friedman, *Emet ve'emunah*, 52–5.
[102] See my 'Letter', 18. [103] 'Hatot ne'urim', 112.

Jewish Congregational Union of America was formed in 1898, it included in its convention statement the following: 'We affirm our adherence to the acknowledged codes of our Rabbis and the thirteen principles of Maimonides.'[104] Half a century earlier in Philadelphia, Isaac Leeser (1806–68) had also declared that the Thirteen Principles were the authoritative Jewish creed.[105]

A prominent Lithuanian rabbi, who insisted that all Jews are obligated to believe in the Principles, also addressed the gentiles, declaring: 'As long as you do not believe in these Thirteen Principles, you have no belief.'[106] A well-known hasidic leader, who did not share Maimonides' views as expressed in the *Guide*, nevertheless declared that all Jews are obligated to believe in the Thirteen Principles.[107] When, in the face of harsh criticism, an anti-Zionist figure wanted to defend his rejection of the Balfour Declaration, he stated simply: 'Does this equal denial of one of the Thirteen Principles?'[108] A nineteenth-century false messiah accused his non-believing antagonists of denying one of Maimonides' Principles.[109] In trying to discredit his kabbalistic opponents, R. Yihyeh Kafih (1850–1932) accused them of contradicting the Thirteen Principles, a charge they vehemently denied.[110] In trying to show the great wickedness of Jews who chose to have their bodies cremated, R. Hayim Eleazar Shapira assumed as a matter of course that they must also deny the Thirteen Principles.[111] More recently, when R. Immanuel Jakobovits (1921–99) announced that he intended to give a lecture under Conservative auspices, a local Orthodox rabbi protested that his 'presence would serve

---

[104] See Mendes-Flohr and Reinharz (eds.), *Jew in the Modern World*, 470.

[105] See Sussman, *Isaac Leeser*, 78.

[106] Broide, *Shir hadash*, 63–4. While not going this far, R. Hayim David Regensberg argues that Maimonides requires a *ger toshav* (a resident alien who keeps the Noahide laws) to accept his Principles; see his *Mishmeret hayim*, 155. R. Abba Mari Astruc of Lunel states that one should not condemn Aristotle for not believing in creation, since it is not included in the seven Noahide commandments. See id., *Minhat kenaot*, ed. Dimitrovsky, 257. (That non-Jews are not obligated to believe in creation is also stated by Kamenetzky, *Emet leya'akov*, 311.) The implication of R. Abba Mari's comment is that Noahides are not obligated to believe in *any* principles of faith, since none is included in the Noahide commandments. Although, to be sure, Noahides are forbidden to practise idolatry, there is no command against *believing* in polytheism. As Aviner, *She'elat shelomoh*, vii, no. 214, points out, it is better for a non-Jew to be an atheist than an idolater, since belief in God is not one of the seven Noahide commandments. See, however, Maimonides, *Mishneh torah*, 'Hilkhot melakhim', 8: 11, who indeed requires Noahides to affirm at least some aspects of a proper theology. Regarding the old question of which is worse, an atheist or an idolater, see Ibn Ezra, commentary on Exod. 20: 1 (end); Albo, *Sefer ha'ikarim*, i. 14; Herzog, *Decisions*, ii, no. 119; Jacobs, *Principles*, 55; Kook's view as interpreted by Naor, 'Rav Kook', and in Naor's translation of Kook, *Orot*, 51 ff.; and the quotation from Abraham Azulai, see below, Ch. 2 n. 3. Maimonides apparently believed that atheism is worse. See *Letters*, ed. Kafih, iii n. 79.

[107] See Safrin, *Heikhal haberakhah*, i. 29a.

[108] M. Friedman, *Hevrah vedat*, 320.

[109] See Goitein, *Zikhron avot*, 50–1.

[110] See Araki et al., *Emunat hashem*, 176 ff., 325 ff. This book reprints Y. Kafih, *Milhamot hashem*, followed by the kabbalists' refutations. See Tobi, 'Who Was the Author?'.

[111] See his responsum in J. J. Weinberg, *Seridei esh*, ii. 282.

to add a great deal of prestige to an institution that denies many of the Thirteen Principles'.[112] The guidelines of a popular Orthodox website state: 'The Rambam's Thirteen Principles of Belief (and/or the *Ani Ma'amin*s and/ or the *Yigdal*) are baseline standards for our discussion group.'[113]

Other contemporary authors in the Orthodox community express themselves similarly: 'It should be stressed that *all* Torah scholars agree on the validity and significance of the Principles'.[114] 'The fact is that Maimonides' Thirteen Principles are all derived from the Talmud and the classic Jewish tradition, *and were never in dispute*'.[115] 'The principles have been discussed for the past eight hundred years, and are still accepted by *all* Jews as the one clear unambiguous creed of Judaism'.[116] 'It is *universally recognized* as definitive halacha that firm belief in, and adherence to each of these Thirteen Principles is the *sine qua non* of Torah faith'[117] (emphasis added to all four quotations). 'From an Orthodox standpoint, though the 13 Principles of Faith have a history, they are obligatory nonetheless.'[118] 'Fundamentalists we are indeed in the original sense of the word. We hold the thirteen Ikkarim [Principles] to be fundamental to Torah Judaism.'[119]

What emerges clearly from what we have seen is that Maimonides' Principles came to be regarded as central to Jewish belief.[120] Once his Principles were accepted, it was only a short step to agreement with Maimonides that any deviation from the Principles was enough to categorize one as a heretic. After this became something of an unofficial dogma, the notion further developed, as seen in some statements cited above, that Torah scholars throughout history have always been in agreement with the Principles. Some interesting flights of fancy were also made in support of the authority of the Principles. For example, Morteira points out that the singular noun *mitsvah* appears thirteen times in the Torah in contexts in which one would have expected the plural, *mitsvot*. Morteira illustrates how each of these examples points to one of the Principles.[121] In more recent years, R. Hayim Eleazar Shapira thought it significant that the *gematriyah* of אחד, signifying God, is 13.[122] Other examples are R. Nathan Adler's (1803–90) assertion that the Principles

---

[112] J. M. Cohen (ed.), *Dear Chief Rabbi*, 259.   [113] <www.aishdas.org>.

[114] Mordechai Blumenfeld in his introduction to Y. Weinberg, *Fundamentals and Faith*, 18.

[115] Genack, 'Ambiguity', 73.   [116] A. Kaplan, *Maimonides' Principles*, 3.

[117] Fendel, *Torah*, 314.   [118] Yaakov Elman, as quoted in *Wellsprings* (Summer 1996), 19.

[119] Danziger, 'Modern Orthodoxy', 5.

[120] For other Orthodox works that reflect this notion, see Sparka, *Yesodei ha'emunah*; Kutner, *Ha'emunah vehahakirah*; Roller, *Ma'amrei be'er hayim mordekhai*; Gottesman, *Emunah shelemah*; Danin, *Sha'ar emunah*; Neriyah, *Yod-gimel ha'ikarim*; anon., *Ma'ayanot ha'emunah*.

[121] *Givat sha'ul*, 129a–132a ('Ekev'). See also ibid. 76a ('Tetsaveh'), where he finds another allusion to the Thirteen Principles in the Torah.   [122] *Divrei torah*, ix, no. 6.

are already present in Onkelos' Aramaic translation of the Torah,[123] and, also in the nineteenth century, R. Elijah Soloveitchik's claim that the Principles are taught in the New Testament, which he believed was written by faithful Jews.[124] R. David Cohen, a contemporary scholar, even claims that one can find the Thirteen Principles in the Passover Haggadah.[125]

Maimonides' rationalism notwithstanding, his Principles became too significant to leave to the philosophers and talmudists, and it therefore should not surprise us that there are also kabbalistic and hasidic interpretations of them.[126] In fact, the prayer book of the Biala hasidim includes an 'updated' version of the Principles. The seventh Principle reads: 'I believe with perfect faith that all the words of the prophets and the [kabbalistic] teachings of Rabbi Simeon ben Yohai, Rabbi Isaac Luria, and the Ba'al Shem Tov and his students are true.' In the Eighth Principle it is stated that these kabbalistic teachings were given to Moses. Apparently, even this is not enough, so the prayer book adds two more Principles: that Israel is the chosen people, and that 'in every generation there are righteous ones like Abraham, Isaac, and Jacob'.[127]

Because Maimonides' Principles were so important, it also should not surprise us that the *maskilim* and early nineteenth-century proto-Reformers, who composed a variety of manuals of Jewish belief, placed great emphasis upon the Thirteen Principles. *Yesodei hadat*, by Judah Leib Ben-Ze'ev (1764–1811), is typical, for it states that all religious people must believe in the Principles.[128] Indeed, 'the Maimonidean creed is hardly ever absent from these presentations'.[129] Needless to say, the Principles were reinterpreted in accordance with these thinkers' Zeitgeist, which placed an emphasis on the 'spirit' of the law while playing down the Torah's ceremonial and ritual components. Thus, books were written which summarized the essence of Judaism without mentioning traditional religious obligations such as *kashrut* and the Sabbath, or even explaining what Jewish law is all about. Mordechai Gumpel Schnaber Levison (1741–97), a prominent *maskil* who wrote *Shelosh-esreh yesodei hatorah* (The Thirteen Foundations of the Torah; Altona, 1792), provides another good example of the importance of the Principles in the maskilic imagination, as well as how they were used (and misused). As David Ruderman puts it: 'Levison began with a putative discussion of Maimonides' thirteen principles of faith only to subvert them radically in the end. . . . He had virtually trans-

[123] Introduction to *Netinah lager*, sect. 4.

[124] *Kol kore*, introduction.   [125] *Masat kapai*, 129–31.

[126] See Safrin, *Heikhal haberakhah*, i. 29a–37b; Gurary, *Thirteen Principles*.

[127] Anon., *Sidur ḥelkat yehoshua*, 291–5 (called to my attention by Rabbi Daniel Yolkut). See also I. D. B. Hakohen, *Ohel yisakhar*, 16–17.   [128] (Vienna, 1811), 2nd introduction.

[129] Petuchowski, 'Manuals', 63. See also Eliav, *Jewish Education*, 73–44, 244, 262.

formed a Maimonidean theology of the twelfth century into a conventional deism of the eighteenth.'[130]

Some modern Reform thinkers have continued along this path, as seen in the recent book by Kerry M. Olitzky and Ronald H. Isaac, *The Thirteen Principles of Faith: A Confirmation Textbook*.[131] Nor could the Dönme, the believers in Shabetai Tsevi after his conversion, overlook the popularity of the Principles. For Maimonides' Ninth Principle (the immutability of the Torah), they substituted the following: 'I believe with perfect faith that the Torah will not be changed and there will not be another Torah; only the *mitsvot* are null but the Torah will be forever and ever.'[132]

Even when Maimonides' original formulation is not the focus, the notion of thirteen principles has remained strong. Thus Ibn Bilia added an extra thirteen principles to those of Maimonides, addressed specifically to the philosophically inclined intellectual.[133] In an example entirely removed from Maimonidean thinking, R. Yekutiel Aryeh Kamelhar (1871–1937) identified thirteen principles of Beshtian hasidism.[134] Concluding that beliefs could no longer 'function as a means of Jewish unity', Mordecai Kaplan (1881–1983), the founder of Reconstructionism, set forth the principles of his new movement in terms of thirteen 'wants'.[135] The Jewish secular humanists have also got in on the act, with their leader Sherwin Wine outlining thirteen principles to guide their movement, including 'selecting an alternative that one believes in, [and] shedding expectations of magical powers'.[136] Further reflecting the popularity of the Thirteen Principles, even the Jewish sectarians were influenced. Thus, Simhah Isaac ben Moses Halutski (1670–1746) enumerates a list of thirteen Karaite principles, which are actually quite similar to those of Maimonides.[137] Finally, even Christian missionaries, in an early 'Jews for Jesus'-type manifesto, developed their own formulation of thirteen principles.[138]

Returning to the statements mentioned above concerning the unanimous agreement accorded the Principles—and many more examples of such rhetoric could be cited—a comment by Gershom Scholem, made in a entirely different context, seems relevant: 'This seems to me an extraordinary example of

---

[130] *Enlightenment*, 129–30.   [131] Hoboken, NJ, 1999.

[132] See Naor, *Post-Sabbatian Sabbatianism*, 8. As Naor points out, Shabetai Tsevi was actually less conservative than his followers, and stated unambiguously that Maimonides' Ninth Principle was untrue (ibid. 151 n. 10).

[133] See Ibn Bilia, *Yesodot hamaskil*, and Kellner, *Dogma*, 77–9.   [134] *Dor de'ah*, i. 46–7.

[135] See Scult (ed.), *Communings*, i. 218; Kaplan and Kohn (eds.), *Sabbath Prayerbook*, 562–5.

[136] *Forward* (15 Oct. 1999), 6.   [137] *Kevod elokim* (Ramleh, 2000).

[138] See Delitzsch, *Bikurei te'enah*, Hebrew introduction. (Not all of these *hanahot*, as Delitzch terms them, are theological.) Is it only a coincidence that the Mormons also have thirteen 'Articles of Faith'? See J. Smith, *Pearl*, 60–1.

how a judgment proclaimed with conviction as certainly true may nevertheless be entirely wrong in every detail.'[139] This is so, for as the present book
seeks to demonstrate, even a cursory examination of Jewish literature reveals
that, both before and after his time, Maimonides' Principles were not regarded
as the last word in Jewish theology.

Nevertheless, it is amazing that so few modern rabbinic scholars have
explicitly acknowledged this fact, even when writing for their peers. It is possible that many scholars simply regarded it as obvious and perhaps others
even began believing their own rhetoric. Whatever the reason, I have found
only three modern traditional scholars who openly acknowledge the validity
of disputes concerning the Thirteen Principles. R. Samuel David Luzzatto
(1800–65),[140] after noting that some sages had disagreed with the Principles,
writes: 'Heaven forbid that we agree with Maimonides in what he said (in his
commentary on *Sanhedrin*, ch. 10), that anyone who does not believe with
perfect faith in the Thirteen Principles that he set up for our religion has left
the fold and is a complete heretic.'[141] R. Reuven Amar writes: 'With regard to
the Principles of Faith, Maimonides' words are not to be regarded as divinely
revealed since he did not receive them via tradition dating back to Moses, but
they are the product of his own reasoning and knowledge.'[142] R. Bezalel Naor
writes: 'The truth, known to Torah scholars, is that Maimonides' formulation
of the tenets of Jewish belief is far from universally accepted.'[143] I have found
one other source that departs from the notion that the Thirteen Principles are
the last word in Orthodox theology, though it is not as blunt as the scholars
quoted above. Surprisingly enough, it is the editors of the Artscroll publishing house, regarded by many as the quintessential Orthodox obscurantists,
who offer a careful formulation, stating that the Principles achieved 'virtually
universal acceptance'.[144] After examining the evidence, I think most readers
will agree that even this statement is wide of the mark.

[139] *Major Trends*, 130.

[140] Although, strictly speaking, Luzzatto should perhaps not be categorized as 'Orthodox', I have
included him because of his strong ties to tradition. In fact, it is probably not helpful to refer to Italian
scholars by categories developed in western Europe. In Italy he was always regarded as a traditional
scholar, and he trained a generation of Italian rabbis. My reluctance to categorize him as Orthodox is
due to the fact that in a private letter he admitted that he did not accept a certain halakhah as set down
in the Talmud, preferring instead Ibn Ezra's interpretation of the verse in question. However, he also
noted that this was a completely private opinion. See Luzzatto, *Letters*, 246 (concerning shaving with
a razor). In one essay, Luzzatto claimed that the book of Ecclesiastes was a heretical work: see *Peninei
shadal*, 161–206. However, he later retracted this view: see Vargon, 'Identity', 365–84. With regard to
Luzzatto's original view of Ecclesiastes, the closest parallel among traditional sources is that of R.
Israel Bruna, who seemingly states that the book of Ecclesiastes was not divinely inspired; see id.,
She'elot uteshuvot, no. 66.

[141] *Studies*, ii. 19.   [142] S. Berlin, *Besamim rosh*, appendix, 40.

[143] *Post-Sabbatian Sabbatianism*, 8. In his note, Naor writes that he heard this insight from his
teacher, R. Shelomoh Fisher of Jerusalem.   [144] Scherman (ed.), *Artscroll Siddur*, 178.

Many years ago Leon Roth wrote: 'O for the masterpiece (but it will have to be published not only anonymously but also posthumously) which will demonstrate to our formula-bound souls that there is no single one of the Thirteen Articles even of Maimonides' alleged creed which was not rejected, explicitly or implicitly, by leading lights in the history of Judaism, including, I fancy (but only whisper the suspicion), no less a person than Maimonides himself.'[145] As we shall see, Roth has exaggerated only slightly in this statement. His basic thrust is certainly on the mark, even with regard to his suggestion about Maimonides himself. Unlike Roth, however, I do not believe that the present book, masterpiece or not, must appear anonymously or posthumously. After all, the Jewish inquisitorial authorities closed up shop a long time ago.[146]

ॐ

The plan of this book is simple enough. After a short examination of the place of dogma in Judaism, I will proceed to examine each of Maimonides' Principles and document the controversies concerning them. Since this is a study of Maimonides' Principles and not Maimonidean philosophy as a whole, I shall generally refrain from detailed discussion of an esoteric Maimonides who would be regarded as a heretic according to his own Principles. However, where Maimonides openly contradicts the Principles in his other writings, further examination is called for.

I must make one more point about the structure of this book. As I have already demonstrated, it is often asserted that Maimonides' Principles were accepted as dogma by the traditionalists—what is today known as the Orthodox denomination of Judaism. This being the case, it would make no sense in the context of this book, which deals with traditional responses to the Principles, to discuss those scholars who are not regarded as acceptable to the traditionalists (and who, in fact, usually did not regard themselves as traditional or Orthodox). To be sure, some figures mentioned in this book have been involved in disputes and opposed by members of the wider community, as was indeed the case with Maimonides himself.[147] However, the scholars dis-

---

[145] L. Roth, *Is There A Jewish Philosophy?*, 11 (called to my attention by Professor Menachem Kellner).

[146] To be sure, there are still some heresy-hunters about. After my original article appeared in the *Torah u-Madda Journal*, both myself and the editor of the journal, Rabbi Dr Jacob J. Schacter, were attacked in a scurrilous fashion by Binyamin Jolkovsky in the Satmar paper *Yidishe tsaytung* (28 July 1995). Jolkovsky, who telephoned me for an interview, was at least honest enough to admit that he had never read the article.

[147] A good example is R. Abraham Isaac Kook, who was regarded as a heretic by many of the anti-Zionist Hungarian rabbis, including a figure who is himself quoted a number of times in this book, R. Hayim Eleazar Shapira of Munkacz. See H. E. Shapira, *Divrei torah*, vi, no. 82; id., *Sha'ar yisakhar*, 373; Weinberger (ed.), *Igerot shapirin*, no. 219.

cussed in this book always regarded themselves as part of the traditional community. They were also regarded as such by significant, if not overwhelming, segments of this community, in particular by the religious and intellectual leadership, both during and after these scholars' lifetimes. In many cases, these men were even leaders of their community. The fact that they differed with aspects of Maimonides' Principles never caused them to lose this status, which itself shows that traditional Jews rejected a central facet of Maimonides' Principles, namely, that denial of any of them turns one into a heretic. For my purposes, this acceptance on the part of their peers and succeeding generations suffices to place these scholars in the traditional or 'Orthodox' category. While it is true that some of these individuals are only minor figures, and thus probably not an acceptable source for those seeking to create a new Orthodox theology, they are still significant from a historical standpoint, that is, when one seeks to document how traditional figures did not feel bound by the Thirteen Principles.

I have omitted those scholars whose overall views place them clearly at odds with what traditional Jews have generally regarded as religiously acceptable. In modern times these scholars are usually, but not always, at odds with the halakhic system (in whole or in part), and do not regard themselves as part of the Orthodox community. When dealing with medieval society, matters are more complex since there is no clear breakdown of denominations. Furthermore, the radical philosophers whose writings have come down to us all seem to have lived in accordance with Jewish law, even if their view of its significance diverged drastically from that of the talmudists. In choosing whom to include, I shall concentrate on figures who were accepted by significant segments of the community and whose religious legitimacy was, when occasion warranted, publicly defended by their colleagues. This explains why, for example, I include R. Samuel ibn Tibbon (*c*.1160–*c*.1232), and his son-in-law R. Jacob Anatoli (*c*.1194–1256),[148] but not Moses ben Joshua of Narbonne (commonly called Narboni; died 1362), Isaac Albalag (thirteenth century),

---

[148] See Gordon, 'Rationalism', 128–33; G. Stern, 'Menahem ha-Meiri', 204; Halbertal, *Between Torah and Wisdom*, 18. R. Abba Mari Astruc of Lunel, who instigated the assault on extreme rationalism in Provence, denied that he was including Anatoli in this category. See Gordon, 'Rationalism', 150 n. 1; G. Stern, 'Menahem ha-Meiri', 204 n. 71. Aside from Maimonides' positive comments about Ibn Tibbon (see p. 77), R. Abraham Abulafia quotes Ibn Tibbon and even agrees with his theory of providence. See Scholem, *Origins*, 377 n. 32. R. Isaac b. Jacob Lattes also refers very positively to Ibn Tibbon and his *Ma'amar yikavu hamayim*. See Halbertal, *Between Torah and Wisdom*, 144. Nahmanides refers to Ibn Tibbon's *Ma'amar yikavu hamayim* in his sermon on Ecclesiastes. See id., *Kitvei ramban*, i. 187. R. Menahem Meiri was influenced by Ibn Tibbon and Anatoli and had a great deal of respect for them, though I think Stern exaggerates somewhat when he writes (p. 205): 'Meiri *reveres* Anatoli and the Tibbons' (emphasis added). See Halbertal, *Between Torah and Wisdom*, ch. 2.

and a host of other radical medieval philosophers who constitute a veritable 'school' of extreme rationalism.[149]

Dogma in Judaism

There is no need for me to attempt here a detailed study of the place of dogma in Jewish intellectual history. Fortunately, this task has already been carried out by other scholars, in particular Louis Jacobs and Menachem Kellner, from whose work I have benefited greatly. However, because of its import-ance it is necessary to make a few comments on this issue.

There is no question that one of the great misinterpretations of Judaism, so frequently repeated that it is often assumed as a matter of course, is that Judaism does not have dogmas. To be sure, all would agree that belief in God and some sort of revelation are dogmas that the tradition has always affirmed, but, aside from these, Judaism has commonly been portrayed as granting complete freedom in matters of thought. However, even if one discounts Maimonides' original advocacy of what can be termed salvific dogmas (namely, dogmas the belief in which guarantees one a place in heaven), the fact remains that for all medieval authorities, as well as the talmudic rabbis, there were certain dogmas which Jews were obligated to believe in, simply because the religion is unintelligible without them. Although it is likely that the talmudic rabbis had fewer of these dogmas than their medieval colleagues, they too were prepared to lay down some parameters of belief. For example, Mishnah *Sanhedrin* 10: 1 states: 'These are they who have no share in the world to come: he who says that there is no resurrection of the dead in the Torah, he who says that the Torah is not from Heaven, and the *epikoros*.'[150] Although it

[149] Dov Schwartz has performed a tremendous service in bringing to light these philosophers, most of whose writings are still in manuscript. In addition to his many articles, see his books, *Old Wine* and *Messianic Idea*.

[150] Although Maimonides understands *epikoros* to have a theological connotation (*Mishneh torah*, 'Hilkhot teshuvah', 3: 8, 'Hilkhot gezelah', 11: 2, 'Hilkhot rotse'ah', 4: 10), and this is clearly the con-text in which it appears in Mishnah *San.* 10: 1, the Talmud offers a few different definitions of the term, none of which has anything to do with theology. Thus, an *epikoros* is defined as one who shows disrespect for the sages, for one's neighbour, or for one's teacher (see BT *San.* 99*b*–100*a*). For analysis of how Maimonides uses the term, see Abraham di Boton, *Leḥem mishneh* on 'Hilkhot teshuvah', 3: 7; Kellner, *Dogma*, 19 ff. In 'Hilkhot avodah zarah', 10: 1, Maimonides states that an *epikoros* is to be killed because he leads people away from God. See also 'Hilkhot edut', 11: 10. In his commentary on Mishnah *San.* 10: 1, Maimonides explains *epikoros* as coming from the root *hefker*, and not from the Greek philosopher Epicurus. This is surprising as Maimonides knew of Epicurus and refers to him in *Guide* iii. 17. (Even if Maimonides had not heard of Epicurus when he wrote his commentary on the Mishnah, we know that he revised it throughout his life and yet he never altered this explanation.) See Nathan b. Yehiel, *Arukh hashalem*, s.v. *epikoros*. Simeon Duran, *Magen avot*, i. 2 (p. 4*b*), and the section of this work on Mishnah *Avot* 2: 14, also called *Magen avot* (Leipzig, 1855), points to the Greek philosopher as the origin of the term *epikoros*.

is hard to know what the Mishnah meant by the term *epikoros* (probably someone who denies God's providence[151]), clearly this mishnaic formulation does not exhaust the list of rabbinic dogmas. It is likely that the Mishnah only mentions those beliefs which were not then obvious, that is, those concerning which there was dispute in the Jewish community. This would explain why nothing appears here regarding belief in God.

In his classic study of the dogmas in Judaism, which totally disproves the notion that Judaism is unconcerned with belief, Solomon Schechter stated the point very well.

Political economy, hygiene, statistics, are very fine things. But no sane man would for them make those sacrifices which Judaism requires from us. It is only for God's sake, to fulfill his commands and to accomplish his purpose, that religion becomes worth living and dying for. And this can only be possible with a religion which possesses dogmas. It is true that every great religion is 'a concentration of many ideas and ideals', which make this religion able to adapt itself to various modes of thinking and living. But there must always be a point round which all these ideas concentrate themselves. This centre is Dogma.[152]

That so many scholars could, in the face of all the evidence, continue to assert that Judaism has no dogmas probably tells us more about their attempts to justify their own freethinking than about the history of Jewish thought. Although the denial that Judaism has dogmas was more common in previous generations, this view continues to be advanced by some modern thinkers. In their opinion, Judaism is a religion of law and one can basically believe what one wishes. Thus, to give one example, the late Zvi Kurzweil, a Modern Orthodox thinker, argues for this position and writes that 'while fundamentalism in Christianity includes dogmatic belief in certain basic tenets of faith, Judaism lacks such dogmas. There is more than a grain of truth in Leon Roth's reference to "dogmalessness as the only dogma in Judaism".'[153]

Kurzweil supports his view regarding the lack of dogmas in Judaism by citing Moses Mendelssohn (1729–86), Isaac Breuer (1883–1946), and Isaiah Leibowitz (1903–94). Leaving aside the question of whether Mendelssohn is a representative of traditional Judaism, Kurzweil is correct that, in his *Jerusalem*, Mendelssohn asserted that Judaism has no dogmas.[154] Yet Kurz - weil neglects to point out that matters are more complicated than this, and it may be that Mendelssohn himself was unsure on this point. Indeed, he often

---

[151] See Schiffman, *Who Was a Jew*, 44. As Schiffman points out, Josephus describes the Epicureans, as well as the Sadducees, as those who deny God's providence. The Sadducees also denied both the resurrection and that the Oral Torah was from heaven, thus making it very likely that this Mishnah was formulated against this latter group. See ibid. 42 ff.   [152] *Studies*, i. 181.

[153] Kurzweil, 'Fundamentalism', 9. See L. Roth, *Judaism*, 125.   [154] *Jerusalem*, 100.

accepted the existence of certain dogmatic principles, although these are not to be understood as dogmas in the Christian sense—that is, articles of faith which have been formulated by an authoritative body or which stand in contradiction to reason. Furthermore, even according to the most liberal understanding of the passage referred to by Kurzweil, Mendelssohn obviously agreed that some beliefs are required, for without them one cannot even speak of a Jewish religion.[155]

As for Breuer, it is true that he had some interesting views regarding the nature of faith and its relation to Jewish law. However, although he put individual faith in the background and acceptance of the law in the forefront, he never denied that Judaism required dogmas, without which, he believed, the religion would be incomprehensible. For Breuer, it was the acceptance of the dogmas by the *community* which was crucial, and it was only for the wavering individual that he emphasized the importance of law over dogma. That is, the dogmas of Judaism are important, though, *ex post facto*, an individual who observes the halakhah is not to be viewed as a heretic because of his lack of belief.[156] However, it is essential to note that Breuer did not regard this situation favourably. According to him, non-believers are in error and every effort must be made to set them right. He was clearly not a relativist in matters of belief.

Only Leibowitz remains to support Kurzweil's contention. However, Leibowitz was the first to admit that his views disregarded vast portions of what has always been regarded as part and parcel of Jewish thought and values.[157] Thus, to give one example of many, Leibowitz did not believe that

---

[155] See e.g. *'Jerusalem' and Other*, 154, where, in his reply to Charles Bonnet's *Palingénésie*, Mendelssohn wrote that Judaism has three principles: God, providence, and legislation (i.e. revelation of the Torah). In his reply to Lavater, Mendelssohn offered the identical opinion. See Altmann, *Mendelssohn*, 544. See also E. Jospe, *Mendelssohn*, 121, for his letter to Elkan Herz, in which he clarified his opinion: 'We have no dogmas *that go beyond or against reason*' (emphasis added). A hundred years ago, Solomon Schechter called attention to this common distortion of Mendelssohn's views: see his *Studies*, 147–8. See also Friedlaender, *Jewish Religion*, 16–18, and Altmann's note in his edition of *Jerusalem*, 217. Mendelssohn also believed that Maimonides' Thirteen Principles had significant religious and educational value, and he therefore translated them into German and included them in a book he published for students: see A. Shohet, *Changing Eras*, 256; A. E. Simon, 'Philanthropism', 163. However, rather than recording them with the formulation 'I believe', he used the phrase 'Ich erkenne für wahr und gewiss' (I recognize it as true and certain). In section I of *Jerusalem* (p. 63 in Altmann's and Arkush's edition) he listed God, providence and future life as the fundamental prin - ciples 'on which all religions agree, and without which felicity is but a dream'.

[156] Not surprisingly, this view encountered opposition. See I. Breuer, *Concepts*, 3–4; M. Breuer, 'Changes', 174 n. 38; id., *Jüdische Orthodoxie*, 493 n. 35; E. Stern, *Ishim vekivunim*, 135 n. 29. Yerahmiel Yisrael Yitshak Domb, in his polemic against the ethos of German Orthodoxy, refers specifically to this view of Breuer; see his *Ha'atakot*, 275–6.

[157] See the numerous refutations of Leibowitz's various positions in Ben Yeruham and Kolitz (eds.), *Shelilah lishemah*.

Israel is the 'Holy Land'. As he explained on numerous occasions, the word 'holy' can only be applied to 'the disciplined and saintly conduct of human beings who master their desires and inclinations and serve the Lord by leading a life of Torah and mitzvot'.[158] This attitude enabled Leibowitz to call for the demolition of the Western Wall, which he considered to be an idol of stone. The fact that Leibowitz was probably the first observant Jew in history who did not view the Land of Israel or the Western Wall as holy was of no concern to him, yet we should keep it in mind whenever someone, such as Kurzweil, tries to quote Leibowitz as an illustration of traditional Jewish thought. What Kurzweil does not mention is that at least since the rabbinic period, every important rabbi, talmudist, Bible commentator, and philosopher believed in dogmas. Salis Daiches is therefore entirely correct in writing that 'all authoritative exponents of Judaism are agreed as to the necessity of making spiritual truth the basis for material action.'[159]

A few more points must be noted in this regard. As we shall see, there have been those who opposed the Principles of Maimonides because they believed them to be mistaken. This is very different from the attitude of Abarbanel,[160] R. David ibn Zimra,[161] and R. Samson Raphael Hirsch (1808–88),[162] who, although they accepted the truth of Maimonides' dogmas, opposed his singling them out as being the most significant aspects of Judaism. According to them, no special dogmas can be established because *everything* contained in the Torah is, in and of itself, a dogma of paramount importance. Thus, one who denies *any* Torah teaching is to be regarded as a heretic. One example of Abarbanel's thought on this matter is as follows:

I, therefore, believe that it is not proper to postulate principles for the divine Torah, nor foundations in the matters of beliefs, for we are obliged to believe everything that is written in the Torah. We are not permitted to doubt even the smallest thing in it. . . . For he who denies or doubts a belief or narrative of the

[158] Kurzweil, *Modern Impulse*, 51. See also Leibowitz, *Judaism*, index, s.v. holiness. Leibowitz cites R. Meir Simhah of Dvinsk, *Meshekh hokhmah*, on Exod. 32: 19, as agreeing with his view, since the latter writes that nothing in this world is intrinsically holy, but rather becomes holy by virtue of our observance of the *mitsvot*. See also the discussion in Fox, 'Holiness', 157 ff. Yet even R. Meir Simhah's view, which I believe is unique in traditional literature, is somewhat different from that presented by Leibowitz, for he posits that if Jews fulfil God's will, physical objects, such as the Temple and the Land of Israel, *do* assume real holiness. See Ben-Sasson, *Philosophical System*, 164–7. Leibowitz, on the other hand, denies that the concept of holiness can ever be applied to inanimate objects. There are, of course, many *halakhot* whose very basis is the holiness of the Land of Israel. See J. D. Bleich, *Contemporary Halachic Problems*, ch. 8, 'The Sanctity of the Liberated Territories'.

[159] 'Dogma', 249.

[160] See Kellner, *Dogma*, 184 ff., for an important analysis of Abarbanel's position.

[161] *She'elot uteshuvot haradbaz*, no. 344.

[162] *Neunzehn Briefe*, 79 (fifteenth letter). See, however, the seventeenth letter, in which he acknow-ledges that Judaism may indeed be based on the Thirteen Principles, but points out that they hardly comprise the entire religion.

Torah, be it small or great, is a sectarian and *epikoros*. For, since the Torah is true, no belief or narrative in it has an advantage over any other.[163]

However, it would seem that this comment misses the mark, because, with the exception of the words of criticism directed against him, Maimonides believed everything advocated here. One who denies the divine origin of anything in the Torah is indeed regarded by him as a heretic, in accordance with the Eighth Principle. It is also quite imprecise for Abarbanel, as part of his polemic against Maimonides, to assert without clarification that a belief which is found in the Torah cannot be denied. Abarbanel's assertion simply begs the question: who is to determine that the belief is really found in the Torah? As this book will demonstrate, the fact that traditional scholars, none of whom would dream of denying a 'belief of the Torah', argued about basic issues of Jewish theology shows that even explicit Torah texts can be interpreted in a variety of ways. Abarbanel also speaks of denying a narrative of the Torah. Again, this begs the question: what does 'deny' mean? Is one who understands a narrative in the Torah allegorically guilty of 'denial'? All this is quite apart from the fact that many of Maimonides' Principles are *not* found expli-citly in the Torah. Maimonides believed them to be latent, but this is not the same as being explicit.

Furthermore, although Abarbanel does not make the distinction, there is a difference between believing something and simply not doubting it. For example, there is a great deal which the masses do not doubt, but which by the same token they do not believe either, because they simply know nothing about the subject. By positing his Thirteen Principles, Maimonides distinguished between obligatory truths (that is, truths which everyone must believe) and non-obligatory truths. With regard to the Thirteen Principles, one cannot remain in blissful ignorance or be agnostic. This is acceptable with regard to other true beliefs, even those recorded in the Torah, but the Principles are in a separate category in that they must be positively affirmed. As R. Hayim Soloveitchik quite properly explained in relation to the distinc-tion between the 613 *mitsvot* and the Principles, if one does not know about a certain *mitsvah* his Judaism is lacking but there is nothing heretical about this person. However, one who does not acknowledge the Thirteen Principles is a heretic.[164] So we see that there are many true beliefs which are not necessarily obligatory beliefs, i.e. beliefs which every Jew must hold in order to be a Jew in good standing. It is this basic point that Abarbanel overlooked.

Returning to the structure of this book, I have already mentioned that I will not generally concern myself with those scholars who opposed Maimonides'

---

[163] *Rosh amanah*, ch. 23.   [164] Gerlits (ed.), *Hagadah*, 197–9.

Thirteen Principles and substituted their own. They did not, for the most part, deny that Maimonides' Principles were correct and indeed obligatory on Jews to believe. Their disagreement with Maimonides concerned which doctrines they viewed as *indispensable* to Judaism, that is, without which Judaism would be inconceivable.

This is most important, for scholars have often tried to show that, because Albo only postulated three articles of faith, this meant that he did not think that the others were essential, or that their denial equalled heresy. In fact, a leading halakhist, R. Jacob Meshulam Orenstein (1775–1839), is among those who advocates this position and even adopts it as his own. According to him, one is only a heretic if he denies the existence of God, Torah from heaven, and reward and punishment, which are Albo's three fundamental principles. One who denies Maimonides' other Principles is to be regarded as completely wicked but, contrary to Maimonides, is not a heretic and thus has not removed himself from the religion.[165]

While Orenstein's liberality is certainly noteworthy, his assertion that he is following Albo is incorrect, at least with regard to Albo's dominant position. Albo's differences with Maimonides regarding dogma relate to 'classification and grading',[166] not substance. Indeed, Albo himself regards one who only accepts his principles as a heretic. Thus, although Albo did not view belief in the messiah as a 'fundamental' principle—without which Judaism would be inconceivable—he still thought that one who denied the coming of the messiah, knowing it was incumbent upon Jews to believe this, should be viewed as a heretic with no share in the world to come.[167] In fact, R. Simeon ben Tsemah Duran, whose reduction of the principles to three was later adopted by Albo, states explicitly that Maimonides' Thirteen Principles are the 'roots of our faith' (*shorshei emunatenu*).[168]

One final point: although we have seen that many traditional thinkers identified heresy with denial of the Thirteen Principles, this should not be taken to mean that they regarded these Principles as the sole determinants of what constitutes heresy. This is certainly a popular conception, and in

[165] *Yeshuot ya'akov*, 'Orah hayim', 126: 1. I have seen a number of other writers who also misrepresent Albo's position, despite the fact that throughout Book I of his *Sefer ha'ikarim* he leaves no room for doubt. See e.g. Graetz, *Structure*, 167; Taenzer, *Religionsphilosophie*, 36; and I. Epstein, *Faith*, 321 n. 13. Moses Mendelssohn also seems to err in this regard; see id., *Jerusalem*, 102.

[166] Husik, *History*, 416.

[167] See *Sefer ha'ikarim*, i. 23. See also Schechter, *Studies*, 171–2; Jacobs, *Principles*, 392–3; and Ch. 10 n. 26 of this book. See also the careful way in which the messianic belief was formulated at the Dispute of Tortosa, in which Albo participated; Lopez, *Disputa*, i. 544. There is, to be sure, a famous contradiction in Albo regarding this point, and this is perhaps what Orenstein had in mind; see p. 144 of this book. [168] Introduction to *Magen avot* on *Avot*.

Orthodox circles departure from a traditional viewpoint is often justified by saying 'This is not one of the Thirteen Principles.' Yet it is unlikely that any rabbinic figure ever adopted this approach. I say this for the simple reason that Maimonides' Thirteen Principles are not all-inclusive. For example, they do not include the idea that the Jews are God's chosen people.[169] In addition, there are a number of dogmas which Maimonides discusses in other places but excludes from the Thirteen Principles.[170] Thus, there is no mention in the Principles about the existence of free will or miracles, despite the overriding importance of these notions in Maimonides' thought. Although creation and resurrection, Principles 4 and 13, are examples of the miraculous, the traditional belief in miracles encompasses much more than this. Nor does Maimonides include providence as a Principle. Reward and punishment are mentioned, but while they can be included under the general rubric of providence, the concept itself implies much more than simply reward and punishment. In fact, most post-Maimonideans include providence in their detailed lists of dogmas, and some of them include it in addition to reward and punishment.[171] Only R. Shem Tov Falaquera (thirteenth century), in his *Sefer hamevakesh*, follows Maimonides in listing reward and punishment as a principle while omitting providence (although in another work he does list it).[172]

[169] Regarding this omission, see *Maimonides' Introductions*, ed. Shailat, 219. For the view that this is a basic principle of Judaism, denial of which is heresy, see M. Klein, *Mishneh halakhot*, introd., 3 (unnumbered).

[170] See Kellner, *Dogma*, 53 ff.

[171] See Kellner, *Dogma*, 200 ff. Albo lists reward and punishment as a basic principle and providence as a 'root' or derivative principle. See ibid. 146–9.

[172] See Kellner, *Dogma*, 74–5. Hyman, 'Maimonides' "Thirteen Principles"', 139, writes: 'Even more striking is Maimonides' omission of the World to Come from the "thirteen principles".' He contrasts this to 'Hilkhot teshuvah', where 'the World to Come forms a part of the discussion of reward and punishment'. This is incorrect, as Maimonides includes the world to come as part of the Eleventh Principle. In his words: 'The greatest reward is the world to come and the greatest punishment is *karet*'. Hyman's assertion that Maimonides does not mention creation of the world in the Principles has also been shown to be inaccurate, with the publication of the Kafih edition of Maimonides' commentary on the Mishnah. For attempts to explain the omission of free will, see Simeon Duran, *Ohev mishpat*, 13*b*; Gedaliah b. Solomon Lipschuetz's commentary on Albo's *Sefer ha'ikarim*, i. 3 (found in the standard editions); Leibowitz, *Faith*, 85–6; *Maimonides' Introductions*, ed. Shailat, 187–8; Goldman, 'Halachic Foundation', 117–18. Goldman concludes that 'free-will was not for him a decisive dogma to be compared with Revelation or Resurrection'. However, in 'Hilkhot teshuvah', 5: 3, Maimonides writes that free will 'is a fundamental concept and a pillar [on which rests the totality] of the Torah and *mitsvot*' (see also ibid. 6: 1). In *Guide* iii. 17 Maimonides terms free will 'a fundamental principle of the Law of Moses our Master'. In his 'Letter on Astrology' he states that free will is not simply a fundamental principle of the Torah, but is also acknowledged by all the philosophers. See *Letters*, ed. Shailat, ii. 486. In *Shemoneh perakim*, ch. 8, Maimonides writes: 'If Man's actions were done under compulsion, the commandments and prohibitions of the Law would be nullified and they would all be absolutely in vain. . . . All of this is utterly absurd and false, contrary to what is

All this may lend credence to Arthur Hyman's argument, anticipated by Duran[173] and Abarbanel,[174] that the Thirteen Principles were never intended to comprise all of the most important aspects of Judaism. Rather, they were formulated so as to correspond with the structure of the Mishnah in tractate *Sanhedrin* upon which Maimonides was commenting. In addition, Duran claims that Maimonides chose as Principles only those that were explicitly found in biblical verses.[175] Another suggestion noted by Duran is that Maimonides' choice of thirteen is parallel to God's thirteen attributes, and this forced him to omit principles which should have been included.[176] According to Albo, Maimonides only included those Principles which can be seen as deriving from Albo's own three foundational beliefs: the existence of God, Torah from heaven, and reward and punishment.[177] R. Joseph Joshua Preil (1858–96) argued that Maimonides' Principles only include those beliefs

grasped by the intellect and perceived by the senses, destructive of the wall around the Law, and a judgement upon God, the Exalted, as being unjust—may He be exalted above that.'

Shlomo Pines and Alexander Altmann have identified Maimonides as a determinist and regard this view as his esoteric doctrine. In fact, this approach was anticipated by Abner of Burgos. See Pines, 'Studies', 195–8; Altmann, *Essays*, 47–59; Gershenson, 'View'. Still, even if correct, this would have nothing to do with the omission of free will in the Principles, since there is no question that the Thirteen Principles represent the *exoteric* teachings of Maimonides. See Altmann, *Essays*, 54: 'There can be no doubt that in the *Mishna Commentary* and kindred texts of a theological character Maimonides subscribes to the theory that, no matter how strong the impact of circumstances and motivations, man is able to overrule them by his free choice.' (Cf. however, W. Z. Harvey, 'Maimonides' Interpretation', 18, and id., 'The *Mishneh Torah*', 24 ff., who does not make any distinction between the *Guide* and the more popular texts.) For recent discussions of this issue, see Gellman, 'Freedom'; Safran, 'Maimonides'.

[173] *Magen avot*, 2b.

[174] *Rosh amanah*, ch. 6. Abarbanel also claims that Maimonides' Thirteen Principles can be derived from the creation story. See id., *Mifalot elokim*, i. 4.   [175] *Ohev mishpat*, ch. 8.

[176] Ibid. 13b. See similarly Albo, *Sefer ha'ikarim*, i. 3. R. Isaiah Horowitz, *Shenei luhot haberit*, i. 96a, also relates the Thirteen Principles to God's attributes, and not merely in terms of their number. He regards them as 'hinted at' in the thirteen attributes of God. See similarly Safrin, *Heikhal haberakhah*, i. 29a and Rothschild, *Oniyah belev hayam*, 33b. On the number 13, see also J. D. Bleich, *With Perfect Faith*, 13 n. 2: 'The notion that the credal principles of faith are thirteen in number may well be an ancient tradition. R. Avraham ha-Levi [sic] Horowitz . . . cites a certain prayer ascribed to Rav Tavyomi, one of the talmudic sages, which contains a reference to thirteen principles.' Actually, Bleich's point was anticipated by R. Moses Sofer, *She'elot uteshuvot*, 'Yoreh de'ah', no. 356. However, both are mistaken. Horowitz, *Shenei luhot haberit*, 97a, never refers to *Rav* Tavyomi. He simply mentions a prayer composed by a certain Tavyomi, which is another way of writing the name Yom Tov. See the letter from Leopold Loew in *Kerem hemed*, 9 (1856), 78; J. Schwartz, *Divrei yosef*, iii–iv, no. 57. (In an earlier responsum, *She'elot uteshuvot*, 'Even ha'ezer', ii, no. 148, Sofer himself realized that Tavyomi's prayer has nothing to do with Maimonides' Thirteen Principles. His change of mind remains a mystery.) This prayer was actually composed by R. Yom Tov Lipmann Muelhausen (14th–15th cents.), and was published by Efraim Kupfer, '*Sefer haberit*', 340–1. For a fanciful explanation as to why Maimonides picked the number 13, see Schueck, *Sidur haminhagim*, iv. 42a; id., *Sidur rashban*, 2a. See also Michael Chilton's ridiculous suggestion that 'the very number thirteen perhaps received an added emphasis in Jewish tradition because it was considered unlucky by Christians', in id., *Christian Effect*, 193.   [177] *Sefer ha'ikarim*, i. 4.

which separate Judaism from other religions, a point he used to explain why the coming of the messiah is included as dogma even though, as pointed out by Albo, it is not indispensable to the religion.[178] All these scholars are thus in agreement that not everything Maimonides regarded as a basic Jewish belief was included in the Thirteen Principles, but this need not imply that it was any less important in his eyes.[179]

Since one can view the Thirteen Principles as less than all-inclusive, it should not surprise us that since Maimonides' day many traditional scholars felt comfortable expanding the list of obligatory beliefs. To give one example, I referred earlier to R. Abraham Isaiah Karelitz's comment that he ordered his life on complete faith in the Thirteen Principles. Yet Karelitz added a new dogma to the list, namely, the belief that *all agadot* in the Talmud have their origin in the sages' prophetic power.[180] As with every dogma, one who denies this is to be regarded as a heretic.

Maimonides himself, however, did not share Karelitz's extreme fundamentalism in this regard, for he rejected the authority of various *agadot* and acknowledged that the talmudic sages could err.[181] Occasionally, one even finds him subtly criticizing the talmudic sages: 'You also know their [the talmudic sages'] famous dictum—would that all [their] dicta were like it.'[182] Maimonides also expresses a tolerant opinion of 'a perfect man of virtue' who, because of his own speculation, improperly rejected *agadot*. According to Maimonides, even though such a man is led to regard various talmudic sages as ignoramuses, 'in this there is nothing that would upset the foundations of belief.'[183]

---

[178] *Eglei tal*, 24a. The same approach is followed by Schechter, *Studies*, 179; Petuchowski, *Theology*, 23; Neumark, *History of Jewish Dogma*, ii. 130; Maimon, *Maimonides*, 63.

[179] See Hyman, 'Maimonides' "Thirteen Principles"', 131 n. 73, 138–9. See also Raffel, 'Maimonides' Fundamental Principles', 77–88. According to these scholars, Kellner is not correct when he says that Maimonides would not regard as a heretic one 'who inadvertently denies some teaching not included in the principles'. It would depend upon which teaching he is denying. See Kellner, 'Heresy', 309.

[180] *Kovets igerot*, i. 42–3.

[181] See my 'Maimonidean Halakhah'. For the numerous *ge'onim* and *rishonim* who did not share Karelitz's embrace of all *agadot*, see Saperstein, *Decoding the Rabbis*, ch. 1.

[182] *Guide* i. 59.   [183] Ibid., introduction.

TWO

The Existence and Unity of God

༄

The First Principle

THE FIRST PRINCIPLE declares that God exists, that he is perfect in every way, and that he is the cause of the existence of all things. The Principle also includes the belief that God is eternal, for he is 'an existent Being which is perfect in all aspects of existence', and perfect existence precludes dissolution. Needless to say, later Jewish thinkers all concurred with Maimonides that God exists, is eternal, and is perfect. Those thinkers who significantly limit God, as we shall see (particularly in our discussion of the Tenth Principle), do not dispute with Maimonides the fact that God is perfect and thus omnipotent. According to them, the fact that even God cannot do the impossible is not an imperfection, and Maimonides agrees with this. He explains his position in *Guide* i. 75: 'We do not call a human individual weak because he cannot move one thousand hundred-weights, and we do not attribute to God, may He be exalted, incapacity because He is unable to corpify His essence or to create someone like Him or to create a square whose diagonal is equal to its side.' In *Guide* iii. 15 he writes:

The impossible has a stable nature, one whose stability is constant and is not made by a maker; it is impossible to change it in any way. Hence the power over the maker of the impossible is not attributed to the deity. This is a point about which none of the men of speculation differs in any way. . . . Likewise, that God should bring into existence someone like Himself, or should annihilate Himself, or should become a body, or should change[1]—all of these things belong to the class of the impossible; and the power to do any of these things cannot be attributed to God.[2]

This view is a non-controversial position reaffirmed by all post-Maimonidean philosophers.[3] Even before Maimonides arrived on the scene, the same

---

[1] See R. Joseph ibn Kaspi's commentary on the *Guide*, *Amudei kesef umaskiyot kesef*, ad loc., where he discusses this point with reference to Christian doctrine.   [2] See also *Guide* ii. 13.

[3] R. Abraham Azulai wrote: 'God can do all things that are impossible according to nature, for he created nature, but it is not to be imagined that he can do things that are impossible according to reason. . . . Yet there is no need to publicize this among the Gentiles . . . because if they hear it they will be led to doubt God's existence': id., *Ba'alei berit avram*, 121. Since the context of this comment shows that he is speaking about Christians, the words just quoted would appear to refer to the Trinity. In other words, if Christians learn that a triune God is an impossibility, it will lead them to complete unbelief, which is worse than their present doctrine.

notion was strongly affirmed by Sa'adiah Gaon.[4] Kabbalists could also feel comfortable with this basic idea, and the great Spanish mystic R. Ezra ben Solomon (died *c*.1238) is just as adamant as Maimonides that it implies no defect in God to assert that he cannot do the impossible.[5] The dispute between Maimonides and those who 'limit' God is only over what constitutes the impossible, with Maimonides having a more restricted understanding of this than some other thinkers.

It is worth noting, however, that there have been Jewish thinkers who reject Maimonides' basic assumption, and believe that God *can* do the logically impossible. They argue that this is only impossible from the human standpoint, and there is no reason to posit that 'because the human intellect cannot conceive the existence of something possessing simultaneously contradictory properties, such existence is necessarily impossible in reality'.[6] Against those, such as Maimonides, who argued that God cannot do the impossible and, in particular, asserted that God can have no physical movement, the Tosafist R. Moses Taku (thirteenth century) wrote: 'They are issuing a decree to the Creator as to how He must be. By so doing they are degrading themselves.'[7] R. Nahman of Bratslav also argued that God can do the logically impossible, and that to claim otherwise is to restrict God's freedom. One of his disciples reported: 'He mentions that it says in their [the philosophers'] books: "Is it possible that a triangle be a rectangle?" Our master said: "I believe that God can make a rectangular triangle. For the ways of God are hidden from us; He is omnipotent, and no deed is beyond Him."'[8] As Arthur Green put it in summarizing R. Nahman's position, 'Faith is to exist even in the face of logical absurdity. . . . The tradition of Tertullian has here found its Jewish parallel.'[9]

---

[4] *Emunot vede'ot*, i. 3, ii. 13. See H. A. Wolfson, *Repercussions*. This view was also standard among both Christian and Muslim philosophers. See id., *Philosophy*, 578–89.

[5] Nahmanides, *Kitvei ramban*, ii. 494 (commentary on Song of Songs 3: 9); Scholem, *Studies*, 28. For a long time R. Ezra b. Solomon's commentary on Song of Songs was mistakenly attributed to Nahmanides. See Chavel's introduction in Nahmanides, *Kitvei haramban*, ii. 474–5; Vajda, *Commentaire*.   [6] Fox, *Interpreting Maimonides*, 30.

[7] *Ketav tamim*, ed. Kirchheim, 82. Although he calls the idea 'strange', R. Elijah Delmedigo, *Behinat hadat*, 82, seems to regard the notion that God can do the impossible as an acceptable belief. See Ross' note, p. 120.

[8] See Green, *Tormented Master*, 306. See, similarly, R. Tsevi Elimelekh of Dynów, *Benei yisakhar*, 'Sivan' 5: 19 (103*a*); Marcus, *Keset hasofer*, 9.

[9] Green, *Tormented Master*, 306. In his note, Green writes: ' "Their books" here may be a garbled reference to Maimonides' *Guide* 3: 15.' Actually, the 'garbled' reference is probably to Albo, *Sefer ha'ikarim*, i. 22, who, unlike Maimonides, actually discusses triangles and squares. R. Nahman's position is also discussed in Jacobs, *Faith*, 201–9, who calls attention to the similar view of R. Aaron b. Moses of Starosselje. See also Jacobs, *Seeker*, 101–2. Tertullian is often quoted as saying 'Credo, quia absurdum est' (I believe, because it is absurd), yet these exact words are nowhere found in his writings. What he does say is, 'Certum est, quia impossibile est' (It is certain because it is impossible) and 'prorsus credibile est, quia ineptum est' (it is by all means to be believed, because it is absurd [senseless]). See *De carne christi*, 5. On what Tertullian meant by these phrases, see Roberts, *Theology*, 75–8.

Maimonides' other point in this Principle is that God is the cause of the existence of all things. This is not an assertion of creation *ex nihilo*, a point that will be discussed in relation to the Fourth Principle. Rather, it establishes God's ontological priority to the universe. In other words, the universe is dependent upon God for its existence. However, Maimonides' formulation leaves open the possibility that the universe has coexisted eternally with God.

The Second Principle

The Second Principle teaches the absolute unity of God, which is unlike the unity of anything else. No Jewish teacher has openly disputed this.[10] To be sure, opponents of kabbalah viewed the mystical doctrine of the Sefirot, the ten aspects, or powers, of the Godhead, in the same way as the Trinity, namely, as a violation of God's absolute unity and thus idolatrous.[11] In a famous responsum, R. Isaac ben Sheshet (1326–1407) quotes a philosopher who argued that, whereas the Christians believe in 'three', the kabbalists believe in 'ten'.[12] The renowned kabbalist R. Abraham Abulafia (thirteenth century) agreed with the philosophers in this regard, seeing the standard kabbalistic understanding of the Sefirot as even worse than the concept of the Trinity.[13]

There can be no doubt that, had Maimonides known of this concept, he would have responded in the same fashion, and opponents of kabbalah have understandably regarded themselves as following in Maimonides' footsteps. It is impossible to reconcile the kabbalistic understanding of God and his various sefirotic manifestations with the simple, unknowable God of Maimonides. This is especially so when dealing with those kabbalists who insist that the Sefirot are actually part of God's essence. For example, R. Moses Cordovero (1522–70) writes: 'At the start of the emanation, the Ein Sof, King of all kings, the Holy One, blessed be He, emanated ten Sefirot, which are from His essence, are one with Him and He and they are all one complete unity.'[14]

The kabbalists, for their part, never regarded the doctrine of the Sefirot as doing violence to God's absolute unity. In their mind, the Sefirot are always united with Ein Sof, God's unknowable essence, and are manifestations of

[10] See Jacobs, *Jewish Theology*, ch. 2.

[11] See R. Meir b. Simeon of Narbonne's letter published in Scholem, *Studies*, 16–18; E. Delmedigo, *Beḥinat hadat*, 91; Halamish, *Kabbalah*, 75.

[12] *She'elot uteshuvot harivash*, no. 157. See also Leone da Modena's comment, quoted in Idel, 'Differing Conceptions', 163. Cf. *Guide* i. 50, where Maimonides compares those who believe that God has attributes with the Christians.

[13] See Jellinek, *Ginzei ḥokhmat hakabalah*, 19. For Abulafia's view of the Sefirot, see E. R. Wolfson, *Abraham Abulafia*, pt. II.

[14] *Pardes rimonim*, iv. 4. For Cordovero's view of the Sefirot, see Ben-Shelomoh, *Mystical Theology*, ch. 2. Regarding Sefirot as part of the divine essence, see Idel, *Kabbalah*, 137 ff.

the various aspects of God's nature. The Zohar asserts that Israel lost its battle against Amalek because they misunderstood this point.[15] Yet the fact remains that, even after accepting the kabbalistic assumptions, there have been times when it is difficult for all but the most vigorous defenders of the sefirotic system not to see in it a departure from the doctrine of the unity of God.

For centuries kabbalists have been adamant that, although Ein Sof, or as it is often referred to, Ilat Ha'ilot (Cause of causes), is unknowable, it is through the 'light' (power) of Ein Sof that the world was created and providence is exercised. Thus, although one should focus on various Sefirot during prayer, the prayer itself is fundamentally directed to Ein Sof (or to its 'light', which envelops the Sefirot and works through them). In this conception, even if it appears that prayer is directed towards the Sefirot, it is never to the Sefirot alone, only to Ein Sof as revealed in the Sefirot. Orthodox kabbalists also regarded as heretical the notion popularized by the Shabatean kabbalist Abraham Miguel Cardozo (1626–1706), that the hidden God, called the 'First Cause', is entirely removed from any contact with the world. According to Cardozo, it is the Demiurge, the 'God of Israel', who created the world and exercises providence. In other words, it was the Demiurge, not the First Cause, who appeared to the Patriarchs, sent the plagues, and took the Israelites out of Egypt. It thus comes as no surprise that it is the Demiurge to whom prayers are addressed. As Scholem put it:

> even the moderate Sabbatians tried to evolve a conception of God which conflicted with the fundamental tenets of Judaism. Their passionate insistence in proclaiming a derivative of something else the supreme object of religion has something strange and perturbing. The furious reaction of Orthodoxy and also of orthodox Kabbalism against this attempt to tear the God of Reason and the Revealed God asunder, is only too comprehensible.[16]

Before looking at the centuries preceding the Shabateans, it must be pointed out that in the succeeding centuries there was at least one rabbinic figure, R. Isaac Lopes of Aleppo (seventeenth century), who saw nothing heretical in Cardozo's view. Lopes even advocated this position himself, quoting from Cardozo's unpublished *Boker avraham*. He stated that he was unaware of the origin of this work; since he believed that a great kabbalist had written it, he was able to evaluate its position and find it acceptable.[17] It is true that some scholars reject Lopes' claim that he did not know the identity of the author of *Boker avraham*, and regard him as a secret Cardozian,[18] yet the fact remains

---

[15] *Zohar* ii. 64*b*; Scholem, *Mystical Shape*, 52–3.

[16] *Major Trends*, 323–4. See also Yosha, 'Philosophical Background'; D. J. Halperin, *Abraham*, chs. 4, 10.   [17] *Kur matsref ha'emunot umare ha'emet*, 101*a*–103*b*.

[18] See Yosha, 'Philosophical Foundations', 192 ff.

that the renowned halakhist and kabbalist R. Joseph Hayim ben Elijah Al-Hakam of Baghdad (1832–1909), who strongly rejects Lopes' Cardozian position,[19] nevertheless had a very high opinion of him.[20] Lopes is also cited a number of number of times by R. Jacob Kassin (1900–94), the late rabbi of Brooklyn's Syrian community.[21]

Although Cardozo's view was regarded as heretical in his day, there were outstanding kabbalists in medieval times who held a very similar position. Like Cardozo, they believed that Ilat Ha'ilot has no involvement with human affairs, being completely impersonal and transcendent. Therefore, no prayers are directed towards it. Instead one prays to the 'God' who is immanent, who created the world and exercises providence in it, that is, the God of Scripture, who is identified with either the first Sefirah (Keter) or the second Sefirah (Hokhmah).[22] Among the kabbalistic works which promulgated this opinion, mention should be made of the influential and anonymous *Ma'arekhet ha'elohut*, which Scholem believes was written around the turn of the fourteenth century.[23] Even if it is incorrect to say that there are two Gods in this conception, there is no escaping the fact that there are two supreme powers in the Godhead—precisely what another religious tradition might call two 'persons'. In line with this, R. Isaac ibn Latif (thirteenth century) describes the immanent 'God' (what he terms the 'First Created Being'), in words that Maimonides would view as blasphemous dualism:

The First Created Being, may He be blessed, knows everything by virtue of His essence, for He is everywhere and everything is in Him, as it is written, *the whole earth is full of His glory* (Isa. 10: 3); and all beings exist through him by way of emanation and evolvement, and nothing exists outside of Him.[24]

Even among 'mainstream' kabbalists, we still find views very much at odds with Maimonidean conceptions. For example, R. Jacob the Nazirite (twelfth century) claimed that the first three and last three benedictions of the Amidah

---

[19] See Joseph Hayim ben Elijah Al-Hakam, *Od yosef hai*, 27 ff. ('Vayeshev'; in the Jerusalem 1910 edition, this appears on pp. 22 ff. of the second pagination). See also id., *Rav pe'alim*, iii, section 'Sod yesharim', no. 11, regarding prayer and Ein Sof.

[20] See *Rav pe'alim*, i, section 'Sod yesharim', no. 1.

[21] See his *Yesod ha'emunah*. There are, to be sure, a number of cases of Orthodox kabbalists who defended problematic passages in Shabatean works. For example, the Yemenite authors of Araki et al., *Emunat hashem*, did so with Nehemiah Hayon's *Oz le'elohim*, which had been attacked as heretical by their opponent, R. Yihyeh Kafih. This says a great deal about the elasticity of apologetics. In the case of *Emunat hashem*, after R. Abraham Isaac Kook, in his *haskamah*, pointed out the true nature of Hayon's book, the authors excised their defence of this work. See *Emunat hashem*, 605. Regarding Shabatean works which have been unknowingly accepted in the Orthodox world, see Naor, *Post-Sabbatian Sabbatianism*.   [22] Heller-Wilensky, '"First Created Being"', 264 ff.

[23] See Scholem, 'Kabbalah', cols. 557–8; Gottlieb, 'Ma'arekhet ha-Elohut', cols. 637–8.

[24] Heller-Wilensky, '"First Created Being"', 263.

prayer are directed to the Sefirah Binah. The middle blessings are directed to Tiferet during the day and to Binah at night. The renowned R. Abraham ben David of Posquières (Rabad; *c.*1125–98) differs in that he believes that the first three and last three blessings are directed to the Supreme Deity (Ilat Ha'ilot), but the middle blessings, which are more personal, are directed to the divine entity which is the manifestation of Ilat Ha'ilot, the Creator (Yotser Bereshit). The logic behind this position is as follows: the early and later blessings contain only praise rather than supplication, and they can therefore be directed towards Ilat Ha'ilot. However, in the middle blessings man beseeches the Lord, and one does not do this with Ilat Ha'ilot. While it is true that Ilat Ha'ilot is the ultimate cause of all, it is not involved in the world in any way and does not hear prayers. Thus, one must direct these prayers to the Creator, who exercises divine providence and in whose image man is created.[25]

On the issue of prayer, it should be noted that there were some kabbalists, such as R. Joseph ben Shalom of Barcelona (thirteenth–fourteenth centuries), author of a famous commentary on *Sefer yetsirah* falsely attributed to Rabad,[26] who even believed that the Sefirot pray to Ilat Ha'ilot![27] With such a view, especially when merged with the popular kabbalistic notion that the Sefirot do not perceive the true nature of Ilat Ha'ilot,[28] it becomes increasingly hard to accept the rhetoric that even in the sefirotic system the unity of God remains uncorrupted. This is doubly so when we consider the view of the great kabbalist R. Azriel of Gerona (thirteenth century), that, with the exception of the first Sefirah, which exists eternally with Ilat Ha'ilot, the other Sefirot all had a beginning in time.[29] Furthermore, what is one to make of the assertion made by R. Isaac Pilitz (nineteenth century), that while it is obvious that Ein Sof knows the future, since it is not subject to time, it is most likely that the Sefirot, which run the world, do not know the future? Pilitz believed that this is the best solution to the old problem of preserving man's free will in the face of God's knowledge.[30] Non-kabbalists will find it difficult to understand why views such as this, where Ein Sof is severed from the Sefirot, do not create a dualism in the divine realm.

Finally, there were also kabbalists who directed prayers to the 'Unique Cherub', an anthropomorphic entity of the divine realm which emanated from, or was created by, God and in whose image man is created.[31] Maimonides

---

[25] Dan, *Jewish Mysticism*, ii. 248–51; id., 'Unique Cherub', ch. 14; Scholem, *Origins*, 212. See also Scholem, 'Concept of Kavvanah', 177 n. 31, where he cites the Oxford manuscript in which the positions held by R. Jacob b. Shalom and Rabad are reversed. See also Idel, 'Kabbalistic Prayer'.

[26] Scholem, 'Chapters from the History'.   [27] Scholem, 'Kabbalah', 567.

[28] Ibid.   [29] Ibid. 568.   [30] *Zera yitshak*, 10*b*–11*a*.

[31] Dan, 'Unique Cherub', 72, 110 (which quotes a manuscript description of the Unique Cherub as having 'an image and form, and a human form, and eyes, and hands . . . and phylacteries are on his head').

would no doubt agree with the judgement of Abraham Epstein that this figure eventually evolved into a 'virtual second God'.[32] Concerning prayer to the Cherub, Dan writes:

The theological necessity dominant in the formulation of the concept of the Cherub, that is, the need to have a divine entity as the subject of anthropomorphic descriptions of God, was probably replaced by mystical devotion to this divine power, which in turn was elevated to the previously forbidden role of accepting prayers from the people of Israel. The theological reservations which had motivated earlier thinkers, forbidding prayer to an entity with an image and limits, did not seem to bother the participants in this later stage of development.[33]

In conclusion, although there is certainly much more that can be said about the nature of kabbalistic prayer, it is not necessary for our purposes. It is true that the kabbalists all believed that their detailed speculations on the Godhead did not damage the fundamental unity of God. Yet from a Maimonidean perspective, which knows only a simple monotheism and a simple divine unity, they indeed violated the intent, if not the letter, of the Second Principle.

[32] *Kitvei*, ii. 239. For a medieval text that refers to the Cherub as the 'lesser YHWH', see Scholem, *Origins*, 216.

[33] '*Unique Cherub*', 238. Regarding R. Elhanan b. Yakar's view that one should pray to the Kavod, which emanated from the Shekhinah, see ibid. 168 ff. See also Abrams, 'Evolution'.

THREE

The Incorporeality of God

❧

The Third Principle

T HE THIRD PRINCIPLE teaches God's incorporeality—that God is without image and form. According to Maimonides, this Principle includes the assertion that God cannot be described as being in movement or at rest, for this would mean that he has form and physical dimensions.[1] Although, as we shall see, the Bible and Talmud speak of a corporeal God, Maimonides' philosophical outlook forced him to insist on divine incorporeality. This is so because a corporeal God is a contradiction in terms, as it is impossible for a corporeal God to have the defining characteristics set down in the First and Second Principles.[2] As noted above, Maimonides also states that God, omnipotent though he is, is unable to assume corporeal form. In fact, Maimonides goes even further and states that one who believes in God's corporeality is worse than some types of idolater.[3] R. Shem Tov ben Joseph ibn Shem Tov (fifteenth century), one of Maimonides' standard commentators, explains this strong statement as follows: the idolater Maimonides refers to at least believes in an incorporeal god (the idol being merely an intermediary or something that has the power to do good or evil). However, a 'corporealist'[4] denies God's existence entirely, for a corporeal being is, by definition, not the Deity. Arthur Hyman has pointed out that, in insisting, as did the Almohad rulers,[5] that the masses be taught God's incorporeality, Maimonides is imparting metaphysical truths which have no political expediency.[6] According to Hyman, this stands as a refutation of Lawrence Berman's thesis that Maimonides' purpose in imparting these metaphysical truths was political in nature without any intrinsic value for the masses.[7]

---

[1] See also *Guide* i. 12, 26; *Mishneh torah*, 'Hilkhot yesodei hatorah', 1: 11.

[2] In 'Hilkhot yesodei hatorah', 1: 7 and *Guide* i. 35, Maimonides argues that the perfection of God (First Principle) and the unity of God (Second Principle) are only applicable to an incorporeal God.

[3] *Guide* i. 36. See, similarly, Hakokhavi, *Sefer habatim*, 'Migdal david: sefer emunah', 39, 'Migdal david: sefer mitsvah', 286.

[4] I prefer this term to 'anthropomorphist' (which I also use when appropriate), since as we shall see, there were those who believed that God is a physical being, although he does not have a human form.   [5] See Heinemann, 'Maimuni'.

[6] 'Maimonides' "Thirteen Principles"', 137–8, 141.

[7] Berman, 'Ibn Bajah', 137–8. See also Pines, *History*, 14.

Whether Maimonides' purpose in teaching the masses the doctrine of an incorporeal God was to instil part of the knowledge required in order for them to attain immortality (as argued by Hyman),[8] was designed to make possible perfect halakhic observance,[9] or was meant to ensure the Jews' *dhimmi* status,[10] makes no difference when one is actually confronted with a corporealist. According to all understandings of Maimonides, such a person cannot attain immortality. This is an important point to which I will later return. For now, I simply note in support of Berman's thesis the fact that the *dhimmi* status of the Jews in Islamic lands would indeed have been endangered had they held to a corporeal conception of God. In other words, contrary to Hyman's assertion, the principle of God's incorporeality certainly did have political expediency.

In addition, I find Hyman's larger argument problematic. According to Hyman, not simply this Principle but all of the Principles dealing with God are intended to impart to the masses knowledge of divine things, thus ensuring them some measure of immortality. Yet would Maimonides ever agree that the masses could attain immortality simply through affirmations lacking any cognitive content, that is, without any actualization of the intellect?[11] At the most, we can say that the Principles are directed towards those non-intellectuals who have the potential of actualizing the intellect. After all, there are gradations of intellectual attainment. Even one who is not a scholar can achieve *some* understanding of these Principles, even though his initial, and to a large extent even continuing, acceptance of them was due to tradition. This is what Maimonides means when, after reviewing his efforts at popularizing religious truth, he writes, 'They [i.e. the philosophically illiterate] will no longer cast the knowledge of God behind their backs, but will exert themselves *to the limit of their power* to attain what will perfect them and bring them nearer to their Creator.'[12] Maimonides also has this population in mind when he writes:

Accordingly if we never in any way acquired an opinion through following traditional authority and were not correctly conducted toward something by means of parables, but were obliged to achieve a perfect representation by means of essential definitions and by pronouncing true only that which is meant to be pronounced true in virtue of a demonstration—which would be impossible except

---

[8] Hyman, 'Maimonides' "Thirteen Principles"'. See also Guttmann, *Philosophies*, 201–3.

[9] See Kellner, *Dogma*, 37 ff. Kellner also offers two other reasons, but this appears to be his main point.

[10] See Silver, *Maimonidean Criticism*, 162. Silver does not exclude the presence of other motivations.

[11] See Nuriel, 'Remarks', 49–50; Hartman, *Maimonides*, 229 n. 31; Mesch, 'Principles', 88.

[12] *Letters*, ed. Shailat, i. 321 (Arabic), 343 (Hebrew); Halkin and Hartman, *Crisis*, 213.

after the above mentioned lengthy preliminary studies—this state of affairs would lead to all people dying without having known whether there is a deity for the world, or whether there is not, much less whether a proposition should be affirmed with regard to Him or a defect denied. Nobody would ever be saved from this perdition except *one of a city or two of a family* (Jer. 3: 14).[13]

We thus see that, for Maimonides, immortality is not exclusively for philosophers. Yet, all of Maimonides' efforts notwithstanding, it also seems clear that the mass of simple people who, especially in medieval times, constituted the overwhelming majority of Jews, have no hope of attaining the Maimonidean world to come. The 'limits of their power' are simply not sufficient to attain any real apprehension of the divine things that are the key to immortality.

Returning to the Principle, it must be stressed that, contrary to popular belief, the notion that God is incorporeal was not always a unanimously accepted Jewish (or Christian[14] or Muslim[15]) view. Before examining the particulars of this corporealism, it should be obvious to all that Maimonides' insistence on God's incorporeality contradicts a simple reading of the Bible. Here God is frequently described as a physical being, with a back, head, and hand. Indeed, *nowhere* in the Bible does it state that God is incorporeal (or invisible, for that matter). Even Deutero-Isaiah, whose prophecies speak of a transcendent and all-powerful God, only states: 'To whom then will ye liken God? O what likeness will ye compare unto Him?' (Isa. 40: 18). This is not a

---

[13] *Guide* i. 34.

[14] In the early Church there were many who took the biblical descriptions of God literally. To combat this heresy, Bishop Theophilus of Alexandria issued a pastoral letter in 399. After being confronted with his error, one old monk found it impossible to pray and declared: 'Woe is me! They have taken my God away from me, and I have none to grasp, and I know not whom to adore or to address.' See Cassian, *Conferences*, 10: 3, in Chadwick (ed.), *Western Asceticism*, 235. See also ibid. 234, where it is reported that nearly all the monks in Egypt received the bishop's letter 'with bitterness and hostility; and a large majority of elders from all the ascetic brotherhood decreed that the bishop was guilty of a grave and hateful heresy, because (by denying that Almighty God was formed in the fashion of a man when Scripture bears clear witness that Adam was created in his image) he seemed to be attacking the text of Holy Scripture'. It is known that rioting broke out when Theophilus' letter was received, and the monks even threatened to kill him. See Clark, *Origenist Controversy*, ch. 2 (called to my attention by Dr Edward Mathews). See also G. Stroumsa, 'Form(s) of God'; Paulsen, 'Early Christian Belief'; Paulsen and Griffin, 'Augustine and the Corporeality of God'. Paulsen writes: 'Ordinary Christians for at least the first three centuries of the current era commonly (and perhaps generally) believed God to be corporeal' ('Early Christian Belief', 105).

[15] See Ibn Tahir al-Baghdadi, *Moslem Schisms*, 67–72; Wensinck, *Muslim Creed*, 67–8, 86–7, 91–2; Tritton, *Muslim Theology*, 48 ff., 74–5; Sweetman, *Islam*, pt. 2, vol. ii, 7. Averroes wrote: 'Most of the Muslim people have come to believe that the Creator is a body, but unlike other bodies. This is what Hanbalites and most of them who follow them accept. . . . The sect which accepts the corporeality of God believes those who deny it to be denying the existence of God.' See Sweetman, *Islam*, pt. 2, vol. ii, 115–16. See also Wolfson, *Philosophy*, 8 ff., 76–7, 102 ff.; R. M. Frank, *Al-Ghazali*, 80; Martin et al., *Defenders*, 68–9.

denial that God has a form, only that this form is unlike anything else. Similarly, when Deuteronomy 4: 15 states: 'Ye saw no manner of form on the day that the Lord spoke to you in Horeb out of the midst of the fire', this is not a denial of divine corporeality, only a statement that God's form was not seen.

While not denying God's corporeality, the Bible does, however, state that seeing the Lord is hazardous to one's health; as God says to Moses, 'Thou canst not see My face for man shall not see Me and live' (Exod. 33: 19). Even before God said this, Moses was aware that seeing God was not easily accomplished. As Exodus 3: 6 states: 'And Moses hid his face, for he was afraid to look upon God.' The danger present in gazing upon God is also expressed by Isaiah, who, after seeing God sitting on his throne, proclaimed: 'Woe is me! For I am undone . . . for mine eyes have seen the King, the Lord of hosts' (Isa. 6: 5). Isaiah nevertheless survived this experience, as did Moses, whom the Pentateuch describes as having beheld 'the likeness of the Lord' (Num. 12: 8). The prophet Micaiah was also able to proclaim, 'I saw the Lord sitting on His throne' (1 Kgs. 22: 19).[16]

From the perspective of Maimonides and his followers, all of these verses obviously have to be understood figuratively. In the words of R. Menahem Me'iri (1249–1316), 'The principles of faith are not tied to the literal meaning of Scripture and *agadot*.'[17] As for the fairness of condemning as heretics those simpletons who do not know any better and take these biblical descriptions of God literally, Maimonides writes:

If, however, you should say that the external sense of the biblical text causes men to fall into this doubt [regarding God's incorporeality], you ought to know that an idolater is similarly impelled to his idolatry by imaginings and defective representations. Accordingly there is no excuse for one who does not accept the authority of men who inquire into the truth and are engaged in speculation if he himself is incapable of engaging in such speculation. I do not consider as an infidel one who cannot demonstrate that the corporeality of God should be negated. But I do consider as an infidel one who does not believe in its negation; and this particularly in view of the existence of the interpretations of Onkelos and of Jonathan ben Uziel, may peace be on both of them, who cause their readers to keep away as far as possible from the corporeality of God.[18]

Maimonides is correct in asserting that the Targumim often shy away from anthropomorphism,[19] but this is hardly the case with talmudic and midrashic

---

[16] Biblical anthropomorphism is a very large topic but lies outside the scope of this book. See E. R. Wolfson, *Through a Speculum*, 13–28, who also provides the relevant bibliography.

[17] *Beit habehirah* on BT *Shab.* 55a.   [18] *Guide* i. 36.

[19] Yet in the Targumim there is still a great deal of anthropomorphism. See M. L. Klein, *Personification*. See also Nahmanides, commentary on Gen. 46: 1; Abarbanel, commentary on *Guide* i. 27; Ishbili, *Sefer hazikaron*, 62 ff.

literature. In this literature there are numerous descriptions of God as a corporeal being, one of the most famous being BT *Berakhot 6a*, which describes God as wearing *tefilin*. As with the biblical descriptions of God's corporeality, Maimonides understood all of the rabbinic passages in a figurative way. As he put it, 'the doctrine of the corporeality of God did not ever occur even for a single day to the Sages, may their memory be blessed, and this was not according to them a matter lending itself to imagination or to confusion'.[20] But is this the only way to read these texts? It would seem not, for there is little doubt that a popular view in rabbinic times was that God indeed had a form. Because medieval theology has been so influential, this statement will no doubt surprise many. Yet, as Alon Goshen-Gottstein has pointed out, 'in all of rabbinic literature there is not a single statement that categorically denies that God has body or form'. Furthermore, 'there is absolutely no objection in all of rabbinic literature' to the idea that man was created in the image of God's physical form.[21] Although this last statement would seem to be an exaggeration,[22] it is not far off the mark, as can be seen from Yair Lorberbaum's recent exhaustive study of the subject.[23]

Furthermore, as Goshen-Gottstein has stressed, there are some examples in rabbinic literature that are very difficult to understand metaphorically.[24] Indeed, they seem to show clearly that at least some of the rabbinic sages believed in divine corporeality. In *Vayikra rabah* 34: 3, we are told of Hillel, who was on the way to the bathhouse:

His disciples asked him: 'Rabbi, where are you going?' He said to them: 'To perform a commandment.' They said to him: 'And what then is this commandment?' He said to them: 'To bathe in the [public] bath.' They said to him: 'And is this a commandment?' He said to them: 'Yes. If the man who is appointed to take care of the images of kings, which [the gentiles] set up in their theaters and circuses, scours them and rinses them, and they provide his livelihood, and not only that, but he occupies an important place among government officials, how much more I, who was created in the image [*tselem*] and in the likeness [*demut*] [of God].'

---

[20] *Guide* i. 46.   [21] 'The Body as Image of God', 172–3. See also M. Smith, *Studies*, ch. 11.

[22] For example, *Bereshit rabah* 27: 1 states: 'Great is the power of the prophets, who liken that which is created to its Creator, as it is written . . . *And upon the likeness of the throne was a likeness as the appearance of a man upon it above* (Ezek. 1: 26).' (The parallel text in *Pesikta derav kahana*, 65, and *Bamidbar rabah* 19: 3 reads: 'Great is the power of the prophets, who compare the likeness [*demut*] of the Power on High to the likeness of man.' See *Midrash tehilim*, 3a, n. 48, regarding the two formulations.) In other words, the prophet portrays God as a man, but he does not actually have a physical form. Maimonides cites this midrash in *Guide* i. 46. However, even this passage has been read anthropomorphically; see Lorberbaum, 'Doctrine'. I find Lorberbaum's interpretation most far-fetched.

[23] 'Image of God'.

[24] S. Friedman, 'Graven Images', also argues that the rabbinic passages that refer to God's image must be understood literally.

Goshen-Gottstein also calls attention to *Avot derabi natan* 2: 4, where, in a list of people born circumcised, Adam is listed first; the prooftext is that he was created in the image of God. 'This prooftext would only work if the correspondence between man's body and the divine body is understood to be exact.'[25] Another good example is found in *Rosh hashanah* 24*b* and *Avodah zarah* 43*b*. In explaining why it is forbidden to make a portrait of a man, the prooftext cited is Exodus 20: 20: 'You shall not make with Me', which is read as 'You shall not make Me'. That is, since man is made in God's image you cannot reproduce the human face, because by doing so you will be doing the same with God's face. In other words, the human face is a literal copy of God's face.

Meir Bar-Ilan has also studied the relevant rabbinic literature and come to an identical conclusion, namely, 'that in the first centuries Jews in the Land of Israel and in Babylon believed in an anthropomorphic God'.[26] In fact, two generations ago Arthur Marmorstein concluded that there was 'a school in Judaism, and an important one too, that believed in a God who accompanies man in human form and shape'.[27] Marmorstein also points to the school of R. Ishmael, which according to him did not understand God in this manner. However, neither Goshen-Gottstein nor Bar-Ilan sees any evidence to justify the conclusion that R. Ishmael's school did not share an anthropomorphic conception of God. Bar-Ilan cites a text which actually shows R. Ishmael referring to an anthropomorphic God.

This is how you are to make it (Gen. 6: 15)—it teaches that God pointed out to Noah with His finger, and told him 'like this you shall make'. It has been taught: Rabbi Ishmael said: five fingers in the right hand of God—all are a great secret; the little finger—with it God showed Noah what to do. . . . The second finger, next to the little, with it God smote the Egyptians. . . . The third finger, the middle one, with it God wrote the tablets. . . . The fourth finger, the index, with it God showed to Moses what Israel should give to save their souls. . . . And the whole hand, with it the Lord will ruin the children of Esau that are His foes, and destroy the children of Ishmael that are His enemies, as it is written, *Your hand shall be lifted up over your adversaries* (Mic. 5: 9), and it is written, *In that day the Lord will extend his hand yet a second time* (Isa. 11: 11).[28]

A revealing passage, which is not cited by Goshen-Gottstein or Bar-Ilan, appears in *Midrash tanḥuma*[29] and *Pesikta derav kahana*:[30]

[25] A. Goshen-Gottstein, 'The Body as Image of God', 175.   [26] 'The Hand of God', 331.

[27] Marmorstein, *Old Rabbinic Doctrine*, ii. 52. I should note, however, that David Stern offers an alternative reading of rabbinic anthropomorphic passages which does not presume a belief in divine corporeality. See his '*Imitatio Hominis*'. See also E. R. Wolfson, *Through a Speculum*, 33 ff.

[28] *Midrash hagadol* on Genesis, 159; *Pirkei derabi eli'ezer*, ch. 48, p. 116*a*.

[29] 'Ha'azinu', 4.   [30] p. 471.

Isaiah said: *Seek ye the Lord while He may be found* (Isa. 55:6), David said: *Seek ye the Lord and His strength* (Ps. 105: 4). [What did he have in mind in going on to say in the same verse] *Seek His face continually* (ibid.)? To teach you that the Holy One, may His name be blessed, is at times seen and at times not seen. . . . Thus he showed Himself to Moses, as is said, *And the Lord spoke unto Moses [face to face]* (Exod. 33: 11). But then He turned away and hid from him, so that Moses had to say, *Show me, I pray Thee, thy glory* (Exod. 33: 18). He likewise showed Himself to Israel at Sinai, as is said: *They saw the God of Israel* (Exod. 24: 10) and *The appearance of the glory of the Lord was like devouring fire* (Exod. 24: 17). But then He turned away and hid from them, as is said: *Take ye therefore good heed unto yourselves—for ye saw no manner of form* (Deut. 4: 15)[31] and *Ye heard the voice of words, but ye saw no form* (Deut. 4: 12).

According to this passage, the anti-anthropomorphic verses in Deuteronomy, which state that God's form was not seen, only refer to a time when God *chose* to turn away. At other times, as the text clearly states, God was indeed visible.[32]

Because Adam was created in the image of God, and thus looks like him, *Bereshit rabah* 8: 10 reports that even the angels were confused.

Rabbi Hoshaya said: When the Holy One, blessed be He, created Adam, the ministering angels mistook him [for God] and wished to exclaim 'Holy' before him. What does this resemble? A king and a governor who sat in a chariot and his subjects wished to say to the king, *Domine!* [Sovereign] but they did not know which it was. What did the king do? He pushed the governor out of the chariot, and so they knew who was the king. Similarly, when the Lord created Adam, the angels mistook him [for God]. What did the Holy One, blessed be He, do? He caused sleep to fall upon him, and so all knew that he was [but mortal] man.

Another revealing text is found in *Pirkei derabi eli'ezer*:[33]

Rabbi Shimon said: When Isaac was bound to the altar he lifted his eyes and saw the Shekhinah [Divine Presence]. But it is written, *Man may not see Me and live* (Exod. 33: 19). In lieu of death his eyes dimmed when he got older, as it says, *When Isaac was old and his eyes were too dim to see* (Gen. 27: 1). From here you learn that blindness is considered as death.

It is hard to understand this passage as meaning anything other than that Isaac actually gazed upon God's Presence.

Matters are necessarily more complicated than I am able to summarize here, and it is possible to argue, following Goshen-Gottstein, that at least some rabbinic passages reflect the notion that God's body is a divine body of

---

[31] This verse only appears in the *Pesikta derav kahana* version.
[32] On Moses' vision of 'the likeness of the Lord', see also BT *Ber.* 7a, quoting R. Joshua b. Korhah and R. Jonathan. [33] Ch. 32, p. 73b.

light rather than a corporeal body.[34] Still, it seems impossible to deny that a widespread rabbinic view was that God does, in fact, have a physical body, even if it is more perfect than the human body that is modelled on it.[35]

Josephus is also part of the anthropomorphic tradition, as he clearly implies that God has a form, although it is beyond our powers of comprehension.

By His works and bounties He is plainly seen, indeed more manifest than all else, but His form and magnitude surpass our powers of description. No materials, however costly, are fit to make an image of Him; no art has skill to conceive and represent it. The like of Him we have never seen, we do not imagine, and it is impious to conjecture.[36]

What can we say about the views of the masses during rabbinic times? Philo, who thanks to Greek philosophical influence was a strong anti-anthropomorphist, claims that the biblical anthropomorphisms are for the benefit of those who 'are very dull in their natures, so as to be utterly unable to form any conception whatever of God apart from a body'.[37] He goes on to say, in opposition to what Maimonides would later argue, that 'we must be content if such men can be brought to a proper state, by the fear which is held over them by such descriptions'.[38] It would appear from this that anthropo-

---

[34] Goshen-Gottstein's 'divine body of light' thesis has been disputed in Aaron, 'Shedding Light'.

[35] In early Jewish mysticism, in particular in the Heikhalot literature, one encounters highly developed anthropomorphic myth. The problem with this type of literature is that it is never clear when descriptions of God are to be taken literally and when they are only symbolic. Furthermore, with regard to some figures, e.g. Akatriel, who is mentioned in BT *Ber. 7a*, it is not clear if what is being discussed is God himself, his 'Glory', or simply an angel. See E. R. Wolfson, *Through a Speculum*, ch. 3; Abrams, 'Divine Shape'; Deutsch, *Guardians*. For the uncertainty surrounding the seemingly grossly anthropomorphic *Shiur komah*, see Dan, *Early Jewish Mysticism*, ch. 4; Sherwin, 'Human Body', 78 n. 2; Farber-Ginat, 'Studies'; Martin Cohen, *Shiur Qomah*. Cohen writes (p. 99):

The single most characteristic feature of the *Shiur Qomah* is the description of the divine body and the revelation of the names and dimensions of the limbs and some of the internal organs of the Deity. Whether or not this notion implies a rejection of the principle of divine incorporeality in the mind of the author, or in the minds of his earliest readers, is not a question that can be decided with certainty. It does seem, however, that if we ask in absolute terms, whether this *must* have been the case, the answer would have to be that it is not so, as evidenced by those gaonic and medieval scholars who praised the text and who accepted it as a valid text of Jewish mystic expression, and who, yet, are known to have held the doctrine of divine incorporeality as a cardinal element in their religious systems.

In his youth Maimonides apparently believed that *Shiur komah* was an authentic rabbinic work. See his commentary on Mishnah *San.*, 142 n. 42; J. Kafih, *Writings*, 475 ff. Later in life he changed his mind and regarded it as a heretical work that should be destroyed. See his *Responsa*, no. 117. See also Jospe, 'Maimonides'.

[36] *Contra apionem* ii. 23. This passage was called to my attention by Professor Louis Feldman.

[37] *De somniis* i. 40: 236. See also *Quod deus immutabilis sit*, xi, xiv, and H. A. Wolfson, *Philo*, ii. 94 ff.

[38] *De somniis* i. 40: 237. See also ibid. 135, that the anthropomorphisms found in the Bible are 'concerned not with truth, but with the profit accruing to its [i.e. the Bible's] pupils'.

morphism among the masses was not uncommon in Philo's day. Evidence for this from a later period can be found in the anthropomorphic representations of God's hand extending from heaven which appear in the excavated synagogues of Dura Europos (third century) and Beit Alfa (sixth century).[39] It is also significant that Justin Martyr (second century) describes the Jews as believing that God 'has hands and feet, and fingers, and a soul like a com-posite creature'.[40]

Yet despite all the evidence that many Jews in rabbinic times believed in some form of divine corporeality, I believe that there were also significant segments of the Jewish world which worshipped an incorporeal God. The evidence for this comes from descriptions of Jewish life and worship by Greek and Latin authors. For example, a very early writer, Hecateus of Abdera (fourth century BCE), reports that Moses was of the opinion that God has no human form. While this perhaps leaves open the possibility that God has some other form, Strabo (first century BCE–first century CE) writes that Moses taught 'that the Egyptians were mistaken in representing the Divine Being by the images of beasts and cattle . . . for, according to him, God is the one thing alone that encompasses us all and encompasses land and sea'. Livy (58 BCE–17 CE) states flatly that the Jews 'do not think that God partakes of any figure'. Tacitus (*c*.55–*c*.117 CE) also reports that according to the Jews God 'is incapable of representation and without end'. It seems most unlikely that a few philosophically oriented Jews of Philo's ilk could have decisively influenced these writers' judgement. These authors, who would have been more than happy to report that the Jews, or at least great numbers of them, were corporealists, offer a very different perspective.[41]

Earlier I noted that Maimonides believed that all anthropomorphic descriptions of God in the Torah must be understood figuratively. However, he also pointed out that anthropomorphic conceptions of God were indeed held in biblical times, even by some important figures. I shall later discuss his shocking explanation as to why the Torah uses anthropomorphic expressions. Here I simply wish to call attention to Maimonides' understanding of Exodus 24: 9–11: 'Then went up Moses, and Aaron, Nadab, and Abihu, and seventy of the elders of Israel; and they saw the God of Israel; and there was under His feet the like of a paved work of sapphire stone, and the like of the very heaven for clearness. And upon the nobles of the children of Israel He laid not His hand; and they beheld God, and did eat and drink.'

---

[39] See Goodenough, *Jewish Symbols*, i. 246 ff., x. 180 ff.; Wischnitzer-Bernstein, 'Jewish Pictorial Art', 210; Sukenik, *Synagogue of Dura Europos*, 119; id., *Synagogue of Beth Alpha*, 41.

[40] *Dialogue with Trypho*, ch. 114.

[41] For the authors cited in this paragraph, see Bland, *The Artless Jew*, 60–1.

According to Maimonides, it was only Nadab, Abihu, and the seventy elders who are described by this text as seeing God. Had the text only mentioned this, it would not have been exceptional, as Moses was also described as seeing God and Maimonides interprets this figuratively. However, this text also speaks of them observing something under God's feet. According to Maimonides, this shows that their apprehension of God was marred, 'inasmuch as corporeality entered it to some extent—this being necessitated by their overhasty rushing forward before they had reached perfection'. For this, they deserved to perish.[42]

According to Albo, Isaiah also almost fell victim to this error.[43] I have already quoted Isaiah 6: 5, where we read that Isaiah saw God and feared that it would be his undoing. Instead of trying to explain Isaiah's vision—'I saw the Lord sitting upon a throne high and lifted up'—in a philosophical manner, Albo claims that Isaiah, through his power of imagination, really did envision a corporeal God. This was because his prophetic ability was not as exalted as that of Moses. Albo adds, however, that Isaiah realized his error and exclaimed 'Woe is me! for I am affected by imagination.'[44] Albo explains, 'The meaning is, I am affected by the power of imagination and my prophetic inspiration is not through a luminous glass like that of Moses, who heard a voice speaking to him without seeing any image before his eyes.'[45] According to the Talmud,[46] this utterance of Isaiah, which contradicted Moses' statement: 'For men shall not see Me and live' (Exod. 33: 20), was one of the reasons Manasseh slew him.

While on the subject of Isaiah's vision, it should be noted that a desire to view God[47] need not imply that God has an actual physical form. Elliot R. Wolfson, in his justly praised book, *Through a Speculum that Shines: Vision and Imagination in Medieval Jewish Mysticism*,[48] has provided us with numerous examples of mystics imagining God in anthropomorphic ways, though this hardly means that they regarded God as having a corporeal form. It is obvious that they were simply imagining him this way. Although this would certainly not be to Maimonides' liking, since these mystics believed in an incorporeal God there was no violation of the Third Principle.

Despite Maimonides' forceful attacks against the belief in divine corporeality, he did not immediately succeed in uprooting it. Furthermore, there were

---

[42] *Guide* i. 5. See, however, ibid. i. 28, ii. 26, for a non-anthropomorphic understanding of the verses in Exodus.   [43] See *Sefer ha'ikarim*, iii. 17.

[44] דמיתי is normally translated as 'I am undone'. As Husik points out in his note on the passage, Albo has connected it with the word דמיון.

[45] See, however, *Sefer ha'ikarim*, ii. 14, where Albo offers a non-anthropomorphic understanding of Isaiah's vision.   [46] *Yev.* 49b.

[47] On this desire see Pedaya, 'Seeing, Falling, Singing'.   [48] Princeton, NJ, 1994.

a number of scholars in medieval times who were corporealists, which should not surprise us since they were simply following the rabbinic tradition already described. This led R. Abraham ben David (Rabad) to his famous defence of the corporealists: 'Why has he [i.e. Maimonides] called such a person a heretic? There are many people greater and superior to him who adhere to such a belief on the basis of what they have seen in verses of Scripture and even more in the words of those *agadot* which corrupt right opinion about religious matters.'[49] Although, unfortunately, we do not have much in the way of written records from these corporealists, there are a number of texts that enlighten us. The most significant is the *Ketav tamim* of R. Moses ben Hasdai Taku, a Tosafist.[50]

Although there is some dispute as to how 'extreme' an anthropomorphist Taku was,[51] there is no question that he rejected Maimonides' Third Principle and viewed God as having an image and form, or at least able to assume these at will. Thus, according to him, when the Bible states that various prophets saw God, it means that they literally beheld the Creator.[52] The philosophical objections raised against such a position were of no significance when contradicted by explicit biblical and rabbinic texts, which attest to both God's omnipotence *and* his corporeality. Directing his ire at Maimonides, Taku writes: 'Is it at all proper for a believer in the Torah to say that the Torah speaks in the language of man?'[53]

Taku's literalism is so extreme that he views as blasphemous the rationalists' denial that God literally sits on his throne. After all, BT *Rosh hashanah* 31*a* clearly states (in Taku's version): 'On the sixth day they said, *The Lord reigneth, He is clothed in majesty* (Ps. 93: 2). He completed His work and ascended and sat on His royal throne in Heaven.'[54] Responding to the view

---

[49] *Hasagah* on 'Hilkhot teshuvah', 3: 7. This is undoubtedly the correct version of the gloss; see Kaufmann, *Geschichte*, 487–8 (many of the medieval sources to which I refer in this chapter were first collected by the astonishingly erudite Kaufmann). See also Twersky, *Rabad*, 282 ff.; W. Z. Harvey, 'Incorporeality'; Gellman, 'Philosophical *Hassagot*', 153 ff.; Gellman writes: 'Rabad probably wanted to support the *permissibility* of the belief in corporeality and not just its not being culpable in certain cases' (p. 155). There is no evidence that Rabad upheld the permissibility of such a belief. On the contrary, Rabad's concluding words show that his comments are merely an *ex post facto* justification for those who erred in this matter.

[50] There were those who referred to the work as כתב טמא; see *Kiryat sefer*, 4 (1928), 338; Kupfer, 'Cultural Image', 137. Before Kirchheim published Taku's *Ketav tamim*, R. Joseph David Sinzheim (1745–1812) saw the manuscript and discussed it in a letter; see his *Minhat ani*, i. 110 (the editor's note is incorrect). Regarding Taku, see Ephraim E. Urbach's edition of Abraham b. Azriel, *Arugat habosem*, iv. 78 ff., Urbach, *Ba'alei hatosafot*, 425 ff.; *Ketav tamim*, ed. Dan, 7–27.

[51] See Hayim Hillel Ben-Sasson's review of the first edition of Urbach's *Ba'alei hatosafot* in *Behinot*, 9 (1956), 51–2; Urbach, *Ba'alei hatosafot*, 423 n. 74*; Davis, 'R. Yom Tov', 51 n. 49; Ta-Shma, *Talmudic Commentary*, ii. 194 n. 8.   [52] *Ketav tamim*, ed. Kirchheim, 83.   [53] Ibid. 77.

[54] Ibid. 85. For a similar version of this text see Rabbinovicz, *Dikdukei soferim*, ad loc.

popularized by Sa'adiah Gaon[55] and the Hasidei Ashkenaz,[56] and quite popular today, that God's presence is to be found everywhere, Taku writes: 'Heaven forbid that the Holy One of all holiness should be found in a place of filth and in the midst of idols. The Torah writes, *Therefore shall thy camp be holy, that He see no unseemly thing in thee, and turn away from thee* (Deut. 23: 15). Thus, the Torah testifies that God is not found in unfitting places.'[57] In Taku's mind, God can at times be found in a definite place, and indeed, 'He does not need to be everywhere to know what He has brought about, for this is His greatness, that He is above all, and knows all, and is [nevertheless] close to all.'[58] How then does this square with Jeremiah 23: 24: 'Do not I fill heaven and earth? saith the Lord'? According to Taku, the greatness of God is seen in the fact that, while filling the world (excluding the filthy areas) with his majesty, he can still occupy one place![59]

In support of his anthropomorphic conception, Taku cites an interesting talmudic passage in *Sanhedrin* 46*b*. In explaining the Torah's prescription that one who is executed should not hang overnight (Deut. 21: 22–3), R. Meir offered a parable:

To what is this matter comparable? To two twin brothers [who lived] in one city; one was appointed king, and the other took to highway robbery. At the king's command they hanged him. But all who saw him exclaimed, 'The king is hanged!', whereupon the king issued a command and he was taken down.[60]

In other words, man's physical appearance resembles that of God. What, then, is one to do with the verse in Isaiah 40: 18: 'To whom then will ye liken God? Or what likeness will ye compare unto Him?' Taku explains that it is stated with reference to God's greatness and the splendour of his glory, that nothing compares to them. The verse does not, however, mean that God has no image.[61]

Another significant anthropomorphic text is that of the *Sefer hamaskil*, written at the end of the thirteenth century by R. Solomon Simhah of Troyes (*c*.1235–1300), a descendant of Rashi (1040–1105) and student of R. Meir of Rothenburg (*c*.1215–93) and R. Peretz of Corbeil (thirteenth century).[62] According to R. Solomon, and this is a major theme of *Sefer hamaskil*, God is identical with the air that is found everywhere. In line with this conception, R. Solomon adds 'blessed be He and blessed be His name' whenever he

---

[55] *Emunot vede'ot*, ii. 13. Taku quotes from a Hebrew paraphrase of *Emunot vede'ot*. Concerning this work, see Kiener, 'Hebrew Paraphrase'.   [56] See Dan, *Esoteric Theology*, ch. 6.

[57] *Ketav tamim*, ed. Kirchheim, 69. Concerning God avoiding places of filth, see also ibid. 82.

[58] Ibid. 97.   [59] Ibid. 61.   [60] BT *San.* 46*b*; Taku, *Ketav tamim*, ed. Kirchheim, 60.

[61] *Ketav tamim*, ed. Kirchheim, 61. For other examples from Taku, see Jacobs, *Principles*, 121–2.

[62] See Ta-Shma, '*Sefer hamaskil*'; Freudenthal, 'The Air, Blessed Be It'.

mentions the air (or better, Air). R. Solomon also claims that in the upper world the Air is of infinite brightness, and that the sun is a window allowing us to glimpse a portion of God's substance.[63] When God is described in human form, as in prophetic visions, this is not to be interpreted in an allegorical fashion. Rather, God, or more precisely an element of God referred to as his *ruaḥ nifrad*, actually assumed such a form.

Since R. Solomon's lineage is traced to Rashi, it is not without interest that both Meir Bar-Ilan and Israel M. Ta-Shma have recently claimed that even Rashi was a corporealist.[64] As proof of this, Bar-Ilan points to Rashi's comment that the measurement of the heavenly Torah, which is said to be 3,200 times bigger than the universe, is arrived at by calculating in accordance with the 'cubit of the Holy One, blessed be He'.[65] Not noted by Bar-Ilan is that, elsewhere in his talmudic commentary, Rashi refers to both God's face and his arm.[66] In his commentary on Exodus 7: 5 ('That I may lay my hand upon Egypt'), in order to prevent one from thinking that in this verse 'hand' means simply 'power', Rashi writes 'An actual hand [*yad mamash*], to smite them'.[67] In his commentary on Genesis 1: 26 Rashi states that, when the Bible records that man was to be created in God's 'image' (*tselem*), it means in God's 'form' (*defus*). This is distinguished from the other biblical expression, which states that man was to be created in God's 'likeness' (*demut*). According to Rashi, this latter expression means that man was created 'to understand and to be intellectually creative'. In other words, both man's physical form and his intellectual ability are modelled on those of God. As if to make sure that no one misunderstands what he is saying, in his comment on the next verse Rashi writes: 'This teaches you that the form that was established for him [i.e. man] is the form of the image of his Creator [*tselem deyukan yotsro*]'.[68]

---

[63] Freudenthal discusses possible influences on R. Solomon's strange view at length, without coming to any definite conclusions.

[64] Bar-Ilan, 'The Hand of God', 326–7; Ta-Shma, *Commentaries*, ii. 194.

[65] BT *Eruv.* 21a, s.v. *esrim*. A cubit is a body-based measurement, being the distance from the elbow to the fingertips.

[66] BT *Yev.* 49b, s.v. *nistakelu*, BT *Ber.* 6b, s.v. *vekhulhu*.   [67] See also Rashi on Exod. 14: 31.

[68] It is noteworthy that, despite the clear anthropomorphic elements found in Rashi's writings, *Maḥzor vitri*, 514, which emanates in large part from Rashi's school, states explicitly that 'God has no likeness or form'. Ginzberg, 'Anthropomorphism', argues that Rashi did not hold anthropomorphic views by citing BT *Mak.* 12a, s.v. *ḥamuts*, where Rashi 'remarks that the angels are not composed of flesh and blood, which, in philosophic phraseology means the "angels are incorporeal".' According to Ginzberg, if the angels are incorporeal, no doubt God must be too. Yet Ginzberg's proof from *Makot* is completely false and has nothing to do with rejecting anthropomorphism. From the Talmud itself it is clear that angels are not made of flesh and blood. Rather, while they look like men, they consist of fire and water: see JT *RH* 2: 4 and *Shir hashirim rabah* 3: 11. With regard to this fire, see Ginzberg, *Legends of the Jews*, v. 21: 'The fact that angels were created of fire does not interfere with their incorporeality, for in legend fire, particularly the heavenly fire, is incorporeal.' Leaving aside the fact that

Martin Lockshin has argued that R. Samuel ben Meir (Rashbam, *c*.1085–
c.1174), Rashi's grandson, was also a corporealist.[69] His major proof is Rashbam's comment on Genesis 48: 8:

Israel saw. Even though below [verse 10] it is written that *he could not see*, it is possible to see a person's shape without recognizing the features of his face. So also
Man may not see Me and live (Exod. 33: 20) and *I saw the Lord* (1 Kgs. 22: 19).

According to Lockshin, what Rashbam is saying is that while one cannot see
God clearly, one can see him 'in the same way that a partially blind man can
see non-detailed images'. Lockshin also cites Rashbam's comment on Leviticus 16: 2 ('For I appear in the cloud upon the ark-cover'). Rashbam writes:
'This is to be understood according to its literal meaning, for at all times I am
beheld from the midst of the cloud upon the ark-cover.'[70]

Another example of anthropomorphism among medieval European Jews
is found in a text published by Ephraim E. Urbach. According to this text,
certain names of God are written on God's forehead which, in *Shiur komah*
fashion, is described as being of gigantic size. The text then continues: 'God
resembles an old man, a handsome man, a Jew, and a sage.'[71] Apparently, the
author of this text shared R. Moses Taku's conception of the deity. Another
anonymous text,[72] which is quite ancient and to this day is recited at the
beginning of the *Avodah* section in the Sephardi and hasidic Yom Kippur

Ginzberg does not explain how water—the other component of angels—can also be incorporeal, it
must be stressed that nowhere in rabbinic literature is it stated, or even implied, that the angels are
incorporeal. The Bible itself (Gen. 18–19, Josh. 5: 13 ff., Judg. 6: 12, Isa. 6: 2, etc.) speaks of corporeal
angels. In BT *RH* 24*a–b* and BT *AZ* 43*a–b* it states that one is forbidden to reproduce an image of an
angel, showing that they indeed have physical form. According to BT *Ḥag.* 16*a*, angels have wings.
Sa'adiah Gaon, who was the leading philosophical opponent of divine corporeality before Maimonides, believed that angels are physical beings; see *Emunot vede'ot*, iv. 2, vi. 4. Medieval Ashkenazi
sages also thought that angels are corporeal; see Rabad, *hasagah* on 'Hilkhot teshuvah', 8: 2; and the
letter published by Scholem, *Origins*, 226. Although Maimonides believed that angels are incorporeal
('Hilkhot yesodei hatorah', 2: 3, 'Hilkhot teshuvah', 8: 2, *Guide* i. 49, ii. 6, *Letters*, ed. Shailat, i. 323,
327 (Arabic), 346–7, 354 (Hebrew)), he did not mind if the masses believed otherwise; see *Letters*, ed.
Shailat, i. 323 (Arabic) 346–7 (Hebrew). In fact, he even recorded the talmudic law that one cannot
reproduce angelic images ('Hilkhot avodah zarah', 3: 11). This is an example of Maimonides recording a law even though it did not fit in with his world view. For other examples, see Levinger, *Halakhic
Thought*, 129–30, and cf. my 'Maimonidean Halakhah', 99 n. 135.

[69] *Rabbi Samuel*, 338.

[70] See, however, Rashbam's commentary on Gen. 1: 26–7, where he argues that man was created in
the image of the angels, not God. If he believed that God has a physical form, why did he depart from
the simple meaning of the biblical text? For further evidence of what seems to be an anti-corporealist
outlook, see Japhet (ed.), *Rabbi Samuel*, 128 ff. Lockshin has argued against identifying the author of
this commentary with Rashbam, but even he acknowledges that it contains a great deal of Rashbam's
comments. See his review essay, '"Rashbam" on Job'.

[71] Abraham b. Azriel, *Arugat habosem*, iv. 76–7. The editor, Urbach (ibid. 78), believes that anthropomorphism was the accepted doctrine among the early German mystics.

[72] אתה כוננת עולם מראש.

liturgy, is a *piyut* which reads: 'You fashioned a clod of earth in your form.'[73] An anthropomorphic conception of God would also appear to be behind the following comment of R. Jacob Moelin: 'Perhaps Moses' eyes beheld [the face of] his Master [God], blessed be He, and he turned to his right, may his Master forgive him.'[74] R. Joseph Ashkenazi, the inveterate opponent of Maimonides, has this to say:

[Maimonides] wrote in *Sefer mada* that anyone who says that God has a form is a heretic. According to this it is certainly the case that the Torah and the believer of its words are also to be regarded as heretics, because it states there [with reference to Moses] *the likeness of the Lord doth he behold* (Num. 12: 8). . . . They say that God is Intellect and does not change, and with this they deny God's seeing and hearing things and His speaking . . . for all these require corporeality [*gashmut*] and even more so His descent on Sinai and ascent to the Heavens.[75]

The great historian of Jewish philosophy Harry A. Wolfson claimed that very few Jews had a corporeal conception of God in the days of Maimonides.[76] This opinion was supported by J. L. Teicher, who also asserted categorically that no medieval scholar held such views.[77] However, even if we ignore evidence provided by Christians,[78] Muslims,[79] and Karaites,[80] there are still many sources which indicate that corporealist views of various sorts were widespread among both ordinary people and scholars, especially among Ashkenazi Jews.[81] Sa'adiah Gaon speaks of people who imagined God as a body, and others who, while not attributing a crude corporeality to God, applied to him characteristics, such as quantity, quality, and location, that only apply to physical beings.[82] R. Abraham ibn Daud (twelfth century) reports that masses of Jews believed God to be a material being.[83] Maimonides, who argues so forcefully against the corporealists, himself speaks of numerous people, including 'the majority' of the ignorant, who held anthropomorphic views.[84] In a revealing passage in his *Essay on Resurrection*, he also writes:

[73] גולם תבניתך מן האדמה יצרת. This is the original text, but some *mahzorim* have eliminated the anthropomorphism by substituting תבנית for תבניתך. Regarding this *piyut*, see J. Karo, *Avkat rokhel*, nos. 27–8; Malachi, 'Yom Kippur', 17–20.

[74] *She'elot uteshuvot maharil*, no. 40. The first bracketed text is found in one of the manuscripts.

[75] See the text published in Scholem, 'New Information', 210, 229.

[76] Wolfson, *Philosophy*, 100 ff.   [77] 'Literary Forgery', 85.

[78] G. Stroumsa, 'Form(s) of God', 269–88; Bonfil, 'Evidence', 332.

[79] See Wolfson, *Repercussions*, 40 ff. In line with his view that Jewish anthropomorphism was very rare, Wolfson regards the Islamic statements he cites as 'misinformation' (ibid. 43).

[80] See Nemoy, 'Al-Kirkisani', 114 ff.; Wolfson, *Repercussions*, 44 ff.

[81] Septimus, *Hispano-Jewish Culture*, 79, writes: 'it seems likely that the views of Moses b. Hasdai [Taku] do approximate a significant body of Franco-German opinion'. See also Sonne, 'Scrutiny'.

[82] *Emunot vede'ot*, ii, introduction.   [83] *Ha'emunah haramah*, 47, 91.

[84] *Letters*, ed. Shailat, i. 322 (Arabic), 346 (Hebrew).

I have met some who think they are among the sages of Israel—by God, they indeed know the way of the Law ever since childhood, and they battle in legal discussions—but they are not certain if God is corporeal, with eyes, hands, and feet, as the Bible says, or if He has not a body. Others, whom I have met in some lands, assert positively that He is corporeal and call anyone who thinks differently a nonbeliever, name him a heretic and Epicurean. They explain the homilies of [BT] *Berakhot* literally. I have received similar reports of some whom I have not met.[85]

In *Guide* i. 1 Maimonides states:

They accordingly believed in it [divine corporeality] and deemed that if they abandoned this belief, they would give the lie to the biblical text; that they would even make the deity to be nothing at all unless they thought that God was a body provided with a face and a hand, like them in shape and configuration. However, He is, in their view, bigger and more resplendent than they themselves, and the matter of which He is composed is not flesh and blood.

R. Yedaiah Bedershi (thirteenth–fourteenth centuries) writes that it is well known that 'in previous generations' (i.e. before Maimonides was able to reverse matters) the belief in God's corporeality was spread throughout virtually all Israel.[86] Other scholars who testify to corporeal views being held by Jews include R. Isaiah of Trani (the Elder; died *c*.1260),[87] R. Moses of Salerno (thirteenth century),[88] R. David Abudarham (thirteenth–fourteenth centuries),[89] the anonymous author of *Ma'amar hasekhel*,[90] R. Shem Tov ben Joseph ibn Shem Tov,[91] and R. Isaac ben Yedaiah (thirteenth century), who refers to 'faithless "Sadducees" who say that God is [composed of] a matter which is finer, purer, and more transparent than the matter of any shining star'.[92] Following in Rabad's path, R. Meir ben Simeon of Narbonne (thirteenth century) is more sympathetic. After noting that the 'majority' of the masses believe in a corporeal God, he asserts that 'verses of the Torah and prophets cannot mislead one and thereby turn him into a heretic'. He therefore assumes that one who is led to his error by misinterpreting the Scriptures remains a Jew in good standing.[93]

---

[85]   *Letters*, ed. Shailat, i. 320 (Arabic), 341 (Hebrew); Halkin and Hartman, *Crisis*, 212. In the forged ethical will attributed to Maimonides, the author harshly attacks the French Jewish scholars for viewing God anthropomorphically. See Lichtenberg, *Anthology*, ii. 40*a*.

[86]   See Solomon ben Adret, *She'elot uteshuvot harashba*, no. 418 (p. 216, s.v. *vehitbonenu*). See also Delmedigo, *Beḥinat hadat*, 86, and A. I. Kook, *Ma'amrei hare'iyah*, 106, who, entirely ignoring R. Sa'adiah, give Maimonides all the credit for discrediting the corporealists. Concerning R. Sa'adiah's efforts in this regard, see Rawidowicz, 'Saadya's Purification'.   [87]   See Ta-Shma, 'R. Isaiah'.

[88]   See Teicher, 'Literary Forgery', 84–5.   [89]   *Abudarham hashalem*, 362.

[90]   14*a*. This work is attributed to R. Eliezer b. Nathan of Mainz (12th cent.).

[91]   See his commentary on Maimonides' introduction to the *Guide* (p. 10*a* in the standard edition).

[92]   See Saperstein, *Decoding the Rabbis*, 185–6.

[93]   See the text published in Halbertal, *Between Torah and Wisdom*, 125–6.

R. Abraham ibn Ezra (1092–1167),[94] R. David Kimhi (1160–1235),[95] R. Abraham Maimonides (1186–1237),[96] R. Meshullam ben Solomon da Piera (thirteenth century),[97] R. Samuel Sapurto (thirteenth century),[98] an anonymous thirteenth century anti-Maimonidean poem,[99] R. Shem Tov Fala-quera,[100] R. Isaac ibn Latif,[101] and R. Moses Alashkar (1466–1542)[102] all speak of corporeal conceptions of God being held by *scholars*. As we see from R. Abraham Maimonides' letter, some of the scholars did not believe that God has a hand or a face, and in their mind this sufficed to remove from them the charge of corporealism. Yet as R. Abraham points out, they remained corporealists without realizing it, for they believed that God is literally to be found in a particular place, which by definition means that he has physical dimensions.

With regard to scholars and corporealism, a particularly revealing passage is found in Nahmanides' famous letter to the French sages. Nahmanides wrote this letter in an attempt to make peace between the two sides in the Maimonidean controversy. The French rabbis had recently proclaimed a ban on study of Maimonides' *Guide* and *Sefer hamada*, the first volume of the *Mishneh torah*. This in turn led to indignation among Maimonides' followers

---

[94] See his commentary on Exod. 33: 21, where he refers to scholars who understood literally the talmudic statement (BT *Ber.* 7a) that God showed Moses his *tefilin*.

[95] See Lichtenberg, *Anthology*, iii. 3c.

[96] See ibid. 16 ff. When Maimonides says that the faith of the sages of Montpellier 'is not far from their [Christian] faith' (ibid. 17a), he is also referring to corporealism and not belief in the Sefirot, as has been suggested by Sendor, 'Emergence', 165.

[97] See his poems, published by Hayim Brody:

אל תאנף באומרים גשמות ואם/לא–ל תמונת האנוש צירו
האומרים כבוד והחשבים דמות/דעות חלוקים הם ולא כפרו
כמה חכמים אמרו שעור והם/העובדים צורם ופיו לא מרו.

('Poems', 102)

ובסוד גשמות/אם הוא בדמות/לדעת זאת אין לך רשיון/אך האמן/ואמור אמן/כי יש מנהיג יושב חביון. (ibid. 34). See also ibid. 91 for another defence of the corporealists.

[98] See the text published (perhaps by Solomon Judah Rapoport) in *Kerem hemed*, 5 (1841), 12. Sapurto is apparently the author of this letter directed to the French rabbis, in which he writes: 'Are there to be found among the foolish of the nations corporealists [*magshimim*] such as you?' See also his letter, published in *Ginzei nistarot*, 4 (1878), 44 ff. (Halberstam, who edited this letter, does not believe that the letter published in *Kerem hemed* was written by Sapurto; see ibid. 37.

[99] *Otsar nehmad*, 2 (1857), 85: וחכמי לב בגשמות מחזיקים ... והגדות עלי שעור מעידות ... ולגשמות ראיה מפסוקים.

[100] See his letter in Lichtenberg, *Anthology*, iii. 23 ff. (This letter also appears in Bislikhis' edition of Abba Mari Astruc of Lunel, *Minhat kenaot*, 183 ff.) The letter is anonymous but there is reason to assume that Falaquera is the author; see Graetz, *Geschichte*, vii. 474. In reference to Rabad's assertion that there were people 'greater and superior' to Maimonides who believed in God's corporeality, Falaquera responds sarcastically: 'Perhaps they were greater than him in height and physical attractiveness.' (Lichtenberg, *Anthology*, iii. 23b). [101] See [Schorr], 'R. Nissim', 91–2.

[102] *She'elot uteshuvot maharam alashkar*, no. 117 (p. 312). Alashkar singles out the French rabbis. In his words, they were guilty of מגשימים בפרהסיא, a phrase which appears earlier in Bedershi's letter.

and eventually to the excommunication of R. Solomon ben Abraham of Montpellier (thirteenth century) and his pupils, the main antagonists of Maimonidean philosophy. In his attempt to make peace between the two parties, Nahmanides wrote to the French rabbis: 'I have heard others say that you have seized upon the *Sefer hamada* for it states that there is no [physical] form or image on high.'[103] Assuming this testimony was correct, and it is certainly in line with the evidence mentioned in the previous paragraph, for at least some of the French rabbis it was not only Maimonides' advocacy of philosophy which was so objectionable but also his opposition to corporealism. From Nahmanides' letter we also see that he shared Rabad's view of the matter, namely, that while corporealism was incorrect, it was not enough to condemn one as a heretic.[104]

Significantly, R. Abraham Klausner, an important fourteenth–fifteenth century Austrian talmudist, was still able to wonder, two hundred years after Maimonides, whether Taku's opinion was the correct one.[105] Even more surprising, in the fifteenth century we find that while R. Elijah Delmedigo (died 1497) acknowledged that denial of God's incorporeality is heretical, he nevertheless argued that if someone believed in a corporeal deity, 'his belief in the essence of God and in God's eternal attributes would not be damaged'.[106]

Although it was difficult for post-medieval scholars to sympathize with the anthropomorphist position, this was not the case for the Italian scholar R. Samuel David Luzzatto, who writes: 'I reject Maimonides on the issue of corporeality . . . I have long believed that the earlier generations ascribed to all spirits (souls, angels, God Himself) a very refined matter.'[107] Elsewhere he writes: 'The early ones ascribed to God and the angels and the souls a very fine spiritual essence, more subtle than any body known to us but nevertheless characterized by form and build.'[108] Not surprisingly, Luzzatto also attacks Maimonides by pointing out that his dogma condemns as heretics generations of pious Jews who did nothing wrong but simply believed what they had been taught.[109]

Yet Luzzatto did not advocate a base corporeality, i.e. a God who resembles humans, but a perfected corporeality. He was also certain that one cannot see God, and that passages that imply otherwise are to be regarded as figurative.[110] As part of the sages' effort to prevent people from falling into

---

[103] *Kitvei ramban*, i. 345.

[104] This was noted by R. Tsadok Hakohen, *Divrei soferim: sefer hazikhronot*, 28a.

[105] See Kupfer, 'Cultural Image', 135.   [106] *Behinat hadat*, 82. See Ivry, 'Remnants', 258–9.

[107] *Letters*, 1196–7. See also Leone da Modena, *Magen vaherev*, 40, who makes the same observation with regard to the medieval rabbis of France who opposed Maimonides.

[108] Luzzatto, *Peninei shadal*, 274. See also id., *Studies*, ii. 205.   [109] *Peninei shadal*, 416.

the mistaken notion that God can indeed be seen, he points to Exodus 34: 23 ('Three times in the year shall all thy males appear (יֵרָאֶה) before the Lord God, the God of Israel'). According to Luzzatto, this text was originally understood as 'Three times in the year shall all males *see* (יִרְאֶה) the Lord God', and the Masoretes, following a tradition going back to Second Temple times, 'corrected' the text.[111] Luzzatto also felt that Maimonides' extreme opposition to corporealism went far beyond his predecessors and was a new position in Judaism. In fact, he regarded the Maimonidean position as dangerous, for it undermined traditional beliefs. Rather than corporealism being heresy, as Maimonides claimed, Luzzatto argued that it is the doctrine of incorporeality which, through its association with philosophy, leads to heresy. He thus felt that it would be infinitely better if Jews were to return to the traditional belief in a corporeal God.[112]

While they did not go as far as Luzzatto, we find other opponents of Maimonides' harsh condemnation of the simple believers in God's corporeality. These sages follow in the footsteps of Rabad, who did not regard belief in an incorporeal God as a fundamental principle of faith, denial of which means exclusion from the Jewish people. R. Simeon ben Tsemah Duran[113] and R. Joseph Albo[114] both argue in this fashion, and, like most of their successors, they emphasize the fact that the corporealist, although he is in error, does not know any better. R. Joseph Yavets (*c.*1435–1507) likewise claims that a simple believer, punctilious in the performance of *mitsvot*, who can only conceive of God in a corporeal fashion, is not to be regarded as a heretic. On the contrary, God prefers him to all the philosophers, whose faith leaves much to be desired.[115] R. Hayim Hirschensohn is another scholar who expresses complete agreement with Rabad's position.[116]

In a fascinating story recorded by R. Moses Hagiz (1671–1751), a simple man in Safed, a former Portuguese Marrano, brought bread to the synagogue every Friday in order for God to eat. The synagogue beadle would actually take the bread but the man was convinced it was God himself who was pleased with his offering. It happened that the local rabbi once saw the man bringing the bread, and upon learning what he was doing harshly rebuked

---

[110] *Commentary on Isaiah*, 1: 12.

[111] *Commentary on the Torah*, ad loc.; id., *Commentary on Isaiah*, 1: 12.

[112] *Letters*, 1195. See M. Harris, 'Theologico-Historical Thinking', 317 ff.

[113] *Ohev mishpat*, ch. 9.   [114] *Sefer ha'ikarim*, i. 2.

[115] *Or hahayim*, 32*b*. See also R. Simeon Sofer, *Igerot soferim*, iii. 41, who adopts a similar approach regarding the masses' ascription of corporeality to divine things (although he does not seem to be referring to a belief in the corporeality of God himself).

[116] *Musagei shav ve'emet*, 118 (second pagination). R. Ishmael Hanina of Valmontone (the teacher of R. Menahem Azariah da Fano), in his apologetic work *Shivah hakirot*, 4*a*, uses Rabad's approach to exonerate Christians from the sin of idolatry.

him, both for his foolishness and for the great sin he was committing by holding an anthropomorphic conception of God. However, when R. Isaac Luria
heard of this, he informed the rabbi that, since the destruction of the Temple,
God's greatest pleasure was when this simple man brought his bread. Since
the rabbi had put a stop to this, it was decreed that he should die, and so it
happened.[117]

R. Moses Cordovero shared Luria's tolerant approach. According to him,
the only people who should be regarded as heretics are those who, knowing
the teaching of the Torah, nevertheless continue to advocate the corporealist
position. Cordovero sees this as parallel to his view that denial of the Sefirot is
only regarded as heresy if one knows that the doctrine is part and parcel of the
Torah and still refuses to accept it.[118] Along these lines, R. Kalonymus
Kalman Shapira (1889–1943) argues that one who has not yet reached a state
of spiritual elevation in which his conception of God is pure is permitted to
visualize God in a physical way. As he rises in spiritual sensitivity this physical
image will disappear on its own.[119]

In line with this attitude, R. Menaham M. Kasher (1895–1983) writes, with
reference to how children are instructed:

We teach them belief in God in a simple and clear fashion, in accordance with their
understanding, until they mature and are able to understand matters in a more
profound way. But there are many who grow up and still retain their early education, and they never have the ability to reach a profound understanding of belief
in God, in accordance with the approach of R. Sa'adiah Gaon and Maimonides.
Can one possibly regard these people as heretics?[120]

As support for this tolerant viewpoint, Kasher cites the rabbinic saying: 'It
is written, *They have forsaken Me, and have not kept My law* (Jer. 16: 11). That is,
would that they had forsaken Me but kept My law, since by occupying themselves therewith, the light which it contains would have led them back to the
right path.'[121] In other words, those who, through no fault of their own, har-
bour false beliefs about God are not condemned as heretics but are encour-
aged to keep the Torah's commandments in the hope that they will eventually
be led to the proper theological understanding. Kasher also cites a very relevant passage from the writings of R. Bahya ibn Pakuda (eleventh century),
which, surprisingly, was not cited by other defenders of the anthropomorphists:

---

[117] *Mishnat ḥakhamim*, no. 220. R. Arele Roth also tells this story in *Shomer emunim*, i. 95*b*.
[118] *Pardes rimonim*, x. 9.
[119] *Benei maḥashavah tovah*, no. 7 (called to my attention by Uriel Frank).
[120] *Torah shelemah*, xvi. 302–3. See also ibid. 320–1 and id., *Hatekufah hagedolah*, 143–4. In writing
this chapter I benefited greatly from Kasher's wide collection of sources.
[121] *Eikhah rabah*, introduction, sect. 2, and see the similar passage in JT Ḥag. 1: 7.

The foolish and simple person will conceive of the Creator in accordance with the literal sense of the Scriptural phrase. And if he assumes the obligation of serving his God and strives to labour for His sake, he is excused by reason of his ignorance and lack of understanding. A man is judged only on the basis of his intellectual ability, his powers of discrimination, and his readiness to act. When this same simple man is able to master this knowledge but is heedless of it, then he is liable to be judged accordingly and punished for his inaction and his neglect of the pursuit of knowledge.[122]

In the same vein, there is a wonderful tale told by R. Israel ben Shabetai Hapstein (1733–1814), the Magid of Kozienice. According to the Magid, after Maimonides proclaimed the corporealists heretics, the souls of many pious Jews who held this view were chased out of Heaven. Only after Rabad defended them were they allowed to return. The Magid continues by pointing out that it was only Maimonides' ignorance of kabbalah that led him to his view. He thus did not know that 'God is clothed in the worlds and the worlds are the measure of the image of His body, as it says "Let us make man in our image".'[123] Although the Magid's quasi-pantheistic conception does not correspond to the primitive corporeal outlook referred to by Rabad, a point he was presumably aware of, his identification with the simple believers of medieval times is quite significant.[124]

Even after the philosophical triumph of God's incorporeality, later thinkers still occasionally express themselves in ways that seemingly contradict this. Perhaps some of them were even anthropomorphists without realizing it, to use R. Abraham Maimonides' words in describing the French rabbis who opposed Maimonides.[125] For example, R. Israel Lipschuetz (1782–1860) writes that Moses, unlike the other prophets, saw, as it were, God's reflection.[126] Obviously, there must be a substance to cause a reflection, unless Lipschuetz

---

[122] *Ḥovot halevavot*, i. 10.

[123] See Jehiel Moses of Komarovka, *Niflaot ḥadashot*, 49*d*, and a slightly different version of the story in H. E. Shapira, *Divrei torah*, v, no. 10 (here the protagonist is R. Jacob Isaac Horowitz).

[124] R. Meir b. Simeon of Narbonne finds Maimonides' opinion so difficult to fathom that he claims that Maimonides agrees with Rabad! According to him, Maimonides' comment is only directed against one whose error has been pointed out to him, yet obstinately holds to his opinion. But he does not refer to someone who arrived at his error accidentally. See similarly R. Samuel Messer Leon, quoted in Benayahu, 'Revolutionary', 148; Tsevi Elimelekh of Dynów, *Ma'ayan haganim*, 32*b*; Serero, *Mishneh kesef* on *Mishneh torah*, 'Hilkhot teshuvah', 3: 7; S. B. Bamberger, 'Open Letter' (called to my attention by R. Chaim Rapoport), and Karelitz, *Ḥazon ish*, 'Yoreh de'ah', 96*a*. They obviously never saw *Guide* i. 36, cited above, p. 48. Hirschfeld, *Mishnat rishonim*, 37 ff. is aware of *Guide* i. 36, but he misunderstands what Maimonides says.

[125] This is how R. Joseph Ergas regarded those, such as R. Raphael Immanuel Hai Ricchi, who understood *tsimtsum* literally. According to Ergas, such a conception must mean that God has a form and occupies space. See Ergas, *Shomer emunim*, 70–2, and, similarly, T. Hakohen, *Divrei soferim*, 32*b*. Needless to say, the advocates of literal *tsimtsum* strongly disagreed with this position.

[126] *Tiferet yisra'el*, on Mishnah *Kelim*, ch. 30, 'Boaz', no. 1.

means that he saw the reflection in a vision. R. Moses Gentili (Hefetz, 1663–1711) offers a similar comment in his discussion of Numbers 14: 9: 'Their defence [literally 'shadow'] is removed from over them, and the Lord is with us; fear them not.' Gentili explains that it is the nature of a shadow to shrink until it entirely disappears if the body casting the light is greater than the darkened body. He continues: 'And God, who is the body [*guf*] that shines, is with us, therefore do not fear them, for our [light] is greater than their [darkness].'[127]

The eighteenth-century *Tsava'at harivash*, which purports to record the testament of R. Israel Ba'al Shem Tov (*c*.1700–60), states that one should 'always be happy, and think and believe with perfect faith that the Shekhinah is at his side and watches over him and one should look upon the Creator, blessed be He, and the Creator will look upon him.'[128] The anthropomorphic element of this passage was actually cited by the (in)famous *mitnaged*, R. Avigdor ben Joseph Hayim of Pinsk (eighteenth–nineteenth centuries) in his memorandum to the Russian government against the hasidim. Commenting on this passage, he wrote: 'With this we see how the wicked express insolence against God and praise themselves falsely, saying that they see the Creator, as if He has a form. With this they deny the Torah of Moses in which all the nations of the world believe. As a result of this they are against all the nations.'[129] R. Avigdor did not mention that just a few paragraphs earlier, *Tsava'at harivash* discusses seeing the Creator with the *mental* eye (*ein sikhlo*), which certainly reflects a non-corporeal understanding of God.

The Talmud, *Ḥagigah* 15*a*, states: 'On high there is no sitting [and no standing][130] no division and no cohesion.' This text is cited by Maimonides in the Third Principle as well as in other places[131] as support for his assertion that God, as an incorporeal being, cannot be described as being in movement or at rest. However, R. Samuel Edels (Maharsha, *c*.1555–1632), one of the most outstanding talmudic commentators, understands this passage to refer to the angels alone, and not to God. This is so for God, unlike the angels, indeed sits, as Micaiah stated: 'I saw the Lord sitting on His throne' (1 Kgs. 22: 19).[132]

R. Jacob Isaac Horowitz (died 1815), the Seer of Lublin, writes that there are people who actually see God, and that one of these was Abraham. Before

---

[127] *Melekhet mahshevet*, 125*a*.

[128] p. 23; regarding this work see Gries, *Sifrut hahanhagot*, chs. 4–5.

[129] Wilensky, *Hasidim umitnagdim*, i. 245.

[130] These words were in Maimonides' text but are lacking in ours. See Rabbinovicz, *Dikdukei soferim*, ad loc.   [131] *Guide* i. 12; *Mishneh torah*, 'Hilkhot yesodei hatorah', 1: 11.

[132] Maharsha, ad loc. Rashi also understands the text to be referring to angels, but he does not tell us why.

his circumcision God only appeared to his soul, but after the circumcision even his body could behold God![133] The Seer would have been quick to point out that he was referring to a spiritual, incorporeal vision, but from a Maimonidean standpoint a vision apprehended by the physical eyes is by definition not incorporeal.

Finally, what is one to make of the following story, told by R. Adin Steinsaltz?

> When I was a young man I met someone in Israel who was at the time a very important political personality.[134] We were talking, and he asked me, 'Where does God put his legs?' For a moment I didn't understand. I thought he was joking, but he was asking this question seriously. When I tried to tell him that, as far as I knew, God has no legs, he told me that I did not know what I was talking about as a religious person, because his father truly believed that God has legs! I tried to remonstrate. I opened the Siddur and showed him that not only do we not believe that, but we should not: it is forbidden. He ended the conversation by telling me that he was very friendly with the *rosh yeshivah* of Mir and that he would warn him that there was a person in Jerusalem who should be destroyed![135]

Although Maimonides is adamant that even children must be instructed in God's incorporeality,[136] not everyone held to this position. Thus, in the medieval *Sefer ḥasidim* we are told that the teacher should instruct children that God lives in Heaven, and he should even point to the sky to illustrate this.[137] I have no doubt that the author of this passage, who was part of an anti-corporealist milieu, would agree that this description crossed the line of strict theological propriety, but he would nevertheless argue that in the education of children one need not be bound by such concerns. In fact, as R. Reuven Margaliyot points out in his notes to the text, the approach of *Sefer ḥasidim* is based on a story told in the Talmud (*Ber.* 48*a*) about Rava and Abaye as children. When asked where God lives, Rava pointed to the roof and Abaye went outside and pointed to the sky. Upon seeing this, Rabbah commented approvingly to the boys, 'Both of you will become rabbis.'

It is possible that this tolerance of childish anthropomorphism has a parallel in tolerance of anthropomorphism that was never intended to be taken seriously. This would explain the artistic personifications of God that have

---

[133] *Zikhron zot*, 10 ('Vayera').

[134] 'It is interesting to note that he was also a son of a very famous rabbi who was a member of the Moetzet Gedolei ha-Torah in Poland' (Steinsaltz's note). Could the reference be to R. Yitshak Meir Levin (1894–1971), the Agudat Yisrael leader and son of R. Hanokh Tsevi Levin (1871–1935), rabbi of Bendin and one of the leading Polish scholars of his time?

[135] 'Where', 162. Because this story is so astounding—testifying as it does to the existence of Orthodox anthropomorphism in the twentieth century—I have my doubts as to its veracity.

[136] See *Guide* i. 35.

[137] No. 304.

not been entirely absent from post-Maimonidean Jewish history.[138] Indeed, as late as 1540, 1698, and 1742 we have title pages from rabbinic works with images of God (see Figs. 1–3 on pp. 163–7). Now this certainly does not mean that Jews at these late dates believed in a corporeal God, and such examples are indeed very rare. In fact, it is probably because there was general agreement that God is incorporeal that some tolerance was given to Jewish artists in portraying God in a physical form (or to the use of such portrayals from non-Jewish artists, if that was the case). In any event, these examples of an anthropomorphic God are certainly very un-Maimonidean.

In concluding our discussion of the Third Principle, one more point must be noted. There is no question that, according to Maimonides, a corporealist has no share in the world to come. This is such an important Principle that even 'children, women, stupid ones, and those of a defective natural disposition' must be instructed in it.[139] One who believes that God is corporeal by definition denies God's unity and is even worse than some types of idolater. It is irrelevant whether or not this mistaken belief is unintentional.[140]

Having said this, Maimonides must explain why the Torah used corporeal expressions to refer to God. His answer is striking.[141] Since the masses needed to be instructed in God's existence but could not conceive of the existence of an incorporeal God, it was necessary for them to be led to this belief in a progressive fashion. First they were taught of the existence of one corporeal God, which was an improvement to believing in many corporeal gods or having no belief. Only following this were they taught about God's incorporeality. (Maimonides does not tell us if this process was be accomplished quickly or took a number of generations.[142]) As Howard Kreisel has noted:

[138] See C. Roth, 'Representation'; Saltman, ' "Forbidden Image" '; Kochan, *Beyond the Graven Image*, 113.   [139] *Guide* i. 35.   [140] Ibid. 36.

[141] R. Bahya ibn Pakuda, *Ḥovot halevavot*, i. 10, adopts the same approach, but since he does not regard the unknowing corporealist as a heretic, his use of this explanation is not as striking as when it is used by Maimonides.

[142] See *Guide* i. 26, 46; *Mishneh torah*, 'Hilkhot yesodei hatorah', 1: 9. See also Bahya ibn Pakuda, *Ḥovot halevavot*, i. 10, and Rawidowicz, *Studies*, i. 182–3. Since the prophets use corporeal expressions, it was apparently a lengthy process. It is only when there is general acceptance of God's existence that children, women, etc. are also to be instructed in his incorporeality. Thus, there is no contradiction between the progressive approach of *Guide* i. 26, 46 and i. 35–6, where Maimonides insists that all must be instructed in God's incorporeality. In his commentary on *Guide* i. 26, Ibn Kaspi gives a similar interpretation, but includes a number of points which are totally at odds with Maimonides' opinion. Thus, he writes that the progressive method described in *Guide* i. 26, 46: ידבר מה שצריך לנהוג עם כל ההמון תמיד whereas as regards Maimonides' assertion in *Guide* i. 35–6 that one must entirely cleanse the nation of anthropomorphism: ידבר מה שצריך לנהוג עם קצת ההמון וקצת עתים ומעט מעט ראשון ראשון (see also his commentary on *Guide* i. 35). Thus, Ibn Kaspi believes that, with some exceptions, the masses are not to be exposed to the notion of God's incorporeality. However, Ibn Kaspi's understanding is directly contradicted, not merely by what Maimonides writes in the Third Principle and in the *Mishneh torah*, but also by his words in *Guide* i. 35–6. In these chapters Maimonides is

'It follows from Maimonides' remarks that the Torah deliberately misleads the people in the matter of the corporeality of God. . . . The Torah has no choice but to compromise with reality in order to educate the people effectively.'[143]

Here we are not dealing with a population that understood the Bible in a corporeal sense rather than turning to the wise men for guidance. Rather, and this is what is so significant, it was the Torah which originally intended the masses to accept God's corporeality. In other words, it is not merely that the Torah 'misleads the people', but rather that *the Torah taught them a heretical doctrine*. Of course, it must be emphasized that for an ancient Israelite to believe in God's corporeality was actually an *improvement* over his earlier state when he had no belief in God. Only when the ancients advanced beyond this stage would they be able to understand that the anthropomorphic expressions in the Torah are to be understood figuratively. If one of the ancients died without having rejected a corporeal conception of God, he would suffer the consequences of his heresy, namely, denial of a share in the world to come. Once again, it must be noted that the spiritual consequences of heresy are not to be viewed as a punishment but rather as a necessary outcome of the world's metaphysical structure. An incorporeal conception of God is a basic necessity for intellectual perfection *at all times and places*.

adamant that the time has come when the masses must be informed of God's incorporeality. (In fact, Ibn Kaspi himself advocates this opinion in his commentary on Isa. 26: 10, printed in *Mikraot gedolot: haketer*, 171.) Even in *Guide* i. 46, Maimonides clearly states that by the time of the sages there was no excuse for anyone to hold corporeal views.

Having said this, I must note that there appears to be an esoteric hint in the *Guide* that not all the sages believed in an incorporeal God. In *Guide* i. 46 Maimonides states that 'the doctrine of the corporeality of God did not ever occur even for a single day to the sages, may their memory be blessed, and that this was not according to them a matter lending itself to imagination or to confusion.' This assumption enables Maimonides to explain why the Talmud and Midrash did not shy away from speaking of God anthropomorphically. In *Guide* i. 3 Maimonides also explains that the Hebrew word *tavnit* refers only to 'the build and aspect of a thing; I mean to say its shape. . . . For this reason the Hebrew language does not use this word with reference to attributes that apply in any way to the Deity.' Yet according to the Talmud, *Ket. 8a*, one of the traditional wedding blessings, recited to this day, states that man was fashioned in the *tavnit* of God. We thus have a contradiction of the seventh cause (see Maimonides' introduction to the *Guide*), and *Guide* i. 3 holds the key to Maimonides' true view. In accord with his practice of not deviating from the text of prayers established by the talmudic sages, the anthropomorphic version is codified by Maimonides (*Mishneh torah*, 'Hilkhot berakhot', 2: 11, 'Hilkhot ishut', 10: 3). Regarding the anthropomorphic element in this blessing, see Berliner, *Writings*, i. 96; Gaguine, *Keter shem tov*, i. 607–8.

[143] 'Intellectual Perfection', 34. See also Leo Strauss's introductory essay 'How to Begin', p. xlii. For a similar approach by Maimonides in order to explain why resurrection is not mentioned in the Torah, see *Letters*, ed. Shailat, i. 334 ff. (Arabic), 368 ff. (Hebrew). See also *Guide* iii. 32, which focuses on Maimonides' view of sacrifices. When Maimonides writes that the Torah and Prophets 'explicitly' set forth that God is not a body (*Mishneh torah*, 'Hilkhot yesodei hatorah', 1: 8), he means only that it is explicit to philosophers and sages.

That the Torah taught a heretical doctrine is certainly a radical position for Maimonides to take. Yet this is not all he says. Elsewhere he explains that both the Torah and the sages use positive attributes with reference to God, since the masses are unable to achieve a representation of him otherwise.[144] Now, although 'the Torah speaks in the language of men', the fact remains that one who continues to regard God as having positive attributes 'has abolished his belief in the existence of the deity without being aware of it'.[145] The far-reaching nature of this statement is grasped when one sees that, according to Maimonides, not only is one not supposed to instruct the masses regarding God's attributes,[146] but the Torah even regards it as *necessary* for the masses to believe in positive attributes, such as the notion that God displays anger.[147] Thus, although the Torah intends the masses to hold these beliefs in order to create a stable society, the result is that they effectively deny the existence of God. Although this certainly appears to be unfair to the masses, I think Maimonides would argue that it is not the Torah that is responsible for these people having no share in the world to come. As far as he is concerned, anyone who believes in positive attributes is, in any event, unable to achieve the intellectual perfection required for immortality. Maimonides might also wonder why the masses would even be interested in the immortality he has in mind, which is, after all, completely intellectual and reserved exclusively for the philosophically enlightened.

Having said this, it is interesting that Maimonides does, in fact, justify the punishment of the corporealist who does not know any better, or who was led to his heretical belief from what he saw in Scripture. I have already quoted at length Maimonides' comments in *Guide* i. 36, in which he states: 'There is no excuse for one who does not accept the authority of men who inquire into the truth and are engaged in speculation if he himself is incapable of engaging in such speculation.' However, it would seem that Maimonides' justification is directed at those who do not grasp his true beliefs. The philosophers are aware that the attainment of immortality is not related to any questions of fairness and that God does not need to be justified for withholding this 'reward'. For Maimonides, the attainment of immortality by means of intellectual perfection is a natural process and not a reward. Thus, there is no difference between the example given by Maimonides and a person who grows up on a desert island and therefore has no wise men to turn to for instruction about God. Since neither of them has achieved the minimum measure of intellectual perfection, their intellects cannot live on.

---

[144] *Guide* i. 26, 59.

[145] Ibid. 60. See also his harsh words in *Guide* i. 50 and *Mishneh torah*, 'Hilkhot yesodei hatorah', 2: 10 that belief in divine attributes is a denial of God's unity.   [146] *Guide* i. 35.   [147] Ibid. iii. 28.

FOUR

Creation Ex Nihilo

ঙ্গ

The Fourth Principle

THE FOURTH PRINCIPLE affirms God's priority to other beings (not his eternity, as has often been assumed),[1] and creation *ex nihilo*, i.e. creation after[2] absolute non-existence.[3] There are no Jewish scholars who question God's priority, however it may be defined. However, this is not the case with regard to the doctrine of creation *ex nihilo*, which has never achieved unanimous acceptance. Thus, in describing creation, Ibn Ezra writes: 'Most biblical commentators explain that the word *bara* indicates creation *ex nihilo*'; he rejects this and concludes: 'The meaning of *bara* is to cut or to set a boundary. The intelligent person will understand [what I am alluding to].'[4] The implication of this, and some other comments of Ibn Ezra, is that he believed that the world was created by giving form to eternal matter. In his commentary on Genesis, Ibn Ezra writes that the entire creation story refers to the sublunar world,[5] implying that the spheres are eternal. This implication is even stated explicitly in his commentary on Daniel 10: 21, where he states that the heavenly bodies 'do not begin, nor do they end'. Among those who interpret Ibn Ezra along these lines are Levi ben Abraham (thirteenth–fourteenth centuries),[6] R. Nissim ben Moses (fourteenth century),[7] R. Joseph ben Eliezer Bonfils (fourteenth century),[8] R. Ezra

---

[1] That God is eternal is implied in the First Principle. This was recognized by R. Nissim b. Moses; see Mesch, 'Nissim', 86.

[2] 'The term "after" would of course have to be purged of any implications of time, inasmuch as time came into existence only with the creation of time [see *Guide* ii. 30]': H. A. Wolfson, *Studies*, i. 215. See also *Guide* ii. 13, and the helpful discussion in Seeskin, *Searching*, 71 ff.

[3] This is explicit in Maimonides' later addition to the Principles, and is found in the Kafih edition, p. 142. See also Maimonides' letter to the scholars of Marseilles (*Letters*, ed. Shailat, ii. 483), and his medical work, *Pirkei mosheh*, ch. 25, where he also expresses this opinion. (This last source was called to my attention by Professor Charles Manekin). The overwhelming majority of scholars believe creation *ex nihilo* to have been implicit in Maimonides' first formulation. See Kellner, *Dogma*, 57. Kellner (ibid. 55–6) attempts to refute this position, and argues that the original formulation only places God ontologically, but not temporally, prior to the universe. In other words, 'without God the universe could not exist; but God and the world may have coexisted eternally' (ibid. 241 n. 218). However, the notion that the world is dependent upon God for its existence was already stated explicitly in the First Principle.   [4] *Commentary*, Gen. 1: 1.

[5] *Commentary*, Genesis, 156 (alternative commentary on Genesis).

[6] See Nissim b. Moses, *Ma'aseh nisim*, 219 n. 31.   [7] Ibid. 219–20.

[8] *Tsofnat pane'ah*, 28–30, 41. See D. Schwartz, 'Creation Theory', 616–18.

Gatigno (fourteenth century),[9] R. Isaac Abarbanel,[10] R. David Arama (sixteenth century),[11] and R. Joseph Solomon Delmedigo (1591–1655).[12] Although there has recently been a great deal of discussion among scholars about Ibn Ezra's view, with some arguing that he advocates an emanationist doctrine, it is fairly clear that he is denying creation *ex nihilo*.[13]

R. Samuel Ibn Tibbon, the translator of Maimonides' *Guide* and a philosopher in his own right, is another of the medieval scholars who did not accept creation *ex nihilo*. According to him, the four elements (i.e. matter) are eternal, as are the heavenly spheres. All creation, such as it was, took place in the sublunar world.[14] Some years later, the outstanding philosopher and biblical commentator Gersonides (1288–1344) maintained that the world was created from eternal formless matter, describing his view at length in Book VI of his *Milḥamot hashem*. He is quite adamant that creation of matter out of nothing is impossible, and this is the basic stumbling-block for creation *ex nihilo* as far as he is concerned. That even God cannot do this does not limit him in Gersonides' eyes, for, as we have already seen, inability to do the impossible implies no imperfection. It is interesting that, while Gersonides sees creation *ex nihilo* as an impossibility, he is quite willing to defend the notion of matter without form, something Aristotle rejected.[15]

R. Shem Tov Falaquera also accepted the notion of creation from eternal matter, which Maimonides identifies with Plato's view.[16] Perhaps afraid of the controversy such a view would engender, as well as worried about the effect this view would have on the religiosity of the masses, Falaquera was

---

[9] See the text published in D. Schwartz, 'Philosophical Supercommentaries', 93.

[10] *Commentary*, Genesis, 3 (first question), 5 (second question), 19; id., *Mifalot elokim*, ii. 2.

[11] *Perush al harambam* (Amsterdam, 1706), 9a.

[12] *Novelot ḥokhmah*, 6b. R. Judah Moscato, *Kol yehudah* on Judah Halevi, *Kuzari*, i. 67, is suspicious of Ibn Ezra but does not come to any definitive conclusion.

[13] See Solomon Franco, quoted in D. Schwartz, 'Worship', 226–7; Rosin, 'Religionsphilosophie', 66 ff.; Orschansky, *Abraham ibn Esra*, 12 ff.; Neumark, *History of Jewish Philosophy*, ii. 276, 280 ff.; Lévy, 'Philosophie', 172; Bernfeld, *Da'at elokim*, i. 179; Greive, *Studien*, 53–60; Sirat, *History*, 106; Rottzoll, *Abraham*, 34 n. 23; Heller-Wilensky, 'Ibn Ezra', col. 1169; Husik, *History*, 190; Guttmann, *Philosophies*, 135–6; Schwartz, *Old Wine*, 102–14; and the comprehensive discussion in J. Cohen, *Philosophical Thought*, 106 ff., 166 ff. Cohen makes a strong case that Ibn Ezra entirely excludes the elements and spheres from creation, *ex nihilo* or otherwise. For scholars who understand Ibn Ezra as affirming creation *ex nihilo*, see Friedlaender, *Essays*, 3 ff.; Lipshitz, *Studies-Ibn Ezra*, 151 ff.; and Prijs, *Abraham*, 6–7, 60. Nahman Krochmal's interpretation does not seem to be in opposition to Maimonides' Principle either: see his *Kitvei ranak*, 306 ff., and the discussion in J. M. Harris, *Nachman Krochmal*, 67 ff.

[14] See Vajda, 'Analysis', 147–9; Rivlin, 'Shmuel Ibn Tibbon', 43 ff.; Nehorai, 'R. Solomon', 133 ff.; Ravitzky, 'Philosophy', 221 ff., id., 'Aristotle's *Meteorologica*', 225–50; Sirat, *History*, 218–20.

[15] *Milḥamot hashem*, v. 2, vi. 18. For detailed discussion of Gersonides' view, as well as a translation of the relevant texts, see Staub, *Creation*; Gersonides, *Wars*, iii. Nahmanides also accepted the notion of formless matter; see his comment on Gen. 1: 1 and C. D. Chavel's note in his edition of Nahmanides' *Commentary*, i. 12.   [16] See *Guide* ii. 13.

somewhat ambiguous in some of his discussions of creation. Nevertheless, a complete reading of the relevant texts clearly demonstrates that Falaquera rejected creation *ex nihilo*.[17] Indeed, not only does he say that Plato's opinion corresponds to the view of the Torah, he even states that Plato received this information from the Jewish sages![18] Two centuries before Falaquera, R. Solomon ibn Gabirol (eleventh century) was also not entirely clear regarding this matter, and some scholars understand him to be denying creation *ex nihilo*.[19] As a curiosity, we should also note the view of R. Judah Halevi (died c.1140), that the patriarch Abraham believed in the eternity of matter when he wrote *Sefer yetsirah*, a work popularly attributed to him. Only later, after receiving God's revelation, did he abandon this view.[20] Yet, according to Halevi, there is no fundamental religious objection to Abraham's original belief. In Halevi's words: 'If a believer in the Torah finds himself obliged to acknowledge and admit pre-existent matter and the existence of many worlds prior to this one, this would not impair his belief that this world was created at some particular time.'[21]

There is also the position advocated by R. Abraham Abulafia (thirteenth century),[22] R. Hasdai Crescas,[23] and R. Joseph ibn Kaspi (1280–1340)[24] that

[17] See R. Jospe, *Torah and Sophia*, 156–64; S. Harvey, *Falaquera's Epistle*, 111–19; R. Jospe and D. Schwartz, 'Shem Tov', 171 ff. For more radical readings of Falaquera, see Abarbanel, *Mifalot elokim*, ii. 1; Yair Shiffman's introduction to his edition of Falaquera, *Moreh hamoreh*, 19 ff.

[18] *Moreh hamoreh*, 117 (introduction), 259 (ii. 13). In the second source he is more hesitant, stating that 'perhaps' this is where Plato learned this view.

[19] See Kaufmann, *Studien*, 66; Husik, *History*, 68; Seeskin, *Searching*, 70. See also S. D. Luzzatto, *Studies*, ii. 19.

[20] See *Kuzari* iv. 25 ff.; Silman, *Philosopher*, 222–3. It is possible that Maimonides' esoteric view is similar. See Turner, 'Patriarch', 148–9.

[21] *Kuzari* i. 67. The proper translation of this passage has been the subject of some controversy. See Kaufmann, *Geschichte*, 138 n. 56; id., 'Jehuda Halewi', and Hartwig Hirschfeld's response, ibid. 374–8; Neumark, *History of Jewish Philosophy*, ii. 304 ff.; Waxman, *Selected Writings*, i. 77 n. 36. According to Neumark, *History of Jewish Philosophy*, ii. 304–5, and id., *Essays*, 240–1, Halevi actually believed in eternal matter.

[22] *Sitrei torah*, 114–21. See W. Z. Harvey, 'Third Approach', 76. To be sure, Abulafia was harshly criticized by perhaps his generation's leading talmudist, R. Solomon b. Adret, who even affixed to his name the curse *shem resha'im yirkav* (may the name of the wicked rot). See id., *She'elot uteshuvot harashba*, no. 548; Idel, 'Solomon', 235–51. Despite this, his writings are quoted by a number of mainstream kabbalists, including R. Hayim Vital and R. Moses Cordovero. See the publisher's introduction to Abulafia's *Razei hayei olam haba* and A. Kaplan, *Meditation*, ch. 3. See also Abulafia, *Sefer haheshek*, which was published with the approbation of R. Israel Jacob Fischer, *av beit din* of the ultra-Orthodox Edah Haredit in Jerusalem, and R. Netanel Safrin, the *rebbe* of Komarno.

[23] *Or hashem* iii. 1: 5. There is a good deal of ambiguity in the text, and my understanding follows that of W. Z. Harvey, *Physics*, 18 ff. For an alternative approach, see Feldman, 'Theory', 289–320.

[24] Commentary on *Guide* ii. 13. This passage is translated in Mesch, *Studies*, 97–100. See also H. Kasher, 'Joseph ibn Kaspi', 54–61. Although Ibn Kaspi had a number of untraditional philosophical views, I have included him in this book since he is given an entry in H. J. D. Azulai, *Shem hagedolim*, 92, and Goldwurm, *Rishonim*, 178–9, published by Artscroll. He is also included as one of the com-

God continually and from eternity 'creates' the world ('eternal creation'), or, to use Averroes' words, God 'convert[s] the world eternally from non-being into being'.[25] What creation means, according to these thinkers, is eternal ontological dependence of all existents upon the Creator, 'or if you will, the continuous information of matter by the Form of the world'.[26] In support of this contention, Abulafia and Crescas cite the words of a prayer from the morning service: 'He creates each day continuously the work of creation.'[27] Similarly, Ibn Kaspi writes: 'Every use of the expression "creation" is true, and how many creations are there in the world every day?' This combination of creation and eternity of the world, while reconcilable with the biblical account, conflicts with the notion of temporal creation after non-existence, which is what Maimonides requires.

Before taking leave of this Principle, one more point must be noted. One need not be an esotericist to see that that there are serious problems with Maimonides' claim that one who doubts creation *ex nihilo* is a heretic with no share in the world to come. Without delving too much into the often discussed problem of whether Maimonides had a secret view of creation, it is clear from Maimonides' *exoteric* teaching in the *Guide* that even he did not regard creation *ex nihilo* as a fundamental religious doctrine. Also significant in this regard is the passage in *Mishneh torah*, 'Hilkhot teshuvah' 3: 7, where Maimonides lists those who qualify as *minim*; there is no mention here of creation *ex nihilo*. Instead, he refers to one who denies 'that He alone is the First Cause and Rock of the Universe'. Another place in which one might have expected some mention of creation *ex nihilo* is at the very beginning of the *Mishneh torah*, but what Maimonides actually says there is somewhat different. It is striking how he seems to go out of his way to avoid any mention of creation:

The foundation of all foundations, and the pillar of all the sciences, is to know that there exists a First Existent, that He gives existence to all that exists, and that all existent beings, from the heaven to the earth and what is between them, exist only due to the true reality of His existence.[28]

mentaries in Artscroll's popular version of the Pentateuch, Scherman (ed.), *Chumash: Stone Edition*, in the new *Mikraot gedolot 'haketer'*, published by Bar Ilan University Press, and in *Otsar harishonim*, published with the approbations of such noted authorities as R. Jehiel Mikhel Feinstein, R. Samuel Wosner, and R. Ya'akov Perlow.

[25] *Tahafut al-tahafut*, 103. See H. A. Wolfson, *Studies*, i. 376–7.

[26] W. Z. Harvey, 'Third Approach', 77. Barzilay, *Delmedigo*, 198–203, believes that R. Joseph Solomon Delmedigo also held this position. To arrive at this conclusion, one must regard the many pages in which Delmedigo defends the philosophical soundness of this approach (*Novelot hokhmah*, 80 ff.) as representing his true view, and ignore his assertion (ibid. 107*a*–*b*) that, despite all that he has written, the Torah does indeed teach creation in time.

[27] See W. Z. Harvey, 'Third Approach', 83 n. 23.   [28] 'Hilkhot yesodei hatorah', 1: 1.

According to this passage, God is the cause or source of all that exists, but this does not mean that he created these existents out of nothing. Rather, 'gives existence' can be understood as meaning that God is the eternal cause or source.[29] In fact, nowhere in the *Mishneh torah* does Maimonides mention creation *ex nihilo*, a point which raised eyebrows and created controversy in medieval times.[30]

In the *Guide* Maimonides discusses at length the Platonic view, which maintained that the world was created by God fashioning eternal matter. He refers to a passage in *Pirkei derabi eli'ezer*[31] which seemingly advocates this position:[32]

Wherefrom were the heavens created? From the light of His garment. He took some of it, stretched it like a cloth, and thus they were extending continually, as it is said: *Who coverest thyself with light as with a garment, who stretchest out the heavens like a curtain* (Ps. 104: 2). Wherefrom was the earth created? From the snow under the throne of His glory. He took some of it and threw it, as it is said: *For He said to the snow, Be thou earth* (Job 37: 6).

Since Maimonides believed this passage to have been written by the important *tana* R. Eliezer, its apparent acceptance of the Platonic position must have been regarded by him as highly significant.[33] Yet, although Maimonides, as well as Duran[34] and Albo,[35] discusses the implication of this passage, neither he nor they entirely discount the possibility that there is another way of understanding it. R. Ezra ben Solomon, however, states without hesitation that this text is 'in accord with Plato's opinion that it is impossible for the Creator to create something from nothing'.[36] Yet, before one concludes that his position is no different from that of Gersonides, it must be noted that as a kabbalist he does not believe that the eternal matter existed in the temporal world. While the matter indeed existed, it was hidden in the Divine Mind and was only brought into the temporal world through a process of emanation.[37] Certainly, the kabbalistic 'existence' that R. Ezra speaks of hardly corresponds to anything the philosophers had in mind.[38]

---

[29] See Ibn Kaspi, commentary on *Guide* ii. 13; W. Z. Harvey, 'The *Mishneh Torah*', 20–2; Kellner, 'Literary Character', 33–4.

[30] See Halbertal, *Between Torah and Wisdom*, 120–5. [31] Ch. 3, 7*b*–8*a*.

[32] *Guide* ii. 26. See also ibid. 30 for a rabbinic passage citing R. Judah and R. Abahu which Maimonides believes might refer to the eternity of time. According to him, eternity of time also means the eternity of the world.

[33] According to V. Aptowitzer, some of the sages believed that light is a sort of prime matter. See his 'Zur Kosmologie'. For a rejection of this view see Altmann, *Studies*, ch. 5.

[34] *Ohev mishpat*, 14*b*–15*a*. [35] *Sefer ha'ikarim*, i. 2.

[36] See Nahmanides, *Kitvei ramban*, ii. 494 (commentary on Song of Songs 3: 9); Scholem, *Studies*, 28. [37] See Altmann, *Studies*, 139; Gottlieb, *Studies*, 82–3.

[38] Even when kabbalists speak of creation *ex nihilo*, they mean creation *out of God*. 'This *Nothing* from which everything has sprung is by no means a mere negation; only to us does it present no

As for Maimonides' view of the Platonic position, he notes that there are many passages in the Torah and other writings that could be interpreted to support it.[39] In contrast to the Aristotelian view that the world is eternal, which according to Maimonides would destroy the Torah, he claims that there is no religious reason to reject the Platonic view. Thus, he would have no difficulty accepting this view and interpreting Scripture in accordance with it if reason so dictated. Marvin Fox has summarized Maimonides' opinion as follows:

it seems evident that, even though he does not consider the Platonic view to be the preferred or the exclusively correct view, Maimonides does admit it, alongside the theory of creation out of nothing, as a legitimate and acceptable opinion on both philosophical and religious grounds. It can be shown to accord with one acceptable reading of Scripture and with the teachings of numerous canonical midrashim. From this evidence, we seemingly must conclude that Maimonides accepts the Platonic position as consistent with prophetic teaching, although it does not follow that he considers it to be the best interpretation of that teaching. . . . If someone finds it persuasive, there is no reason to object, since it does not contradict any principle of the Torah or of philosophy.[40]

It must be emphasized that Fox is not describing any hidden view of Maimonides. As he puts it, 'this acceptance of the Platonic position should not be viewed as an esoteric position; it is perfectly open and direct'.[41] Taking note of this fact, and not having access to Maimonides' corrected edition of the Principles, it made perfect sense for R. Gedaliah ben Solomon Lipschuetz (seventeenth century) to suggest that the reason Maimonides did not include creation *ex nihilo* in the Principles is precisely because he did not regard it as an essential belief, even for the masses to whom Lipschuetz believed the Principles were addressed.[42] Having thus seen that Maimonides himself was fully prepared to deny creation *ex nihilo*, there is simply no way one can take seriously his contention that someone who even doubts this Principle is a heretic.[43] As to his

attributes because it is beyond the reach of intellectual knowledge. In truth, however, this *Nothing*—to quote one of the Kabbalists—is infinitely more real than all other reality. . . . For this *Nothing* comprises a wealth of mystical reality although it cannot be defined': Scholem, *Major Trends*, 25. See also id., 'Kabbalah', 562–3.

[39] *Guide* ii. 25. He does not say what these other writings are, but is undoubtedly referring to the other books of the Bible and rabbinic literature.

[40] Fox, *Interpreting Maimonides*, 291, 295. R. Simeon ben Tsemah Duran, *Ohev mishpat*, 15a–15b, goes further than Maimonides and claims that, if necessary, he could even reinterpret the Torah in accord with the Aristotelian view that the world is eternal. See Kellner, *Dogma*, 257 n. 70.

[41] *Interpreting Maimonides*, 291.

[42] Commentary on Albo, *Sefer ha'ikarim*, i. 3, 15 (found in the standard editions).

[43] The contradiction between *Guide* ii. 13, where Maimonides claims that from a religious standpoint Plato's view does not differ from Aristotle's, and *Guide* ii. 25 has been dealt with by a number of authors. See most recently Fox, *Interpreting Maimonides*, 290–6.

reasons for saying something he does not really believe, I will return to this in my discussion of the Eighth Principle.

Although, as noted already, this book does not devote much attention to the esoteric reading of Maimonides, with regard to this Principle it must be mentioned that not only does Ibn Tibbon deny creation *ex nihilo*, but he can also be read as implying that Maimonides' secret teaching denies it as well.[44] This must be taken very seriously for the simple reason that Maimonides himself said that Ibn Tibbon completely understood the secrets of the *Guide*.[45] Ibn Kaspi,[46] R. Nissim ben Moses,[47] R. Profiat Duran (fourteenth century),[48] R. Shem Tov ben Joseph ibn Shem Tov,[49] and Moses of Narbonne[50] also thought that Maimonides' secret teaching was not in accord with his exoteric affirmation of creation *ex nihilo*. Among modern scholars who have argued this point, mention should be made of Herbert Davidson,[51] who adduces evidence that Maimonides held the Platonic view, and Abraham Nuriel[52] and Warren Zev Harvey,[53] who believe that Maimonides accepted the Aristotelian position.

There are even those who have argued that not just the *Guide* but also the *Mishneh torah* teaches the eternity of the world. This is in contradiction to Maimonides' exoteric view that his method of demonstrating the existence of God in the *Mishneh torah*, based on eternity, does not represent his true view.[54] Among those who advocate this position are Isaac Albalag,[55] Shlomo Pines,[56] and Warren Zev Harvey. Harvey makes the following striking statement. 'An examination of Maimonides' statements in his great Code, the *Mishneh Torah*, reveals that the Aristotelian premise of eternity is indeed *required* for the fulfillment of the divine *commandments* to know God and to know that he is one, and that Abraham our father had in fact come to know God on the basis of the Aristotelian premise of eternity.'[57]

[44] See Ravitzky, 'Philosophy', 221 ff.

[45] Maimonides' words of praise for Ibn Tibbon were recorded by his son. See Lichtenberg, *Kovets*, iii. 16c. This comment does not, however, appear in any of the three manuscripts used by Reuven Margaliyot in his edition of R. Abraham Maimonides, *Milḥamot hashem*: see ibid. 53 n. 17. R. Solomon b. Abraham of Montpellier, Maimonides' great opponent, writes that Ibn Tibbon revealed that which Maimonides had concealed. See Solomon's 'No. 7: A Copy of the Letter', 100, and Halberstamm (ed.), *Letters*, 52.   [46] Commentary on *Guide* i. 9, ii. 13.

[47] *Ma'aseh nisim*, 223.   [48] Commentary on *Guide* i. 9.

[49] Commentary on *Guide* i. 9. See also A. I. Kook, *Otsarot hare'iyah*, ii. 945, for R. Kook's reaction to this. Shem Tov's opinion, while clearly alluded to, is contradicted by an explicit statement in his commentary on *Guide* ii, introduction, 'Eighteenth Premise'. Like Maimonides, Shem Tov made expert use of the method of contradictions.

[50] *Pirkei mosheh*, 302–3; M.-R. Hayoun, *Philosophie*, 128 ff.

[51] 'Maimonides' Secret', 16–40. See also Samuelson, 'Maimonides' Doctrine', 249–71.

[52] 'Question', 372–87.   [53] 'Third Approach'; id., 'The *Mishneh Torah*', 15 ff.

[54] See *Guide* i. 71.   [55] *Tikun hade'ot*, 50–1.   [56] 'Philosophic Purport', 5.

[57] 'Third Approach', 76–7. See also id., 'The *Mishneh Torah*', 15 ff.

FIVE

Only God is to be Worshipped

ॐ

The Fifth Principle

THE FIFTH PRINCIPLE teaches that only God is to be worshipped. Stars, spheres, angels, and elements and their compounds have no free will, and as such must not be used as intermediaries to reach God.[1] As Maimonides puts it, 'our thoughts should be directed towards Him, may He be exalted, and we should leave aside everything else'. Apart from employing philosophical reasons in support of this Principle, Maimonides would have been able to point to a passage in the Jerusalem Talmud, *Berakhot* 9: 1:

If a man who has a friend is faced with a time of distress, he does not enter his [friend's] house suddenly but goes and stands beside the courtyard door of his protector and calls upon his [friend's] servant or a member of his family, who reports to him, 'A certain person is standing outside.' The Holy One, blessed be He, is not so. Instead, He has said: 'If a time of distress comes upon you, appeal neither to Michael nor to Gabriel to answer you; appeal to Me, and I will immediately answer you.'

There is no dispute among later authorities about the first part of this Principle, namely, that only God is to be worshipped, but there is a great deal of debate on Maimonides' comment about intermediaries.[2] The Talmud discusses how angels bring man's prayers to God, concluding that therefore one should not pray in Aramaic, as the angels do not understand this language.[3] The Talmud simply refers to prayers directed towards God, which are then brought before him by the angels. While there is no indication from this source that the person engaged in prayer has the angels in mind, this is only a short step from actually asking the angels to intercede on one's behalf.

---

[1] See also *Mishneh torah*, 'Hilkhot avodah zarah', 2: 1. Since Maimonides does not explicitly mention anything about asking the dead to intercede, I have not discussed this subject, although it may be implicit in this prohibition.

[2] The most comprehensive discussion is Sprecher, 'Controversy'.

[3] BT *Shab.* 12b, *Sot.* 33a. Not willing to countenance any intermediaries between God and man, Maimonides omitted this from the *Mishneh torah*: see my 'Maimonidean Halakhah', 81. However, it is regarded as halakhah by numerous other authorities, including *Shulḥan arukh*, 'Oraḥ ḥayim', 101: 4.

It is thus not surprising that such intercession is indeed found in talmudic literature.[4] For example, BT *Berakhot* 60*b* records a prayer directed towards the angels upon entering the privy.[5] BT *Sanhedrin* 44*b* states: 'Rabbi Johanan said: One should ever implore mercy that all [heavenly beings] may support his effort [in prayer] so that he may have no enemies on high.' According to Rashi and R. Samuel Strashun (1794–1872), this text refers to requests for angelic assistance. *Midrash tanḥuma*[6] portrays Moses asking the earth, stars, mountains, valleys, sea, and the angel *Sar hapanim* (Metatron) to intercede with God on his behalf.

It is possible that similar requests for angelic intercession led the anti-Christian polemicist Celsus (second century) to believe that contemporary Jews actually prayed to angels,[7] though it is also possible that some Jews did direct certain prayers to angels. In later years we find that one of the *ge'onim*, either Sherira (*c*.906–1006) or Hai (939–1038), defended the practice of requesting favours from angels, either directly or through amulets.[8] As is well known, Jewish magical texts and amulets often invoke angels.[9]

Among *rishonim*, R. Eleazar ben Judah of Worms (*c*.1165–*c*.1230),[10] a leader of the Hasidei Ashkenaz, and R. Zedekiah ben Abraham Anav (thirteenth century)[11] defend the practice of asking angels to intercede with God, citing rabbinic sources to buttress this opinion. In line with this, a prayer attributed to R. Jacob ben Meir (Rabenu Tam; *c*.1100–71) begins, 'I entreat you, Michael, Gabriel, and Raphael, that you stand in prayer before the King of Kings, the Holy One, blessed be He.'[12] R. Samson Morpurgo (1681–1740) also defends this practice, arguing that, since all power lies with God, there can be no harm in asking the angels for assistance.[13] The numerous other sages who agree with this view include R. Israel Bruna (*c*.1400–1480),[14] R. Gedaliah

---

[4] Numerous sources are found in the writings of those who permit the practice. See especially Medini, *Sedei ḥemed*, viii. 288 ff. ('Ma'arekhet rosh hashanah', 1: 2); Zunz, *Poesie*, 148–51. A relevant midrashic text, which, as far as I recall, has not been noted by earlier authors, is *Eikhah rabah* 2: 6 (brought to my attention by Rabbi Jay Zachter).   [5] See my 'Maimonidean Halakhah', 102–4.

[6] 'Va'ethanan', 6.   [7] Origen, *Contra Celsum*, i. 26 and v. 6.

[8] See Lewin, *Otsar hage'onim, Shabat: Teshuvot*, 4–6, *Ta'anit*, 24; Sherira Gaon, *Teshuvot*, no. 8 (see n. 1 regarding the authorship of this responsum).

[9] See Gaster, *Sword*; *Ḥarba demosheh*; Trachtenberg, *Jewish Magic*, 97 ff., 139 ff.; Baron, 'A Unusual Excommunication Formula', 32 (a request that the wicked be cursed by angels); Swartz, 'Scribal Magic', 173 ff.; id., *Scholastic Magic*. A very strange anonymous work from the talmudic era, *Sefer harazim*, explains how to invoke angels for a variety of purposes, but, as Margulies shows in his introduction, this book is clearly sectarian.

[10] See his responsum, published in Zachter, 'Roke'ah's Responsum', 41–6. See also ibid. 46 n. 32, where Zachter quotes a passage from R. Eleazar b. Judah's unpublished work *Hashem* in which the author offers a formula for requesting angelic assistance.   [11] *Shibolei haleket*, no. 282.

[12] Hahn, *Yosif omets*, no. 484. See Kanarfogel, 'Peering through the Lattices', 172–6.

[13] *Shemesh tsedakah*, 'Oraḥ ḥayim', nos. 23–4.   [14] *She'elot uteshuvot*, no. 275.

Lipschuetz,[15] R. Jacob Emden (1697–1776),[16] R. Judah Aszod (1794–1866),[17] and R. Samson Raphael Hirsch.[18]

It thus comes as no surprise that a number of commonly recited *seliḥot* (penitential prayers) contain requests for angelic assistance.[19] For example, the *seliḥah Makhnisei raḥamim*, which appears in the prayer book of R. Amram Gaon (821–75), includes the plea 'Angels of mercy, usher in [our petition for] mercy before the Lord of mercy. . . . Intercede [for us] and multiply prayer and entreaty before the King, the most high God. Mention before Him, and let Him hear of the [observance of the] Torah and of the good deeds [performed] by those who repose in the dust.'[20] A similar request for angelic intercession, recited during the sounding of the shofar, is found in the Habad *maḥzor*.[21] The best-known request for angelic assistance is actually recited by many Jews on a weekly basis, for it is found in the third paragraph of the Friday night hymn *Shalom aleikhem*, which reads 'Bless me for peace, O angels of peace, angels of the Exalted One.'[22] Also noteworthy is the phrase in the Grace after Meals, which reads 'On high, may merit be pleaded upon them and upon us.'[23]

The following prayer is directed towards the angel Zevadyah and appears in many contemporary hasidic and Sephardi prayer books: 'Zevadyah, preserve me and keep me alive; so shall it be Thy will, Living God and King of the universe who has all living things in His hand, Amen.' The prayer, which first appears in R. Raphael Immanuel Hai Ricchi's *Mishnat ḥasidim* (Amsterdam, 1727)[24] is supposed to be recited three times after Hallel on Rosh Hodesh as a special prayer for long life. Recognizing the problematic nature of this request, some prayer books instruct the reader only to have the prayer in mind, rather than actually verbalizing it. Other modern prayer books substitute 'God' for 'Zevadyah', thus solving the theological problem of addressing prayers to angels. This emendation also makes the prayer correspond to Psalm 41: 3: 'The Lord preserve him and keep him alive.'

---

[15] See his commentary on Albo, *Sefer ha'ikarim*, ii. 28 (found in the standard editions).

[16] *Mor uketsiah*, no. 3.   [17] *Yehudah ya'aleh*, 'Oraḥ ḥayim', no. 21.

[18] See his responsum published in Sprecher, 'Controversy', 728.

[19] See ibid. 707–9, for a list of such *seliḥot*.

[20] Rosenfeld (trans. and ed.), *Selichot*, 21.   [21] *Maḥzor hashalem-ḥabad*, 116.

[22] Surprisingly, although there is a great deal of discussion in rabbinic literature about the recitation of *seliḥot* that entreat the angels, the third paragraph of *Shalom aleikhem* has not been the focus of much attention. There were, however, some rabbinic figures who refused to say it, such as the Vilna Gaon (*Tosefet ma'aseh rav, She'elot*, no. 128); R. Hayim of Volozhin (see Katzenellenbogen, *Sha'arei raḥamim*, 9a, no. 26), and R. David Feinstein (see Feinstein, *Igerot mosheh*, viii. 146).

[23] במרום ילמדו עליהם ועלינו זכות. See Y. D. Berg's note in *Beit aharon veyisra'el*, 14 (Nisan–Iyar, 5754/1994), 109. See, however, Sprecher, 'Controversy', 710 n. 14, who claims that this prayer is not directed to the angels and should be interpreted as a prayer to God that he should command the angels to plead merit on our behalf.   [24] Page 100a in the Brooklyn, NY, 1975 reprint.

Although he personally opposed all prayers directed towards angels as a violation of Maimonides' Fifth Principle, R. Samuel Leib Kauders (1768–1838) recognized their history and popularity, and was forced to conclude, 'We must not regard all of Israel as erring, God forbid, and in particular since the great ones of the generation saw and heard this and did not protest, this means that they did not regard the practice as forbidden.'[25] In other words, acceptance of Maimonides' Fifth Principle was regarded by him as a matter of choice, and this is how matters stand today throughout the Orthodox world.

Although Maimonides includes as part of the Principle the notion that angels do not have free will, there are numerous sources that disagree with this. For example, BT *Yoma* 77a reports that God punished the angel Gabriel for not fulfilling his command properly. That one can have a philosophical bent and still not share Maimonides' view on this matter is apparent from the fact that both R. Sa'adiah Gaon and R. Samuel ben Hofni (died 1013) believed that angels have free will.[26] R. Meir ben Simeon of Narbonne, best known for his vitriolic attack on the doctrine of the Sefirot, also asserted that angels have free will.[27] Of course, the very notion of requesting angelic assistance would make no sense unless the angels possess this freedom.

Many important authorities, including R. Sherira Gaon (or R. Hai Gaon),[28] R. David Kimhi,[29] R. Bahya ben Asher (died *c.*1340),[30] and R. Hayim ben Attar (1696–1743)[31] even claim that angels have the authority to alter their divine mission. Their proof comes from the story of Lot (Gen. 19). After the angels tell Lot that they are going to destroy the entire plain of Sodom and Gomorrah, as God has commanded them, Lot asks them to spare one of the cities so that he can flee to it. One of the angels replies, 'See, I have accepted thee concerning this thing also, that I will not overthrow the city of which thou hast spoken.' Another relevant passage, not noted by these scholars, is Genesis 32: 27, where Jacob demands, and receives, the angel's blessing. This too shows that angels have free will and that they can make 'on the spot' decisions independently of God.

R. Bahya further points out that there is an explicit biblical text that supports the notion that angels can use their free will in opposition to God's plan. Job 4: 18 reads: 'Behold, He putteth no trust in his servants, and His angels He chargeth with folly.' As if this were not enough, R. Bahya even speaks of angels who 'sin',[32] as does R. Hezekiah ben Abraham (fourteenth–

---

[25] *Olat shemuel*, no. 88. [26] See Greenbaum, 'Shmuel Hofni Gaon's Commentary', 276–9.
[27] See Halbertal, *Between Torah and Wisdom*, 124 n. 23. [28] See above, n. 8.
[29] Commentary on Gen. 19: 21, 32: 29.
[30] Commentary on Gen. 3: 6, 19: 13, Exod. 23: 20. For the 'fallen angels' motif in R. Bahya, see Lipshitz, *Studies-Bahya ben Asher*, 33.
[31] Commentary on Gen. 19: 20. [32] Commentary on Gen. 3: 6.

fifteenth centuries)[33] and R. Jonathan Eybeschuetz (*c.*1690–1764).[34] In support of this notion, Eybeschuetz calls attention to the famous High Holiday *piyut*, *Unetaneh tokef*, traditionally attributed to R. Amnon of Mainz (tenth century), which reads: 'Behold, it is the Day of Judgement, to muster the heavenly host for judgement.' Eybeschuetz remarks: 'If there is punishment, there must be sin.' Although he believes that angels have free will, Eybeschuetz also agrees with some rabbinic sources that assert that angels do not have an evil inclination.[35] How then, he asks, could they come to sin? He responds that their sins are not acts of rebellion, but rather the product of good intentions. Equally uncomfortable with the idea that angels can deliberately disobey God, R. Moses Hayim Luzzatto (1707–46) claims that there are times when an angel is not given full knowledge of his mission and has to exercise his own free will, which sometimes leads to error.[36]

Although it undoubtedly makes many moderns uneasy, the idea that angels can challenge and even rebel against God, as well as the notion of 'fallen angels', can find support in a number of rabbinic and zoharic texts,[37] as well as in Philo.[38] For example, *Bereshit rabah* 50: 9 states: 'Because the ministering angels revealed God's secrets, they were banished from their precincts for a hundred and thirty-eight years. . . . Rabbi Hama ben Hanina said: [They were punished] because they expressed themselves boastfully.' The first part of this midrash is cryptic, since it is not clear what secrets the angels revealed. There is no confusion about the last part, which is alluded to by Rashi;[39] it refers to the idea that the angels overreached themselves by taking personal responsibility for the destruction of Sodom and Gomorrah, saying 'for we will destroy this place' (Gen. 19: 13). In *Devarim rabah* 11: 10 we read how 'two angels, Uzah and Azael, came down from near Thy Divine Presence and coveted the daughters of the earth, and they corrupted their way upon the earth until Thou didst suspend them between earth and heaven.' Confronted with the evidence, even as modern a scholar as R. David Tsevi Hoffmann (1843–1921) is forced to conclude that the belief in fallen angels is part of the rabbinic tradition, accepting it even though he acknowledges that it is difficult to understand.[40]

---

[33] *Malki'el*, 13 ff.   [34] *Ya'arot devash*, i. 15b–16a (Derush 2).

[35] See *Bereshit rabah* 48: 11, *Vayikra rabah* 24: 8; Moses of Coucy, *Sefer mitsvot gadol*, introduction to positive commandments.

[36] *Ginzei ramhal*, 40–1. See, similarly, *Sefer hasidim*, no. 530. Luzzatto's position is not entirely clear, for while he claims that angels can only err through lack of knowledge but not through sin, on page 40 he says that Samael rebelled against God.

[37] See Jung, *Fallen Angels*; Marmorstein, 'Discussion'; B. J. Bamberger, *Fallen Angels*; Schulz, 'Angelic Opposition'; Lauterbach, *Studies*, 149 ff.; Schäfer, *Rivalität*; Bodoff, 'Real Test', 90–2; Altmann, *Essays*, ch. 1; M. Kasher, *Torah shelemah*, Gen. 6: 2. Modern scholars agree that the 'fallen angels' motif is the product of non-Jewish influence.   [38] See H. A. Wolfson, *Philo*, i. 382 ff.

[39] Commentary on Gen. 19: 22.   [40] *Commentary*, 133.

Although Maimonides considers these beliefs heretical and would either reject or, more probably, interpret any objectionable rabbinic passages allegorically,[41] the sources quoted illustrate that such views are part and parcel of the Jewish tradition and that Maimonides' Fifth Principle has not been accepted. As for Maimonides' opinion, it has been suggested (correctly) that his views on this matter were influenced by Greek philosophy, and 'we do not say that one is required to follow after and believe that which Maimonides said as a philosopher.'[42] R. Joseph Messas (1892–1974) goes so far as to suggest that Maimonides did not truly deny the validity of prayers containing requests for angelic intercession. Rather, his opinion was only stated as a protective measure (*lemigdar milta*) and was directed towards the masses of his time, in order to prevent them from thinking that angels could act independently of God, for good or bad. 'But in our generation, when there is no one who believes this', Messas concludes that even Maimonides would permit such prayers![43]

Leaving aside the obvious error of Messas' assertion, his comment is interesting for two reasons. First, it is a good illustration of a common phenomenon in which post-Maimonidean scholars attempt to bring Maimonides' views, in particular his philosophical views, into line with popular practice and conceptions.[44] Since Maimonides is such a central figure, many regard this tactic as preferable to saying that Maimonides' view should be rejected. (For those who were not satisfied with explaining 'problematic' passages in Maimonides' philosophical works on an *ad hoc* basis, there arose, as early as medieval times, the view that towards the end of his life Maimonides became a kabbalist.[45] Those who accepted this legend were no longer troubled by Maimonides' now irrelevant philosophical views.) The second point of interest in Messas' comment is his claim that Maimonides did not actually accept everything he stated in the Principles. This notion, that there

[41] He would do the same for all the examples assembled in Aptowitzer, 'Rewarding'. According to Maimonides, since there is no providence for individual animals, there can be no reward and punishment. See *Guide* iii. 17. For those who disagreed, including Sa'adiah Gaon, see Malter, *Saadia Gaon*, 210 n. 482.

[42] See the anonymous responsum published by Lampronte, *Paḥad yitsḥak*, vii. 37*b*, 53*b* (s.v. *tserakhav*; the quotation comes from the second reference). The discussion of this issue in *Paḥad yitsḥak* extends to fifty pages.　　　　　　　　　　　　　　　　　　　　[43] *Mayim ḥayim*, no. 159.

[44] See my 'Maimonidean Halakhah', 73, concerning R. Hayim Eleazar Shapira's view that Maimonides did not really reject the existence of demons and other supernatural phenomena. As with Messas, he argues that Maimonides' comments in this regard were only directed towards the masses.

[45] See Scholem, 'From Scholar to Kabbalist'; Shmidman, 'On Maimonides' "Conversion"'. The other tactic is to deny that Maimonides wrote the *Guide*; see above, Ch. 1 n. 77, for a claim to this effect by R. Jacob Emden. R. Hayim Eleazar Shapira also denied the authenticity of certain sections of the *Guide*: see id., *Divrei torah*, vii. no. 70.

are 'necessary beliefs' in the Principles, is something I will return to in greater detail in my discussion of the Eighth Principle.

Another opponent of Maimonides, although in a less extreme way, is R. Nissim Gerondi (fourteenth century), who puts forth the strange and original position that there is one particular angel before whom prostration is permitted.[46] R. Nissim makes this claim in the course of explaining how it was that Joshua prostrated himself before an angel (Josh. 5: 14), an act which should be forbidden, just as it is forbidden to sacrifice an animal, burn incense, or pour a libation to an angel. (Prostration, sacrifice, incense-burning, and libation are the four forms of worship singled out by the Talmud as always being forbidden, even if this is not how the deity in question is usually worshipped.[47]) R. Nissim does not suggest that prostration to an angel performed as an act of honour is permitted, just as it is with humans.[48] This is probably because the Talmud (BT *San.* 61*b*) specifically exempts prostration to humans from the prohibition if it is not done as an act of worship.[49] The implication is that prostration is by definition to be regarded as a form of worship with regard to angels. According to R. Nissim, however, there is one angel who is special in this regard, and before whom one can prostrate oneself. This is the angel spoken of in Exodus 23: 20–2, concerning whom God says 'My name is in him.' It is because this angel in some way shares an aspect of God's divinity that it is treated differently from the other angels. As R. Nissim put it, 'Prostrating before him is as if one is prostrating before God.'

R. Menahem Recanati (thirteenth–fourteenth centuries)[50] and R. Joseph ben Solomon Alashkar (sixteenth century)[51] offer an alternative approach, suggesting that one is permitted to prostrate oneself before an angel if it assumes human form, just as one is permitted to do this in front of a real human. R. Isaiah of Trani (the Elder) and Albo propose a different reason,

[46] *Derashot haran*, 57–8.

[47] BT *San.* 60*b*. See Maimonides, *Mishneh torah*, 'Hilkhot avodah zarah', 2: 1, 3: 3, 6: 8.

[48] This approach is, however, adopted by R. Isaiah of Trani (the Elder) in *Kuntres hare'ayot*, 57–8, and Abarbanel, *Rosh amanah*, ch. 12.

[49] R. Aaron Samuel of Kremenets (d. *c.*1620) put forth the bold view that one can indeed prostrate oneself as an act of worship before a *tsadik*. Since the *tsadik* is infused with God's divinity, one who does this is not worshipping the *tsadik per se*, but rather the divinity within him. See id., *Nishmat adam*, 100. This strange text has been a focus of dispute in the current debate over the religious legitimacy of Habad messianism; see Berger, *Rebbe*, 165–6.

[50] *Commentary*, Exod. 20: 3. See also the similar justification of R. Abraham b. Eliezer Halevi, 'Ruling', 144, and the discussion of Halevi's view in Robinson, 'Abraham', 208 ff.

[51] See Abrams, 'Boundaries', 315–16. In this article Abrams offers a comprehensive discussion of the ambiguous figure of Metatron, who at times is portrayed as the highest angel and to whom prayers are addressed.

claiming that one may prostrate oneself before an angel, but only in recognition of its role as a messenger of God.[52]

Before concluding this discussion of the Fifth Principle, it must be noted that, despite the clarity of Maimonides' formulation, difficulties are presented by his other writings. Indeed, it appears that Maimonides later changed his view from that expressed in this Principle. In *Guide* ii. 7 he writes:

> The spheres and the intellects apprehend their acts, choose freely, and govern, but in a way that is not like our free choice and our governance, which deal wholly with things that are produced anew. . . . All this indicates that they apprehend their acts, and have will and free choice with regard to the governance committed to them, just as we have will with regard to that which from the foundation of our existence has been committed to us and given over to our power.

This passage directly contradicts Maimonides' statement in the Fifth Principle, as well as in his letter to Obadiah the Proselyte,[53] that the angels (= intellects[54]) and spheres have no free will. One of the biblical prooftexts cited by Maimonides in the *Guide* is already familiar to us—Genesis 19: 21, in which the angel, in response to Lot's request that he spare one of the cities of the plain, replies, 'See, I have accepted thee concerning this thing also, that I will not overthrow the city of which thou hast spoken.'[55]

To be sure, the free will of which Maimonides is speaking is different from human choice, for humans 'sometimes do things that are more defective than other things, and our governance and our action are preceded by privations; whereas the intellects and the spheres are not like that, but always do that which is good, and only that which is good is with them.'[56] Thus, the angels and spheres have free will that they exercise consciously, yet they always choose the same thing, the good. This means that, while there is a theoretical difference between what Maimonides writes in the Principles and what he writes in the *Guide*, there is no real practical difference with regard to angelic actions. For our purposes, however, the difference is quite significant, for in

---

[52] Isaiah of Trani, *Kuntres hare'ayot*, 57–8; Albo, *Sefer ha'ikarim*, ii. 28. Halperin, *Ḥemdah genuzah*, 39 n. 121, points out that this opinion is the same as the heretical error of Enosh and his generation, as described by Maimonides, *Mishneh torah*, 'Hilkhot avodah zarah', 1: 1. R. Abraham b. Eliezer Halevi, 'Ruling', 148, rejects this approach, for if it is correct, one should then be able to offer sacrifices, libations, or incense to angels under the same pretext, which he regards as an absurd proposition.

[53] *Letters*, ed. Shailat, i. 236.

[54] According to Maimonides, the angels are identical with the Aristotelian 'separate intellects' (or 'intelligences' (*sekhalim nifradim/nivdalim*)): see *Guide* ii. 6; Blumberg, 'Separate Intelligences'. Maimonides also states that natural and psychic forces are referred to as angels, as well as prophets and those with 'all the intellectual and moral virtues'. See his commentary on Mishnah *Avot*, 5: 13; *Guide* ii. 6–7, 42.

[55] See Shem Tov's comment ad loc., which discusses Maimonides' use of this verse.

[56] *Guide* ii. 7.

the Principles Maimonides requires one to affirm a theological notion that is contradicted by the *Guide*.

Maimonides also contradicts the Fifth Principle in the *Mishneh torah* ('Hilkhot tefilah', 7: 5), where he records a talmudic ruling (BT *Ber.* 60*b*): 'Whenever one enters the privy, before entering, he says, "Be honoured, holy honourable ones, servants of the Most High. Guard me, guard me. Wait for me until I enter and come out, as this is the way of humans".'[57] This prayer is directed to the angels which are said to accompany every man; their protection is needed at this point since the privy was regarded as a place inhabited by demons (it would not be proper for the angels to accompany one inside). Leaving aside the problems created by the fact that Maimonides does not acknowledge the existence of demons, and that in *Guide* iii. 22 he interprets the idea of two angels accompanying every man to refer to the good and evil inclinations, this halakhah stands in direct contradiction to his admonition in the Fifth Principle not to turn to the angels, as 'our thoughts should be directed towards Him, may He be exalted, and we should leave aside everything else'.[58]

Finally, there is one more place where Maimonides contradicts the Fifth Principle. In his *Essay on Martyrdom* he speaks of God punishing the ministering angels after they have criticized the Jewish people.[59] If angels do not act on their own, as Maimonides states in this Principle, they obviously cannot be 'punished'. Even according to the *Guide*, which states that angels have free will, they never exercise this will wrongly. This contradiction can probably be explained by noting that Maimonides' *Essay on Martyrdom* is not a philosophically sophisticated treatise; rather, it is a popular work designed to get a point across, and, as Haym Soloveitchik has argued, it should be regarded as a work of rhetoric. As he put it, the *Essay on Martyrdom* 'aimed not at truth but at suasion, at moving people by all means at hand toward a given course of action'.[60] Even without positing the existence of an esoteric Maimonides, it is axiomatic in Maimonidean scholarship that the opinions expressed in such popular works do not necessarily represent Maimonides' true view.

[57] I discuss this passage in 'Maimonidean Halakhah', 102–4.

[58] For R. Meir b. Simeon of Narbonne's attempt to explain this halakhah in a Maimonidean fashion, see S. E. Stern (ed.), *Me'orot harishonim*, 32–3.

[59] *Letters*, ed. Shailat, i. 36.

[60] H. Soloveitchik, 'Maimonides' *Iggeret*', 306.

Prophecy and the Uniqueness of Moses

֍

The Sixth and Seventh Principles

THESE PRINCIPLES teach the existence of prophecy, and that Moses was the greatest prophet who ever lived. He prophesied with intellect alone, without the imaginative faculty playing any role.[1] In addition to listing four ways in which Moses' prophecy differed from that of all other prophets,[2] the Seventh Principle also includes the belief that no prophet as great as Moses will ever arise again. 'He reached a greater understanding of God than anyone who has lived or will ever live.' Thus even the messiah is not regarded as Moses' prophetic equal, and elsewhere Maimonides says explicitly that the messiah will approach, but not surpass, Moses' level.[3]

There are, to be sure, great disputes about the nature of prophecy,[4] but no thinker denies it outright. Indeed, to do so would be to reject the notion that Judaism is a revealed religion. As to the unsurpassed greatness of Moses' prophecies, most see this as established in Deuteronomy 34: 10, a verse which seemingly could only have been written many years after Moses' generation: 'And there has not arisen a prophet since in Israel like unto Moses, whom the Lord knew face to face' (ולא קם נביא עוד בישראל כמשה אשר ידעו ה' פנים אל פנים). This notion is widely assumed in talmudic and midrashic literature, though there is a talmudic passage, concerning Ezra, and a couple of strange midrashim, dealing with Balaam and Samuel,[5] that seem to take a different approach.

On Ezra, BT *Sanhedrin* 21*b* states:

It has been taught: Rabbi Jose said: Had Moses not preceded him, Ezra would have been worthy of having the Torah presented to Israel through him. Of Moses

[1] See also *Guide* ii. 36, 45 (end).

[2] Shamir, 'Allusions', 216 ff., and Kraemer, 'Naturalism', 72–3, have argued that Maimonides' distinctions between prophets (which are also repeated in *Mishneh torah*, 'Hilkhot yesodei hatorah', 7: 6) are directed against Muslim views of Muhammad. However, everything Maimonides records has a basis in *Bamidbar rabah* 14: 34.

[3] 'Hilkhot teshuvah', 9: 2; *Letters*, ed. Shailat, i. 106 (Arabic), 154–5 (Hebrew). See also *Guide* i. 54: 'For what has been apprehended by [Moses], peace be on him, has not been apprehended by anyone before him nor will it be apprehended by anyone after him.' The same formulation is found in 'Hilkhot yesodei hatorah', 1: 10 and *Letters*, ed. Shailat, i. 90 (Arabic), 126–7 (Hebrew). See also *Guide* ii. 35, 39.   [4] For medieval discussion of the issue, see most recently Kreisel, *Prophecy*.

[5] On Samuel, see Ginzberg, *Legends*, vi. 228–9. See also Septimus, 'Piety', 199, 209–10.

it is written, *And Moses went up unto God* (Exod. 19: 3), and of Ezra it is written *He, Ezra, went up from Babylon* (Ezra 7: 6). As the going up of the former refers to the receiving of the Torah, so does the going up of the latter. Concerning Moses, it is stated: *And the Lord commanded me at that time to teach you statutes and judgements* (Deut. 4: 14) and concerning Ezra, it is stated: *For Ezra had prepared his heart to expound the law of the Lord, to do it and to teach Israel statutes and judgements* (Ezra 7: 10).

This passage certainly seems to imply that Ezra was as great a prophet as Moses.[6] While the text itself is careful to state only that Ezra would have been *worthy* of receiving the Torah, R. Joseph Messas declares: 'This shows that Ezra was equal to Moses, and if he had preceded Moses, it [i.e. the Torah] would have been given through him.'[7]

On Balaam, there is a famous passage in *Bamidbar rabah* 14: 34:

> It was taught: *And there has not arisen a prophet since in Israel* (Deut. 34: 10): *In Israel* there has not arisen one like him, but there has arisen one like him among the nations of the world. This was in order that the nations of the world might have no excuse for saying, 'Had we possessed a prophet like Moses we would have worshipped the Holy One, blessed be He.' What prophet did they have who was like Moses? Balaam the son of Beor.

The midrash continues by enumerating three ways in which Moses' prophecy surpassed that of Balaam, as well as three ways in which Balaam surpassed Moses. For example, God only spoke 'face to face' with Moses. On the other hand, Balaam spoke to God whenever he wished, which was not the case with Moses.[8] Although many post-talmudic authorities reinterpret this midrash so that Balaam is no longer regarded as Moses' equal,[9] there are those who do indeed take it in its simple sense. For example, R. Samuel of Rushino (twelfth century) quotes the midrash without comment.[10] Abarbanel states plainly that Maimonides' Principle contradicts this rabbinic teaching about Balaam.[11] Among post-talmudic authorities who disagree with Maimonides with regard to prophets other than Balaam and the messiah is R. Abraham Hayim Viterbo (seventeenth century). In the midst of his polemic against

---

[6] See Kellner, *Maimonides*, 14.   [7] *Naḥalat avot*, vol. v, pt. 1, p. 298.

[8] This midrash and its variants are discussed in Heschel, *Theology*, ii. 328–32. See also Urbach, *From the World of the Sages*, 537–55.

[9] See e.g. Nahmanides, commentary on Num. 24: 1; id., *Kitvei ramban*, i. 265; Menahem Recanati, commentary on Num. 22: 2 (printed in Jaffe, *Levushei or yekarot*, 283 ff.); Efodi on *Guide* ii. 35; Gersonides, commentary on Num., 136; I. Arama, *Akedat yitshak*, Num., Gate 85; Bahya b. Asher, commentary on Num. 24: 4; Albo, *Sefer ha'ikarim*, iii. 20; Abarbanel, commentary on Deut. 34: 10; Eybeschuetz, *Ya'arot devash*, ii. 7a (Derush 2); Meklenburg, *Haketav vehakabalah*, on Deut. 34: 1.

[10] *Sefer rushino* on Deut. 34: 10.

[11] Commentary on *Guide* ii. 35. An alternative approach appears in his commentary on Deut. 34: 10.

Maimonides concerning the immutability of the Torah,[12] Viterbo states that God may indeed speak to us by means of a prophet as great as Moses.[13] In another instance of conflict with this Principle, R. Kalonymus Kalman Epstein (died 1823) writes that, with proper preparation, 'anyone can reach Moses' [prophetic] grasp'.[14]

The issue becomes more complicated in relation to the messiah. It must be remembered that Deuteronomy 34: 10, cited above, is speaking of the past and says nothing about a future prophet.[15] According to a midrashic tradition the messiah 'shall be more exalted than Moses'.[16] Although one can perhaps quibble about the exact meaning of the word 'exalted', there seems to be no question that this midrash opposes Maimonides' Principle, since the Seventh Principle includes the belief that Moses achieved the highest perfection possible for a human being. Indeed, both Albo[17] and R. Tsevi Hirsch Chajes[18] understand this passage as contradicting the Principle. Nahmanides clearly disagrees with the Principle, for he says that the messiah will attain a more complete knowledge of God than Moses.[19] Gersonides also disagrees with Maimonides, for he believes that the messiah will equal, and even surpass, Moses' level of prophecy.[20] R. Hayim ben Attar (1696–1743), while not coming to any definitive conclusion, leaves this open as a possibility.[21]

It is interesting to see how Gersonides uses the verse 'And there has not arisen a prophet since in Israel', which Maimonides and others see as a proof that no future prophet can surpass Moses. Gersonides focuses on the words 'in Israel', which he believes are a clear proof that a prophet like Moses will arise among the nations. After explaining why this prophet could not be Balaam, he concludes that the messiah is intended, for he will not simply be a prophet for Israel but for the nations as well. Thus, the verse means that, while a prophet like Moses will not arise *in Israel*, that is, to prophesy for Israel exclusively, one will arise to prophesy for *both* Israel and the nations.

---

[12] See Ch. 8 n. 22.   [13] *Emunat hakhamim*, 28b.   [14] *Maor vashemesh*, 255 ('Terumah').

[15] Although Maimonides does not mention this verse in the Principle, he does mention it in *Guide* ii. 35. Abarbanel, in his commentary ad loc., notes that were it a real prooftext, the verse would have said, 'There *will* never again arise a prophet in Israel like unto Moses'. See Reines, *Maimonides and Abrabanel*, 68 n. 18. For explanations as to why Deut. 34: 10 also refers to the future, see Hayim b. Attar, *Or hahayim*, ad loc.; Maimonides, *Letters*, ed. Kafih, 51 n. 28. They both claim that the word קם refers to the past, and that עוד refers to the future. According to R. Nissim Gerondi, the word קם is actually a participle and refers to both past and future. See *Derashot haran*, 49. Surprisingly, none of these sources notes that the Talmud, BT *RH* 21b, understands Deut. 34: 10 as referring to the future. For another approach, see Hayim of Volozhin, *Nefesh hahayim*, iii. 14.

[16] *Midrash tanhuma*, ed. S. Buber, i. 70a.   [17] *Sefer ha'ikarim*, iii. 20.   [18] *Kol sifrei*, ii. 527.

[19] See *Kitvei ramban*, i. 322–3. Referring to Abraham, Moses, and the heavenly angels, Nahmanides writes: 'None of them approaches the knowledge of God as closely as the messiah.'

[20] See his *Commentary* on Num. (pp. 136–7), Deut. (pp. 344–5, 352); and the comprehensive discussion in Kellner, 'Gersonides on Miracles', 9 ff. (English section).   [21] *Or hahayim* on Lev. 19: 2.

Finally, I must mention R. Isaac Luria's view that Moses' understanding of divine matters was inferior to that of certain kabbalists (including himself!). This notion is elaborated upon by R. Shneur Zalman of Lyady (1745–1813), who asks, 'How did Rabbi Isaac Luria, of blessed memory, apprehend more than he, and expound many themes dealing with the highest and most profound levels [*penimiyut*], even of many Sefirot?' According to R. Shneur Zalman, because Moses only used prophetic powers he was not able to reach the heights of R. Simeon bar Yohai, Luria, and other kabbalists, who attained their understanding through wisdom and knowledge (*ḥokhmah veda'at*). According to R. Shneur Zalman, this means that, while these kabbalists had a more profound understanding of divine matters, none of them actually reached Moses' *prophetic* level. Thus, there is no conflict with Deuteronomy 34: 10, since this verse only states only that another *prophet* as great as Moses will never arise again.[22]

According to R. Shneur Zalman, this superior understanding of the kabbalists in comparison to Moses explains the talmudic saying, 'A wise man is better than a prophet.'[23] R. Shneur Zalman comments: 'Because by his wisdom he can apprehend exceedingly beyond the levels that can descend netherwards in a mode of revelation to the prophets in the vision of their prophecy. For only the lowest ranks can descend and become revealed to them.'[24] Yet Maimonides' Principle includes the notion that Moses 'reached a *greater understanding of God* than anyone who has lived or will ever live'. The assertion that certain kabbalists were privy to exalted theological matters of which Moses, *for whatever reason*, was ignorant is thus clearly a violation of Maimonides' Principle.

[22] *Likutei amarim*, 'Igeret hakodesh', no. 19.
[23] BT *BB* 12a.
[24] *Likutei amarim*, 'Igeret hakodesh', no. 19.

SEVEN

Revelation of the Torah

☙

The Eighth Principle

T HE EIGHTH PRINCIPLE teaches that the Torah was divinely revealed and that the Torah in our hands is exactly the same as the Torah that Moses presented to the Children of Israel. In addition, there is no difference in holiness between any parts of the Pentateuch. The Principle also declares that the Oral Law is likewise of divine origin.[1]

There has never been dispute about the Written and Oral Laws being divinely inspired, but agreement ends at that. J. David Bleich has correctly noted that 'this principle is, in effect, an affirmation of the authenticity of the Masoretic text'.[2] It is also much more than that. The Principle declares that the Masoretic text established by Aaron ben Moses ben Asher (tenth century) is, in its entirety, of Mosaic authorship.[3] Consequently, it suggests, there is no such thing as a history of the pentateuchal text, that is, of the development of the *textus receptus*. As with the other Principles, one who denies this, or even expresses doubt with regard to it, is a heretic with no share in the world to come.[4]

In popular circles this aspect of the Principle is often repeated dogmatically as if traditional Judaism is unimaginable without it. For example, J. Newman writes: 'The version [of the Torah] in our hands today is identical with that which Moses received. . . . [T]he entire text, in every detail, now in our possession is the one given to Moses at Sinai.'[5] Louis I. Rabinowitz writes: 'The Masoretic text is the sole *textus receptus* of the Torah. All other readings represent man-altered variations from that authentic text.'[6] Avraham Kushelevsky

---

[1] On the question of which aspects of rabbinic tradition qualify as divine Oral Law according to Maimonides, see Blidstein, 'Oral Law'. [2] *With Perfect Faith*, 365.

[3] The standard version of Maimonides' *Commentary on the Mishnah* does not contain the words 'this entire Torah which is found in our hands today'. It does appear in the accurate Kafih edition as well as in the *Ani ma'amin*. Not having the correct text of Maimonides' Eighth Principle, Hirschensohn, *Malki bakodesh*, ii. 234–5, was able to argue that Maimonides could not have presented the accuracy of the Masoretic text as dogma. D. Cohen, *Masat kapai*, 92, also errs in this regard.

[4] In 'Hilkhot teshuvah', 3: 8, Maimonides does not go to such an extreme. All he says here is that it is heretical to say that a part of the Torah, even one word, was added by Moses without divine inspiration (*mipi atsmo*). According to this formulation, Maimonides is not concerned with the issue of textual accuracy but with whether or not the divine word was falsified, thus turning Moses into a charlatan.   [5] *Faith*, 60–1.   [6] 'Torah', 39–40.

writes: 'The text of the Torah has been preserved as it was given more than 3,000 years ago, without an addition or deletion of a verse, a single word, or even a single letter.'[7] The intricate system of 'codes' which was discovered in the Masoretic text, popularized by Orthodox proselytizers, and made famous through Michael Drosnin's bestseller, *The Bible Code*,[8] depends on this Principle for its validity. As Drosnin puts it: 'All Bibles in the original Hebrew language that now exist are the same letter for letter. . . . The Bible code computer program uses the *universally accepted original* Hebrew text. Therefore, there is no question that information about today's world is encoded in a book that existed at least 1000 years ago, and almost certainly 2000 years ago, *in exactly the same form it exists today*.'[9]

Nevertheless, there are a number of points, based only upon traditional sources, which make this aspect of the Principle extremely problematic. As Herbert Loewe put it: 'It stands or falls by an absolutely uniform text. If the manuscripts of the *textus receptus* differ in one single iota, the doctrine is irreparably shattered. Which, in that case, was the reading revealed to Moses and recorded by him?'[10] As quoted above, this Principle is seen to affirm the Masoretic text. Yet strictly speaking, there is no such thing as *the* Masoretic text. One can only speak of the texts established by various Masoretic scholars, which differed in minor details. Technically speaking, all of these disparate texts must be termed 'Masoretic'.[11] It is thus only natural that

---

[7] *Meetings*, 86. [8] New York, 1997.

[9] *Bible Code*, 194–5; emphases added. Here is not the place to comment on Drosnin's incredible ignorance regarding the age of the Pentateuch.

[10] Loewe and Montefiore (eds.), *Rabbinic Anthology*, p. lxii. I have refrained from commenting on the differences between the script in contemporary Torah scrolls (*ketav ashuri*) and ancient Hebrew script. Although Maimonides insists that current Torahs are exactly the same as the original one in Moses' day, it is hard to know whether the issue of script is included in this Principle. Maimonides believed that Moses' Torah was written in *ketav ashuri* (see his commentary on Mishnah *Yadayim* 4: 5). However, this does not mean that he included this as part of the Eighth Principle. Presumably he also did not include the issue of the enlarged or reduced letters or other textual peculiarities, regarding which there is no uniformity in biblical manuscripts and Masoretic lists. (See his *Shemot kodesh veḥol*, 7–8 (Hebrew numerals), which notes that the unusual letters are of rabbinic origin. However, it is doubtful whether Maimonides is truly the author of this work. See Levinger, 'On the Book *Be'ur shemot*'.) Maimonides himself admits that in his day there was no uniformity with regard to the *tagim* (the letters' ornamental crownlets), even though they are of Mosaic origin. See his *Responsa*, ii, no. 154. Nor do I believe that Maimonides is referring to the issue of open and closed sections, although this is less certain since here more significant halakhic considerations enter the picture; see e.g. 'Hilkhot sefer torah', 7: 11, 8: 3, and Penkower, 'Maimonides', 39 ff.; M. Goshen-Gottstein, 'Keter', 880 ff. I understand Maimonides to mean that the *words* which now appear in the Torah are identical with those that appeared in Moses' Torah.

[11] I say 'technically', for there is no question that it is not improper, at least for purposes of simplicity, to continue to refer to 'the Masoretic text', and in the pages that follow I shall do so. The minor variations simply reinforce the fact that there is an overwhelming measure of agreement. As Moshe Goshen-Gottstein has noted, 'the *receptus* tradition emerges clearly from the vast majority of the codices'. See his 'The Rise of the Tiberian Bible Text', 117 n. 122, and also his introduction to the

Me'iri, to mention one example of many, speaks of 'Masoretic works', rather than of a single Masoretic text.[12] In fact, he could not have spoken of *the* Masoretic text because this characterization is not part of traditional Jewish terminology, but is, rather, a relatively recent invention of printers and editors.[13] When we currently speak of the Masoretic text or the *textus receptus*, we refer to the edition of the Bible edited in 1525 by the future apostate Jacob ben Hayim (*c.*1470–*c.*1538), including the corrections made to it by the Masoretic scholars R. Menaham de Lonzano (1550–*c.*1620) and R. Yedidyah Solomon Norzi (1560–1616).[14] Before this time, pentateuchal texts, even though they can be termed Masoretic, were not united around a single text.

As early as talmudic times, it was understood that the Babylonian rabbis were no longer aware of the proper defective and plene spellings.[15] According to such outstanding sages as R. Isaiah Horowitz (*c.*1565–1630),[16] R. Tsevi Hirsch Ashkenazi (1660–1718),[17] R. Jacob Reischer (*c.*1670–1733),[18] and R. Moses Feinstein (1895–1986),[19] this explains why R. Moses Isserles (*c.*1530–72) ruled that if such an error is found in a Torah scroll, there is no need to take a new one out of the ark.[20] Although, as a practical matter, scribes are instructed

---

Jerusalem 1972 reprint of the *Biblia Rabbinica*, para. 19 (hereafter 'Introduction'); Menachem Cohen, '"Masoretic Text"'; Barr, *Variable Spellings*, 5–6. Mordechai Breuer's more extreme conclusions in his *Aleppo Codex* are based on a methodological error, as has been shown in Penkower, 'Jacob ben Hayim', 437–8, and Menachem Cohen, 'Introduction', 54*–5*. My thanks to Dr Penkower for a lengthy and detailed letter in which he clarified a number of points relevant to this discussion.

[12] *Beit habehirah*, on BT *Kid.* 30*a*.

[13] See M. Goshen-Gottstein, 'Introduction', paras. 13, 17.

[14] Ibid., para. 21; id., 'Editions', 226–7. Of course, this does not mean that Jacob b. Hayim created a new text. Rather, he viewed his job as simply correcting errors, and his role was limited to choosing between one of the given variants, making his text very similar to earlier ones. However, as Penkower has shown, his method was eclectic, and does not appear to be based on any system. See id., 'Jacob ben Hayim', 51–2, 134. To give a few examples: in Gen. 19: 13, his text is את המקום although the Spanish manuscript which he normally used read אל המקום. In Exod. 19: 4, his text is למצרים, despite the fact that he noted that there was another reading, במצרים, and he did not have any Masoretic notes to guide him. He decided on his own which version should be recorded. In Gen. 16: 12, he has ועל פני, even though he acknowledges that, according to the Masoretic notes he used, it should be על פני. For these examples see Penkower, 'Jacob ben Hayim', 127, 135.

As for the apostasy of Jacob b. Hayim, earlier scholars were often unaware of this and thus referred to him in glowing terms: see e.g. Basilea, *Emunat hakhamim*, 41*b*; Penkower, 'Jacob ben Hayim', 412–14. Communications not being what they are today, this is not so surprising. However, in our day, when anyone can open an encyclopedia and learn this information, it is truly remarkable that a book could be published, in Benei Berak no less, which describes Jacob b. Hayim as one of the great scholars of Israel. I refer to Mosheh Tsuriel's *Masoret seyag latorah*, i. 9, 94 ff. See Mordechai Breuer's harsh review of this work in *Megadim*, 20 (1993), 91–6.

[15] Plene refers to a system of full orthographic notation, whereby vowel sounds are indicated by vocalic signs (in particular the letter *vav*). BT *Kid.* 30*a*. Presumably this is the reason why there is no uniformity as to the number of letters in the Torah. See the various numbers recorded in A. Kaplan, *Handbook*, 135.   [16] *Shenei luhot haberit*, ii. 2*b*.   [17] *Hakham tsevi*, no. 54.

[18] *Shevut ya'akov*, ii, no. 3.   [19] *Igerot mosheh*, 'Yoreh de'ah', iii, no. 114.

[20] *Shulhan arukh*, 'Orah hayim' 143: 4.

to write these words in a certain way, since we do not truly know how defective and plene words should appear, the new Torah scroll will not necessarily be any better than the first. The upshot of all this is that, as Feinstein writes, 'the *kashrut* of our Torah scrolls is not so certain'. Not surprisingly, Masoretic biblical manuscripts exhibit a good deal of variety in this regard, and there is no consistent orthography.[21]

Similarly, it was recognized long ago that a number of quotations from the biblical text, including the Pentateuch, found in the Talmud and Midrashim differ from the accepted (Masoretic) text.[22] In a famous responsum, R. Solomon ben Adret (Rashba, *c.*1235–*c.*1310) discussed when Torah scrolls should be corrected in accordance with the Talmud's pentateuchal text.[23] As R. Jacob Hagiz (1620–74) points out, these differences are not simply in matters of defective and plene, but even extend to actual words.[24] There are numerous examples of this, and one of them is even found in the Ten Commandments, a text that one would have assumed would not exhibit alternative versions, because of its great significance and popularity. Yet this is not so: according to the Jerusalem Talmud, *Sukah* 4: 3, the very first verse of the Decalogue reads: אנכי ה' אלהיך אשר הוצאתך מארץ מצרים, although our versions of the Decalogue, in both Exodus and Deuteronomy, have הוצאתיך.

It is well known that medieval authorities also had differing versions of the Pentateuch,[25] and we often have manuscript evidence to support these

---

[21] On medieval textual traditions, see the important studies by Menachem Cohen: 'Basic Features' and 'Consonantal Character'. On the Babylonian Masoretic tradition, see Ofer, *Babylonian Masorah*, ch. 11.

[22] Among *rishonim*, see e.g. Tosafot on BT *Shab.* 55*b*, s.v. *ma'avirim* (and R. Akiva Eger's note ad loc.), and on BT *Nid.* 33*a*, s.v. *vehinaseh;* Me'iri, *Beit habehirah*, on BT *Kid.* 30*a*; id., *Kiryat sefer*, 57–8; Halaveh, *Teshuvot maharam halaveh*, no. 144; Nissim Gerondi on BT *Ned.* 37, s.v. *at*; Isaac b. Sheshet, *She'elot uteshuvot harivash*, no. 284. Regarding this issue, see J. Z. Stern, *Tahalukhot ha'agadah*, ch. 16; Aptowitzer, *Schriftwort*; D. Rosenthal, 'Rabbinic'; Maori, 'Rabbinic Midrash'; Leiman, 'Masorah'; B. Levy, *Fixing God's Torah*.

[23] *She'elot uteshuvot harashba hameyuhasot leramban*, no. 232. For comments on the textual aspects of this responsum, which appears here in a mutilated form, see Penkower, 'Maimonides', 40 n. 3. Rashba contended that, when the Talmud derived *halakhot* from words, these words should then appear in our Torah scrolls as they do in the Talmud (see also Me'iri, *Beit habehirah* on BT *Kid.* 30*a*; id., *Kiryat sefer*, 57–8, and David ibn Zimra, *She'elot uteshuvot haradbaz*, nos. 1020, 1172). Although this opinion found a number of outstanding defenders, it is not in accord with current scribal practice. See Hirschensohn, *Malki bakodesh*, ii. 227; Maori, 'Rabbinic Midrash', 123 ff.; Leiman, 'Masorah'; B. Levy, *Fixing God's Torah*.   [24] *Halakhot ketanot*, i, no. 14.

[25] Most of these are very minor differences. For example, our texts of Exod. 25: 22 read את כל אשר אצוה. However, Ibn Ezra and some versions of Rashi have ואת. Although much has been written regarding textual variations in talmudic and midrashic literature, we still await a comprehensive study of this phenomenon with regard to the medieval writers, texts by whom are constantly being published. Aptowitzer, *Schriftwort*, provides the initial spadework. Future research must establish when we are confronting scribal errors and lapses of memory and when we are presented with a different textual tradition. For a step in this direction see Esh, 'Variant Readings'.

readings. Even R. Samuel David Luzzatto, who doubts that there were any differences in medieval Torah scrolls and attributes all variations to memory lapses, has to admit that this can only be said from the period of the Masoretes onwards. Before this time, however, even he admits that variations occurred in the text.[26] R. Aryeh Loeb Guenzberg (1695–1785) and R. Eleazar Fleckeles (1754–1826) advance the startling view that, as far as biblical law is concerned, Jews are no longer required to fulfil the commandment of writing a Torah scroll, since it can no longer be carried out properly because of uncertainty about defective and plene spellings.[27] Fleckeles and R. Moses Sofer (1762–1839) both cite this uncertainty as the reason why no blessing is said before writing a Torah scroll. Perhaps the Talmud's version is correct, which would mean that the Torah scroll being written would actually be invalid.[28]

Scholars have also called attention to textual variations in the Dead Sea Scrolls, Samaritan Pentateuch, Septuagint, Peshitta, and Targumim.[29] To be sure, many of these variants are due to scribal errors, and with regard to the translations, it is often difficult to know whether we are confronted with a different textual tradition or whether the translator has simply taken liberties with the text. However, there is universal agreement that at least some of the examples do reflect traditions at variance with the Masoretic text.[30] In fact, with regard to the Dead Sea Scrolls it is incorrect simply to speak of alternative readings, since the reality is more significant. For example, the text of the books of Exodus and Numbers preserved in the Dead Sea Scrolls (and often paralleled in the Samaritan version), shows us that there were basically two

---

[26] *Peninei shadal*, 338; id., *Ohev ger*, 86, and his letter in Yolles, *Hatorah vehahokhmah*, 148–9. See however, id., *Letters*, 277, where he points to a textual variation in Ibn Ezra's Pentateuch.

[27] Guenzberg, *Sha'agat aryeh*, no. 36; Fleckeles, *Teshuvah me'ahavah*, iii. 58*a*. R. Abraham Tsevi Hirsch Eisenstadt, *Pithei teshuvah*, 'Yoreh de'ah', 270: 10, argues that, according to Guenzberg, there is no longer even a rabbinic commandment to write a Torah scroll. R. Ephraim Hiksher, *Adnei faz*, no. 13, claims that if one finds a mistake in a Torah scroll which does not require a new one to be taken out—for example, if a defective word is written plene—then when lifting the scroll at the end of the Torah reading one does not say: 'This is the Torah that Moses placed before the Children of Israel' (Deut. 4: 44). This view is difficult to understand, for the Talmud makes clear that *none* of our Torah scrolls is letter perfect.

[28] Fleckeles, *Teshuvah me'ahavah*, iii. 56*b*; M. Sofer, *She'elot uteshuvot*, 'Orah hayim', nos. 52, 54.

[29] An interesting phenomenon which has not yet been studied adequately is the attitude of some Orthodox scholars who refuse to accept the notion that the Talmud, Targum, and other ancient writings had textual variants. What makes this approach so interesting is that its adherents are not content with accepting a view that was supported by numerous rabbinic authorities. See Maori, 'Rabbinic Midrash', 102 ff. To the sources cited by Maori, add Ehrenreich, 'Variations'.

[30] Although traditional rabbinic scholars have not generally dealt with the Septuagint, Peshitta, and Dead Sea Scrolls, they have written numerous commentaries on the Targumim and have sometimes pointed to divergences between the Masoretic text and the text upon which the Targum is based. See e.g. Berkovitz, *Halifot simlot*, and Schmerler, *Ahavat yehonatan* on Exod. 34: 30. R. Jehiel Jacob Weinberg noted that there are passages in the Peshitta which are based on variant readings; see my *Between the Yeshiva World and Modern Orthodoxy*, 169 ff.

editions of these books in Second Temple times.[31] The Dead Sea Scrolls version of these books is quite expansive, and is without question an elaboration
of a version similar to what we call the Masoretic text, but this certainly does
not mean that we can dismiss all the textual variants found in the Scrolls.[32]

Indeed, that there were differences in pentateuchal texts in Temple days is
indisputable. It was because of this that R. Akiva and R. Ami emphasized the
importance of using a corrected text.[33] According to a number of midrashic
sources, R. Meir himself had a Torah text that differed from that of his
colleagues.[34] For example, while the standard version of Genesis 1: 31 reads:
'And God saw every thing that He had made, and, behold, it was very good'
(טוב מאד), R. Meir's text read: 'Behold, death was good' (טוב מות).[35] The
standard version of Genesis 3: 21 reads 'garments of skin' (עור), but R. Meir's
text read 'garments of light' (אור). According to Nahmanides, the former
example was not the result of an error made by an ignorant scribe, but rather
R. Meir himself was responsible for the variant.[36] In fact, it is possible that R.
Meir's scroll was related to the so-called Severus scroll mentioned in *Bereshit
rabati*. This midrash lists a number of textual variants found in a Torah scroll
which 'came out of Jerusalem in captivity and went up to Rome and was
stored in the synagogue of Severus'. These variants include additions and
deletions of letters and even an occasional word. Some of them correspond
to what appeared in R. Meir's text.[37]

R. Isaac Safrin agrees with Nahmanides that R. Meir was responsible for
writing 'garments of light' in his scroll, and he offers a kabbalistic reason for
this. According to him every Jew has an obligation to write a Torah scroll in
accordance with the 'root' of his soul. Since the word אור corresponded to
the root of R. Meir's soul, this was what he wrote. In what appears to be a
unique halakhic position, Safrin states that while a Torah scroll which contains the word אור should be changed to agree with the standard reading,
even without the change it remains a kosher scroll which can be used in the
synagogue. Safrin also claims that all of the disagreements over defective and

---

[31] See Ulrich, *Dead Sea Scrolls*, 25–6, 64–5.

[32] I exclude from this statement the orthography of the Dead Sea Scrolls, which is distinctive in
being 'very full', and is a later development than the orthography reflected in the Masoretic text. See
Tov, *Textual Criticism*, 108, 222.

[33] See BT *Pes.* 112*a*, *Ket.* 19*b*. This point was noted by R. Jehiel Jacob Weinberg; see my *Between the
Yeshiva World and Modern Orthodoxy*, 169–70.

[34] *Bereshit rabah* 9: 5, 20: 12, 94: 9; *Bereshit rabati*, 209.

[35] See *Guide* iii. 10, for Maimonides' view that this only reflects R. Meir's interpretation of the
verse, rather than a different reading in the text he used.

[36] *Kitvei ramban*, i. 184. See also Lieberman, *Hellenism*, 25.

[37] *Bereshit rabati*, 209–12. See Loewinger, 'Torah Scroll'; Siegel, *Severus*; Tov, *Textual Criticism*,
119–21.

plene spellings, as well as over the occasional letter, actually go back to the revelation at Sinai. Whereas Maimonides establishes as dogma that Moses received the Torah, gave it to the children of Israel, and that it is this very Torah which is in use today, Safrin claims that Moses received the Torah together with all the variants. He also states that Moses gave each tribe a *different* Torah, each one in accordance with the root of that tribe's soul.[38]

Faced with all the textual differences, even Maimonides' son R. Abraham agreed that there was no authoritative text, and he was therefore unwilling to invalidate scrolls that differed from Maimonides' prescriptions.[39] Maimonides' establishment of the authority of the Ben Asher Masoretic text as dogma means that the sages of the Talmud and Midrash, the Babylonian Masoretes,[40] and countless medieval scholars stand in opposition to Maimonides' Principle, thus making them heretics! Even today the Yemenites have a slightly different text from that used by the rest of Jewry.[41] It is thus impossible to speak about the Torah 'found in our hands today' without clarifying that there is no such single text. Considering all that has been mentioned with regard to the non-uniformity of the Torah text, it should not be surprising that R. Jacob Kamenetzky (1891–1986) argued that perhaps Maimonides' text of the Pentateuch differed from the one in use today.[42] In fact, with the publication of Jordan Penkower's monograph on the Aleppo Codex, we see that the letters in Maimonides' pentateuchal text (the Ben Asher text) were identical to those of the current Yemenite text.[43] This means that if contemporary Ashkenazim and Sephardim accept Maimonides' Eighth Principle with regard to *their* versions of the Pentateuch, they stand condemned as heretics by Maimonides himself for refusing to accept *his* version as the proper one.[44]

[38] *Heikhal haberakhah*, i. 7a, 87b, 261a.

[39] *Teshuvot rabenu avraham ben harambam*, no. 91. This responsum is concerned with open and closed sections; however, I do not see why questions of defective and plene spelling would not also be included by R. Abraham.

[40] e.g. in Num. 11: 21 the Tiberian Masoretes read להם while the Babylonians read לכם. See Ginsburg, *Introduction*, 189.

[41] There are nine differences in single letters, seven of which concern defective and plene spelling. The other two are Gen. 9: 29: ויהי (Ashkenazi-Sephardi) vs. ויהיו (Yemenite) and Deut. 23: 2: דכה (Ashkenazi-Sephardi) vs. דכא (Yemenite). See Korah, *Se'arat teman*, 103–4; Penkower, *New Evidence*, 68 n. 180. For the halakhic ramifications, see Yosef, *Yehaveh da'at*, vi, no. 56.

[42] *Emet leya'akov*, 388. To support this view he cites information obtained from the critical apparatus of the apostate C. D. Ginsburg's edition of the Pentateuch (London, 1908).

[43] See Penkower, *New Evidence*, 67 ff. In five places Ben Asher and the Yemenite text differ with regard to the proper separation of words.

[44] I have cited Kamenetzky's view simply to show that a leader of the right-wing yeshiva world had no difficulty rendering the Masoretic aspect of the Principle non-binding. This does not imply that there is any validity to his claim that, in the instance he discussed, Maimonides had a different text of the Pentateuch. Even before the publication of Penkower's book, the textual variant was adequately

Rabbinic sources speak of *tikunei soferim*, that is, textual changes introduced by the Scribes, some of which concern the Torah.[45] The unifying characteristic of almost all of these passages is that before the 'correction' the biblical verse could be regarded as offensive to God or grossly anthropomorphic. A famous example, recorded in various early lists of the 'corrections', occurs in Genesis 18: 22: 'The men turned from thence and went toward Sodom, but Abraham stood yet before the Lord.' In truth, it was God who came to Abraham, not the other way around, and therefore the text should have said, 'God stood yet before Abraham.' However, since this is offensive to God, for it is not fitting to say that God was waiting for Abraham, the text was 'corrected'.

According to *Midrash tanhuma*[46] and *Yalkut hamakhiri*,[47] it was the Men of the Great Assembly who changed certain words in the Torah. The anonymous Masoretic work *Okhlah ve'okhlah* (tenth century?)[48] and R. Joshua Falk (eighteenth century)[49] credit Ezra with the textual changes.[50] R. Nathan ben Jehiel (d. 1106),[51] Rashi,[52]

explained as the result of Maimonides citing from memory. Some of the other examples cited by Kamenetzky are simply manuscript or printing errors, which do not appear in the most recent critical editions of Maimonides' works. (Neuhausen, *Torah or leharambam*, the only comprehensive study of biblical passages in Maimonides, is severely flawed, primarily because it relies on faulty texts.) Still, Kamenetzky's readiness to posit a different pentateuchal text in order to answer a difficulty is an essential tool in biblical exegesis. A good example of this is provided by Shmuel Ashkenazi in his note in *Or torah*, 24 (Nisan 1992), 567. Lev. 19: 33 reads: וכי יגור אתך גר בארצכם. R. Hayim b. Attar, *Or hahayim*, ad loc., seeks to explain why the verse begins with the singular and ends with the plural. While any number of imaginative answers can be given for this difficulty, it is important to realize that the reading אתכם is found in biblical manuscripts, the Samaritan Pentateuch, and the Babylonian and Jerusalem Talmuds, and is the basis for the translations found in Onkelos, Pseudo-Jonathan, Neofiti, Septuagint, Vulgate, Peshitta, and Sa'adiah Gaon. Thus, almost certainly the answer to *Or hahayim*'s question is that the Masoretic text preserves an inauthentic reading.

[45] For all his radical ideas, it is actually Ibn Ezra who rejects the idea of *tikun soferim*. See his Introduction to the Pentateuch (end), in his *Commentary*, and his comment on Num. 11: 15, 12: 12, and especially *Sefer tsahut*, 74a, where he claims that the notion of *tikun soferim* is merely a solitary opinion, not accepted by the sages. Still, he has no doubt that, according to this opinion, *tikun soferim* meant exactly that, namely, a post-Mosaic correction of the biblical text.

[46] 'Beshalah' 16.   [47] *Yalkut hamakhiri*, on Zech., 30–2.   [48] p. 113.

[49] *Binyan yehoshua* on *Avot derabi natan*, 34: 5. Although Falk quotes R. Meir Eisenstadt, the latter's comments are not quite the same as Falk's interpretation.

[50] See also Ginsburg, *Masorah*, ii. 710, who quotes a Masoretic note that, in the opinion of some Masoretic schools, it was Ezra who was responsible for the changes. Another such note attributes the changes to Ezra and Nehemiah; see Ginsburg, *Introduction*, 351. A Genizah fragment (Taylor–Schechter Collection, Job[a]) refers to a '*tikun* of Ezra and the Scribes'. Another fragment (Taylor–Schechter Collection, Job[b]) refers to a '*tikun* of Ezra and Nehemiah and Zechariah and Haggai and Baruch'. See Barnes, 'Ancient Corrections', 403. See also Sachs, 'Investigation', 53; McCarthy, *Tiqqune Sopherim*, 42–52; Zipor, *On Transmission*, ch. 3.   [51] *Arukh hashalem*, iv. 181, s.v. כבד.

[52] Commentary on Gen. 18: 22. The relevant passage does not appear in a number of manuscripts; see Abraham Berliner in his edition of *Rashi al hatorah*, pp. xiv–xv. Those who deny the authenticity of this passage seem to have overlooked Rashi's comment on Job 32: 3, where he reiterates this view. Barnes, 'Ancient Corrections', 403, 405, offers a radically different interpretation of Rashi's comment

R. David Kimhi,[53] various Masoretic notes,[54] and *Shemot rabah* as explained by the standard midrashic commentary *Matnot kehunah*[55] (which actually presents the *peshat*, the literal meaning of the midrashic text), also state explicitly that the biblical text was changed by the Scribes. Although missing from the standard edition, there are some versions of *Shemot rabah* 13: 2 which contain this explanation.[56] R. Elijah Mizrahi (1450–1525) rejects the notion that the various *tikunei soferim* are actual corrections in the Torah text, but acknowledges that Genesis 18: 22 (mentioned above) is different in nature from the other examples referred to in rabbinic literature. In the case of this verse, he believes that the Scribes actually did alter the Torah text.[57]

It is not important for us to determine whether this meaning of *tikun soferim* is correct, since our primary focus remains the sources that conflict with Maimonides' Principle. Not surprisingly, this view of the term was subject to harsh criticism by those who refused to countenance that the Torah text could ever have been purposely altered.[58] According to their reading, the meaning of *tikun soferim* is that the original biblical text contained the euphemistic 'scribal correction', and it is referred to as such only to show its similarity to what human scribes would be expected to do in such cases. Saul

on Gen. 18: 22. However, contrary to Barnes's suggestion, Rashi cannot possibly mean that *rabotenu* or *soferim* are identical with 'the original writers or redactors of books of Scripture'. Rashi's comments on Num. 11: 15 and Job 32: 3 make clear what is implied elsewhere (see his commentary on Hab. 1: 11, Mal. 1: 3, Job 7: 20), that for him there is no distinction between corrections of the Scribes and what is known as כינה הכתוב ('The text substitutes [one word for another]').

[53] See his commentary on Hab. 1: 12. When this is taken together with what he writes in his commentary on Ezek. 8: 18 and 1 Sam. 3: 13, it is obvious that, as with Rashi, he understands כינה הכתוב to mean a correction of the Scribes. Bearing in mind both this and what Hayim Zalman Dimitrovsky has recently written in Solomon b. Adret, *Teshuvot harashba*, i. 177–9, one can confidently reject Uriel Simon's interpretation in 'R. Abraham', 228–9. In addition, Kimhi usually refrains from mentioning the *tikunei soferim* in his explanations of the text, which probably means that he did not accept them.

[54] See Ginsburg, *Introduction*, 350–1.

[55] *Shemot rabah* 30: 15. See also *Matnot kehunah* on *Bereshit rabah* 49: 5. This commentary was written by R. Issachar Baer b. Naftali Hakohen (16th cent.).

[56] See Lieberman, *Hellenism*, 28; *Midrash shemot rabah*, ed. Shinan, 256.

[57] See his supercommentary on Rashi, Gen. 18: 22, Num. 11: 15; Hirschensohn, *Nimukei rashi*, on Gen. 18: 22. Commenting upon Mizrahi's view, R. Samuel Jaffe b. Isaac Ashkenazi (16th cent.) writes: 'It is not correct, for if we admit that the Scribes altered [the text] in one place, what prevents us from saying so with regard to the other places?' See his *Yefeh to'ar* on *Bereshit rabah* 49: 12. See also the rejection of Mizrahi's view by R. Issachar Baer Eylenburg (1570–1623), *Tsedah laderekh*, on Gen. 18: 22. According to Eylenburg, in addition to such a view being heretical, the phenomenon it describes should not be called *tikun soferim* but rather *kilkul soferim* (corruption of the Scribes). Norzi, *Minhat shai*, on Zech. 2: 12, writes that it should be called *tikun kesilim* (fools' correction).

[58] R. Saul Cohen's comment is typical, in explaining why *tikun soferim* cannot mean an actual correction in the text of the Torah: 'For this is one of the Thirteen Principles, that the Holy Torah was not changed and will never be changed.' See id., *Karnei re'em*, 61, and also 62, where he acknowledges the existence of rabbinic sources that understand *tikun soferim* in a way that he regards as heretical. His way of dealing with them is two-pronged: either they are not authentic or they are individual opinions that have been rejected by the rabbinic tradition.

Lieberman claims that the divergent views about the nature of *tikun soferim* actually go back to rabbinic times.[59]

There are other scholars who assert that the Torah's text has changed since Moses' day. Ibn Ezra states that whether a word was written defective or plene was left to the scribe, as it is the sense of the word that is important, not its textual form.[60] In line with this, R. Samuel Tzartza (fourteenth century) explains that according to Ibn Ezra, God dictated the Torah and Moses wrote it down without paying any regard to defective or plene spellings.[61] R. Joseph Solomon Delmedigo claims that whether a word is defective or plene is not accidental, but is due to the wisdom of the Masoretes.[62] In the Pentateuch edited by R. Joseph H. Hertz (1872–1946), widely used by Orthodox Jews, it is stated that the *alef* in the first word of Leviticus (ויקרא) is not part of the original text but was added at a later date.[63]

There is a well-known passage which appears with minor variations in the Jerusalem Talmud,[64] *Avot derabi natan*,[65] *Masekhet soferim* (6: 4), and *Sifrei devarim*:[66]

Three books they found in the Temple court: the book מעוני, the book זעטוטי, and the book היא. In the one they found written מעון אלהי קדם and in the two they found written מעונה (Deut. 33: 27), and they upheld the two and set aside the one. In the one they found written וישלח את זעטוטי בני ישראל and in the two they found written וישלח את נערי בני ישראל (Exod. 24: 5) and they upheld the two and set aside the one. In the one they found written nine times היא, and in the two they found written eleven times היא, and they upheld the two and set aside the one.

Obviously there is no reason why we should assume that the texts that were in the majority were correct. However, as with all halakhic decisions, objective 'truth' is set aside, and the decision of the sages, in this case based on

---

[59] *Hellenism*, 28–37.

[60] *Safah berurah*, 7a–7b. See also id., *Sefer tsahut*, 71b–72a; id., Introduction to the Pentateuch (fifth approach), in his *Commentary*, and his comments on Gen. 18: 13, Exod. 11: 5, 18: 21, 20: 1, 25: 31, Deut. 5: 5.

[61] *Mekor hayim*, on Exod. 20: 1. This approach conflicts with the halakhic view that it is precisely the uncertainty regarding defective and plene letters that makes the *kashrut* of our Torah scrolls questionable. See above, pp. 93–4. From the standpoint of practical halakhah, since a certain text has been accepted, a scribe is not permitted to decide independently between defective and plene, for a wrong decision makes the scroll *pasul*. See BT *Men*. 29b–30a, 32b; Maimonides, 'Hilkhot sefer torah', 7: 11, 13; 10: 1; *Shulhan arukh*, 'Yoreh de'ah', 275: 6, 279: 4. Regarding Maimonides' understanding of the texts in *Menahot*, see M. Goshen-Gottstein, 'Keter', 875 n. 12, 881 n. 28.

[62] *Matsref lehokhmah*, 10b.

[63] *Pentateuch*, on Lev. 1: 1. Although R. Samuel David Luzzatto is quoted, his view actually differs significantly from that of Hertz. Luzzatto does not agree that the Scribes inserted a letter which was not in the original text. See his *Commentary on the Torah* on Gen. 26: 46.

[64] *Ta'an*. 4: 2. This version will be quoted below. For discussion of the passage and its textual variants, see Israel M. Ta-Shma's note in Steiner, 'Linguistic Features', 52–3; Havlin, 'Establishing Correct Manuscript Readings', 244 ff.   [65] (B), ch. 46.   [66] *Piska* 356.

the majority principle, is determinative. Indeed, R. David Kimhi,[67] R. Profiat Duran,[68] Me'iri,[69] and R. Joseph ibn Waqar (fourteenth century)[70] admit that there were occasions when the rabbis could not determine the proper text, and that this is why they instituted the *keri ukhetiv* (a word read differently from the way in which it appears in the text).[71] As Kimhi puts it:

These variant words apparently developed because during the First Exile, the texts were lost, the scholars were dispersed, and the Torah scholars died. The Men of the Great Assembly who restored the Torah to its former state found differences in the texts and followed the reading of those which they believed to be in the majority. When they were unclear about this, they wrote one version without pointing it, or they wrote it in the margin and not in the text, or they wrote one version in the margin and one version in the text.[72]

As can be imagined, despite the great efforts made by the sages, not all difficulties were cleared up. This explains another passage found in *Bamidbar rabah* 3: 13 and *Avot derabi natan* 34: 5, which discusses the placing of dots over certain words in the Torah:

Wherefore are the dots? Thus said Ezra: 'If Elijah will come and say, Why have you written these words? I shall say unto him: I have already put dots over them. And if he will say, thou hast written well, I shall remove the dots over them.'

As David Weiss Halivni has observed, this passage 'implies that Ezra had the right to delete a word if he was sure of its spuriousness'. In these instances he was unsure of the reliability of the text, 'but Elijah's question to Ezra, "Why have you written these words?" implies that Ezra possessed the power of textual emendation'.[73] According to R. Hayim Hirschensohn, it was not only

---

[67] Introduction to his commentary on the Prophets; commentary on 2 Sam. 15: 21, 1 Kgs. 17: 14.

[68] *Ma'aseh efod*, 40.   [69] *Kiryat sefer*, introduction; id., *Beit habehirah* on BT *Ned.* 37b.

[70] See Steinschneider, *Jewish Literature*, 270 n. 15. He refers to the *keri ukhetiv* as נוסחאות.

[71] They say this despite the fact that, according to BT *Ned.* 37b, the *keri ukhetiv* is a tradition from Sinai. In addition, the Talmud seems to derive laws from the *keri ukhetiv*. See Ben-Yitshak, 'Keri ukhetiv'.   [72] Introduction to his commentary on the Prophets.

[73] *Peshat*, 141. Regarding this passage, see also Spiegel, *Pages*, 64–5. See Halivni, *Peshat*, 141, 218, for the rejection of R. Moses Feinstein's assertion that this passage is a heretical interpolation (Feinstein, *Igerot mosheh*, 'Yoreh de'ah', iii, no. 114, p. 358). For authorities who cite the passage, see Halivni, *Peshat*, 216 n. 18, 218 nn. 25–6, to which add Hizkuni on Gen. 16: 5 ('Ezra the Scribe was in doubt about all the marked letters in the Torah'); di Illescos, *Imrei no'am*, 197; H. J. D. Azulai, *Penei david*, 174a, quoting the Tosafists; Levinson, *Hatorah vehamada*, 267; Yadler, *Tiferet tsiyon* on *Bamidbar rabah* 3: 13 ('Ezra was also in doubt about all these words and did not know what to do, other than writing them and placing a dot above').

Feinstein's rejection of the authenticity of this passage should be viewed as part of his pattern of discarding sources that do not fit in with his understanding. He does so even when the sources are neither contradicted by other writings of the authors involved nor by other versions of the text in question. See e.g. *Igerot mosheh*, 'Orah hayim', iii, n. 9, v, no. 20: 2, 'Yoreh de'ah', ii, no. 7, iii, nos. 114–15, 'Even ha'ezer', i, nos. 63, 64 (pp. 161, 163), 'Hoshen mishpat', ii, nos. 69, 70 (pp. 295, 297). For rejections of Feinstein, see Waldenberg, *Tsits eli'ezer*, xiv, no. 100 (p. 183); M. Bleich, 'Role', 45–8.

Ezra who doubted whether certain words should be included in the Torah, but also the author of Targum Onkelos (the early Aramaic translation of the Pentateuch) and the *amora* R. Yose.[74] As for the use of dots to mark doubtful readings, Lieberman has noted that this convention was also used by the Greek grammarians of Alexandria.[75]

Acceptance of Maimonides' Principle presumably means that the extra inverted *nun*s at the end of the tenth chapter of Numbers are also Mosaic. However, the unknown author of *Ginzei mitsrayim* (eleventh century) quotes 'some midrashim' which state that it was the sages who added the inverted *nun*s.[76] R. Solomon Luria describes twelve different ways of writing them, and adds that the entire notion of inverted *nun*s has no basis in the Talmud but is rather based on the kabbalah. Furthermore, according to Luria, the way in which the inverted *nun*s are currently written, with the addition of two extra letters, invalidates the Torah scroll![77] In other words, there is no question according to Luria and the midrashim referred to above that present-day Torah scrolls are not identical to the Torah given to Moses.

Based on these sources, and many others not cited here, one must conclude that acceptance of the Masoretic text as being entirely of Mosaic authorship is neither compelling nor 'Orthodox', and by definition excludes the pentateuchal text quoted in the Talmud. On this basis, R. Hayim Hirschensohn declares that it is not heretical to believe that our pentateuchal text suffers from corruptions. Indeed, one's thoughts in this regard are even considered Torah study.[78] This also leads Hirschensohn to declare that there is no religious objection to Lower Biblical Criticism.[79] The issue of which text is 'correct' is thus viewed separately from the issue of which text appears in our Torah scrolls. It is only the latter which has been sanctified by halakhah, and this halakhic decision follows its own rules, which do not correspond to how a biblical scholar would determine which text is original.[80] As

---

[74] *Malki bakodesh*, ii. 218, 221–2.   [75] Lieberman, *Hellenism*, 44   [76] See ibid. 41 n. 28.

[77] *She'elot uteshuvot maharshal*, no. 73. See id., *Ḥokhmat shelomoh* on BT *Shab.* 115*b*, where he also states that it is forbidden to add the extra *nun*s. However, in the case of a Torah scroll which contains the extra letters (which in his responsum he flatly declared invalid), he is a little more hesitant, stating: 'It *appears to me* to be invalid.'   [78] *Malki bakodesh*, ii. 219.

[79] Ibid. 229, 247. See also Menachem Cohen, 'The Idea of the Sanctity of the Biblical Text', 67–9. Cohen's article is worth careful study. He discusses how, why, and when the Masoretic text came to be viewed as the only authentic text and why contemporary Orthodox Jews are reluctant to engage in textual criticism of it, and concludes with suggestions on how Orthodox Jews should integrate the results of textual criticism into their *Weltanschauung*. See also Levy, *Fixing God's Torah*, 38 ff.

[80] For example, in the introduction to his *Masoret seyag latorah*, R. Meir Abulafia states that, in questions regarding the pentateuchal text, he made a decision based upon the majority of reliable scrolls and Masoretic works. R. Yom Tov Lippmann Muelhausen is even uncertain about the possibility of making a halakhic determination: 'I have toiled to find a Torah scroll with the proper letters and open and closed passages, but have found none, not to mention a scroll which is accurate with

R. Abraham ben Mordekhai Halevi (seventeenth century) states, once the halakhah has been decided we treat our Torah text as if (*ke'ilu*) it is from Sinai, even though in reality it is the product of our scholars' decision.[81]

Up until this point I have only dealt with differences that either crept into or were purposely inserted into a text which was of Mosaic authorship. Yet what of Maimonides' assertion that the entire (original) Torah was revealed to Moses? This is certainly a very popular notion in Orthodox circles. For example, in the introduction to the Artscroll Pentateuch, which is now the standard Pentateuch in many English-speaking Orthodox synagogues, Rabbi Nosson Scherman writes with reference to this Principle: 'Rambam sets forth at much greater length the *unanimously held view* that every letter and word was given to Moses by God.'[82]

However, contrary to Scherman's claim, Maimonides' view is hardly unanimously accepted. To begin with, we must note that nowhere in the Bible does it state that Moses wrote the entire Torah. In fact, as is pointed out by Israel Knohl in *Megadim*,[83] an Orthodox journal of biblical scholarship, there seems to be evidence that the authors of the biblical books of Ezra and Daniel did not regard Moses as having written the entire Torah. Ezra 9: 10–12 reads:

For we are bondsmen; yet our God hath not forsaken us in our bondage, but hath extended mercy unto us in the sight of the kings of Persia, to give us reviving, to set up the house of our God, and to repair the ruins thereof, and to give us a fence

regard to defective and plene spellings, which have been completely lost to our entire generation. Therefore, we are forced [to rely on our Torah scrolls].' See Loewinger and Kupfer, 'Yom Tov', 251. See also Rabenu Tam's comment in *Mahzor vitri*, 654: '[Scribes] are not expert in the accuracy of the text, as R. Joseph said at the end of chapter one of [BT] *Kidushin* [30a], "They [in the Land of Israel] are expert in defective and plene spelling; we are not expert." And because "it is a time to act for the Lord" [i.e. it is an exigent circumstance], therefore our Torah scrolls are also considered kosher.' After describing the great efforts that went into guarding the Torah's text from corruptions, R. Isaac Pulgar, *Ezer hadat*, 156, writes as follows: 'Despite their great diligence and efforts in Masoretic matters, there are today some differences in the Scriptures, and this is known to anyone who examines the famous Torah scroll which is known to have been written by Ezra the priest, for you will find in it words that differ in various ways from the corrected Torah scrolls in our possession.' Norzi, *Mikdash yah* (introduction to id., *Minhat shai*, 9) writes: 'Not only has the Torah become two Torahs, but innumerable Torahs due to the many variations.' Bearing all this in mind, it is shocking to find J. D. Bleich write: 'It is indeed remarkable that despite the vicissitudes of time, and the many upheavals and wanderings to which the Jewish nation has been subjected, the Scrolls of the Law in the possession of even the most far-flung and widely separated Jewish communities are identical in virtually every respect. The variant spellings of the word *daka* in Deuteronomy 23: 2 are the exception which proves the rule' (*With Perfect Faith*, 365). The reason contemporary Torah scrolls are the same is because the invention of printing enabled the *textus receptus* to triumph. There is nothing 'remarkable' in this. As a statement of fact, as opposed to one of polemical value, Bleich's comment would not have even been imaginable before the printing press. As for his point about *daka*, it too is mistaken. See above, n. 41.

[81] *Ginat veradim*, 'Orah hayim', *kelal* 2, no. 6.

[82] *Chumash: Stone Edition*, p. xix (emphasis added).   [83] 'Between Faith and Criticism'.

in Judah and in Jerusalem. And now, O our God, what shall we say after this? For we have forsaken Thy commandments which Thou hast commanded by Thy servants the prophets, saying: The land unto which ye go to possess it is an unclean land through the uncleanness of the peoples of the lands, through their abominations, wherewith they have filled it from one end to another in their filthiness. Now therefore give not your daughters unto their sons, neither take their daughters unto your sons, nor seek their peace or their prosperity for ever; that ye may be strong, and eat the good of the land, and leave it for an inheritance to your children for ever.

The prohibition against intermarrying with the inhabitants of Canaan is stated in Exodus 34: 15–16 and Deuteronomy 7: 3–4, yet the book of Ezra portrays this prohibition as originating with the prophets, thus implying that the Torah also includes the words of various post-Mosaic figures.

Knohl also points to Daniel 9: 10–11:

Neither have we hearkened to the voice of the Lord our God, to walk in His laws [*torotav*], which He set before us by His servants the prophets. Yea, all Israel have transgressed Thy law [*toratekha*], and have turned aside, so as not to hearken to Thy voice; and so there hath been poured out upon us the curse and the oath that is written in the Law of Moses [*torat mosheh*] the servant of God, for we have sinned against Him.

According to Knohl, all three references to 'Torah' refer to the same book. 'God's Torah is the Torah of Moses the servant of God, and it also contains laws that were given into the hand of "His servants the prophets".'[84]

Turning to the Talmud, there is a tannaitic opinion, accepted by a number of post-talmudic authorities, that the last eight verses in the Pentateuch, which contain the account of Moses' death and his 'obituary', were written by Joshua.[85] In BT *Makot* 11a this suggestion is even supported by a prooftext, 'And Joshua wrote these words in the book of the Law of God' (Josh. 24: 26). However, another tannaitic opinion is also offered here, which understands this verse as referring to the section dealing with the cities of refuge. Although the Talmud interprets this to mean that Joshua wrote in his own book (i.e. the book of Joshua) the information which already appears in 'the book of the Law of God', the simple meaning of the tannaitic text is that the sections in the Pentateuch dealing with the cities of refuge (Num. 35: 9–34, Deut. 19: 1–13) were indeed written by Joshua.[86]

Returning to the notion that Joshua wrote the last eight verses of the Pentateuch, R. Joseph ibn Migash (1077–1141), a figure whose influence on

---

[84] 'Between Faith and Criticism', 125.
[85] BT *BB* 15a, *Mak.* 11a, *Men.* 30a; *Sifrei devarim*, *piska* 357. This opinion is attributed to either R. Judah or R. Nehemiah.   [86] See Jacobs, *Principles*, 222.

Maimonides was enormous,[87] stands out as one who adopts this position.[88] R. Tsevi Hirsch Ashkenazi explains that, according to this view, the revelatory status of the last eight verses is not equivalent to that of the rest of the Torah.[89] R. Tsevi Hirsch Grodzinski (1858–1947) states: 'Joshua wrote them [i.e. the last eight verses] and they do not have as much holiness as the other sections of the Torah which Moses wrote.'[90] In an even more striking formulation, R. Abraham Hayim Schor (nineteenth century) writes that, since the last eight verses concern the period after Moses' death, 'their holiness is not so weighty'.[91] R. Joseph B. Soloveitchik (1903–93) is reported to have held a similar view.[92] Quite apart from the issue of Mosaic authorship, positions

---

[87] See Twersky, *Introduction*, 8–9.

[88] *Ḥidushei hari migash* on BT *BB* 15a. Maimonides studied this work and refers to it in *Responsa*, i, no. 82, ii, nos. 251, 393. For other *rishonim* who believed that Joshua wrote the last eight verses, see Heschel, *Theology*, ii. 388. To these sources, add Roke'ah, *Perush haroke'ah* on Deut. 34: 5 Bekhor Shor, *Commentaries*, on Deut. 34: 5.

[89] *Ḥakham tsevi*, no. 13. Baron, *Social and Religious History*, vi. 143, calls attention to R. Abraham ibn Daud, *Ha'emunah haramah*, 102, as being in opposition to Maimonides' Principle, for Ibn Daud claims that not all of the portions of the Torah are equal in rank. For example, sacrifices are on a lower level than matters of faith. (For a similar downgrading of sacrifices, see R. David Kimhi's commentary on Jer. 7: 22.) However, Maimonides agrees with this view. The Thirteen Principles are themselves of more importance than other parts of the Torah. All Maimonides says is that every verse in the Torah is of divine origin and of equal 'perfection, purity, sanctity, and truth', a point with which Ibn Daud would also agree. This is not the same as saying that all portions of the Torah are of equal importance. 'Hear, O, Israel, the Lord our God, the Lord is One' is a more important verse than 'And the sons of Ham were Cush and Mitzraim and Put and Canaan.' However, since both verses were dictated by God, their sanctity (and perfection, purity, and truth) is equivalent. Sanctity is due to revelation, importance is due to philosophic and religious content. (This is similar to the way in which the Islamic creed known as *Fikh akbar* II describes the Koran: all of its verses have equal 'excellence and greatness', but some are pre-eminent with regard to recitation or content. See Wensinck, *Muslim Creed*, 196.)

Jacob Haberman has noted in this regard, 'Did any martyr go to his death proclaiming his faith in a sentence such as "Timna was a concubine" as thousands did with the *Shema* on their lips?': see his *Maimonides and Aquinas*, 265 n. 2. Maimonides' comments in *Responsa*, ii, no. 263, about standing up during the reading of the Ten Commandments, should also be read in this fashion. In this regard, note too the subtitle of Norman Lamm's recent book, *The Shema: Spirituality and Law in Judaism as Exemplified in the Shema, the Most Important Passage in the Torah*. See also *Mishneh torah*, 'Hilkhot keriat shema', 1: 2, where Maimonides explains that one recites Deut. 6: 4–9 as the first paragraph of the prayer known as Shema, 'because it contains a commandment concerning God's unity, love of God, and study, *which is the basic principle upon which all depends*'. In his commentary on Mishnah *Tam.* 5: 1, Maimonides himself states that the Ten Commandments are 'the foundation of [God's] command and its beginning'. It is Abarbanel and others who, in some respects, see no layers or levels in the Torah, and that is why they do not believe one can single out any particular principles. See H. Kasher, 'Principal and Subsidiary'.

[90] *Mikra'ei kodesh*, i. 189. On whether the last eight verses of the Torah are less important than the rest, see Duenner, *Ḥidushei harav yosef tsevi duener* on BT *Men.* 30a.

[91] אין קדושתן חמורה כל כך; id., *Torat ḥayim* on BT *BB* 15a.

[92] Schachter, *Nefesh harav*, 321–2. Lawrence Kaplan has questioned the accuracy of Schachter's presentation: see id., 'Multi-Faceted Legacy', 79 ff.

such as these contradict the Eighth Principle's additional affirmation that all verses of the Torah share the same sanctity,

Also worth noting is the view, shared by R. Isaac Ze'ev Soloveitchik (1886–1959)[93] and R. Joshua Leib Diskin (1817–98),[94] that not all parts of the Torah were revealed to Moses in the same fashion. As Lawrence Kaplan has pointed out, this notion 'directly contravenes the fundamental principle set down by the Rambam *that every single verse of the Torah* was received directly by Moses from God like a scribe taking down dictation!'[95] R. Shalom Schwadron (1835–1911) also contradicts this aspect of the Principle, for he distinguishes between Deuteronomy and the rest of the Torah, claiming that Moses' prophetic level in the revelation of Deuteronomy was at a lower level than when the rest of the Torah was revealed.[96]

To return to the issue of Mosaic authorship, although Maimonides regards it as heretical, the view that Joshua had a hand in writing the Pentateuch is also affirmed by Ibn Ezra, who claims that the last twelve verses were written by Joshua. He does not regard this opinion as controversial and feels comfortable in stating it openly.[97] R. Meyuhas ben Elijah (twelfth century?) agreed with Ibn Ezra,[98] and R. Moses Sofer also sympathized with this position.[99] Presumably, these authorities did not see anything radical in this notion since they were merely expanding upon the rabbinic view mentioned above.[100] This is different from suggesting post-Mosaic authorship for a portion of the Torah not discussed in the Talmud.

Significantly, as R. Ya'akov Hayim Sofer has pointed out,[101] Nahmanides believed that Joshua was involved in the writing of the poem 'Ha'azinu' (Deut. 32: 1–43).[102] The same view is found in a Tosafist work.[103] According

---

[93] *Ḥidushei hagriz al hashas* on BT *Men.* 30*a* (pp. 159–60). See, similarly, Schulman, 'Essay', 509–10.

[94] *She'elot uteshuvot maharil diskin*, 71*b*.

[95] 'Multi-Faceted Legacy', 81 n. 62 (emphasis in original).

[96] *She'elot uteshuvot maharsham*, iii, no. 290.

[97] *Commentary* on Deut. 34: 1. See also Reifman, *Studies*, 40.

[98] *Commentary*, Deut. 34: 1.   [99] *Torat mosheh* on Deut. 34: 1.

[100] See also Tosafot, *Meg.* 21*b*, s.v. *tana*. The expression 'eight verses' is used here to refer to the entire last chapter of Deuteronomy. See Heschel, *Theology*, ii. 392–3.   [101] *Yehi yosef*, 194.

[102] See his commentary on Deut. 31: 19 ('Now therefore write [plural] this song for you [plural]'). In a comment perhaps directed against Nahmanides, Abarbanel writes: 'It does not mean that both of them will write it in God's Torah, because Heaven forbid that Joshua should write even one letter.' However, Nahmanides is not entirely clear since, in the same comment, he also seems to deny that Joshua had a hand in writing part of the Torah. See Heschel, *Theology*, ii. 399–400 n. 26. In his introduction to the Torah, Nahmanides explicitly states that Moses wrote the entire Pentateuch. However, Abarbanel is just as explicit that Nahmanides believed that there were non-Mosaic elements in the Torah; see his commentary on Num. 21: 1 (although there is hardly any doubt that Abarbanel is mistaken in this example). It is perhaps significant that Nahmanides, who is so quick to criticize Ibn Ezra, says nothing about the latter's view of Mosaic authorship.

[103] *Hadar zekenim* on Deut. 32: 44.

to R. Nissim Gaon (*c.*990–1062) the 'Ha'azinu' poem was written by Moses together with seventy-seven of the elders of Israel.[104] R. Moses Schick (1807–79) goes further and states that, 'according to one opinion', Moses wrote the Torah up until, but not including, this poem, and Joshua finished the book.[105] Schick does not mention where this opinion is found, and I have been unable to find any source which states that Joshua wrote the *entire* poem, though there are midrashim which state that, although Moses began to write the poem, he died before completing it.[106] This means that more than forty verses were added to the Torah after Moses' death.

Ibn Ezra's views on the Mosaic authorship of the Pentateuch cover considerably more than just the end of the Torah. In his comment on Deuteronomy 1: 2 (which actually deals with the first verse in Deuteronomy: 'These are the words which Moses spoke unto all Israel beyond the Jordan'), Ibn Ezra writes: 'If you know the secret of the twelve, and of *And Moses wrote* (Exod. 24: 4, Num. 33: 2, Deut. 31: 9, 22), and of *And the Canaanite was then in the land* (Gen. 12: 6), and of *In the mount where the Lord is seen* (Gen. 22: 14), and of *Behold his bedstead was a bedstead of iron* (Deut. 3: 11), you will discover the truth.' This passage has long been regarded as meaning that Ibn Ezra considered Deuteronomy 1: 1–5, as well as all the other verses mentioned, as similar to the last twelve verses in Deuteronomy in that they too are post-Mosaic.[107] Quite apart from modern academic scholars, Ibn Ezra has been understood along these lines by R. Solomon ben Samuel (*c.*1160– 1240),[108] an anonymous student of R. Solomon ben Adret (thirteenth century),[109] R. Moses ibn Tibbon (thirteenth century),[110] R. Isaiah of Trani (the Elder),[111] R. Samson Kino (thirteenth century),[112] R. Eleazar ben Mattathias (thirteenth

---

[104] See *Maḥzor vitri*, 388, and Heschel, *Theology*, ii. 398 n. 20. According to the anonymous medieval work *Pitron torah*, 149, the words 'And the Lord spoke unto Moses saying', which appear frequently in the Torah, were added by the elders.   [105] *Maharam shik al taryag mitsvot*, no. 613.

[106] *Devarim rabah* 11: 10; *Midrash tanḥuma*, 'Ha'azinu' 5. According to the latter source, Deut. 32: 5 was the last verse Moses wrote. These midrashim seem to be contradicted by Deut. 32: 44–5, which portrays Moses as having recited the entire poem.

[107] The anachronisms in these verses are explained by Jacobs, *Principles*, 232–3. As already noted, Ibn Ezra explicitly asserts the post-Mosaic authorship of the last twelve verses. Thus, the 'secret of the twelve' must mean that the principle of post-Mosaic authorship, stated regarding these twelve verses, is also applicable to other verses.

[108] See the text published in Ta-Shma, 'On Bible Criticism', 455–6.

[109] See Friedlaender, *Essays*, 235.

[110] See the text published in Dov Schwartz, *Astrology and Magic*, 330 ff. According to Ibn Tibbon, Ibn Ezra also identified other post-Mosaic additions. See also U. Simon, 'Interpreting the Interpreter', 102–6.

[111] See D. Schwartz, *Astrology and Magic*, 332–4. Since R. Isaiah of Trani the Elder wrote a commentary on the Pentateuch (extracts from which appear in H. J. D. Azulai's *Penei david*), the reference is undoubtedly to him. R. Isaiah of Trani the Younger, though the author of commentaries on the Prophets and Hagiographa, is not known to have written a commentary on the Five Books of Moses.   [112] See U. Simon, 'Interpreting the Interpreter', 102.

century),[113] the commentary attributed to Ibn Kaspi,[114] R. Samuel Motot (fourteenth century),[115] R. Joseph ben Eliezer Bonfils,[116] R. Shem Tov ben Joseph Shaprut (fourteenth century),[117] R. Eleazar Ashkenazi ben Nathan Habavli (fourteenth century),[118] R. Solomon Franco (fourteenth century),[119] R. Moses ben Judah ben Moses Nearim (fourteenth century?),[120] the anonymous author of *Avat nefesh* (fourteenth century),[121] R. Ezra Gatigno,[122] R. Yedidyah Solomon Norzi,[123] R. Azariah dei Rossi (sixteenth century),[124] R. Eliezer Ashkenazi (sixteenth century),[125] R. Moses Almosnino (sixteenth century),[126] R. Aviad Sar-Shalom Basilea (*c*.1680–1743),[127] R. Gad del Aquilla (eighteenth century),[128] R. Benjamin Ze'ev ben Solomon (eighteenth–nineteenth centuries),[129] R. Samuel David Luzzatto,[130] R. Moses Tedeschi (nineteenth century),[131] R. Solomon Netter (nineteenth century),[132] and the contemporary Orthodox biblical scholar, R. Mordechai Breuer.[133]

It is significant that R. Solomon ben Samuel, Ibn Tibbon, Bonfils, R. Shem Tov ben Joseph Shaprut, R. Eleazar ben Mattathias, Franco, del Aquilla, R. Benjamin Ze'ev ben Solomon, and Netter all defend Ibn Ezra. According to

[113] Simon, 'Interpreting the Interpreter', 106–9, and the text published in Ben-Menahem, *Jewish Treasures*, 128 ff. He explains the 'secret of the twelve' in an original fashion.

[114] See H. Kasher, 'Ibn Caspi's Commentary', 108.

[115] Supercommentary on Ibn Ezra, Deut. 1: 2. The version of Motot's commentary that appears in Lazi (ed.), *Margaliyot tovah* is not merely censored, as is Bonfil's, but is actually an example of forgery. It explains Ibn Ezra to mean that Moses wrote all these passages prophetically. However, this does not appear in Motot's commentary. In any case, what then would the 'secret' be? To say that Moses wrote these passages prophetically is the traditional view and does not need to be hidden. Since, as Lazi says in his introduction, Motot's commentary was very inaccessible, this was what probably led him to believe he could get away with this forgery.

[116] *Tsofnat pane'ah* on Gen. 12: 6, 22: 14, 36: 31, Deut. 1: 2. See the discussion in Jacobs, *Principles*, 234–7.   [117] Friedlaender, *Essays*, 223.   [118] *Tsofnat pane'ah*, 46.

[119] See the text published in D. Schwartz, 'Worship', 236–7.   [120] Friedlaender, *Essays*, 239.

[121] See the commentary on Gen. 12: 6, published in Gartig, 'Critical Edition'.

[122] See the text published in D. Schwartz, 'Philosophical Supercommentaries', 109.

[123] *Mikdash yah*, 10. Although he never actually mentions Ibn Ezra by name, there is no doubt that he is referring to him.   [124] *Me'or einayim*, ch. 39 (p. 324).   [125] *Ma'asei hashem*, i. 79*d*.

[126] See the text published in Ben-Menahem, 'Additional Explanation', 153.

[127] *Emunat hakhamim*, ch. 2 (p. 12*a*).

[128] See the text published in Ben-Menahem, *Inyanei ibn ezra*, 326.

[129] See the text of his commentary *Ben yemini* on Deut. 34: 6, published in Fleischer, 'Supercommentaries', 54–5. In addition to this passage, see his comments on Gen. 12: 6 and Deut. 1: 2. For some reason, this is a very rare book; the only copy I was able to locate in the United States is at Yeshiva University. This work was published with approbations and letters by, among others, R. Ezekiel Banet and R. Moses Sofer. The commentary on Deut. 34 is missing from the copy I examined.

[130] *Commentary on the Torah*, 507; id., *Hamishtadel*, on Deut.1: 1.   [131] *Ho'il mosheh*, 204.

[132] Supercommentary on Ibn Ezra (Vienna, 1859), Deut. 34: 6. (See, however, his comment on Gen. 3: 21 and Deut. 1: 2.) As he often does, Netter has simply incorporated R. Benjamin Ze'ev's words into his own commentary.

[133] 'Divine Origin', 131. Breuer adds: 'I do not know if the sages approve of these words. Yet they were stated by Ibn Ezra, and thus no one is able to deny their legitimacy.'

Ibn Tibbon and Bonfils, one must distinguish between the post-Mosaic addition of commandments, which is objectionable, and narrative additions, which are not. (Bonfils adds that positing post-Mosaic additions of *entire* portions of narrative is also objectionable.) With the possible exception of R. Eleazar ben Mattathias (see below), all agree that any additions to the Pentateuch were written through prophetic inspiration. This point is especially stressed by del Aquilla, who points out that it is heresy to suggest that Moses (or someone else) added a verse to the Bible at his own discretion. However, if one assumes that the entire Torah is written through divine inspiration, post-Mosaic additions cease to be problematic. It is only because of this, del Aquilla adds, that the tannaitic view which asserts that Joshua wrote the last eight verses is not heretical.

R. Eleazar ben Mattathias goes even further. According to him, Ezra, who was responsible for renewing knowledge of the Torah among the common people, did not change any of the *mitsvot* which were given to Moses. However, he did not hesitate to enlarge the narrative portion of the Torah and 'likely' did this at God's command. In one case, R. Eleazar says, he even deleted a verse from the Torah. R. Benjamin Ze'ev explains that the statement 'Moses wrote the Torah' is comparable to statements in 1 Kings 6: 10 and 9: 1 that Solomon built the Temple. That is, Solomon need not have literally participated in the building for him to be credited with its construction. Similarly, a few post-Mosaic prophetic insertions do not alter the fact that Moses is regarded as the author of the Torah. R. Ya'akov Hayim Sofer, an important contemporary rabbinic scholar, accepts this analysis.[134]

Ibn Ezra is not unique in this regard among *rishonim*. Two leading Ashkenazi sages, R. Judah Hehasid (*c*.1150–1217)[135] and R. Avigdor Katz (the teacher of R. Meir of Rothenburg; thirteenth century), maintain that there are post-Mosaic additions in the Torah inserted by Joshua and the Men of the Great Assembly.[136] They obviously agreed with Maimonides that the latter were also prophets,[137] yet the implications they drew from this diverged sharply from Maimonides' view. According to them, one of the post-Mosaic

[134] *Yehi yosef*, 194.

[135] See his *Torah Commentaries*, 64, 138, 198 (uncensored version). R. Judah Hehasid's view is discussed in Brin, 'Studies', 215–26; Katz, 'Judah he-Hasid', 23–30; Jacobs, *Beyond Reasonable Doubt*, 63–5.

[136] See the text by R. Avigdor Katz published in Zimmels, 'Manuscript', 259. R. Avigdor's wording in this passage is virtually identical to that of R. Judah Hehasid, which I assume means that he copied R. Judah's comments directly. It is also possible that one of R. Avigdor's students inserted them into the text. Incidentally, R. Avigdor's version enables us to explain the mysterious word לעכבו that appears in Judah Hehasid, *Torah Commentaries*, 198. It should actually read לעכו ('to Acre').

[137] See *Guide* i. 59. According to Maimonides, the Men of the Great Assembly were members of Ezra's *beit din* (see his introduction to the *Mishneh torah*).

additions is Genesis 36: 31–9, which contains a list of the kings of Edom 'before there reigned any king over the children of Israel'. This comment is particularly interesting, for the view advocated here, focusing on the alleged anachronism in these verses, was actually declared heretical by the other 'critic', Ibn Ezra. As Bonfils explained, Ibn Ezra's strong feelings about this are due to the fact that, unlike R. Judah Hehasid, he believed it illegitimate to posit that an *entire portion* was added after the death of Moses.[138]

According to *Moshav zekenim*, a medieval Tosafist collection of Torah commentaries, the famed R. Samuel ben Meir (Rashbam) also identified Genesis 36: 31–9 as post-Mosaic, believing that it was added in the days of the Judges.[139] In his commentary on Numbers 22: 1, Rashbam focuses on the phrase 'beyond the Jordan', which concerned Ibn Ezra in his commentary on Deuteronomy 1: 2. The difficulty is that 'in Moses' day the Israelites had not yet entered the Promised Land and the term "beyond the Jordan" would not have been used for the side of the Jordan on which they were encamped'.[140] According to Rashbam, this phrase was written 'after they [the Israelites] had crossed [to the western side of] the Jordan. From their point of view the plains of Moab [on the eastern side of the Jordan] are called "beyond the Jordan"'.[141] In other words, this phrase was only added after Moses' death, which occurred *before* the Israelites crossed the Jordan.

Returning to R. Judah Hehasid, in addition to pointing to post-Mosaic additions, he makes another fascinating remark. Commenting on Numbers 21: 17 ('Then sang Israel this song'), he claims that the 'song' referred to is the 'Great Hallel' (Psalm 136). It was only in a later generation that King David removed it from the Pentateuch, together with all the other anonymous psalms written by Moses, and placed them in the book of Psalms.[142] R. Avigdor Katz, in his comment on this verse, also claims to have heard that it refers to the 'Great Hallel' which was removed from the Torah by David.[143] Apparently, there was some tradition regarding this verse, the source and nature of which is unknown. Significantly, both R. Avigdor Katz and the late fourteenth-/early fifteenth-century kabbalist R. Menahem Zioni, who cites R. Judah Hehasid,[144] quote this opinion without a hint of objection.

As Israel M. Ta-Shma has noted, there were other Ashkenazi *rishonim* who believed that the Scribes took material out of the Torah.[145] They focus on a cryptic text in BT *Nedarim* 37*b* which speaks of *itur soferim*, usually translated

[138] *Tsofnat pane'ah* on Gen. 36: 31.
[139] See the text published in Isaac Lange, 'Moshav zekenim', 83.
[140] Jacobs, *Principles*, 222–3.
[141] See Lockshin, *Rashbam's Commentary*, 260–1.
[142] *Torah Commentaries*, 184–5.
[143] Zimmels, 'Manuscript', 261.
[144] *Commentary*, 64*d*.
[145] Ta-Shma, 'Open Bible Criticism', 421 ff.

as 'scribal embellishment'. However, according to both R. Abraham ben Azriel (thirteenth century)[146] and R. Asher ben Yehiel,[147] the phrase actually means 'omission of the Scribes', because the Scribes (presumably the Men of the Great Assembly) removed particular letters from the Torah. Although R. Abraham adds that this was done on the basis of tradition (*al pi hakabalah*), he is explicit that before the Scribes' emendations earlier generations had a different Torah text. For example, originally the Torah read ואחר תעברו (Gen. 18: 5). The Scribes deleted the initial *vav*, so it now reads אחר תעברו.[148] While Me'iri strongly rejects this opinion, declaring 'Heaven forbid that the Scribes would remove one letter from the Torah',[149] R. Naftali Tsevi Judah Berlin (1817–93) quotes R. Asher ben Yehiel's comment without objection.[150] The medieval commentary on *Nedarim* attributed to Rashi[151] which appears in standard editions of the Talmud interprets the passage somewhat differently. According to this commentary, the Scribes never removed any letters, but they did switch the order of words. In the example mentioned above, while originally the Torah read תעברו אחר, the Scribes changed it to אחר תעברו. Again, Me'iri rejects this opinion, 'for the Scribes did not change the order, to place earlier that which comes later'.[152]

Ta-Shma has also recently published another text from R. Judah Hehasid's school, written by R. Solomon ben Samuel.[153] He studied under both R. Judah and his father R. Samuel, and he too speaks of post-Mosaic additions to the Torah. In commenting on Leviticus 16: 10, R. Solomon assumes that the word *azazel* is Aramaic. He then asks why this word is not written in Hebrew, as is the rest of the Torah, and claims that this is not problematic since Moses did not write this verse.[154] (According to this explanation Moses also did not write Leviticus 16: 8, 26 where *azazel* also appears.) R. Solomon continues: 'Do not be surprised at what I say, that another wrote it, because this is not unique, and there are many [verses] which Moses did not say, such as [from] *And Moses went up* (Deut. 34: 1) until *In the sight of all Israel* (Deut. 34: 12). Similarly, [*Behold, his bedstead was a bedstead of iron;*] *is it not in Rabbah of the children of Ammon?* (Deut. 3: 11), was certainly[!] not written by Moses.'

---

[146] *Arugat habosem*, iii. 136.

[147] Commentary on BT *Ned*. 37*b* (found in the Vilna edition of the Talmud).

[148] This reading is found in biblical manuscripts and the Samaritan version, and is reflected in Targum Pseudo-Jonathan, Onkelos manuscripts, the Septuagint, and the Peshitta. See C. D. Ginsburg's edition of the Pentateuch, ad loc.; Tov, *Textual Criticism*, 67.

[149] *Beit habehirah* on BT *Ned*. 37*b*.　　　　[150] See *Meromei sadeh*, on BT *Ned*. 37*b*.

[151] See J. N. Epstein, 'Commentaries', 175 ff.; id., 'Rashi's' Commentary', 110; Y. H. Sofer, *Torat ya'akov*, 886–90.　　　　[152] *Beit habehirah* on BT *Ned*. 37*b*.

[153] Ta-Shma, 'On Bible Criticism', 455–6.

[154] According to R. Moses ibn Tibbon, Ibn Ezra also believed that the word *azazel* was post-Mosaic (though not the entire verse). See D. Schwartz, *Astrology and Magic*, 330–1.

R. Solomon then explains why it is incorrect to believe that Moses said this last verse prophetically, and nowhere does he imply that his opinion has any great theological significance. He certainly did not regard his approach as violating any essential Jewish doctrine.[155]

Although in later centuries the notion that a prophet other than Moses added to the Torah was regarded as theologically unacceptable, this approach was not entirely eliminated. Thus, R. Shneur Zalman Dov Anushiski, a nineteenth-century Lithuanian talmudist and scholar of the Zohar, writes: 'Ezra the Scribe also added material to Moses' Torah as he saw fit.[156] The reason he was able to do so is explained in BT *Sanhedrin* 21b: "Had Moses not preceded him, Ezra would have been worthy of having the Torah presented to Israel through him".'[157] Another view which may reflect a break with Maimonides' Principle is advanced by R. Solomon Tsevi Schueck (1844–1916). While agreeing that Moses wrote the entire Pentateuch, he maintains that the portion dealing with Balak and Balaam was inserted in the Torah by the elders and prophets after the Children of Israel had already entered the Promised Land.[158]

Although the scholars who accept post-Mosaic additions to the Torah are in dispute with Maimonides, are they also in dispute with the Talmud? The classic passage in this regard appears in BT *Sanhedrin* 99a:

Because he hath despised the word of the Lord (Num. 15: 31). This refers to one who says there is no Torah from Heaven. And even if he said that the whole of the Torah is from Heaven, excepting a particular verse, which [he says] was not said by the Holy One, blessed be He, but by Moses of his own accord, he is included in *because he hath despised the word of the Lord*.[159]

It is possible that some of the scholars we have quoted understood this passage as condemning, not the denial of complete Mosaic authorship, but the denial of divine inspiration. That is, what the Talmud regards as heresy is the assertion that Moses composed the Torah on his own, without receiving it from God.[160] Yet once the Torah's divinity is acknowledged, it is not heretical to posit that some verses were revealed to post-Mosaic prophets. Indeed, the Mishnah includes in its list of heretics 'he who says that the Torah is not from

---

[155] As is well known, the medieval Ashkenazi pietists were greatly influenced by Ibn Ezra. Perhaps his view of post-Mosaic authorship also found a following in this circle, which included R. Judah Hehasid, R. Solomon b. Samuel, and R. Avigdor Katz. See Kanarfogel, *'Peering through the Lattices'*, 96 n. 6.   [156] כפי שהי' נראה דעתו.

[157] Anushiski, *Matsav hayosher*, ii. 28b. The first volume of this work appeared with glowing approbations from numerous prominent rabbis, including Joseph Saul Nathanson, Tsevi Hirsch Kalischer, Elijah Guttmacher, Jacob Ettlinger, Meir Leibush Malbim, Naftali Tsevi Judah Berlin, and Isaac Elhanan Spektor.   [158] *Torah shelemah*, i. 83a–83b, iii. 25b.

[159] See also *Sifrei bamidbar*, piska 112; Heschel, *Theology*, ii. 94–7.

[160] See Hirschensohn, *Malki bakodesh*, ii. 234 ff.

Heaven'.[161] In other words, the stress is on the divine origin of the Torah, not on whether Moses alone received the revelation.

To be sure, there are a number of rabbinic sources that mention that Moses said (and did) certain things *mipi atsmo* (of his own accord), without having been commanded to do so by God.[162] One famous talmudic passage states that the curses in Deuteronomy were offered by Moses of his own accord.[163] There is even a zoharic statement that Moses composed the entire book of Deuteronomy on his own.[164] Whatever their original meaning(s), which are far from clear and, as Heschel has shown, may reflect a variety of views, as far as later rabbinic authorities were concerned, passages such as these were not regarded as relevant to the issue discussed here, and thus were not seen as contradicting the passage in *Sanhedrin* cited above. These authorities have always stressed that when these portions, originally stated independently by Moses, were later included as part of the Torah given to the Children of Israel, it was done at God's direction. This, and only this, is what sanctified the text.[165]

Nevertheless, despite this explanation we still find views that seem to contradict Maimonides' Principle. For example, in discussing the talmudic view that the curses in Deuteronomy originated with Moses, not God, R. Nissim Gerondi writes: 'God *agreed* that they be written in the Torah.'[166] It is hard to see how this approach, in which God is no longer directing but concurring, can be brought in line with Maimonides' insistence that the entire Torah was prophetically revealed. Even if one asserts that God's prophetic concurrence satisfies Maimonides' Principle, R. Nissim's comment still seems to contradict another of Maimonides' statements, namely that, upon receiving the revelation, Moses 'acted as a scribe to whom one dictates and who

---

[161] *San.* 10: 1.

[162] For a comprehensive survey of talmudic and post-talmudic sources, see Heschel, *Theology*, ii, chs. 6, 8–9, 11; M. Kasher, *Torah shelemah*, xix. 333 ff. Heschel's collection of sources is breathtaking and has been of great benefit to me. For Ibn Ezra's views in this regard, see Brin, 'Question', 125 ff.

[163] BT *Meg.* 31b.

[164] Zohar, iii. 261a. See Heschel, *Theology*, ii, 184–5. For rabbinic authorities who agree with this position, see ibid. 205–6 (Heschel is mistaken in citing Moses b. Joseph Trani, *Beit elokim*, ch. 33, as also agreeing with this notion). An unusual passage, which admittedly does not contradict the principle, is found in R. Eliezer b. Nathan (12th cent.), *Even ha'ezer*, no. 34. According to R. Eliezer, although all the Torah was revealed by God, Moses himself arranged the book of Deuteronomy. Therefore, it is only with regard to the first four books of the Pentateuch that one can apply the principle that the Torah lacks chronological order (*ein mukdam ume'uhar*).

[165] See I. Karo, *Toledot yitshak*, 411 (beginning of his commentary on Deut.); Abarbanel, introduction to his commentary on Deut. (Jerusalem, 1984), 6–7; Solomon Duran, *She'elot uteshuvot harashbash*, no. 21; Schwadron, *She'elot uteshuvot maharsham*, iii, no. 290. Contrary to the impression left by Heschel's discussion of this issue, *Theology*, ii. 209 ff., he did not identify any post-talmudic authorities who disagreed with this point.

[166] Commentary on Alfasi on BT *Meg.* 31b (p. 11a in the Vilna edn.).

writes all of it including its chronicles, its narratives, and its commandments'. Yet according to R. Nissim, this was not the case with regard to the curses, since here God simply *permitted* Moses to include his *own* curses in the Torah.

It is possible that R. Nissim's view was anticipated in the following passage from *Shemot rabah*:[167]

Another explanation for *Write thou these words* (Exod. 34: 27): The angels began to say before the Holy One, blessed be He: 'Dost Thou grant permission to Moses to write down anything he wishes, so that he may then say unto Israel, "I have given the Torah to you and it was I who wrote and gave it to you?"' But God replied: 'Far be it from Moses to do such a thing, and in whatever he does he can be fully trusted, for it says, *My servant Moses is not so; he is trusted in all My house*' (Num. 12: 7).

As Heschel has noted, the implication of this comment is that God allowed Moses to have a hand in writing the Torah.[168] In support of this, Heschel cites the commentary of R. Ze'ev Wolf Einhorn (nineteenth century) on this passage: 'Even if Moses will write something in the Torah on his own, it is not so that he will say, Heaven forbid, that he personally thought of it. Rather, he is trusted in the entire house of the Torah, and to him I have given all the principles and ways of the Torah . . . and all that he will expound he can say in God's name.'[169] Commenting on this passage in his midrashic commentary *Yefeh to'ar*, R. Samuel Jaffe ben Isaac Ashkenazi (sixteenth century) writes that, unlike other prophets, Moses was able to understand on his own what God wanted him to include in the Torah. Contrary to what Maimonides states, 'he did not need God to read it to him word for word.'

Another relevant passage, which, in contrast to Maimonides' assertion, describes Moses as having a role in the authorship of the Torah and God's acceptance of this, appears in *Midrash hagadol*:[170]

Rabbi Samuel bar Nahmani said: Why does it say concerning each thing [Moses did] *As the Lord commanded Moses*?[171] This may be compared to [the case of] a king who commanded his servant, saying to him, 'Build me a palace.' The servant expertly built him a great and spectacular palace. He wrote on everything [he built] the name of the king. When he finished, the king entered and saw it and was very pleased. He said: 'All this honour has my servant done me, including inscribing my name on every place, yet while I am inside, he is outside! Call him that he may come right in.' So, too, when Moses finished the work of the Tabernacle, and he wrote in every section, *As the Lord commanded Moses*, God appeared and His Shekhinah dwelt in it [the Tabernacle] and He saw it and it pleased Him. . . . He

---

[167] 47: 9.   [168] Heschel, *Theology*, ii. 294.

[169] See also the commentary of R. David Luria ad loc.   [170] *Midrash hagadol*, Shemot, 796.

[171] See Exod. ch. 39, which describes the building of the Tabernacle. Every paragraph concludes with these words.

said: 'The son of Amram [Moses] has done Me all this honour and he is outside! He is worthy to enter My presence and come under the shade of My Shekhinah.'

In other words, Moses independently added the phrase 'Even as the Lord commanded Moses', and because of this he was rewarded. Using the words of R. Nissim, we can say that God *agreed* that these words should appear in the Torah, but they certainly were not dictated to Moses in the scribal fashion described by Maimonides.[172]

Taking into account all the pre-Maimonidean sources cited in this chapter, and in particular, the discussion regarding the text of the Pentateuch, it is impossible to believe that Maimonides should be taken at his word when he writes that all are obligated to believe that our Torah scrolls are the same as the one given to Moses. Who better than Maimonides knew the problems implicit in such a statement? He was perfectly aware of the textual differences in various scrolls, and it was he who went to such great lengths to establish a correct pentateuchal text[173] that the legend developed that he even travelled to France to examine the mythical 'scroll of Ezra' thought to be kept there.[174] Significantly, nowhere in the *Mishneh torah* does he mention an obligation to believe that our Torah scrolls are identical with that given to Moses. Instead, he defines a 'denier of the Torah' as one 'who says that the Torah was not given by God, even if he says that a single verse or word thereof was spoken by Moses on his own authority'.[175] The point here is not the textual (Masoretic)

---

[172] See Heschel, *Theology*, ii. 345–6. See also ibid. 182 for a citation from *Midrash tanḥuma*, 'Shoftim', 19, where, once again, God is portrayed as agreeing with Moses' addition. According to R. Elijah Benamozegh, *Introduction*, 23, only the content of the book of Deuteronomy was prophetically revealed. Moses himself was responsible for the actual words.

[173] See *Mishneh torah*, 'Hilkhot sefer torah', 8: 4. This passage concerns open and closed sections. According to Moshe Goshen-Gottstein, Maimonides never intended to rule on issues of spelling, accentuation, etc.: see id., 'Authenticity', 23, and 'Keter', 874–5. Still, as he himself points out elsewhere, it stands to reason that Maimonides regarded the Ben Asher codex as being authoritative in all areas. See id., 'Hebrew Bible', 49–50. This latter point is stressed by Penkower in *New Evidence*, 54 n. 32. According to Penkower, it would simply have been impractical for Maimonides to list the thousands of defective and plene words in the *Mishneh torah*. As he notes, Maimonides rules that a missing letter invalidates a Torah scroll ('Hilkhot sefer torah', 10: 1). Such a halakhah would be incomprehensible if there did not exist a letter-perfect text which would serve as the 'master copy'. This text is the Ben Asher codex.

[174] See dei Rossi, *Me'or einayim*, ch. 9 (end). See also other versions of the story in Loewinger and Kupfer, 'Yom Tov', 239–41. For other references to the 'scroll of Ezra', see Benayahu, 'Letter', 205–6. It is possible that the legend of Maimonides' journey to France was invented precisely in order to explain just how Maimonides could have put forth such a bold claim, namely, that his copy of the Torah was identical with that of Moses. If Maimonides had examined the scroll of Ezra, which presumably was the same as the scroll of Moses, this problem disappears. Of course, the story of the three Torahs in the Temple, which shows that there was no scroll of Ezra in existence, is ignored in creating this legend. See M. Goshen-Gottstein, 'Authenticity', 46, who explains the legend in another plausible fashion.

[175] 'Hilkhot teshuvah', 3: 8.

aspect of the Torah but the assertion that Moses (or someone else) intentionally added material not transmitted by God. However, this says nothing
about mistakes that naturally crept in. In fact, I believe, as suggested above
with regard to BT *Sanhedrin* 99*a*, that even Maimonides should be understood here as concentrating not on denial of complete Mosaic authorship,
but on denial of divine inspiration. In other words, denial of complete Mosaic
authorship, while certainly false according to Maimonides, would not be
regarded as heretical.

Bearing in mind all the evidence cited here, one should not be surprised to
read the comments of the late *rosh yeshivah* of Yeshivat Ner Yisrael, R. Ya'akov
Weinberg (1923–99). After mentioning some of the points already made,
Weinberg states:

> Rambam knew very well that these variations existed when he defined his Prin-
> ciples. The words of Ani Ma'amin and the words of the Rambam, 'the entire
> Torah in our possession today', must not be taken literally, implying that all the
> letters of the present Torah are the exact letters given to Moshe Rabbeinu. Rather,
> it should be understood in a general sense that the Torah we learn and live by is
> for all intents and purposes the same Torah that was given to Moshe Rabbeinu.[176]

Weinberg is specifically referring to Maimonides' claim that our Torah scrolls
are exactly the same as that given to Moses. However, what about Maimonides' other assertion, namely, that one must believe that the entire Torah
was written by Moses? I think that this too must be taken with a grain of salt.
While there is no question that Maimonides affirmed complete Mosaic
authorship,[177] holding something to be true is very different from establishing it as dogma. By doing the latter, Maimonides would have rendered any
other opinion heretical. Yet there is no question that Maimonides did not
regard Ibn Migash and Ibn Ezra—men who denied complete Mosaic authorship—as heretics.

That Maimonides could not have truly believed that all those who differed
with this principle were heretics is seen from another angle as well. Speaking
of rabbinic disputes concerning theoretical matters, Maimonides declares on
a number of occasions that one cannot decide which opinion must be fol-

---

[176] *Fundamentals and Faith*, 90–1. This book is an authorized presentation of Weinberg's
shiurim.

[177] Complete Mosaic authorship is also affirmed in Maimonides' *Commentary on the Mishnah*, i. 2;
Introduction to the *Mishneh Torah*; 'Hilkhot tefilah', 13: 6; *Letters*, ed. Shailat, i. 90, 405 (Arabic), 127,
410 (Hebrew); and Maimonides, *Ḥidushei harambam*, 104. The authenticity of this last work has
been challenged by Levinger in *Maimonides*, 172–6. See also ibid. 54–5, where Levinger argues that
Maimonides' esoteric view is that the last eight verses are, in fact, post-Mosaic. Cf. Levinger's earlier
Halakhic Thought, 96 n. 24, where this approach is only advanced as a 'daring' possibility. I see no
compelling evidence to support Levinger in this regard.

lowed as one does in questions of practical halakhah.[178] This does not mean that one does not offer one's own view; indeed, Maimonides chooses between different rabbinic opinions in these matters on several occasions. What he means is that one cannot render another opinion invalid and therefore forbidden to be held. This is no different from that which occurs in halakhic disputes, where the opposing opinion is also not rendered invalid. It is just that, for practical purposes, one opinion must be followed. Maimonides' point is that, when there are no practical implications, one cannot *compel* belief in one opinion to the exclusion of another. As he puts it: 'If sages differ regarding some belief or opinion that has no practical outcome, one does not say in this instance, "the halakhah is like so and so".'[179] Since Maimonides' philosophical views were rejected by his rabbinic contemporaries, it is obvious that he had to advocate this approach, if only to ensure that his own opinions would not be rendered invalid.

As we have already noted, there is an opinion in the Talmud that the last eight verses of the Torah were written by Joshua. For Maimonides to declare a talmudic opinion heretical appears extremely unlikely, especially when one bears in mind his view on the impossibility of deciding authoritatively between rabbinic opinions in theoretical matters. In response to this it may be protested that, as seen above, Maimonides acknowledges that there are rabbinic opinions which seem to accept the Platonic view of creation, but he nevertheless regards creation *ex nihilo* as dogma. A number of answers to this difficulty are possible. To begin with, Maimonides does not suggest that these rabbinic opinions accept the Platonic view, only that they *may*. Also, we have already seen how Maimonides' position on creation in the Thirteen Principles is contradicted by what he writes in the *Guide*, and cannot be taken as his true belief.

However, even if one chooses to disregard the *Guide* entirely, a distinction can be made between creation and the authorship of the Torah. It could be that Maimonides felt he had to insist on creation *ex nihilo* in the Fourth Principle because this is a fundamental aspect of Jewish theology. It was not as if he had to decide between two theologically acceptable opinions. Rather, one opinion was totally at odds with the Jewish outlook, and therefore it was not a question of deciding between two opinions but rather of affirming the only

---

[178] *Commentary*, Mishnah *Sotah* 3: 3, *San.* 10: 3, *Shevu.* 1: 4; *Sefer hamitsvot*, negative commandment no. 133; *Letters*, ed. Shailat, i. 327 (Arabic), 354 (Hebrew). This position was put forth earlier in *Mavo hatalmud*, found at the end of tractate *Berakhot* in the Vilna edition of the Talmud and attributed to R. Samuel Hanagid: כל מחלוקת שלא חייב במעשה אלא המחלוקת במעשה אלא בדעת לבד לא נגדור בו הלכה כפלוני. (Concerning the authorship of this work, see Margulies, *Hilkhot hanagid*, 68–73; Abramson, 'Some Teachings', 22–3.) See similarly Rashi, BT *San.* 51b, s.v. *hakhi*; Cordovero, *Elimah rabati*, i. 1.

[179] *Commentary*, Mishnah *Sotah* 3: 3 (translation in Naor, *Kabbalah and the Holocaust*, 10).

correct one. The same could be said with regard to rabbinic passages that speak of angels as intermediaries. Since these passages are theologically untenable, they are not regarded as valid opinions any more than a view which permits Sabbath desecration is a valid halakhic opinion. What we have, therefore, is simply one opinion which Maimonides records, not two opinions of which he chooses one. *Where issues of dogma are concerned, there is never more than one option.* This is not the case with regard to the last eight verses of the Pentateuch. Theologically, it makes little difference if the last eight verses were written by Moses or by Joshua under divine inspiration. There is thus no reason why Maimonides should establish one rabbinic opinion as dogma and, by so doing, classify the other rabbinic opinion as heresy.[180]

I present this argument only to satisfy those who do not wish to deal with what Maimonides writes in the *Guide*. However, for those who are prepared to do so—and this is the only way to achieve a true understanding of Maimonides—there is little doubt that Maimonides' assertions regarding creation *ex nihilo* (that it is an obligatory belief) and the text of the Torah are to be viewed in the same light. Both the Fourth and the Eighth Principles contain things Maimonides did not accept, and yet he wrote that all Jews must believe in them in their entirety. How is this to be explained?

I propose to solve this problem by comparing the *Commentary on the Mishnah* (where the Principles appear) to Maimonides' other works, in particular the *Guide*. In the *Guide* Maimonides adopts the 'daring method of admitting right off to misspoken utterances (as we might call them today) and to half-truths. . . . His endorsement of these views is necessary for obvious political reasons, reasons which he obviously cannot divulge.'[181] According to the fifteenth-century Cretan kabbalist R. Michael Balbo, even in the *Mishneh torah* Maimonides said things which did not reflect his true view, but were 'formulated according to the conventional manner of speaking, in order to

---

[180] Y. H. Sofer, *Yeḥi yosef*, 191 ff., attempts to understand Maimonides by placing the issue in a halakhic context, but this strikes me as far off the mark. A halakhic decision would not leave the rejected opinion in the category of heresy. Sofer takes note of Maimonides' view regarding the inapplicability of halakhic decisions in theoretical matters, but understands this to mean that normal procedures of halakhic decision-making are suspended (כללי ההלכה לא נאמרו בכהאי גוונא). This interpretation is completely unfounded and cannot possibly be foisted on Maimonides' words. It is, however, typical of those scholars who choose to view everything Maimonides wrote from a halakhic perspective. In this regard, see R. S. Kanevsky, *Siaḥ hasadeh*, 29*b*, who tries to explain why it is that Maimonides 'decided in accordance with R. Simeon that Moses wrote the entire Torah. This requires investigation for it is accepted that in a dispute between R. Judah and R. Simeon the halakhah is in accordance with R. Judah' (see BT *Eruv.* 46*b*). See similarly Lichtman, *Benei tsiyon*, 'Oraḥ ḥayim' 428: 7. There is actually no difficulty whatsoever, for Maimonides, in advocating the view that Moses wrote the entire Torah, is expressing an ideological position, not a halakhic ruling, and this has no connection with the rules of halakhic decision-making referred to by these authors.

[181] Ivry, 'Islamic and Greek Influences', 141–2.

ease the way for beginners' who were not yet able to grasp metaphysical concepts.[182] Interestingly enough, Balbo's great opponent, the philosopher R. Moses Ashkenazi, agrees with this statement.[183] The same tendency is apparent in Maimonides' Principles. Here, however, we do not simply find Maimonides putting forth 'misspoken utterances', but rather stating them as dogma. This may be easier to understand if we find an appropriate context in which to place these 'half-truths'.

In *Guide* iii. 28 Maimonides discusses the differences between what he terms 'true beliefs' and 'necessary beliefs'. 'True beliefs' are those which teach, in a literal fashion, some truth about God, such as his existence, unity, eternity, and omnipotence. Their purpose is to enable one to attain intellectual perfection. 'Necessary beliefs', which are based on tradition rather than philosophy, are expressed in a figurative manner and fulfil a political function in that, by instilling obedience to the Torah, they regulate the social relations of human beings. In addition, they enable people to acquire noble qualities. For example, the Torah teaches that God is angry with those who disobey him. Although in truth God does not possess the characteristic of anger, the Torah found it advantageous to use this concept for the effect it would have. It is 'necessary' for the masses to believe that God is angry if they disobey him in order for them to control their behaviour. In addition, it is 'necessary' for the masses to believe that God responds instantly to the prayer of someone wronged or deceived; for them to believe otherwise would be damaging to their faith.

Arthur Hyman has pointed out that Maimonides' understanding of 'necessary beliefs' is dialectical rather than sophistic; that is, they are 'propositions which are true in some respect though not in another'.[184] Although Hyman uses this distinction to make a different point, it would appear that it is also relevant to the problem under discussion. In formulating the Eighth Principle, Maimonides was aware that it is not entirely 'true'. It is true that the Torah is divine and was given to Moses. It is also true that the traditional interpretations are divine. It is even true that Moses wrote the entire Torah, from beginning to end. However, certain other elements are not true but only 'necessary'. It is necessary for the masses to believe that the Torah in their hands is identical to the Torah of Moses. It is also necessary for them to believe that it is heretical to express a doubt as to whether Moses wrote the entire Torah. These 'necessary beliefs' are the equivalent of telling someone

---

[182] See Ravitzky, *Al da'at hamakom*, 193–4, 201. As Ravitzky points out, 193 n. 74, the same position was also expressed in the anonymous 14th-cent. German work, *Alilot devarim*.

[183] See Ravitzky, *Al da'at hamakom*, 194–5.

[184] 'Spinoza's Dogmas', 189. This point had already been made by Albo in *Sefer ha'ikarim*, ii. 14.

that God gets angry or that He responds immediately to prayer, in that all these beliefs have in common the fact that, through them, people are kept from straying from the proper path.[185] This insight will also explain the other problem noted above, namely, why Maimonides lists creation *ex nihilo* as a dogma when he clearly did not view it in this way.

The reason that Maimonides believed it important to insert these 'necessary beliefs' into the Eighth Principle appears obvious. In his time, Muslims were challenging the Jews, claiming that they had altered the text of the Torah. This accusation began with Muhammad, who, as quoted in the Koran, had charged the rabbis with falsifying and tampering with the original Torah text. He proclaimed: 'Do you then hope that they would believe in you; a party from among them indeed used to hear the word of God, then altered it after they had understood it, and they know [this]. . . . Woe then to those who write the Book with their hands and then say this is from God' (II. 75, 79). This charge was elaborated by early Islamic scholars, with the theologian Ibn Hazm (994–1064) taking a lead in publicizing the doctrine of Jewish falsification of Scripture (*taḥrif*).[186]

In the face of such an assault, it is not hard to see why Maimonides felt it was important for the masses to believe that their text was the exact equivalent of Moses' text. The masses then (and today) could not be expected to understand the problems relating to the biblical text. Exposing them to some of this knowledge could have undermined their unquestioned faith, especially in the face of Islamic polemics. It was thus necessary for the masses to affirm what, in reality, was not true, namely, that the text of the Torah in their hands was entirely free from any textual corruptions, even to the last detail.

That this interpretation of Maimonides is correct is further illustrated by a passage in his *Letter to Yemen*. Referring to the Muslim accusation that the Jews had altered the text of the Torah, Maimonides responds by saying that in both East and West 'there exist no differences at all in the text, not even in the vocalization'.[187] Here Maimonides is not simply saying that the Torah in

---

[185] According to the esoteric interpretation of Maimonides' view of revelation, and contrary to what he writes in the Eighth Principle, the Torah was not prophetically dictated to Moses by God. This view turns virtually the entire Principle into a 'necessary belief'. Supporters of this approach include Reines, 'Maimonides' Concept', 325–61; Bland, 'Moses', 49–66; Kaplan, '"I Sleep"'; Ivry, 'Isma'ili', 294–5; Levinger, *Maimonides*, ch. 4. Though he did not attribute this view to Maimonides, it is also advocated by R. Nissim b. Moses, *Ma'aseh nisim*, 177–8 (only the general commands came from God, and Moses supplied the particulars).

[186] See Perlmann, 'Eleventh-Century Andalusian Authors', 271–7; Baron, *Social and Religious History*, v. 88 ff.; Lazarus-Yafeh, 'Ezra'; id., *Intertwined Worlds*; N. Roth, 'Forgery'; Adang, *Muslim Writers*, ch. 7. For similar accusations in the Christian world, see Resnick, 'Falsification'.

[187] *Letters*, ed. Shailat, i. 93 (Arabic), 131–2 (Hebrew). Penkower, 'Jacob ben Hayim', 414–15, calls attention to the *Letter to Yemen* in the context of *taḥrif*, and also notes the similar, though not so extreme, formulation given by Abraham ibn Daud, *Ha'emunah haramah*, 80. As with Maimonides,

his possession is identical to that of Moses, thus making it the only correct version. Rather, he is denying a fact which was obvious to anyone with even a perfunctory knowledge of the Pentateuch, namely, that there were differences in texts. As for denying differences in vocalization, this is the equivalent of denying that the Masoretes ever existed. An Islamic opponent would be excused had he charged Maimonides with a bald-faced lie. However, Maimonides' comments were not directed against such a person, but towards the masses of Jews of simple faith who had never heard of Ben Asher and Ben Naftali and may not have been able to deal with the fact that there were differences in biblical vocalization.[188]

It should be noted that this presumed fear of Maimonides finds expression among later scholars. One of the reasons Bonfils gives for not making Ibn Ezra's hints known to the masses is the ammunition they would provide for the Muslims.[189] R. Hayim ben Attar strongly assails the view that the end of the Torah was written by Joshua, because, as he states, many Jews were confused by this assertion and were led to heresy. In addition, the very notion that Moses did not write the entire Torah gives support to the Islamic view that the Jews altered the holy text after Moses' time.[190] The Muslim accusation of *taḥrif* is also mentioned by R. David ibn Zimra in two responsa. In one he discusses a variety of Masoretic details and states that if one explains matters in a different way (for example with regard to *tikun soferim*), one gives support to the Islamic polemicists. In the other responsum, he mentions *taḥrif* in refusing to sanction the correction of Torah scrolls according to the pentateuchal text found in the Zohar.[191]

Ibn Daud was well aware of the facts, but he too had a polemical battle to wage. The same is true for Albo, who wrote: 'The Torah is exactly the same today without any change among all Israel who are scattered all over the world from the extreme east to the farthest west' (*Sefer ha'ikarim*, iii. 22). See similarly Moses Mendelssohn, *Gesammelte Schriften*, xiv. 213, and E. Breuer, *Limits*, ch. 5, on Mendelssohn's motivations.

[188] Seeing the extremes to which Maimonides was willing to go, perhaps my judgement in n. 10 above is mistaken. Assuming that the Eighth Principle teaches 'necessary beliefs', perhaps Maimonides cast his net as wide as possible, including as part of the Principle issues of script, exceptional letters and anything else found in the text of the Torah. In fact, Maimonides made some other peculiar, and apparently untrue, assertions. For example, his claim that there are no disputes with regard to *halakhot lemosheh misinai* is virtually impossible to justify (*Commentary on the Mishnah*, i. 10). Levinger, *Halakhic Thought*, 63 ff., cites this as an example of Maimonides responding to the needs of the masses by presenting them with an understanding of Judaism which would enable them to withstand the onslaught of Islamic polemics (or possibly Karaite assaults; see *Letters*, ed. Shailat, ii. 442, Baron, *Social and Religious History*, v. 22). With such a goal, namely, the creation of a religious myth, absolute truth is not important. [189] *Tsofnat pane'aḥ* on Gen. 12: 6.

[190] *Or ḥaḥayim* on Deut. 34: 6. [191] *She'elot uteshuvot haradbaz*, nos. 1020, 1172.

EIGHT

Eternity of the Torah

The Ninth Principle

T HE NINTH PRINCIPLE teaches that the Torah will never be abrogated, in whole or part, and that God will never give another Torah.
Maimonides repeats his insistence that the biblical *mitsvot* and the Oral Law
will never be abrogated, not even in messianic days, in a few other places.[1]
While this is certainly a popular position among rabbinic authorities, and has
a talmudic source,[2] it is hardly unanimously accepted.

A number of rabbinic sources speak of future changes in the Torah.[3] The
classic statement is made by R. Joseph: 'The *mitsvot* will be abolished in the
Time to Come' (BT *Nidah* 61*b*). Scholars have debated whether this passage
refers to the messianic age or the time of the resurrection.[4] However, none of
this is relevant to Maimonides, for he explicitly states that the resurrection will
occur 'in the lifetime of the Messiah, or before him, or after he dies'.[5] In other
words, the resurrection will not usher in some new eschatological world.[6]

---

[1] See *Mishneh torah*, 'Hilkhot yesodei hatorah', 9: 1, 'Hilkhot teshuvah', 3: 8, 'Hilkhot megilah', 2:
18, 'Hilkhot melakhim', 11: 1, 3; *Guide* ii. 39, iii. 34.   [2] JT *Meg.* 1: 5, *Sifra* on Lev. 27: 34.

[3] See Palache, *Lev hayim*, 'Orah hayim', no. 32; J. Rosenthal, 'The Idea of the Abrogation of
Mitsvot'; Davies, *Setting of the Sermon on the Mount*, 156–90; Biller, 'God Will Not Change'; Heschel,
Theology, iii. 49–81.

[4] See Tosafot ad loc., s.v. *amar*; Urbach, *Sages*, 819 n. 43. *Midrash tana'im* on Deut. 19: 9 explicitly
distinguishes between the 'days of the messiah', in which *mitsvot* are still obligatory, and the 'Time to
Come', in which there will be no commandments. R. Yeruham Meir Leiner of Radzyn attempts to
prove that, according to both Rashi and Nahmanides, R. Joseph's statement does indeed refer to the
messianic era. See Medini, *Sedei hemed*, iv. 306–7 (*ma'arekhet mem* 218). See also ibid., vol. ix, 'Divrei
hakhamim', no. 53 (pp. 34–6), where Medini discusses the view that only the negative commandments will be abolished. R. Menahem Mendel of Vitebsk also thinks that R. Joseph's statement refers
to the messianic era; see his *Peri ha'arets*, 24 ('Toledot'). According to R. Isser Yehudah Unterman,
Maimonides understood this passage as referring to the afterlife. See his *Shevet miyehudah*, iii. 315–16.
Although this is not the simple meaning of the phrase 'Time to Come', as Unterman points out, this
view was actually held by R. Solomon ben Adret, R. Yom Tov Ishbili, and R. Nissim Gerondi. It is,
however, possible that these sages advanced this view as an apologetic response to Christian polemicists who cited R. Joseph's statement. See Lieberman, *Sheki'in*, 80–1. As part of his polemic against
Shabatean antinomianism, R. Eleazar Fleckeles also claimed that R. Joseph's statement referred to
the afterlife. See Naor, *Post-Sabbatian Sabbatianism*, 152 nn. 13, 15.

[5] *Letters*, ed. Shailat, i. 329 (Arabic) 359 (Hebrew).

[6] This opinion, which Maimonides rejects, namely that the resurrection will be the beginning of a
new spiritual era, was held by a number of scholars and was used to explain how R. Joseph's view—
which in their opinion refers to a post-resurrection world—does not contradict the notion of the

Apart from this uniquely occurring miracle, the world of the resurrection will not differ from the world in which we currently live—a world in which, according to Maimonides, the Torah remains binding in its entirety.

Another famous passage is found in *Vayikra rabah* 13: 3, which seeks to explain the rabbinic tradition that in the Time to Come the righteous will consume the mythical beasts Behemoth and Leviathan. The problem is that the same tradition portrays these beasts as killing one another, hardly a valid method of *sheḥitah*. Playing upon Isaiah 51: 4—'Instruction [*torah*] shall go forth from Me'—R. Abin ben Kahanah proclaimed: 'The Holy One, blessed be He, said: "A new Torah [*torah ḥadashah*] shall go forth from me", that is, a new Torah law [*ḥidush torah*] shall issue from me.'[7] Similarly, *Yalkut shimoni* speaks of a 'new Torah which will be given through the messiah'.[8]

Aside from these general statements speaking of future changes in the Torah, there are a number of other rabbinic passages which specify certain *mitsvot* that will no longer be in force. For example, *Yalkut shimoni*, *Mishlei*, no. 944 says: 'All the festivals are to be abolished in the future [messianic era], but Purim will never be abolished. R. Eleazar said: Also Yom Kippur will never be abolished.'[9] BT *Kidushin 72b* asserts: '*Mamzerim*[10] and *netinim*[11] will become pure in the Time to Come: this is Rabbi Jose's view . . . Rabbi Judah said in Samuel's name: The halakhah agrees with Rabbi Jose.' *Midrash tehilim* (146: 4) states:

> *The Lord looseth the bound* (Ps. 146: 4). What does the verse mean by the words *looseth the bound*? Some say that of every animal whose flesh it is forbidden to eat in this world, the Holy One, blessed be He, will declare in the Time to Come that the eating of this flesh is permitted. . . . [Others offer a different interpretation:] Though nothing is more strongly forbidden than intercourse with a menstruous woman—for when a woman sees blood the Holy One, blessed be He, forbids her to her husband—in the Time to Come, God will permit such intercourse.

Another midrashic passage on this verse, which is attested to by Albo[12] but is not found in our texts, reads: '*The Lord looseth the bound* [מתיר אסורים]: He

---

immutability of Torah law. In other words, Torah law is only immutable in our present world. See e.g. Loew (Maharal), *Tiferet yisra'el*, chs. 52–3; Jacob Emden's note on BT *RH 30a* (printed in the Romm edition of the Talmud); Shneur Zalman of Lyady, *Likutei amarim*, iv ('Igeret hakodesh'), ch. 26; A. I. Kook, *Igerot hare'iyah*, i. 173, ii. 250–1; Messas, *Mayim ḥayim*, i, no. 124; T. Y. Kook, *Linetivot yisra'el*, i. 38.

[7] Some manuscripts lack the word *ḥadashah*, but this does not change the meaning of the passage. See *Midrash vayikra rabah*, ed. Margulies, 278. The version I cite is also found in Abraham ben Azriel, *Arugat habosem*, i. 242.   [8] On Isaiah, no. 429.   [9] See also *Pirkei derabi eli'ezer*, ch. 46.

[10] *Mamzer*: the issue of an incestuous or adulterous relationship. He or she is forbidden to marry other Jews of pure pedigree.

[11] *Netinim*: an ancient nation whose members were forbidden to intermarry with Jews of pure pedigree. See *EJ* vii, cols. 551–4.   [12] *Sefer ha'ikarim*, iii. 16.

permits the forbidden [מתיר איסורין].' Other rabbinic passages speak of the *mitsvot* of remembering the Exodus and offering sacrifices as being abolished in the future.[13]

R. David ben Samuel Hakokhavi (thirteenth century) accepts the notion that in the Time to Come certain *mitsvot* will be abolished. According to him, during this time, when 'the earth shall be full of the knowledge of the Lord' (Isa. 11: 9), the nature of humans will change so that they will be like angels and their intellects will rule over their bodies. Thus there will be no need for the many negative commandments that, Hakokhavi believes, are intended to bring about the control of the sensual urges by the intellect.[14] R. Bahya ben Asher adopts a similar approach in explaining why the prohibition on mixing milk and meat is to be abolished.[15]

Another medieval scholar, R. Joseph Albo, is the most important philosopher to disagree with Maimonides. Although in Book I, chapter 23 of his *Sefer ha'ikarim* he states that 'it is incumbent upon everyone who professes the Law of Moses' to believe that the Torah will never be repealed nor changed, in Book III, chapters 13–20 he presents an entirely different position.[16] Although he considers his position only theoretical, he acknowledges that, were a new prophet to arise whose mission could be verified in the same public and miraculous way in which Moses' mission was verified, it would be possible for the commandments of the Torah to be abolished. The only exception to this is the Ten Commandments, which have a different status from that of the rest of the laws of the Torah, having been proclaimed to the Israelites directly by God.[17] While it is true that humans are commanded neither to add nor subtract from the Torah, 'what can there be to prevent God Himself from adding or diminishing as His wisdom decrees?'[18] According to Albo, the view that the commandments can be abolished 'belongs neither to the category of the necessary nor to that of the impossible'.[19] As he elaborates in another passage:

There is nothing therefore to prevent us from supposing that the divine law may in the future permit some things which are forbidden now, like fat or blood or the slaughter of [sacrificial] animals outside the Temple. These things were originally

---

[13] See Heschel, *Theology*, iii. 60–8; Y. Hayoun, *Otsarot aharit hayamim*, ch. 12. Regarding the famous apocryphal midrash that in the Time to Come pork will be permitted, see Zavihi, *Ateret paz*, i, 'Yoreh de'ah', no. 6; Korman, *Hatahor vehatame*, ch. 7. On the possibility that the consumption of the sinew of the sciatic nerve will be permitted, see Medini, *Sedei hemed*, ii. 18–19 (*ma'arekhet gimel* 76).

[14] *Sefer habatim*, i. 183–4. [15] *Commentary*, Exod. 23: 19.

[16] Albo's view in these chapters did not escape the eyes of Christian polemicists. See the apostate Christfels, *Gespräch*, 177–8.

[17] *Sefer ha'ikarim*, iii. 18–19. According to Albo, the first two of the Ten Commandments, unlike the remaining eight, cannot even be abolished as a temporary measure.

[18] Ibid. 14. [19] Ibid. 19.

forbidden when the Israelites left Egypt because they were addicted to the worship of evil spirits, and ate the flesh with the blood and also ate fat and blood. . . . But when this form of worship has been forgotten, and all people shall worship God, and the reason for the prohibition will cease, it may be that God will again permit it. . . . To sum up, I see no evidence, nor any necessity, from Maimonides' arguments, that the immutability or irrepealability of the law should be a fundamental principle of a divine law generally or of the Law of Moses in particular.[20]

Albo's opinion is quoted without objection by R. Moses Sofer.[21] Similar views, advocating the possibility of God changing aspects of the Torah or giving an entirely new Torah, are independently propounded by R. Tobias ben Moses Cohn (1652–1729),[22] R. Jacob Emden,[23] and R. Abraham Hayim Viterbo.[24] After repeating a point originally made by Albo, that although Adam was forbidden to eat meat Noah was permitted to do so,[25] Viterbo continues as follows:

They were permitted to consume the sinew of the sciatic nerve, but this was forbidden to Jacob; Noah and Abraham offered sacrifices outside the Land [of Israel]; and Jacob was permitted to marry two sisters, and later this was forbidden in the Torah of Moses. What will the rabbi [Maimonides] say [about this]? For everything is good and proper in its time and with the passage of time the law will change and there is no regret, for it is possible that at one time a certain practice is beneficial and years later another practice will be beneficial. Since the divine law changed a few times before the giving of the Torah, why should the rabbi decree that the Torah of Moses will never change?

Most disturbing to Viterbo is what he views as Maimonides' presumptuousness in instructing God, as it were, on how He can conduct Himself.[26] Emden makes a similar point:

We absolutely do not admit that which Maimonides laid down, that the entire Torah will not change, for there is no decisive proof for this—neither from reason and logic nor from the Bible. Verily, the Sages tell us that the Holy One will give a new Torah in the future. If our King should wish to change the Torah, or exchange it for another, whatever the King wishes, whether it be to descend on Mount Sinai or another of the mighty mountains, or even a valley, there to appear a second time before the eyes of all the living, we would be the first to do His will, whatever be His bidding.[27]

---

[20] Ibid. 16. At iii. 18 he quotes in support of this view *Sifrei* on Deut. 18: 5: 'If a prophet . . . says that *we should violate the Sabbath* or transgress some of the commandments as a temporary measure, *or even permanently, provided he does not subvert the foundations of the religion*, we must listen to him.' Our version of the *Sifrei* does not include the italicized text. See *Sifrei devarim*, piska 175. The phrase 'foundations of the religion' (*shorshei hadat*) would certainly not have been used in the classical rabbinic period.　　　　[21] *Torat mosheh* on Deut. 34: 12.

[22] *Ma'aseh tuviyah*, 'Olam ha'elyon', *ma'amar* 3, chs. 2–3.　　　　[23] *Migdal oz*, 26b–c.

[24] *Emunat hakhamim*, 27–9.　　　　[25] See *Sefer ha'ikarim*, iii. 14.

[26] *Emunat hakhamim*, 28b.　　　　[27] Translation in Naor, *Post-Sabbatian Sabbatianism*, 8–9.

In order to show that God's law can change, both Albo and Viterbo cite examples of things which were at first permitted but later forbidden (or, in the case of Adam and meat, first forbidden and later permitted). In some of the examples, it was only before the giving of the Torah that they were permitted, and they became forbidden with the subsequent revelation of Torah law. Surprisingly, neither Albo nor Viterbo cites *Devarim rabah* 4: 6, 9, according to which divine law was changed even after the giving of the Torah. The example given is that of Leviticus 17, where it is stated that when one wishes to eat meat it must be slaughtered at the sanctuary as a sacrificial act. However, in Deuteronomy 12: 15–16 this provision is revoked. It is significant that the midrash does not say that the prohibition was only intended to be temporary, due to the conditions of desert life. Rather, it says 'God prohibited many things and He again made them permissible elsewhere [in Scripture].' In speaking of the new permission in Deuteronomy 12, the midrash links it to the verse in Psalm 146: 7, 'The Lord looseth the bound', which is interpreted here as meaning that the Lord permitted that which was previously forbidden.

Turning to the kabbalists, in discussing the world of the messianic era, the section of the Zohar known as *Raya mehemna*[28] states: 'The Tree of Good and Evil,[29] which is the forbidden and the permitted, uncleanness and cleanness, will no longer rule over Israel, for they will derive their sustenance only from the Tree of Life,[30] where there are no problems from the evil side, and no arguments from the spirit of uncleanness.'[31] In a later passage, the *Raya mehemna* clarifies this by pointing out that only kabbalists will be freed from the commandments in the messianic era. But 'the forbidden and the permitted, uncleanness and cleanness, will not forsake the ignorant, because on their side the only difference between the age of exile and the Messianic Age will be [the destruction of] oppressive political power, for they will not taste of the Tree of Life, and they will need the halakhic teachings of the forbidden and the permitted, the unclean and the clean'.[32] In commenting on the first *Raya mehemna* passage, R. Menahem Mendel of Vitebsk (1730–88) writes:

---

[28] iii. 124*b*; translation in Tishby, *Wisdom*, iii. 1150–1. See also the analysis of Gottlieb in *Studies*, 545 ff.

[29] 'The direction of the world by the opposing forces of good and evil, which necessitates the inclusion in the Torah of regulations concerning the forbidden and the permitted, unclean and clean, will come to an end, as far as the Kabbalists are concerned, in the Messianic Age' (Tishby, *Wisdom*, iii. 1150 n. 275).

[30] 'They will receive their spiritual and physical nourishment from the Tree of Life, and not from the Tree of Knowledge, and therefore they will not be subject to the laws of the forbidden and the permitted' (Tishby, *Wisdom*, iii. 1150 n. 277).

[31] 'Under the rule of the Tree of Life there will be no room for problems and arguments in the study of halakhah, for these originate in evil and uncleanness' (ibid. 1150 n. 278).

[32] iii. 125*a*; trans. in Tishby, *Wisdom*, iii. 1151.

The statement of our teachers, of blessed memory, that in the days of the Messiah all commandments will be abolished rests on [the belief] that in the Time to Come the earth shall be full of the knowledge of God as the waters cover the sea [cf. Isa. 11: 9], and they will have a different Torah . . . and that this knowledge will penetrate to the root of the Torah and the commandments, that is, to the absolute Unity, the Ein Sof as expressed in the words *I am the Lord thy God* (Exod. 20: 2, Deut. 5: 6). When this goal is reached all commandments will 'let down their wings' and all statutes will be suspended because the evil urge will then have been overcome.[33]

R. Isaac of Radzivilov (died 1835) writes:

Regarding that which is stated in the *Zohar ḥadash*, that in the future God will give us a new Torah in the days of the redeemer, may he come speedily in our days, it is not the Torah which is currently in our possession, and also not the Torah which was given at Mount Sinai. Not this shall God give us, but a new Torah which was in existence two thousand years before the creation of the world. The Torah which God will give us in the future is hidden in the Torah currently in our possession . . . and it is certain that it is with regard to the Torah in our possession that the Sages of blessed memory stated that the *mitsvot* will be abolished in the future.[34]

According to R. Jacob Joseph of Polonnoye (died *c*.1782), in the future the *mitsvot* will no longer have a physical component but only a spiritual one. So, for example, one will be able to wear wool and linen as this is only the external form of the *mitsvah*, which in the future will be obsolete. Only the spiritual component of the *mitsvot* is eternal.[35]

R. Isaac Luria, as quoted by R. Hayim Joseph David Azulai (1724–1806),[36] states that in messianic days the *kohanim* and the Levites will exchange roles. R. Hayim Halberstam (1793–1876) claims that the firstborn will take the place of the *kohanim*.[37] Both of these scenarios are certainly a change in the Torah's scheme, according to which only the descendants of Aaron are to be priests. In fact, in speaking of Phinehas, the Torah is explicit that his descendants will have an 'everlasting priesthood' (*kehunat olam*; Num. 25: 13). Presumably, Luria and Halberstam understood 'everlasting' to mean until messianic times, when a new spiritual era will begin.[38]

In Temple days the priests' primary duties revolved around the sacrificial order, and, as mentioned previously, there are rabbinic sources which speak

[33] *Peri ha'arets*, 28 ('Toledot'), trans. in Mendelssohn, *Jerusalem*, 237.

[34] *Or yitshak*, 'Pekudei', quoted in Heschel, *Theology*, iii. 73, and see the similar passage from this author quoted by Heschel, ibid., n. 22.   [35] *Toledot ya'akov yosef*, 31 (introduction).

[36] *Midbar kedemot*, 34*a* (*ma'arekhet kaf*, no. 14).   [37] *Divrei ḥayim*, i. 92 ('Yitro').

[38] See BT *Kid.* 15*a*, where the Talmud understands the word *le'olam* in Exod. 21: 6 as meaning 'until the Jubilee'.

of sacrifices being abolished in the future. R. David Kimhi, relying on Ezekiel's eschatological vision, which portrays the sacrificial order differently from the version specified by the Torah, writes that in messianic days there will indeed be changes in this regard. While most of the changes have to do with the type and number of animals and accompaniments offered at the various sacrifices, there will also be at least one completely new feature in the new sacrificial order. The Torah commands that a burnt offering be offered daily, both morning and evening (Exod. 29: 38–42, Num. 28: 1–8), but according to Kimhi, in messianic days the daily evening sacrifice will be abolished in its entirety.[39] (Maimonides understands Ezekiel's vision to be referring to a special service which will take place once, at the dedication of the Third Temple.[40])

A more striking passage is found in *Vayikra rabah* 9: 7 (and parallels): 'In the Time to Come all sacrifices will be annulled, but that of thanksgiving will not be annulled.'[41] This passage is cited by numerous authorities, including Nahmanides in his commentary on Leviticus 23: 17. It appears to be a reference to the messianic era and not the time of resurrection, since the prooftext cited from Jeremiah 33: 11 is a messianic prophecy.[42]

The great kabbalist R. Joseph Gikatilla (1248–*c*.1325) writes that only the sacrifices slaughtered on the north side of the Temple courtyard will be abolished in messianic days. These include the burnt offering, the sin offering, the guilt offering, and the communal peace offering (all regarded as 'holy of holies', *kodshei kodashim*). In his comment on this passage. R. Mattathias Delacrut (sixteenth century) claims that Gikatilla's words are an explanation of the *Vayikra rabah* passage cited in the previous paragraph.[43] However, this is incorrect, for while it is true that the individual peace offering, which is also known as a thanksgiving offering, can be slaughtered in any part of the Temple court, the same is true of a number of other sacrifices, including the sacrifice of the firstling and the paschal sacrifice, all of which are regarded as *kodashim kalim* (sacrifices of lesser sanctity).[44] Thus, while according to the *Vayikra rabah* passage cited by Delacrut only the thanksgiving offering will

[39] Commentary on Ezek. 45: 22, 46: 4, 13. This is perhaps contradicted by his comment on Jer. 31: 30, where Kimhi denies that there will ever be another Torah other than 'that which was given at Sinai'. It is possible that he distinguished between a completely new Torah and changes in the existing Torah.   [40] *Mishneh torah*, 'Hilkhot ma'aseh hakorbanot', 2: 14–15.

[41] Recognizing the radical nature of this passage, a number of commentators have explained that 'all sacrifices' means all sin offerings, which will no longer be needed since people will not be sinning. However, according to these scholars communal sacrifices will indeed continue to be offered. See David Sperber, 'Future Sacrifices', 100; Aviner, 'Sacrifices', 8 (Aviner appears to have made great use of Sperber's article without acknowledgement).

[42] See Davies, *Setting of the Sermon on the Mount*, 162–3.   [43] Gikatilla, *Sha'arei orah*, 75a.

[44] Mishnah *Zev.*, ch. 5; *Mishneh torah*, 'Hilkhot ma'aseh hakorbanot', 5: 2–4.

exist in messianic days, according to Gikatilla all *kodashim kalim* will continue to be offered.

On the subject of sacrifices, we must also call attention to the view of R. Abraham Isaac Kook, as expressed in his commentary on the prayer book.[45] While agreeing that there will be sacrifices in the messianic era, Kook argues that these will only be vegetable sacrifices. Employing kabbalistic arguments, he claims that in messianic days animals will themselves be full of the knowledge of God and thus will not need to be sacrificed in order to achieve the *tikun* ('correction', 'perfecting') that brings them close to God. Kook's biblical prooftext is Malachi 3: 4: 'Then shall the offering [מנחת] of Judah and Jerusalem be pleasant unto the Lord, as in the days of old, and as in ancient years.' This verse, in speaking of a sacrificial offering in messianic days, mentions the *minḥah* sacrifice, which is not an animal offering but consists of fine flour, oil, and frankincense. This is also how Kook explains the passage in *Vayikra rabah*: animal sacrifices will be abolished, but their place will be taken by vegetable sacrifices.[46] Kook's opinion, which alters the Torah obligation of animal sacrifices by substituting vegetable offerings, must be understood as part of his eschatological vision of vegetarianism.[47] As for all the passages in the Talmud, prayer book, and Kook's own writings[48] that speak of a return to animal sacrifices, presumably he understood them as referring to an early period in the messianic era, before the vegetarian ideal could be realized.[49] This view is in fact suggested independently of Kook by R. Hayim David Halevi (1924–98), late chief rabbi of Tel Aviv.[50]

R. Hayim Hirschensohn argues that in messianic days the sacrificial system will undergo significant alterations in accordance with the mindset and conceptions that will then prevail, conceptions that people today cannot grasp.[51] Although he does not elaborate on this position in as much detail as could be wished, it is clear that he is saying that cultured minds of the future will not find meaning in the sacrificial system as it existed in days of old. Since it is hard to imagine moderns finding spiritual meaning in any form of sacrificial

---

[45] *Olat re'iyah*, i. 292. [46] See A. I. Kook, *Otserot hare'iyah*, ii. 756. [47] Ibid. 742 ff.
[48] *Igerot lare'iyah*, iv. 24; David Sperber, 'Future Sacrifices', 97 n. 5.
[49] David Sperber, 'Future Sacrifices', and Aviner, 'Sacrifices', argue that Kook's comments regarding vegetable sacrifices refer to a post-resurrection world. However, this does not correspond to Kook's view, since he believes that *mitsvot* are to be abolished in the post-resurrection era. He also states explicitly that since there will be no eating at this time, there will be no sacrifices (or at least no sacrifices which leave parts to be consumed). See A. I. Kook, *Igerot hare'iyah*, ii. 250. As we have seen, Kook writes that in the future the only sacrifice offered will be a vegetable *minḥah*. Since the *minḥah* sacrifice is eaten, it is obvious that Kook is speaking of the messianic pre-resurrection era. R. Shelomo Goren, 'Building the Temple', 246 ff., also understands Kook to mean that there will only be vegetable sacrifices in messianic days.
[50] *Aseh lekha rav*, ix. 120–1, id., *Torat ḥayim*, ii. 18–20. [51] *Malki bakodesh*, i. 37.

system, even a completely revised one, Eliezer Schweid is no doubt correct in understanding Hirschensohn to mean that in messianic days there will be absolutely no sacrificial rituals. Rather, 'worship will be spiritual in nature, revealing the inner meaning of the sacrifices offered in the past'.[52] Kook understood this to be Hirschensohn's implication, and in a very conservative letter in which he accepts the return of animal sacrifices, urged Hirschensohn not to be too enamoured of Western culture, which regards sacrifices as an immature form of worship. Rather, he should remember that behind the physical act of the sacrifice stands profound holiness.[53] Despite this criticism, Hirschensohn continued to maintain his position. As for Kook's assumption that Hirschensohn had been taken in by what modern society regarded as intellectually respectable and cultured, and that this could change in the future, Hirschensohn defended himself by declaring: 'Knowledge and discernment will not regress, and lack of culture will not be considered culture.'[54]

There have been other traditional thinkers in modern times who denied that there would be a revival of sacrifices in the messianic era. In 1919 R. Solomon Isaac Scheinfeld (1860–1943), the leading rabbi of Milwaukee's Orthodox community, published an anonymous and controversial article in which he argued that, since sacrifices would never be revived, they were now irrelevant to Judaism and that therefore all references to them should be removed from the prayer book.[55] While he was not an outstanding thinker, it is noteworthy that R. Sabato Morais (1823–97) also denied that there would be a revival of sacrifices.[56]

From what we have seen so far, it is obvious that there is a significant rabbinic position which declares that the commandments will be abolished in messianic days. In fact, Bezalel Naor has speculated that perhaps it was this knowledge—that Maimonides' Principle was subject to such dispute—that prevented many great Torah scholars from reacting more strongly to the false messiah Shabetai Tsevi's violations of halakhah. Since they knew that many authorities believed that Jewish law would change in the messianic era, as long as it had not been established that Shabetai Tsevi was *not* the messiah, his violations of Jewish ritual were not a sufficient reason to condemn him.[57]

The question that must be asked once more is how Maimonides could regard the immutability of the commandments as a dogma, denial of which is

---

[52] *Demokratiyah vehalakhah*, 82.   [53] *Igerot hare'iyah*, iv. 24.   [54] *Malki bakodesh*, iv. 8.

[55] 'Even Shayish' (pseud.), 'Reform'. On Scheinfeld, see Swichkow and Gartner, *History*, 208–11.

[56] See Eisenstein, 'Between Two Opinions', 133. On Morais, see Nussenbaum, 'Champion'. While not offering a definite opinion, R. Jehiel Jacob Weinberg left open the possibility that sacrifices would not be reinstituted. See id., 'Über Opferwesen', 11 Jan. 1918.

[57] Naor, *Post-Sabbatian Sabbatianism*, 7–9.

heresy, when a good number of talmudic and midrashic texts do not accept this position. As I suggested with regard to the Fourth Principle and aspects of the Eighth, it is likely that here too, as Jacob Levinger has argued,[58] Maimonides was formulating a 'necessary belief', directed towards the masses and designed to help them deal with ideological assaults from the Islamic world. I do not claim, as does Levinger, that the belief itself is 'necessary', rather than 'true'. On the contrary, according to Maimonides, as expressed in a number of places in his writings, the belief is indeed true. What was 'necessary' was for Jews to be convinced that denial of this true belief was tantamount to heresy. This is why it was included as one of the Thirteen Principles.

In fact, there seems to be proof to support this reading of Maimonides in the *Mishneh torah*. I have already argued that the Fourth Principle and aspects of the Eighth Principle are 'necessary', in that, while Maimonides may have believed them to be true, he did not believe that one who denies them is a heretic. I have also pointed out that, when Maimonides offers a halakhic definition of heresy in the *Mishneh torah*, he omits mention of these 'necessary' beliefs. That is, he nowhere states that it is heresy to deny that God created the world *ex nihilo*, that the entire Torah was revealed to Moses, and that our current Torah text is identical with the Torah given to Moses. It would therefore be expected that in this case too, Maimonides' formulation in the *Mishneh torah* would not categorize someone who rejects the Ninth Principle as a heretic. In fact, this is exactly what we find, for in 'Hilkhot teshuvah' 3: 8, Maimonides writes: 'There are three individuals who are considered as one who denies the Torah. . . . One who says that though the Torah came from God, the Creator has replaced this Law with another and nullified the Torah, as for example the Christians and the Muslims.' That is, Maimonides defines a heretic as someone who says that God has *already* abrogated the Torah. There is no mention here of someone who asserts that there will be an abrogation in the future.

[58] Levinger, *Maimonides*, 62.

NINE

God's Knowledge; Reward and Punishment

☙

The Tenth Principle

THE TENTH PRINCIPLE states that God knows the actions of men. This would appear to be obvious to all religious people, and Isaac Husik described any view which limits God's knowledge as 'surely very bold as theology, we might almost say it is a theological monstrosity'.[1] However, theological monstrosity or not, such a view is not lacking among Jewish philosophers.

To begin with, it is important to point out, and this is emphasized by the Moroccan sage R. Raphael Berdugo (1747–1821),[2] that Maimonides does not refer to God's knowledge of the contingent, that is, future choices that have not yet been made. He certainly did believe that God had complete foreknowledge,[3] but this does not appear to be included here as dogma. In addition, as pointed out by R. David Cohen,[4] Maimonides mentions nothing here about God knowing the *thoughts* of humans. Similarly, in the *Mishneh torah*, 'Hilkhot teshuvah', 3: 8, he defines a heretic as one who denies that God knows the *actions* of man. This is noteworthy, if only because the popular *Ani ma'amin* formulation for this Principle reads: 'I believe with perfect faith that the Creator, Blessed be His Name, knows all the deeds of human beings and their thoughts, as it is said, *He fashions their hearts all together, He*

---

[1] *History*, 346.

[2] *Rav peninim*, 414, quoted in Maimeron, *Freedom*, 82. Berdugo mentions this as support for his own view that God's knowledge of the contingent is not a required belief. In fact, Berdugo actually argues that the notion that God knows the contingent is contradicted by the Torah and is thus theologically unacceptable! See Berdugo, *Mei menuhot*, 32 ff.; Maimeron, *Freedom*, 77–89; Manor, 'Raphael', 132. Other sages who denied that God knows the contingent include Ibn Daud, *Ha'emunah haramah*, ii. 6: 2; Eliezer Ashkenazi, *Ma'asei hashem*, i. 100 ff.; I. Horowitz, *Shenei luhot haberit*, introduction, sect. 'Beit habehirah'. This position might also be held by R. Isaac Polgar; see Pines, 'Isaac Polgar', 396 ff. I was surprised to learn that Nathan Aviezer, a scientist whose religious writings are popular in Orthodox circles, holds the same opinion. See his *Fossils*, 101 (called to my attention by Rabbi Jay Kelman).

[3] See *Shemoneh perakim*, ch. 8; *Mishneh torah*, 'Hilkhot teshuvah', 5: 5, *Guide* iii. 20.

[4] *Masat kapai*, 92.

comprehends all their deeds (Ps. 33: 15)'.[5] Similarly, the *Yigdal* formulation reads: 'He scrutinizes and knows our innermost secrets.'

Ibn Ezra should be mentioned among those who limit God's knowledge, although his view is not entirely clear. His comment on Genesis 18: 21 states: 'The Whole [God][6] knows the individual in a general manner rather than in a detailed manner', adding that this idea contains a 'great secret'. In this passage, as well as some others, Ibn Ezra appears to be advocating the Islamic Aristotelian view that God only knows the particular in a general way but not the particular as such, since it is constantly changing. This is how Ibn Ezra was understood by Nahmanides, who refers to him pejoratively as 'pleasing himself with foreign offspring [i.e. philosophy]'.[7] Ibn Ezra is also understood in this manner by Gersonides,[8] the commentary attributed to Ibn Kaspi,[9] Abarbanel,[10] Falaquera,[11] R. Eleazar Ashkenazi ben Nathan Habavli,[12] R. Aviad Sar-Shalom Basilea,[13] and by later scholars such as Orschansky,[14] Rosin,[15] Husik,[16] Guttmann,[17] Lévy,[18] Sirat,[19] and Joseph Cohen.[20]

Although this may indeed be Ibn Ezra's view, it must be noted that there is another possible reading which does not fit in with any philosophical system. The implication of his comment, when taken together with the verse, appears to be that God can, if he wishes, attain knowledge of the particular. If this is so, then we are not talking of a God who is constrained by forces beyond his will, but rather of a God who *chooses* not to be aware of particulars.[21] This would

[5] Maimonides does not cite this biblical verse, which happens to be the only verse mentioned in the *Ani ma'amin*. On this, see S. Y. Shohet, *Ahavat sha'ul*, 98; Prins, *Parnas ledorot*, 272–3. That God knows the thoughts of men is a concept found throughout the Bible: see e.g. Gen. 17: 17, 18: 12, 27: 41, 1 Sam. 27: 1, 2 Sam. 6: 16, Ps. 94: 11; Esther 6: 6.

[6] See E. R. Wolfson, 'God, the Demiurge, and the Intellect'; Kreisel, 'The Term *Kol*'.

[7] *Commentary*, Gen. 18: 20. [8] *Milḥamot hashem*, iii. 6.

[9] *Perush hasodot*, 152–3 (see H. Kasher, 'Ibn Caspi's Commentary', 89–108). However, this author understands Ibn Ezra to exclude the righteous, i.e. those who are under the care of God's providence, from this lack of knowledge. [10] *Commentary*, Gen. 18: 20.

[11] *Moreh hamoreh*, iii. 16. [12] *Tsofnat pane'aḥ*, 46. [13] *Emunat ḥakhamim*, vi. 17a.

[14] *Abraham ibn Esra*, 10–11. [15] 'Religionsphilosophie', 62–3.

[16] *History*, 189. See also ibid. 193, where Husik agrees with the commentary attributed to Ibn Kaspi (see above, n. 9). [17] *Philosophies*, 135–6. [18] 'Philosophie', 171. [19] *History*, 107.

[20] *Philosophical Thought*, 256 ff. Cohen's discussion is very comprehensive and discusses all relevant sources. For those who oppose this interpretation, see I. Arama, *Akedat yitshak*, Genesis, Gate 19, 165a–b; Friedlaender, *Essays*, 24; Lipshitz, *Studies . . . Ibn Ezra*, 32–4, 178–80; Frimer and Schwartz, *Life and Thought*, 135.

[21] This seems to be how Ibn Ezra is interpreted by Bonfils, *Tsofnat pane'aḥ*, ad loc.:

וأראה אם עשו כולם כרעה הזאת אף על פי שלא אדעה כלומר אראה ואשגיח
בפרט אף על פי שאינני משגיח תמיד בפרטים . . . ישגיח עליהם ועד עתה לא היה
משגיח . . . ולא היה משגיח השם בהם בתחלה ועל כן אמר ארדה נא ואראה עתה

See also Shem Tov, *Sefer ha'emunot*, 4a; Ibn Ezra, *Commentary*, i. 64 n. 40; Frimer and Schwartz, *Life and Thought*, 174–5. See, however, J. Cohen, *Philosophical Thought*, 264 ff., who explains Ibn Ezra's comment in an Aristotelian fashion.

then be similar to the point made independently by R. Hayim ben Attar,[22] that at times God chooses not to have knowledge of human actions. It is unclear whether this opinion too contradicts Maimonides' Principle. Yet, Principle or not, as far as Maimonides is concerned it is a philosophical impossibility for God to be able to limit himself in this way, just as he is unable to make himself into a body or create another god equal to him.[23]

Among those who oppose Maimonides' Principle, Gersonides famously develops the distinction between God's knowledge of the universal and the particular in Book 3 of his *Milḥamot hashem*. Following in the footsteps of Avicenna,[24] Gersonides argues that God knows particulars in a universal way—that is, in accordance with how they are 'ordered by the universal laws of nature'.[25] But the actual doings of individuals, which are infinite and undergo change through free choice, fall outside God's knowledge and he can do nothing to alter this. It is hard to imagine a view more at odds with traditional Jewish conceptions of God,[26] and Gersonides was indeed subjected to withering criticism. Nevertheless, despite this radical view, Orthodox Jews continue to regard him as one of the outstanding medieval sages (*rishonim*).

The Eleventh Principle

The Eleventh Principle is that of reward and punishment. Although there is considerable disagreement about the nature of this doctrine, with some thinkers, including Maimonides, adopting a naturalistic stance, there is none who denies it outright. However, one cannot help but wonder whether any of the Orthodox spokesmen who have advocated acceptance of the Thirteen Principles are really aware of Maimonides' view of reward and punishment, for it diverges sharply from the mainstream rabbinic tradition.

Without going into great detail, since the issue has recently been discussed by Menachem Kellner,[27] it can be stated that according to Maimonides there is no heavenly reward for the performance of *mitsvot* per se. As he makes clear on a number of occasions in the *Guide*, and as his opponents were well aware,[28]

---

[22] *Or haḥayim* on Gen. 6: 5. See the discussion of his view in Novak, 'Self-Contraction', 311–12. Cf. Ricchi, *Yosher levav*, ii. 1: 3–6 (pp. 29*b*–30*b*), who claims that God chooses not to be aware of the future.

[23] See also Hefetz, *Melekhet maḥshevet*, 162*a*.   [24] See Marmura, 'Avicenna's Theory'.

[25] Husik, *History*, 345. For detailed discussion of Gersonides' view, as well as a translation of the relevant texts, see Samuelson, *Gersonides*.

[26] See e.g. Kellner, 'Gersonides, Providence'.   [27] *Must a Jew Believe Anything?*, appendix 1.

[28] See Crescas, *Or hashem*, ii. 6: 1 (see W. Z. Harvey, 'Critique'); Aaron ben Elijah, *Ets ḥayim*, chs. 88, 105 (see Husik, *History*, 384, and D. Frank, 'Religious Philosophy', p. civ); Joseph Ibn Yaḥya, *Torah or*, ch. 8; Abarbanel, commentary on *Guide* i. 1; id., *Mifalot elokim*, viii. 8; Shem Tov, *Sefer*

Maimonides believed that immortality is entirely consequent upon an intellectual grasp of divine things. He states this explicitly in *Guide* iii. 27:

[Man's] ultimate perfection is to become rational *in actu*, I mean to have an intellect *in actu*; this would consist in his knowing everything concerning all the beings that it is within the capacity of man to know in accordance with his ultimate perfection. It is clear that to this ultimate perfection there do not belong either actions or moral qualities and that it consists of opinions toward which speculation has led and that investigation has rendered compulsory. . . . Once the first perfection [perfection of the body] has been achieved, it is possible to achieve the ultimate, which is indubitably more noble and is *the only cause of permanent preservation*.[29]

In *Guide* iii. 54 he writes similarly:

The fourth species is the true human perfection; it consists in the acquisition of the rational virtues—I refer to the conception of intelligibles, which teach true opinions concerning the divine things. This is in true reality the ultimate end; this is what gives the individual true perfection, a perfection belonging to him alone; and it gives him permanent perdurance; through it man is man.[30]

In fact, this radical view of Maimonides, that intellect is the source of immortality, is also stated explicitly in his *Commentary on the Mishnah*[31] as well as in the *Mishneh torah*.[32] Although Abarbanel terms this view 'a nonsensical falsehood and repugnant opinion',[33] it was also held by Ibn Ezra,[34] R. Abraham ibn Daud,[35] R. Samuel ibn Tibbon,[36] R. Jacob Anatoli,[37] Gersonides,[38] and, apparently, R. Netanel ben Isaiah (fourteenth century).[39]

There are, to be sure, passages in Maimonides' non-philosophical writings which give a different impression, namely, that the performance of *mitsvot*

---

ha'emunot, i. 1; Luzzatto, *Studies*, ii. 168, 183–4; id., *Letters*, 247; id., *Yesodei hatorah*, 71. For a typical example of apologetics in seeking to remove the radicalism of Maimonides' position, see R. Hayim Bleich's introduction to Ankawa, *Sha'ar kevod hashem*, 11 ff. (2nd pagination).

[29] Emphasis added. As Ibn Kaspi, ad loc., points out, Maimonides' view follows that of Aristotle; see *Nicomachean Ethics*, x. 7.

[30] See also *Guide* i. 30, 70, and the complete discussion in Altmann, *Aufklärung*, 60–91.

[31] *Commentary on Mishnah, San.*, 138: 'The survival of the soul consists in the survival of the objects of its knowledge inasmuch as the one is identical with the other.' This passage is part of Maimonides' Introduction to Mishnah *San.*, ch. 10, where the Thirteen Principles also appear.

[32] 'Hilkhot yesodei hatorah', 4: 9, 'Hilkhot teshuvah', 8: 2–3, 'Hilkhot mezuzah', 6: 13.

[33] *Mifalot elokim*, viii. 6.

[34] See Friedlander, *Essays*, 24 ff.; J. Cohen, *Philosophical Thought*, 268 ff., 286 ff.

[35] *Ha'emunah haramah*, i. 7.   [36] See Ravitzky, 'Samuel', 102 ff.

[37] See Gordon, 'Rationalism', 301 ff. As Gordon shows, Anatoli actually required very little in the way of intellectual attainment in order to achieve some degree of immortality.

[38] *Milhamot hashem*, Book I.

[39] *Maor ha'afelah*, 26. This view was also held by some of the 15th- and 16th-cent. rabbis of Saddeh, Yemen: see their letter published in J. Kafih, *Writings*, iii. 1219–20.

also leads to heavenly reward.[40] That different emphases and even outright contradictions appear in Maimonides' works is of course well known, but with regard to these contradictions, or at least some of them, it seems possible to come to a resolution. For example, when Maimonides speaks of the performance of *mitsvot* leading to heavenly reward in his commentary on Mishnah *Makot* 3: 17, one must pay careful attention to his stress on performing the *mitsvah* 'properly', with 'the most complete perfection', and 'for its own sake out of love'. These are code words pointing to an intellectual element—a knowledge of the Divine.[41] In other words, as R. Joseph Kafih (1917–2000) stresses, Maimonides is stating that performance of *mitsvot* *together* with their intellectual component leads to immortality.[42] It is not the performance of a *mitsvah* per se that brings immortality, but the philosophical knowledge that accompanies this performance.

This connection between observance of the *mitsvot* and knowledge of divine things as a prerequisite for immortality is also seen quite clearly in the *Mishneh torah*. For example, in 'Hilkhot teshuvah' 9: 1 Maimonides begins by pointing out that there is a heavenly reward for observing the *mitsvot*; later in the paragraph, however, he clarifies that this reward comes to someone who observes the *mitsvot* and *also* 'knows it [i.e. the Torah] with a complete and correct knowledge'. This 'complete and correct knowledge' refers to knowledge of divine things. Throughout this passage Maimonides continues to stress the combination of *mitsvot* and intellectual attainments as a prerequisite for heavenly reward:

According to the greatness of his deeds and abundance of his knowledge will be the measure in which he will attain that [heavenly] life. . . . Thus we will not be engaged all our days in providing for our bodily needs, but will have leisure to study wisdom and fulfil the commandments and thus attain life in the world to come. . . . For if wisdom is not acquired and good deeds are not performed here, there will be nothing meriting a recompense hereafter.

In 'Hilkhot teshuvah' 10: 1 we find the same approach: 'Let not a man say, "I will observe the precepts of the Torah and occupy myself with its wisdom . . . in order to attain life in the world to come."' Thus we may conclude that, while Maimonides certainly regarded the *mitsvot* as central to Jewish life, he believed that without the accompaniment of the knowledge of divine things

---

[40] See e.g. his comment on Mishnah *Mak.* 3: 17; *Mishneh torah*, 'Hilkhot teshuvah', 9: 1, 'Hilkhot isurei biah', 14: 3. See also *Letters*, ed. Shailat, i. 51, that all who are martyred receive a portion in the world to come.

[41] See W. Z. Harvey, 'Critique', 114–15. For the claim that love of God means knowledge of him, see Maimonides, *Shemoneh perakim*, ch. 5, *Mishneh torah*, 'Hilkhot yesodei hatorah', 2: 2, *Guide* i. 39.

[42] See his commentary on *Mishneh torah*, 'Hilkhot isurei biah', 14: 3.

the *mitsvot* alone do not bring heavenly reward. In fact, as already noted, according to Maimonides immortality should not even be regarded as a 'reward' bestowed by God, but rather as something that man achieves in a completely natural fashion. This is what Maimonides means by 'heavenly reward'.[43]

The flip side of heavenly reward is divine punishment, which is traditionally understood as some sort of torment suffered in the afterlife. However, Maimonides' entire philosophical approach to the attainment of immortality leads to the conclusion that if one does not achieve the world to come (in other words, if one dies without attaining some knowledge of divine things), then one simply ceases to exist. Since the soul has not achieved any immortal knowledge, it cannot live on. In other words, there is no continuing punishment after death.[44] In this conception, when Maimonides speaks of people who are punished after death and yet retain their share in the world to come,[45] the 'punishment' is simply a lesser 'heavenly reward', but not any active form of suffering.

Of course, reward and punishment do not merely refer to what happens after death. Here too Maimonides parts company with the traditional Jewish belief that God is responsible for all that happens to a person in this world. Throughout history Jews have regarded their sufferings as divine punishment and their successes as divine reward. Not surprisingly, this viewpoint is reflected throughout the Jewish liturgy, most vividly in the High Holiday service, where the worshipper testifies that God determines the fate of every individual for the coming year.

In his halakhic writings Maimonides also uses this type of religious language.[46] In the *Guide*, however, where he explains his view of providence at length,[47] he paints a completely different picture. Here he asserts that the extent of a person's divine providence depends on his or her understanding of divine things.[48] The closer intellectually one is to God, the more one is under the watchful eye of providence. According to this view, bad things happen to people, not as a direct result of God ordering them to occur, but as a result of the lack of divine providence which leaves people open to all sorts of

---

[43] See H. Kasher, '"Torah"', 157. Me'iri offers a similar naturalistic view of how one attains the world to come: 'The wise one [*hehakham*] said, concerning this, that the world to come is not a reward for one's actions but their fruit, in other words, it derives from them like a fruit from a tree': *Ḥibur hateshuvah*, 541. See also ibid. 441, where Me'iri quotes this assessment in the name of *ḥakhmei hamada*. However, he does not completely share Maimonides' intellectualism, for he believes that the performance of *mitsvot* also gives one immortality. See Halbertal, *Between Torah and Wisdom*, 30.   [44] See Kellner, *Must a Jew Believe Anything?*, 132 n. 12.

[45] *Mishneh torah*, 'Hilkhot teshuvah', 6: 1.   [46] Ibid. 3: 3, 5.   [47] *Guide* iii. 16–18, 51.

[48] On the role of the *mitsvot* as a means to this end, see Kellner, *Must a Jew Believe Anything?*, 135 ff.

misfortunes. Thus, contrary to the usual view of God punishing people, for example, by giving them a disease, in Maimonides' opinion the disease is not an active punishment sent by God but simply the chance outcome for people left without divine providence. Whether a particular individual will contract the disease, and if so, how bad it will be, is not due to God's intervention but is a result of God's providence being removed, thus allowing the natural world to operate unfettered. Speaking of those who are completely ignorant, Maimonides states that they are like animals. Just as animals cannot grasp intelligibles, and their lives are therefore entirely given over to chance, so too the completely ignorant do not benefit from any measure of providence. Thus, when Maimonides speaks of God decreeing death on someone as a punishment for his sins, this statement must be understood as only symbolically true, not literally so.

The Messiah; Resurrection of the Dead

⟡

The Twelfth Principle

THE TWELFTH PRINCIPLE is the coming of the messiah.[1] It is somewhat surprising that although Maimonides speaks of the revival of the
Davidic dynasty, he says nothing in this Principle about what else will occur in
messianic days. While it is true that Maimonides discouraged speculation
about the details of the messianic era, since there is no authoritative tradition in
these matters,[2] one wonders why he did not include any of the basic messianic
concepts about which there is no dispute in rabbinic literature, such as that
'there will be neither famine nor war'.[3] Since Maimonides omits these central
elements of the messianic idea, it is significant that he includes the following,
which he obviously did not regard as an unimportant detail: 'Included in this
fundamental Principle is that there will be no king of Israel except from David
and from the seed of Solomon exclusively. Whosoever disputes [the sovereignty
of] this family denies God and the words of His prophets.'

This stress on an actual messianic figure is noteworthy, since a number of
prophets and midrashim appear to disregard it. These sources speak instead
of a messianic era in which God alone will be the redeemer, and there is no
mention of a messiah–king. As Jacobs points out, this conception is found in
Nahum, Zephaniah, Habakkuk, Malachi, Joel, and Daniel.[4] In the sixteenth
century R. Samuel Jaffe ben Isaac Ashkenazi, the renowned midrashic commentator, pointed to some other biblical texts that in his opinion ruled out
any notion of a personal messiah.[5] For example, Jeremiah 31: 10 states: 'He
that scattered Israel doth gather him.' Isaiah 11: 12 says: 'And He will set up an
ensign for the nations, and will assemble the dispersed of Israel.' According to
Ashkenazi, the meaning of these verses is that God himself will redeem the
Jews.

Among midrashim that share this conception, R. Menahem M. Kasher[6]
points to *Midrash tanḥuma*:[7]

---

[1] On Maimonides' understanding of the messianic era, see Ravitzky, *Al da'at hamakom*, 74–104;
Kraemer, 'Messianic Posture'.   [2] *Mishneh torah*, 'Hilkhot melakhim', 12: 2.   [3] Ibid. 2: 5.
[4] See Jacobs, *Principles*, 373.   [5] *Yefeh to'ar* on *Bereshit rabah* 98: 14.
[6] *Hatekufah hagedolah*, 118. In addition to the two midrashim I quote, Kasher adduces two more
examples from *Midrash tehilim*.   [7] 'Aḥarei mot', 12.

God said: 'In this world you were redeemed by humans. In Egypt [you were redeemed] through Moses and Aaron, in the days of Sisera through Barak and Deborah, among the Midianites [read: Philistines] though Shamgar the son of Anath, as it says: *And he also saved Israel* (Judg. 3: 31), and also through the Judges. Since they were human therefore you continued to be enslaved, but in the future I Myself will redeem you and you will never again be enslaved, as it says: *O Israel, that art saved by the Lord with an everlasting salvation* (Isa. 45: 17).'

Midrash tehilim (107: 1) expresses the same idea:

Rabbi Berechiah said in the name of Rabbi Helbo who taught in the name of Rabbi Samuel: Who are meant by *the redeemed* in *Let the redeemed of the Lord say* (Ps. 107: 2)? The people of Israel. Isaiah made this explicit in saying: *And the ransomed of the Lord shall return and come with singing unto Zion* (Isa. 35: 10). He did not say 'the ransomed of Elijah', nor 'the ransomed of the king Messiah', but *the ransomed of the Lord*. Even so, the Psalm speaks of *the redeemed of the Lord*.

According to Kasher, denial of a personal messiah, in accordance with these midrashim, is 'perhaps' to be regarded as an acceptable belief.[8]

Going further than Kasher, Isaiah Levy, a contemporary rabbinic scholar, states without hesitation that 'anyone who believes in the coming of the redemption, either through the Son of David or by the hand of God Himself, is not to be regarded as a heretic'.[9] In fact, he claims that even Maimonides agrees with this, for although the Twelfth Principle speaks of a personal messiah, Levy notes that when Maimonides lists various types of heretic in *Mishneh torah*, 'Hilkhot teshuvah', 5: 6, he speaks of one who denies 'the coming of a redeemer', a designation that can also apply to God. However, contrary to Levy, there is no reason to doubt that this text indeed refers to a human messiah. Furthermore, in another *Mishneh torah* passage, 'Hilkhot melakhim', 11: 1, Maimonides writes that 'one who does not look forward to the coming of the Messiah denies not only the teachings of the prophets but also those of the Law and Moses our Teacher'. He then cites biblical verses in support of this contention. Although Levy points out that these verses can also be understood to speak of a messianic era rather than a personal messiah, and this may indeed be Maimonides' hidden teaching, his exoteric view, as seen in the *Commentary on the Mishnah* and the *Mishneh torah*, is clear: denial of a personal messiah is heresy.

While the midrashic texts mentioned previously exclude any mention of a personal messiah, they do retain the notion of a future messianic era. In contrast, there is a radical opinion in the Talmud which goes so far as to reject the

---

[8] *Hatekufah hagedolah*, 145. In support of this contention, Kasher also cites R. Hillel, as interpreted by 'Rashi' (see n. 10 below).   [9] 'Resurrection', 786.

messianic idea in its entirety. According to the *amora* R. Hillel, 'There shall be no messiah for Israel, because they have already enjoyed him in the days of Hezekiah.'[10] Upon hearing this apparently heretical statement, R. Joseph responded, 'May his Master [God] forgive him [for saying so].' It is concerning this view of R. Hillel that R. J. David Bleich makes a number of significant points. After pointing out that matters of belief are 'inherently matters of *Halakhah*', he continues:

The concept of the Messiah is one example of a fundamental principle of belief concerning which, at one point in Jewish history, there existed a legitimate divergence of opinion, since resolved normatively. . . . Rav Hillel certainly denied that reestablishment of the monarchy and restoration of the Davidic dynasty are essential components of the process of redemption. Rabbi Moses Sofer quite cogently points out that were such views to be held by a contemporary Jew he would be branded a heretic.[11] Yet, the advancement of this opinion by one of the sages of the Talmud carried with it no theological odium. The explanation is quite simple. Before the authoritative formulation of the *Halakhah* with regard to this belief, Rav Hillel's opinion could be entertained. Following the resolution of the conflict in a manner which negates this theory, normative *Halakhah* demands acceptance of the belief that the redemption will be effected through the agency of a mortal messiah.[12]

This passage is problematic for several reasons. To begin with, we have already seen that Maimonides explicitly states that issues of belief are not matters of halakhah that can be decided using the method described by Bleich. Furthermore, Bleich's analogy of principles of faith and halakhah fails for

[10] BT *San.* 99a. In identifying R. Hillel as an *amora* I am relying upon Urbach, *Sages*, 680–1. Others identify him as a *tana*. Regarding this passage, see also Hadas-Lebel, 'Il n'y a pas de messie pour Israël'. According to the commentary attributed to Rashi, R. Hillel only denies a personal messiah, but acknowledges that there will be a messianic era. (There is widespread agreement among both academic and traditional scholars that another medieval sage, perhaps R. Judah b. Nathan, Rashi's son-in-law, wrote the commentary on the last chapter of *Sanhedrin*. See Lieberman, *Sheki'in*, 92 ff.; Y. H. Sofer, *Torat ya'akov*, 884–5; Grossman, *Early Sages*, 217 n. 278. Grossman also refers to those scholars who disagree with this assessment.) As Herzog, *Decisions*, ii. 533, points out, according to 'Rashi's' understanding, 'R. Hillel's view accentuates, rather than limits, the miraculous nature of the ultimate redemption'. See, however, BT *San.* 98b where Rav is quoted as saying that in messianic days the Jews will have years of plenty. In answer to the question that this is obvious, the Talmud replies that Rav's statement was made in opposition to R. Hillel, who maintained that there would be no messiah for Israel. This clearly implies that R. Hillel believed that there would be no years of plenty in Israel's future, i.e. no messianic era whatsoever, and this is how he is understood by R. Meir Abulafia in his *Yad ramah*. See also Schechter, *Aspects*, 346; Marmorstein, 'Messianische Bewegung', 176 n. 1. Forced reinterpretation of R. Hillel's view came about, as is sometimes stated explicitly, simply because many viewed it as impossible that an *amora* would deny something so basic to Judaism. A good example of such reinterpretation is Abarbanel's view that all R. Hillel meant was that 'the messiah would not come by virtue of Israel's meriting him'. See *Rosh amanah*, ch. 14. For other reinterpretations of R. Hillel's statement, see M. Kasher, *Hatekufah hagedolah*, 133 ff.

[11] *She'elot uteshuvot*, 'Yoreh de'ah', no. 356.   [12] *With Perfect Faith*, 4.

another reason. Unlike matters of belief, it is essential for halakhic disputes to be settled because everyone must know how to act. This is a purely practical consideration, entirely absent when dealing with matters of belief. In fact, when it comes to deciding halakhah, Jewish scholars never claimed infallibility. On the contrary, the famous story of the 'oven of Akhnai' (BT *Bava metsia* 59*b*) shows us that, in the sages' minds, human consensus outweighs even divine original intent. Central to this understanding of the halakhic process is that one can continue to believe in the correctness of one's halakhic position even if the final halakhah has been decided otherwise. It is forbidden to advocate a rejected position only if this is done for the sake of practical application. Even in the days of the Sanhedrin it was this, and this alone, which turned a dissenting sage into a *zaken mamre* (rebellious elder).[13] Theoretical disagreement with the accepted halakhah is always permissible, and the sage in the minority remains hopeful that his view will be adopted at some future time.[14] Contrary to Bleich, if I were to make an analogy between halakhah and matters of belief, it would be between the *theoretical* halakhah — where an authoritative sage's view still retains its legitimacy even if it is not accepted — and matters of belief advocated by such a sage. The latter are also theoretical and cannot therefore be delegitimized simply because the majority of sages disagree.

However, as far as Maimonides is concerned, true principles of faith are not *and have never been* subject to debate. As we have seen, anyone who even expresses a doubt about a Principle, not to mention denying it outright, is a heretic with no share in the world to come. This judgement is applicable to the years before Maimonides as well as to those after him. In fact, I am unaware of any *rishonim* who hold the view Bleich describes.[15] Furthermore, I

---

[13] Mishnah *San.* 11: 2; *Mishneh torah*, 'Hilkhot mamrim', 3: 6, 8.   [14] See Mishnah *Edu.* 1: 5.

[15] It is, however, the view of R. Moses Sofer (*She'elot uteshuvot*, 'Yoreh de'ah', no. 356). R. Abraham I. Kook, *Ma'amrei hare'iyah*, 105, also sees the majority principle as valid in matters of belief, even if it means rejecting the view of Maimonides (see, however, ibid. 56, where Kook discounts this approach). In *Igerot hare'iyah*, i, no. 302, Kook cites Maimonides' view that 'in matters of opinions [*de'ot*] there is no *pesak halakhah*'. He claims that this is in line with the Babylonian Talmud as well as R. Bahya ibn Pakuda, *Hovot halevavot*, introduction (s.v. *ha'ehad*), who says that Deut. 17: 8–10, which speaks of disputes being brought to the judges for ultimate decision, does not refer to matters of theology. Kook also cites the Jerusalem Talmud, which he believes holds that in matters of *de'ot* there are indeed binding halakhic decisions. In *Igerot hare'iyah*, i, no. 103, he makes the same point, but adds that the Jerusalem Talmud's position is a 'Land of Israel' position. For those in the Diaspora, who do not reach the spiritual heights found in the Land of Israel (and this includes the authors of the Babylonian Talmud), theological matters, which are the basic feature of *agadah*, have no connection to halakhah and there is no binding halakhic authority with regard to them. See also *Igerot hare'iyah*, iii, no. 793. Since my major concern is with Maimonides' view, I have only touched the surface of this complicated question. A separate study is needed in order to provide a comprehensive analysis of views of *rishonim* and *aharonim* concerning whether matters of belief (both principles and less important issues) can be decided in a halakhic fashion.

do not believe that there are any *rishonim*, and certainly not Maimonides, who believed that R. Hillel's opinion could ever be entertained. In their mind it was always regarded as being a mistaken, if not heretical, opinion, and for that reason was rejected by R. Joseph. When Maimonides lists the coming of the messiah as a principle of faith he is not deciding between two contradictory opinions but merely giving the only opinion on the subject. As far as he is concerned, a mistaken and even heretical utterance by one of the *amora'im* does not suffice to create a valid opinion which he must then consider in rendering a 'decision'. Had he thought otherwise, the doctrine of the messiah would not have been listed as a dogma (unless it was to be understood as a 'necessary belief').

Since Bleich has inserted this principle of faith (and indeed all of Jewish theology) in a halakhic context, I will use a halakhic example from his own writings to illustrate my point further.[16] It is a well-established halakhah, perhaps even of biblical authority, that the Jewish status of an individual is determined by the mother. Needless to say, this is also how Maimonides records the law.[17] The fact that there is one opinion in the Talmud[18] that disagrees with this law does not mean that Maimonides, or the Talmud for that matter, ever 'ruled' on the issue. Rather, the law was always clear and unambiguous. The errant statement by someone who lived in talmudic times did not change matters. *This was not a valid opinion which needed to be considered.* Indeed, it was not an opinion at all, as far as Jewish law is concerned. Rather, as the Talmud states, the originator of it (Jacob of Naburaya) was to be flogged. When Maimonides recorded the halakhah, he was simply recording the one, and only, opinion which had the stamp of truth. Similarly, the talmudic rabbis and Maimonides never *decided* that the coming of the messiah was a dogma. They simply expressed what they believed to be the indisputable view of the Torah.

As for Bleich's contention that R. Hillel's view carried no theological odium, this is certainly difficult to fathom. R. Joseph's reply, 'May God forgive him', undoubtedly shows that Bleich is mistaken. As R. Abraham Bibago puts it, 'They prayed to God so that He would forgive him for his heresy'

---

[16] *Contemporary Halachic Problems*, 96–102.

[17] *Mishneh torah*, 'Hilkhot yibum veḥalitsah', 1: 4, 'Hilkhot isurei biah', 12: 7.

[18] JT *Kid.* 3: 12 and parallels. I refer to a certain Jacob of Naburaya. Bleich calls him a 'talmudic sage'. Whoever he was, he certainly was no sage: a sage would not have been ignorant of such an obvious law. In *Bereshit rabah* 7: 2 and parallels, we find another opinion of Jacob of Naburaya which is equally outrageous. Either in total ignorance of, or rebellion against, the halakhah, he claimed that one needed to ritually slaughter fish. In *Kohelet rabati* 7: 47, he is referred to as a 'sinner', and put in the same category as Elisha (b. Avuyah?) and other heretics. See the complete discussion in Irsai, 'Yaakov'.

(*haminut vehakefirah*).[19] If, as Bleich claims, this was indeed 'a legitimate divergence of opinion', why would R. Hillel need God's forgiveness? In the absence of any retraction, he is certainly to be regarded as a heretic according to Maimonides. Albo makes this perfectly clear and says nothing about any 'legitimate divergence of opinion, since resolved normatively'.[20] Like Maimonides, Albo believes that there is only one opinion which was ever valid and that R. Hillel's opinion is heretical. However, according to Albo, one who errs unintentionally regarding a principle of faith, although he has sinned, is not to be regarded as a heretic. In other words, R. Hillel's view was heretical, but this did not mean that he himself was a heretic. Alternatively, and in contradiction to this approach, Albo suggests that, although R. Hillel sinned by this belief, denial of the messiah is not the equivalent of denying the entire Torah, and that therefore he is not to be regarded as a heretic.[21]

David Weiss Halivni has recently commented on the passage in BT *Sanhedrin* 99*a* and his words, exactly the opposite of Bleich's, also deserve to be quoted at length:

Issues of doctrine, in contrast [to halakhah], cannot be definitively settled merely through the consensus suggested by a vote of the majority nor by the judgment rendered by the passage of history. . . . Quantitative superiority can play no role in the qualitative realm of speculation. Although matters of science, logic, and theology—of objective reality—can be debated, they cannot ultimately be settled in the chambers of the Sanhedrin. Additionally, a theological doctrine that was once considered legitimate cannot simply be branded heretical through the mere passing of time, for historical, and thus contingent, factors have no role to play in the resolution of purely intellectual matters. If an authoritative figure in the Jewish past maintained a certain speculative standpoint, the truth or falsity of such cannot be determined by tradition or consensus, and thus its legitimacy cannot be judged by the systemic principles which govern the halakhic process. Avenues of intellec-

---

[19] *Derekh emunah*, 102*b*. See also the similar comment of E. Delmedigo, *Behinat hadat*, 87: 'The sages said about him that which is said concerning those who profane God's name and who are involved with heretical books. Their saying is "May God forgive Hillel." We see therefore that they thought that one who makes this statement [about the messiah] is like a heretic.' According to 'Rashi's' reinterpretation (see above, n. 10), R. Hillel's view was merely mistaken but not heretical. This is seen from how he explains R. Joseph's reply: 'May God forgive him, for what he said is incorrect.' But even 'Rashi' does not hold Bleich's view. According to 'Rashi', R. Hillel never had the right to advance his view. It was always regarded as being in error and he therefore needed God's forgiveness.

[20] See *Sefer ha'ikarim*, i. 1: 'According to Maimonides this sage would have to be classed as a heretic and excluded from a share in the world to come.'

[21] Ibid. 1–2. Albo's second position is also advocated in Cohn, *Ma'aseh tuviyah*, 'Olam ha'elyon', *ma'amar* 6, ch. 1 (called to my attention by David S. Zinberg). R. Simeon Duran, *Ohev mishpat*, 14*b*–15*a*, has a similar, but not identical, formulation. See also Ibn Zimra, *She'elot uteshuvot haradbaz*, no. 1258; Wasserman, *Kovets ma'amarim*, 19.

tual speculation once considered theologically sound cannot be thwarted merely because they are no longer popular.[22]

Chaim Rapoport has similarly written:

It borders on the absurd to suggest that theological truths depend upon the temporal state of the majority opinion. If one were to assume such an approach to theological matters, one would possibly have to conclude that one who in the middle ages believed in the doctrine of *gilgul neshamot* (the reincarnation or transmigration of souls) was a heretic, whereas one who nowadays does not subscribe to this belief is a heretic. Could it be that whether or not souls are reincarnated depends upon the majority opinion?[23]

I agree entirely with these sentiments. Indeed, Maimonides himself writes, with reference to speculative matters:

For when something has been demonstrated,[24] the correctness of the matter is not increased and certainty regarding it is not strengthened by the consensus of all men of knowledge with regard to it. Nor could its correctness be diminished and certainty regarding it be weakened even if all the people on earth disagreed with it.[25]

However, Weiss Halivni continues with a more problematic assertion:

The famous passage in *b. Sanh.* 99a that discusses the dating of the messianic era illustrates the continued viability, despite unpopularity, of minority theological positions. . . . The fact that R. Hillel's opinion was recorded and transmitted in the Talmud despite its obvious unpopularity exhibits the multifariousness and license of rabbinic theology, and preserves this speculative viewpoint as a viable one within the spectrum of traditional Jewish thought.[26] One would have expected,

---

[22] *Peshat*, 94–6.　　　　　　　　　　　　　　　　　　　[23] *Messiah*, 114.

[24] We obviously do not feel as confident as Maimonides concerning the possibility of demonstrating such matters.　　　　　　　　　　　　　　　　[25] *Guide* ii. 15.

[26] In a note, Weiss Halivni cites Albo, *Sefer ha'ikarim*, i. 1. However, as I have already pointed out (p. 34), Albo did not think that denial of the messiah was an acceptable option. In this chapter Albo states that denial of the messiah is a sin and elsewhere (i. 23) he says it is heresy! The following are Albo's exact words in i. 1: 'R. Hillel was guilty of a sin for not believing in the coming of the redeemer, but he was not a heretic.' In i. 2, Albo states that this is called 'sinning through error', and such a sin requires atonement. In iv. 42 Albo writes: 'Every adherent of the Law of Moses is obliged to believe in the coming of the Messiah.'

Having seen what Albo's true view of the messiah is, it is instructive to compare this to what Graetz wrote (*Structure*, 167), for the number of errors in one sentence is staggering. Albo's opinion, according to Graetz, is that the 'messianic belief was definitely not a basic article or dogma of Judaism, that it was merely a tradition[!], and that a disbelief in the coming of the Messiah could never[!] be labelled heresy since even some[!] Talmudic teachers had repudiated it.' Graetz continues by saying that, because of Albo's view, Abarbanel accused him of heresy. He provides no source for this latter comment, which is not surprising since Abarbanel never makes such an accusation. Equally unfounded is Steven Schwarzschild's assertion: 'In effect, Albo proclaimed not only that a Jew need not necessarily believe in the Messiah but actually, by implication, recommended against such belief[!].' See id., 'Personal Messiah', 20.

not unreasonably, that such a controversial theological claim would be purpose-fully excluded from the purview of rabbinic literature.[27]

The problem with Weiss Halivni's point is his assumption that, because the Talmud records the view of R. Hillel, this makes it a 'viable' option in traditional Jewish thought. As far as I know, no traditional authority has ever advocated this position. By adopting Weiss Halivni's approach, one could even say that the view of Jacob of Naburaya was a viable halakhic alternative before it was rejected by the majority. I have already shown the untenability of this view. Had R. Hillel's view been recorded in the name of a significant figure, I would agree with Weiss Halivni. However, as Bibago points out, R. Hillel does not merit such a classification, since he was only a minor scholar.[28] For the same reason that I have refrained from quoting the views of Isaac Albalag, Moses of Narbonne, and Isaiah Leibowitz—men who were never regarded as authority figures—one should also not quote R. Hillel when seeking to define traditional Jewish thought.

Weiss Halivni anticipated this objection by claiming that the Talmud would not have recorded this passage if it did not see it as being viable. How-ever, the same point could be made regarding passages in which the Talmud quotes the views of sectarians. Are we thus to say that the opinions of sect-arians are also viable? As Weiss Halivni well knows, these passages are quoted in order to be refuted, and R. Moses Sofer makes the very same point with regard to R. Hillel's view, i.e. that it was only recorded in order to show its untenability.[29] Even if this were not the case with regard to R. Hillel's view, and indeed Albo specifically rejects this approach,[30] I know of no traditional Jewish sources which assert that *every* rabbinic view mentioned in the Talmud or Midrash has validity and must be taken seriously.[31] Certainly no tradition-al Jewish thinker has ever granted validity to R. Hillel's view.

Returning to Maimonides, it is worth mentioning R. Abraham Hayim Viterbo's sharp criticism of him for including the messianic belief among his Principles. While he acknowledged that all are obligated to believe in Maimon-ides' Principles, he agreed with Albo that if someone is led through study to

---

[27] *Peshat*, 96.

[28] *Derekh emunah*, 102*b*. He also claims that R. Hillel was one of the last *amora'im*, but this may not be correct.

[29] This is what Sofer means when he writes: והא דתני׳ במס׳ עדיות למה נישנו דברי היחיד ע״ש מילתא אחריתי כמובן. Sofer directs the reader to look at Mishnah *Edu.* 1: 6 and *not* 1: 5. The same point was made earlier by the 15th-cent. R. Hayim ibn Musa; see Lawee, '"Israel has no Messiah"', 267.

[30] *Sefer ha'ikarim*, i. 1.

[31] I am well aware that there are numerous sources which pay lip service to this notion. However, after they have explained the 'objectionable' passages, what we are left with usually bears little resemb-lance to the text's original meaning.

disagree with them he is not a heretic. Viterbo's polemic against Maimonides is noteworthy, because while Albo attempted to uphold the importance of the messianic idea while still defending the unwitting non-believer, Viterbo's defence leads to a significant downgrading of the doctrine's importance. After noting that Maimonides had included the coming of the messiah among his Principles, and, in the *Mishneh torah*, had counted those who deny this among the heretics,[32] Viterbo writes:

This is wondrous. From where did he derive it? Moses our teacher did not speak of this at all and did not require us to believe in the coming of the redeemer. How then can the Rabbi say that one who does not believe in his coming, even though he observes all the commandments of God, the Torah and its laws, is a complete heretic and is not regarded as one of Israel? . . . For this is not a Torah matter nor even *a halakhah lemosheh misinai* ['a law given to Moses at Sinai'] but a rabbinic matter . . . and many outstanding people[!] from our nation did not believe in it, and nevertheless the sages of the Talmud did not, Heaven forbid, separate them from the community and refer to them as heretics. . . . If one denies the coming of the redeemer and believes that God will reward and punish in the next world, giving everyone his due in accordance with his actions, whether good or bad, and holds to the opinion of Rabbi Hillel, why does the Rabbi remove him from the people of Israel? . . . After all, he believes in reward and punishment.[33]

Another significant point in the Twelfth Principle is that Maimonides says that the messiah will be descended from Solomon. R. Joseph Kafih apparently did not consider this section essential (i.e. that denial of it equals heresy). I say this because in his note on the passage, he explains this formulation as directed against the Christians, who trace Jesus' lineage to Nathan, another son of David.[34] Since Kafih explains this point as the result of polemical considerations, he implies that it would not be included in the Principle in the absence of these considerations. In fact, the stipulation of Solomonic descent is missing from Maimonides' discussion of the messiah in the *Mishneh torah*, where only Davidic descent is mentioned.[35] However, Kafih's point is only speculative, and I doubt that Maimonides knew anything about the genealogy of Jesus recorded in the New Testament. The fact is that Maimonides *does* include Solomonic descent as part of the Principle, denial of which *is* equated with heresy. As he puts it: 'Included in this fundamental Principle is that there will be no king of Israel except from David and from the seed of Solomon exclusively. Whoever disputes [the sovereignty of] this family denies God and the words of His prophets.' One must conclude from this that even

---

[32] 'Hilkhot teshuvah', 3: 6.   [33] *Emunat ḥakhamim*, 26–7.
[34] This is not entirely correct. While Luke 3: 31 gives Nathan as the ancestor of Jesus, Matthew 1: 6 has Solomon as Jesus' forefather.   [35] 'Hilkhot melakhim', 11: 1.

if there had never been a Christian religion, Maimonides would still have considered it obligatory to believe that the messiah would be of Solomonic descent.

Before noting the sources that disagree with Maimonides, it is necessary to call attention to the comments of R. Meir Dan Plotzki (1867–1928). Plotzki notes that, although Maimonides also mentions Solomonic descent in the *Sefer hamitsvot*,[36] this does not appear in the *Mishneh torah*. On the basis of this, Plotzki claims that Maimonides changed his mind and that his final view on the subject excludes Solomonic descent from the messianic doctrine.[37] Not noted by Plotzki is the fact that Maimonides also mentions the necessity of Solomonic descent in his *Letter to Yemen*, another early work.[38] It is certainly significant that, although he mentioned this element in three of his early works, he omitted it when he wrote the *Mishneh torah*. However, it must also be noted that Maimonides' *Commentary on the Mishnah* went through a few different versions, and in a couple of places he even made corrections to the Principles.[39] Despite this, he never altered the original formulation of the Twelfth Principle.

A number of post-Maimonidean scholars did not feel bound by Maimonides' insistence on Solomonic descent. For example, R. Jacob Hazan (thirteenth century), in his discussion of the messianic era, follows the *Mishneh torah* and therefore mentions only Davidic descent.[40] In discussing Jewish kingship, the anonymous *Sefer hahinukh* (thirteenth century) states that it is eternally reserved for the descendants of David, making no mention of Solomonic descent.[41] R. Azariah dei Rossi,[42] R. Gedalyah ibn Yahya,[43] and R. Jehiel Heilprin (1660–1746)[44] each quote without objection the view, falsely attributed to Philo,[45] that all of Solomon's descendants were wiped out and only Nathan's line survived. This opinion is also supported by a statement in the Zohar that the messiah will be descended from Nathan's wife.[46] Although this passage does not explicitly state that the messiah is descended from Nathan, this is the obvious implication, and a recent commentator on the Zohar has elaborated on the kabbalistic reasons behind the choice of Nathan, rather than Solomon, as the messiah's forebear.[47]

---

[36] Negative Commandment no. 362. [37] *Ḥemdat yisra'el*, i. 14b (final numbering).

[38] *Letters*, ed. Shailat, i. 104 (Arabic), 151 (Hebrew).

[39] See Kafih's notes to the Fourth and Seventh Principles. [40] *Ets hayim*, iii. 301 ff.

[41] No. 498. This point is noted in Katan, 'I Believe', 43 n. 3. [42] *Me'or einayim*, ch. 32.

[43] *Shalshelet hakabalah*, 38. In his usual fashion, Ibn Yahya copied the information from dei Rossi without acknowledgement. See Baron, *History*, 315, for Steinschneider's comment regarding Ibn Yahya's plagiarism. [44] *Seder hadorot*, 58a.

[45] See Joanna Weinberg, 'Azaria'. [46] Zohar iii. 173b. See Aptowitzer, *Parteipolitik*, 113 ff.

[47] Daniel Frish, *Matok midevash*, ad loc. See also Chajes, *Kol sifrei*, ii. 523, 528; I. Luria, *Zohar harakia*, 35b; H. E. Shapira, *Divrei torah*, iv, no. 84; and the discussion in Warhaftig, 'Messiah'.

The Thirteenth Principle

The Thirteenth Principle concerns resurrection, the belief that the dead will rise from their graves to live again.[48] Pines has written that many of the Thirteen Principles 'run counter to philosophic truth'.[49] This is nowhere more apparent than in the dogma of resurrection. For Maimonides, the ultimate reward is eternal spiritual life, in which one basks in the glory of God.[50] For someone to be removed from this state of beatitude in order to be placed again in a physical body runs counter to Maimonides' entire conception of eternal life, which, as we have seen, he views as a completely natural phenomenon. Maimonides' claim, expressed in his *Essay on Resurrection*, that the dead will be raised up only to die again and return to eternal spiritual life is even more confusing. The traditional view was always that the righteous would live for ever in their resurrected bodies. As Jacobs puts it, 'So far as we know, Maimonides was the only philosopher in the Middle Ages to commit

Warhaftig calls attention to R. Menahem Azariah da Fano's attempt at a reconciliation between the two views, in that the descendants of Solomon married those of Nathan, which enables the messiah to be descended from both. See da Fano, *Ma'amar me'ah kesitah*, no. 92. Plotzki, *Ḥemdat yisra'el*, i. 14*b*, mentions that there were those who called attention to the conflict between Maimonides and the Zohar in order to find fault with the latter. On this, see Samson Bloch's letter in *Otsar neḥmad*, 1 (1856), 44–5. R. Jacob Emden refers to this passage in his criticism of the Zohar; see *Mitpaḥat sefarim*, 43. R. Moses Kunitz, in his polemic against Emden, *Ben yoḥai*, 89, responds to some of Emden's criticisms of this passage, but does not mention anything regarding Solomonic descent. R. Reuven Rapaport, in his response to Emden entitled *Itur soferim*, printed as an appendix to the Lvov 1871 edition of *Mitpaḥat sefarim*, p. 44, defends the Zohar's position and cites in support of it the passage of 'Philo' mentioned by dei Rossi. See also the anonymous article 'Notes', 155–8.

[48] Although most scholars agree that the doctrine of a general resurrection must be dated to the later biblical period, the notion of resurrection per se is already found in Isa. 26: 19: 'Thy dead shall live, my dead bodies shall arise; Awake and sing, ye that dwell in the dust; for Thy dew is as the dew of light, and the earth shall bring to life the shades.' Other relevant biblical texts include Deut. 32: 39: 'I slay and revive', as well as the stories of Elijah and Elisha raising the dead (1 Kgs. 17: 17 ff., 2 Kgs. 4: 18 ff.). The book of Daniel, in a passage scholars assign to the Maccabean period, states: 'And many of them that sleep in the dust of the earth shall awake, some to everlasting life, and some to reproaches and everlasting abhorrence' (12: 2). The Pharisees later advocated this position and it is recorded in the Mishnah as dogma: 'The following have no portion in the world to come: one who says that resurrection is not a biblical doctrine' (*San.* 10: 1). Resurrection is also mentioned in the second benediction of the daily Amidah prayer. However, Philo never speaks of resurrection and no doubt understood the concept to be identical with immortality of the soul; see H. A. Wolfson, *Philo*, i. 404. Origen (d. 253) refers to Jews who denied resurrection (*Contra Celsum* v. 14, 274), but it is hard to know to whom he is referring. Perhaps these Jews were the last vestiges of those influenced by Sadducean or Essene doctrine, which denied the resurrection. Since the Talmud does not see fit to polemicize against this view, it does not seem to have posed a significant threat to the rabbinic outlook. The Emperor Justinian, however, as late as 553 felt it necessary to declare that Jews were obligated to believe in resurrection of the dead, or suffer dire consequences, showing that this was not a universally held view in the Jewish community. See Kahle, *Geniza*, 316.

[49] Translator's introduction to *The Guide of the Perplexed*, p. cxviii.

[50] See *Commentary on the Mishnah*, San., 138; *Mishneh torah*, 'Hilkhot teshuvah', ch. 8.

himself definitely to the view that the future existence is ultimately incorporeal.'[51]

The fact that resurrection is never discussed in the *Guide* could certainly lead one to believe that Maimonides did not really accept it in its literal sense.[52] Indeed, even Harry A. Wolfson, generally a very conservative Maimonidean scholar, stated that Maimonides 'fought passionately against the literal interpretation of the belief in resurrection'.[53] This was also the opinion of a number of Maimonides' medieval interpreters, who believed that, when Maimonides used the term 'resurrection', he really meant 'the world to come', i.e. eternal spiritual life.[54] Most notable among the medieval figures was Sheshet Benveniste (*c*.1131–1209), who engaged in a polemic on this issue during Maimonides' lifetime.[55] Benveniste stridently insisted that any physical descriptions of the resurrection in traditional texts were only given 'for the sake of fools who are unable to understand'.[56] Maimonides' student Joseph ben Judah ibn Simeon (twelfth–thirteenth centuries), for whom the *Guide* was written, also interpreted resurrection figuratively, forcing Maimonides to clarify his position in a letter to him.[57]

Rabad, in his critical gloss on *Mishneh torah*, 'Hilkhot teshuvah', 8: 2, had already interpreted Maimonides' words in this way, writing: 'The words of this man appear to me to be similar to one who says that there is no resurrection for bodies, but only for souls.' Rabad was led to this view because

[51] *Principles*, 407. As Jacobs (ibid. 406) notes, Ibn Ezra on Dan. 12: 2 may anticipate Maimonides. Yet his comment is not entirely clear, for he writes that in messianic days the righteous will be resurrected and then 'will die a second death only to be resurrected in the world to come'. The question is, does resurrection in the 'world to come' mean eternal spiritual life? Bleich thinks not: see *With Perfect Faith*, 620.

[52] Maimonides mentions resurrection twice in the *Guide*. In i. 70, he quotes BT *Ḥag.* 12*b* concerning 'the dew by means of which the Holy One, blessed be He, will revive the dead'. As Maimonides explains, this 'dew' is not to be understood literally, perhaps implying that the resurrection should also be understood figuratively. In iii. 23 he quotes BT *BB* 16*a* that 'Job denied the resurrection of the dead'.

[53] 'Escaping Judaism', 81 (this passage was called to my attention by Professor Zev Harvey). On the other hand, Arthur Hyman writes: 'To be sure, the literal belief in the resurrection does not fit readily into his philosophic scheme, but I see no reason to classify him with such Muslim philosophers as Avicenna who consider the principle as a concession to the imagination of the masses who can only conceive of the existence of corporeal substances'. See id., *Eschatological Themes*, 79.

[54] In a number of talmudic passages, the phrase 'the world to come' refers to the era following the resurrection, in which the righteous will live for ever in their resurrected bodies. This is also how it was understood by Maimonides' opponents. The abode of the souls after death was referred to as 'the Garden of Eden'. See Nahmanides, *Kitvei ramban*, ii. 294 ff.; Albeck, *Mishnah: Nezikin*, 454.

[55] See Benveniste's letter published in Alexander Marx, 'Texts', 406–28, esp. p. 425; Septimus, *Hispano-Jewish Culture*, ch. 3.   [56] Marx, 'Texts', 425.

[57] See *Letters*, ed. Shailat, i. 310. See also ibid. 324 (Arabic), 348–9 (Hebrew), where Maimonides informs us that there were many people who relied on his writings in order to deny a physical resurrection.

Maimonides mentions nothing about resurrection in his discussion of life after death in the *Mishneh torah*, 'Hilkhot teshuvah', chapter 8. This could also imply that elsewhere, when Maimonides writes that one must believe in resurrection,[58] he is actually identifying it with the world to come. In support of this approach, I would also suggest the following. In 'Hilkhot teshuvah', chapter 3, Maimonides defines the different types of heretics who have no share in the world to come. In his various lists he includes all of the Thirteen Principles with the exception of the Eleventh Principle (reward and punishment). Many have wondered how Maimonides could have omitted this, especially since the most fundamental aspect of reward and punishment is the fate of the soul in the next world. Isn't denial of spiritual reward, which is actually a denial of the soul's immortality, a prime example of heresy, indeed even more so than almost all of the others he lists? However, if we assume that the resurrection of the dead, which *is* included in this chapter, really means the immortality of the soul, then everything makes sense. In fact, in 'Hilkhot teshuvah', 3: 6, Maimonides lists 'resurrection' before the 'coming of the messiah'. If resurrection refers to life after death, then it makes sense that he would place it before the messiah, just as reward and punishment precedes the messiah in the Thirteen Principles.

Rabad had no knowledge of Maimonides' *Essay on Resurrection* and was basing his gloss entirely on what Maimonides wrote in the *Mishneh torah*. So too R. Meir Abulafia, who arrived at the same conclusion as Rabad and fiercely attacked Maimonides in his *Kitab al-rasail*.[59] It is significant that, even though these sages believed that Maimonides rejected the notion of physical resurrection, they did not regard him as a heretic. Despite what they viewed as Maimonides' serious doctrinal error, he remained for them a great man who had been led astray by philosophy. This shows, once again, that Maimonides' opponents were uncomfortable using the neat Maimonidean categorizations when seeking to define a heretic.

Even after Maimonides confronted the accusations that he denied physical resurrection and publicly set forth his position in his aforementioned *Essay*, a number of Maimonidean interpreters, both supporters and opponents, refused to be swayed. They regarded the *Essay on Resurrection* as a tract directed towards the masses which did not reflect Maimonides' true views.[60] One

---

[58] 'Hilkhot teshuvah', 3: 6.

[59] See Septimus, *Hispano-Jewish Culture*, ch. 3. When Maimonides' *Essay on Resurrection* later arrived in Spain, Abulafia disagreed with it as well. See his *Yad ramah* on BT *San.* 90*a*. R. Samuel b. Eli's famous attack on Maimonides' view of resurrection, which also focuses on the *Mishneh torah*, has now been published. See Langermann, 'Rabbi Samuel'; S. Stroumsa, *Origins*.

[60] See D. Schwartz, *Messianic Idea*, 133–44; Langermann, *Yemenite Midrash*, 300–1; Shem Tov, *Sefer ha'emunot*, 6*a–b*; S. D. Luzzatto, *Studies*, ii. 166.

modern scholar has even claimed that the *Essay on Resurrection* itself has a hidden meaning. In Howard Kreisel's words: 'There are many hints in the Treatise on Resurrection that it contains an esoteric level pointing to this conclusion [i.e. that resurrection is not to be understood literally]. The only "resurrection" that takes place is the immortality of the perfect intellect.'[61] Yet for those who do not posit an esoteric Maimonidean doctrine in this matter, there can be no denying that Maimonides did indeed believe in a literal resurrection, albeit of limited duration.[62]

While virtually all traditional Jewish thinkers have rejected an esoteric reading of Maimonides as concerns resurrection (or any other issue), there have been exceptions. Aside from those who opposed Maimonides, and thus were quick to find evidence of non-traditional views in his works,[63] R. Shem Tov Gaguine (1884–1953), *av beit din* (head of the rabbinical court) of the Sephardi community of London, also held this opinion. In support of it, he made the following interesting point. In the *Mishneh torah*, 'Hilkhot berakhot', 10: 10, Maimonides writes:

A person who sees Jewish graves should recite the blessing: Blessed are You, Lord our God, King of the universe, who created you with justice, gave you life with justice, nourished you with justice, sustained you with justice, took your lives with justice, and will ultimately raise you up in judgement to the life of the world to come. Blessed are You, Lord, who resurrects the dead.

This passage is based on BT *Berakhot* 58*b*, though there it simply states that God 'will ultimately raise you up in judgement'. It is Maimonides who adds 'to the life of the world to come'. Only after this does he conclude 'Blessed are You, God, who resurrects the dead.' On the face of it, it seems obvious that Maimonides is equating resurrection with the world to come, which is exactly what he was accused of doing. For if he indeed believes that people will literally rise from the dead, why would he change the talmudic version of the blessing and interpret it metaphorically, so that God 'raising you up in judgement', which in its original context means physical resurrection, becomes 'raising you up to the life of the world to come', i.e. to eternal life? According

---

[61] *Prophecy*, 312 n. 227. See, similarly, Kirschner, 'Maimonides' Fiction'.

[62] Unlike our versions of Mishnah *San.* 10: 1 (ואלו שאין להם חלק לעולם הבא האומר אין תחיית המתים מן התורה), Maimonides never requires one to believe that resurrection is revealed in the Torah. These words were probably lacking in his text of the Mishnah; see Rabbinovicz, *Dikdukei soferim*, ad loc.; Lowe, *Mishnah*, 128*a*; *Faksimile-Ausgabe*, 303; M. Abulafia, *Yad ramah*, ad loc. (p. 340) for texts that omit this requirement. See also Sinzheim, *Yad david: Sanhedrin*, 173. If Maimonides did have our version of the Mishnah, he might have ignored it in light of Tosefta *San.* 13: 1, where this condition does not appear. It is also possible that, despite what the Mishnah says, he believed it was too extreme to regard one who accepted the belief as a heretic merely because he denied its pentateuchal origin.

[63] See Shem Tov, *Sefer ha'emunot*, 6*a–b*; S. D. Luzzatto, *Meḥkerei hayahadut*, ii. 166.

to Gaguine, this is proof that, for Maimonides, 'resurrection' will be in the world to come, and is simply another term for eternal spiritual life. Recognizing the controversial nature of what he proposed, Gaguine does not elaborate on this striking interpretation, instead concluding with Ibn Ezra's famous comment, 'and the intelligent will understand'.[64]

While not referring to Maimonides' view on the subject, R. Isaac Arama (c.1420–94), author of the biblical commentary *Akedat yitshak*, also seems to have denied a physical resurrection. Although he discusses the soul and the spiritual world to come at great length, only once does he mention resurrection. In this passage he makes clear that, in the opinion of the talmudic sages, the two are nothing more than synonyms.[65] Since, according to Arama, the world to come is entirely spiritual, the fact that the term 'resurrection' is used as a synonym must also mean that *tehiyat hametim* (resurrection of the dead) is not to be understood literally. To support this position he quotes the following passage from BT *Kidushin* 39b:

---

[64] *Keter shem tov*, 651–2. According to Gaguine, R. Amram Gaon also held this interpretation. See also Kafih, comment in his edition of Maimonides, *Mishneh torah*, 'Hilkhot berakhot', 10: 10, who notes the identification of 'the world to come' and *tehiyat hametim*. Gaguine's interpretation should be read together with a point made by Isaiah Leibowitz. The latter noted that the text of the Thirteenth Principle reads: 'Resurrection of the Dead, and we have already explained it.' Earlier in the chapter Maimonides states that resurrection is a fundamental principle and that one who does not believe in it has no religion and no tie to the Jewish people. He also states that the wicked will not be resurrected: 'How can the wicked live again, since they are considered dead even while alive? Thus have our Sages said, "The wicked, even in their lifetime, are called dead, but the righteous, even after death, are called alive" [BT *Ber.* 18a–b].' According to Leibowitz, this shows that Maimonides identifies resurrection with life after death, i.e. the world to come. See Leibowitz, *On the World*, 108; id., *Conversations*, 226. Although I do not find Leibowitz's reading textually compelling, one could support it with the following argument: Maimonides says that one who denies the resurrection has no religion. This is very difficult to understand. Why should denial of resurrection, if it means a temporary physical reappearance, merit such opprobrium, especially if one still believes in eternal spiritual life? If, however, the 'resurrection' here spoken of means eternal spiritual life, then Maimonides' formulation makes perfect sense. Denial of eternal spiritual life means that there is no ultimate reward and punishment and thus no chance for salvation. As Jacobs puts it, 'a religious faith denuded of the belief in the immortality of the soul loses all its spiritual power, a faith without the doctrine of the physical resurrection is not affected at all' (*Principles*, 415). Abarbanel also writes, with reference to the doctrine of physical resurrection: 'Even though this is a true belief . . . why should the Torah collapse in its entirety and its commandments be refuted if one believes that divine retribution occurs [both] in this world and in the world to come, but that there is no bodily resurrection after death?' (*Rosh amanah*, ch. 3).

[65] *Akedat yitshak*, i. 71b: דתחיית המתים ועולם הבא בשם אחד נקראו אצלם. See Heller-Wilensky, *Rabbi Isaac*, 145; E. Kafih, 'Nature of the Soul', 161–2. Me'iri, *Beit habehirah: Avot*, 107, also identifies *tehiyat hametim* and the world to come. But in *Beit habehirah: Sanhedrin*, 334, he adopts the exoteric Maimonidean model and distinguishes between the two. See also Me'iri, *Hibur hateshuvah*, 386. R. Jacob Anatoli's position is ambiguous, for though he speaks of a literal resurrection, he also refers to it as a 'necessary belief'. As noted above, in Maimonidean terminology this phrase means a belief that it is necessary for the masses to adopt but which is not literally true. See D. Schwartz, *Messianic Idea*, 142–3.

Rabbi Jacob said: There is not a single precept in the Torah whose reward is [stated] at its side which is not dependent on the resurrection of the dead. [Thus] in connection with honouring parents it is written: *that thy days may be prolonged, and that it may be well with thee* (Deut. 5: 16). In reference to the dismissal of the nest it is written: *that it may be well with thee, and that thou mayest prolong thy days* (Deut. 22: 7). . . . And where is this man's prolonging of days? *That it may be well with thee* means on the day that is wholly good and *that thy days may be prolonged*, on the day that is wholly long.

In Abulafia's opinion, this passage shows that R. Jacob identifies the world to come ('the day that is wholly good . . . the day that is wholly long') with resurrection.[66] For Arama, however, it is just the opposite. R. Jacob is identifying resurrection with the world to come, which, as noted, is an entirely spiritual realm in Arama's view.

A more recent Orthodox thinker, R. Joseph Seliger (1872–1919), also denied the notion of physical resurrection. He regarded it as a primitive, foreign import, and composed an entire essay in support of this proposition. According to him, the rabbinic concept of *teḥiyat hametim* is identical with the world to come, and any texts which reflect a different approach are not to be understood literally.[67] As Jacobs has noted, R. Joseph H. Hertz, Chief Rabbi of the British Empire, also implied that there is no religious objection to viewing resurrection as identical to spiritual immortality.[68] Hertz cites Maimonides as holding this position, and Jacobs objects by quite naturally pointing to Maimonides' comments in his *Essay on Resurrection*.[69] Presumably, Hertz agreed with those scholars who do not regard the *Essay on Resurrection* as reflecting Maimonides' true view, for, as mentioned above, Maimonides' philosophical system as set out in the *Guide* has no place for physical resurrection. From my own experience, a large percentage of the contemporary Modern Orthodox community agrees with Seliger and Hertz and interprets the notion of physical resurrection in symbolic fashion, or at least regards this as a possible interpretation.[70] However, with one notable exception,[71] this position has not yet been defended in print by Modern Orthodox leaders.

One other noteworthy understanding of resurrection is that of the late R. Joseph Kafih, the renowned Yemenite scholar and authority on Maimon-

---

[66] *Kitab al-rasa'il*, 64.

[67] Seliger, *Kitvei*, 71–96. See, however, Kook's response in his *haskamah* to this work. This source was noted in Jacobs, *Principles*, 414. [68] Hertz, *Prayer Book*, 255.

[69] See Jacobs, *Principles*, 415–16.

[70] This is not a new phenomenon. In R. Meir Abulafia's letter to the French sages he writes that the belief in resurrection has been abandoned by most of his contemporaries. See *Kitab al-rasa'il*, 13.

[71] See Hartman, *Living Covenant*, 257.

ides. In fact, Kafih was more than simply an authority on Maimonides. He was a true Maimonidean, following the master in all particulars, no matter how controversial. As a conservative Maimonidean, he had to accept the *Essay on Resurrection* as proof that Maimonides did indeed believe in a physical resurrection. He also attacked Moses of Narbonne for appearing to deny this.[72] Nevertheless, Kafih was well aware that the traditional view of resurrection cannot be reconciled with Maimonides' philosophical view of immortality.

In an attempt to have his cake and eat it—to maintain that Maimonides believed in resurrection and still see him as affirming a completely spiritual immortality—Kafih offers a new interpretation, which is based on the understanding of resurrection put forth by the medieval Yemenite sage R. Perahyah ben Meshulam (*c*.1400). According to Kafih, when Maimonides refers to a physical resurrection he is only speaking of the return of the impersonal 'life force' to the body. This life force comes into being with man's creation and is responsible for the continuance of physical life. In addition to this life force, which is common to all people, Maimonides also speaks of the perfected intellect. This is unique to each individual, is formed through the knowledge of divine things, and is what remains after death. Once it has left the body, Kafih asserts, it does not return.

In other words, since Kafih understands resurrection as encompassing only the life force, it is a completely new birth, *tabula rasa*! Since there is no resurrection of the developed intellects of actual people who once lived on earth, in what sense can one then speak of resurrection? The answer, according to Kafih, is that it is the body, pure and simple, which is resurrected. As he explains, this is the meaning of the blessing recited in the morning prayers, 'Blessed art Thou, Lord, Who restores souls [*neshamot*] to dead bodies.'[73]

In Kafih's conception, resurrection thus means nothing other than God imparting a life force into dead bodies, but the newly alive body has no essential connection to the individual who previously lived in this body. This is also stated explicitly by R. Perahyah, who writes that God will create a soul for the dead body, separate from the soul that already left it.[74] Thus, according to R. Perahyah and Kafih, individuals who have left this world never return to it, and Moses, R. Akiva, and the other great figures of the past remain for ever pure intellect. In Kafih's words, 'If the righteous one immediately upon his

---

[72] See his edition of *Moreh hanevukhim* (Jerusalem, 1977), 29 (1st pagination). R. Joseph Rozin had earlier attacked Moses of Narbonne in this regard; see M. Kasher, *Mefane'ah tsefunot*, 13.

[73] *Mishneh torah, Sefer hamada*, ed. J. Kafih, 646–7. See 'Hilkhot teshuvah', 8: 3, where *neshamah* is used in the sense of 'life force', and *nefesh* refers to the perfected intellect.

[74] See J. Kafih, *Writings*, i. 190.

death merits the world to come and enjoys the divine splendour in accordance with his attainments [lit. 'his canopy', see BT *BB 75a*], how is it possible for God to uproot him from this great spiritual delight which the eye has not beheld [cf. Isa. 64: 3] and return him [to earth] to eat, drink, have sex, and enter latrines to fulfil his needs? Is this a privilege? Is this not rather a degradation and a punishment greater than all else?'[75] What then, according to Kafih, is the purpose of resurrection if not to reward the dead? He does not tell us, but an examination of Maimonides' *Essay on Resurrection* provides the answer. According to this work, resurrection vividly demonstrates that God is not bound by the constraints of the natural order. By the same token, denial that God can breathe life into a dead body 'leads to the rejection of all miracles which is equivalent to denying the existence of God and abandoning the Faith'.[76] This is undoubtedly where R. Kafih saw the true significance of the doctrine.

[75] *Mishneh torah: Sefer hamada*, ed. J. Kafih, 646. In fact, the kabbalist R. Azriel of Gerona regarded resurrection—which in his mind appears to be identical with *gilgul*—as nothing more than a punishment. The righteous, however, 'have no interruption [in their incorporeal existence] for ever and all eternity'. See Septimus, *Hispano-Jewish Culture*, 111–12.

[76] *Letters*, ed. Shailat, i. 328 (Arabic), 356–7 (Hebrew).

Conclusion

❦

W HEN THE ARTICLE upon which this book is based first appeared, it
created something of a sensation in Orthodox circles. Some were over-
joyed upon learning of the wide-ranging beliefs expressed by Jewish scholars
over the centuries; others were horrified for the same reason. Still others were
simply confused, since the article refuted what had been a strongly held conviction indoctrinated in them since their youth. (For this reason, one reader
called me an 'iconoclast', which I suppose is not a bad thing.) In one well-
known yeshiva, the article was passed from student to student as if it were
Haskalah literature in late nineteenth-century Volozhin. Because of the great
student interest, a teacher at this yeshiva was even forced to speak about it
with his students.

What was it about the article that created such acclaim, aversion, and confusion? Why were the opinions of great sages not only unknown, but, for
many, even unacceptable? The main reason why the views I discussed were so
unfamiliar is that Jewish theology is not taken seriously in contemporary
Orthodoxy. Unlike earlier generations, which had their 'professional' theologians or, at the very least, scholars who devoted a great deal of time to this
field, today we have talmudists, who at best merely dabble in it.

Since the sources of Jewish theology are not part of the curriculum in
yeshivot, the students know nothing about them. Nor is the typical *posek*,
who has mastered the Talmud, codes, and responsa, acquainted with the
theological literature, and he often does not even recognize the issues.[1] As a
consequence of both the conservatism of these sages and their general lack of
knowledge of the history of Jewish thought, certain theological views have
become *de rigueur* in traditional circles. These conservative views are repeated
and expounded upon, but the wide-ranging opinions of sages of past generations are rarely given a hearing. This is why much of what I have discussed in
this book will be surprising to readers who have been raised in Orthodoxy,
even if they received an extensive yeshiva education.

---

[1] R. Joseph Kafih's commentary on the *Mishneh torah* cites many examples of sages who misinter-
preted Maimonides because they were unaware of his philosophical views. A particularly surprising
example of this appears in Feinstein, *Igerot mosheh*, 'Yoreh de'ah', ii. 239. Although R. Moses
Feinstein was the greatest *posek* of his time, he seems to have had no knowledge of Maimonidean
philosophy. He was therefore able to state that Maimonides believed in the protective power of holy
names and the names of angels, as used in amulets. For Maimonides' rejection of this, see his commentary on Mishnah *Sotah* 7: 4 and *Guide* i. 61–2.

While the issues I have discussed are not part of the traditional curriculum, I believe them to be central to a proper understanding of Judaism. Together with the turn to the right in Orthodoxy, which has led to increasing stringency in many areas of halakhah, an ever-increasing dogmatism in matters of belief is also apparent. Many views that were once generally considered 'acceptable' are no longer regarded in this way. If, as with the original article, controversy breaks out over this book, it is because many fear that exposing people to what the great figures of the past have written will break down the walls of theological conformity that have been so patiently erected. I am not a theologian; my approach is that of an intellectual historian. I do, however, hope that traditional Judaism will once again create theologians, as well as great talmudists who will also concern themselves with the theological heritage explored in this book.

I wrote this book to examine the claim that Maimonides' Principles are the last word in Jewish theology. Simply by looking at traditional Jewish sources, I believe it has been clearly demonstrated that many of his Principles were not regarded as authoritative, either before his time or afterwards. The fact that Maimonides placed the stamp of apostasy on anyone who disagreed with his Principles did not frighten away numerous great sages from their search for truth. The lesson for moderns is clear.

APPENDIX I

Other Areas of Dispute

ô

T HIS BOOK has focused on Maimonides' Principles, his assertion that denial of any of them equals heresy, and the rabbinic authorities who rejected many of these positions. This appendix will concentrate on four *practices* which Maimonides stamped as heretical, or at least taken from the heretics. As with his Principles, his assertions in this regard met with widespread rejection, although in two of the cases Maimonides' opinion eventually prevailed.

1. In *Mishneh torah*, 'Hilkhot talmud torah', 3: 10 Maimonides writes:

One, however, who makes up his mind to study Torah and not to work but to live on charity, profanes the name of God, brings the Torah into contempt, extinguishes the light of religion, brings evil upon himself, and *deprives himself of the world to come*, for it is forbidden to derive any temporal advantage from the words of the Torah.

Maimonides elaborates on this position in his commentary on Mishnah *Avot* 4: 7, where he claims that the great scholars of the past refused to take money from the community, earning their living by various pursuits instead. However, as is well known, Jews throughout history, wherever they lived, have scrupulously ignored Maimonides' words. Maimonides himself acknowledged that 'the majority, or possibly all' of his fellow Torah sages disagreed with him.[1] Not surprisingly, men continue to enter the rabbinate expecting to be supported by the community, and contemporary Orthodoxy has established a *kolel* system, in which tens of thousands of young men are paid to study Torah exclusively. In the words of R. Moses Feinstein, 'Those who feign piety basing themselves on Maimonides' opinion are acting at the instigation of the evil inclination. This is done in order to stop their Torah study so as to engage in work, business, etc. In the end they forget even that little which they have already learnt and no longer have even a small amount of time for Torah study.'[2]

2. In *Mishneh torah*, 'Hilkhot avodah zarah', 11: 12, Maimonides writes:

One who whispers a spell over a wound and then recites a verse from the Torah, one who recites a verse over a child to save it from terrors, and one who places a scroll or phylacteries on an infant to induce it to sleep, are not in the category of sorcerers and soothsayers, but *they are included among those who deny the Torah*; for they use its words to cure the body, whereas these are only medicine for the soul, as it is said, *They shall be life to your soul* (Prov. 3: 22). On the other hand, anyone in the enjoyment of good health is permitted to recite verses from the Scriptures or a Psalm, so that he may be shielded by the merit of the recital and saved from trouble and hurt.

---

[1] Commentary on Mishnah *Avot* 4: 7, and see Yitshak Shailat's important comments in his edition of Maimonides' commentary on *Avot*, 73–5. [2] *Igerot mosheh*, 'Yoreh de'ah', ii, no. 116.

In 'Hilkhot teshuvah', 3: 6, Maimonides writes that those who deny the Torah have no share in the world to come. Nevertheless, throughout Jewish history his words have been ignored and pious Jews have indeed used the Torah 'to cure the body'. The *mezuzah* in particular became popular as a protective amulet, and Joshua Trachtenberg reports that during the First World War 'many of the Jewish soldiers carried *mezuzot* in their pockets to deflect enemy bullets'.[3] Even today there are Orthodox Jews who will place a small book of Psalms underneath a baby's pillow, thinking that it will protect the infant.

3. In *Mishneh torah*, 'Hilkhot mezuzah', 5: 4 Maimonides writes:

It is a universal custom to write the word Shaddai on the other side of the *mezuzah* opposite the blank space between the two sections. As this word is written on the outside, the practice is not objectionable. Those however, who write names of angels, holy names, a biblical text, or [angelic] seals within the *mezuzah* are among those *who have no portion in the world to come*. For these fools not only fail to fulfil the commandment, but they treat an important precept that expresses the unity of God, the love of Him, and His worship, as if it were an amulet to promote their own personal interest, for according to their foolish minds the *mezuzah* is something that will secure for them advantage in the vanities of the world.

Today, one cannot find *mezuzot* that violate Maimonides' proscription. This was not the case in medieval times, however, when such *mezuzot* were common in Ashkenazi lands, many of whose sages supported the practice. For example, R. Judah Hehasid is known to have had holy names in his *mezuzah*,[4] and R. Eliezer ben Samuel of Metz (twelfth century) gives descriptions of how to write *mezuzot* complete with angelic names.[5] *Mahzor vitri* prescribes that 'one should be careful' to include the names of angels and their seals,[6] and both *Sidur rashi* and *Sefer hapardes* go even further, regarding the practice as an obligatory aspect of the commandment.[7]

4. In *Mishneh torah*, 'Hilkhot isurei biah', 11: 15, Maimonides writes:

There is a custom which prevails in some places and which is mentioned in the responsa of some of the *ge'onim*, whereby a woman who has given birth to a male child may not have intercourse until the expiration of forty days, and in the case of a female child eighty days, even if she has had a flow for seven days only. This, too, is not a well-founded custom, but the result of an erroneous decision in these responsa. *It is a heretical practice* in these localities and the inhabitants learned it from the Sadducees. Indeed, it is one's duty to compel them to get it out of their minds, so that they return to the words of the Sages, namely that a woman should count no more than seven days of cleanness.

As Maimonides indicates, this practice of adding on to the days of impurity following childbirth could find support in geonic responsa. It is therefore understandable that, despite Maimonides' harsh words, the practice, which included a number of local variations concerning how many days to add, was not uprooted, and remained well established in communities throughout the world, often receiving the support of

---

[3] *Jewish Magic*, 147.   [4] Anon., *Sefer hapardes*, 26.   [5] *Yere'im*, no. 400.   [6] pp. 648–9.
[7] Anon., *Sidur rashi*, 231; anon., *Sefer hapardes*, 26. See Daniel Sperber, *Minhagei yisra'el*, ii. 103 ff., who refers to all the literature on the subject.

leading scholars.[8] R. Jacob Moelin (*c*.1360–1427, Germany) is known to have advocated the practice.[9] R. Alexander Suslein Hakohen (fourteenth century, Germany) testified that the custom was widespread.[10] R. Isaac ben Sheshet (1326–1407, North Africa),[11] R. Joseph Colon (*c*.1420–80, Italy),[12] R. Samuel Aboab (1610–94, Italy),[13] R. Ezekiel Landau (1713–93, Prague),[14] and R. Aaron Worms (1754–1836, Metz),[15] to mention just some authorities from later years, record that this was the practice of certain communities in their day. Both Ben Sheshet and Colon refused to abolish the practice if there were grounds to believe that it arose not in error but as an extra stringency. R. Moses Isserles (*c*.1530–72, Poland) offered what he regarded as clear halakhic justification for the practice.[16] He also ruled that women must follow this routine in a place where the custom is to do so.[17] R. Jacob Reischer (*c*.1670–1733, Prague, Germany) recorded that the sages of Prague supported the practice, and he too offers a justification for it.[18] R. Joel Sirkes (1561–1640, Poland) went even further, declaring that those who abandon this custom, as Maimonides had demanded, 'commit a great sin' and violate the biblical warnings 'Do not forsake the teaching of thy mother' (Prov. 1: 8) and 'whoso breaketh though a fence, a serpent shall bite him' (Eccles. 10: 8). He concludes that a rabbi who rules otherwise requires atonement.[19]

Nevertheless, the influence of Maimonides, together with that of his powerful supporters, was such that the popularity of the practice was significantly reduced. We know of certain rabbinic leaders, such as R. Tsevi Hirsch Ashkenazi (1660–1718, Germany, Amsterdam)[20] and R. Jonathan Eybeschuetz (*c*.1690–1764, Prague, Metz, Germany),[21] who took active steps to abolish the practice in their communities. Virtually all other Ashkenazi *posekim*, while not going to the extreme of formally abolishing the practice, were firm in their insistence that it was without basis and that women did not need to follow it.[22] This Ashkenazi opposition was so successful that R. Abraham Danzig (1748–1820, Lithuania) could write that in his part of the world women did not follow this practice.[23] Some years later, R. Yehiel Mikhel Epstein (1828–1909, Belorussia) declared that he knew of no community where the practice was still followed.[24]

---

[8] See Zimmer, *Olam keminhago noheg*, 220–39, for the most recent and detailed discussion of this practice, focusing exclusively on the medieval period. For additional sources see Sperber, *Minhagei yisra'el*, ii. 76 ff.

[9] See Moelin, *She'elot uteshuvot maharil*, no. 140; id., *She'elot uteshuvot maharil hadashot*, no. 93: 3; id., *Sefer maharil: minhagim*, 595. In this latter source, Moelin is quoted as saying that the practice has biblical authority! On this problematic quotation, see the Makhon Yerushalayim edition of the *Tur*, 'Yoreh de'ah', 194 n. 7.

[10] *Sefer ha'agudah: pesahim*, 190 (no. 96); id., *Sefer ha'agudah: nidah*, 70a (no. 18).

[11] *She'elot uteshuvot harivash*, no. 40.   [12] *She'elot uteshuvot maharik*, no. 144.

[13] *Devar shemuel*, no. 196. On this practice in Italy, see also the responsum of R. Aaron ben Israel Finzi in Bonfil, *Rabbinate*, 281, and Sinigaglia, *Shabat shel mi*, 'Ya'akov lehok', no. 44.

[14] *Noda biyehudah*, 1st ser., 'Yoreh de'ah', no. 54.   [15] *Me'orei or: kan tahor*, 135b.

[16] *Darkhei mosheh*, 'Yoreh de'ah', 194. See also id., *She'elot uteshuvot rema*, no. 94.

[17] *Shulhan arukh*, 'Yoreh de'ah', 194: 1.   [18] *Shevut ya'akov*, iii, no. 77.

[19] *Bayit hadash*, 'Yoreh de'ah', 194.   [20] See Emden, *She'elat ya'avets*, ii. 15.

[21] *Tiferet yisra'el*, 'Yoreh de'ah', 194: 4 (printed together with id., *Kereti ufeleti*).

[22] See the sources quoted in Yosef, *Yabia omer*, iv. 251.

[23] *Hokhmat adam*, 115: 19.   [24] *Arukh hashulhan*, 'Yoreh de'ah', 194: 23.

In the Sephardi world the popularity of the practice also declined, although there remained some who spoke in its favour. Among these should be mentioned R. Jacob Saul Elyashar (1817–1906), the Rishon Letsiyon (Sephardi chief rabbi) of the Land of Israel. He responded very sharply to an attempt by one rabbi to abolish the practice, quoting Sirkes' strong comments mentioned above.[25] This position was reaffirmed by his son, R. Hayim Moses Elyashar (1845–1924), who also served as Rishon Letsiyon.[26] R. Joseph Hayim ben Elijah al-Hakam of Baghdad (1833–1909), while not personally advocating the practice, regarded it as an authentic custom that could not be abandoned without the consent of a *beit din* (*hatarat nedarim*).[27] The custom of Fez, Morocco, was also identical to that which Maimonides blasts as heretical. As R. Yedidyah Monsenego (*c*.1800–68) made clear, this practice had the support of generations of rabbinic leaders of Fez.[28] R. Moses Toledano (died 1773) of Meknes, Morocco likewise advocated this practice.[29] Maimonides' opinion was also ignored in Djerba, Tunisia, where the practice was to wait forty days after the birth of a male. With regard to a girl, however, there were different customs, with some waiting sixty-five days and others the full eighty.[30] In Algeria[31] and Aden[32] the practice was in opposition to Maimonides' opinion. Many people in Yemen did likewise,[33] paying no regard to their sage, R. Hoter ben Shelomoh (fourteenth–fifteenth centuries), who condemned those who followed this practice as violating Maimonides' Ninth Principle, which speaks of the immutability of Torah law.[34]

[25] *Yisa ish*, 'Yoreh de'ah', no. 4. [26] *Sha'al ha'ish*, 'Yoreh de'ah', no. 12.

[27] *Rav pe'alim*, ii, 'Yoreh de'ah', no. 23, id., *Ben ish ḥai*, ii, 'Tsav', no. 20.

[28] *Kupat harokhlim*, 123.

[29] *Hashamayim hahadashim*, 'Yoreh de'ah', no. 30. There was disagreement in Meknes regarding this practice; see Ovadiah, *Natan david*, 389. In many outlying villages of Morocco, Maimonides' opinion was ignored. See Blumenthal, *Commentary*, 161 n. 1.

[30] See M. Hakohen, *Veheshiv mosheh*, 'Yoreh de'ah', no. 36; K. M. Hakohen, *Berit kehunah*, i. 254–5 (s.v. *yoledet*; see also R. Meir Mazuz's note at the end of the book); R. H. Hakohen, *Zikhrei kehunah*, 566. [31] See Tseror, *Dinei*, 45; Blumenthal, *Commentary*, 161 n. 1.

[32] See Tsalah, *Piskei maharits*, iii. 273 (Ratsaby's commentary).

[33] See ibid. R. Yahya Tsalah (1725–1806) says that in a 'few places' people waited forty days for a boy and eighty for a girl: see ibid. 269. However, Ratsaby testifies that in more recent years this was the practice in almost all communities. [34] Blumenthal, *Commentary*, 160–1.

1. Frontispiece to *Arba'ah turim* by R. Jacob ben Asher (Augsburg, 1540). The two scenes at the bottom show God creating first the animals, and then Eve from Adam (Gen 2: 21–2). Courtesy of the Jewish Theological Seminary of America

ספר
עיר בנימן

אשר כפה חומת העיר ומגדליה ועמודים עשה
לבית כית ישראל חלק השני · מותיב וספרך
כמי יתמני · וזה דתנא ונייר הוא חברון אשר לא יובל
ולהלכות · כי דבר פורים מעות קומות · ובמאי דקמינן נראה
וחזה · יבא וזה וילמד על זה · אשר הכל יאמרו עליו כי
כח זה זה · מה בן מזה · דורש כאין חומר · כל מיך שמותנו
לי אומר · שעמהו כנפשית כרנבם זריחו לא נאמר · ה ה
כנוד הרב הגדול המופלא ותוכלג · נ״ים ע״ה כבוד
מיהרר כב מן וגב מאלף גלו · אכ״ד ול״ת דק״ק וויגרלוד
י״ו נסדרב הגדול האמונה מוהרר שמואל דרשן ול״ל ה״ס ·
 המן המותת הסר ונגיד התופלג כתפרה וחכמה כאהורר
הנרהם סג״ל ול״ל · מתן הנחאן המפורסם רכן של כני
הגולה מוהרר יוסיע ול״ל אכ״ד ול״ת דק״ק קרלקפק יכ״ו

ותהי השלמת הספר יוסו טניסן לבנימן
אמרדיד ישבון לבסחלפה
פה קק פרנקפורט דאור

תחת ישולת חרונינו חרוכם הגדול מורחם וחוד האהל·
וכאדיר פריודר השלישי קרופורשט גן בכאבי כאדר
כ״ה ויתנבה לבגתיותו ·

קייש אויה ויכט הלזכן יוחנן קריומטף בטקרן דקטר
ופריופאשר בעיר הגדולה האהללג פרנקפורם דאור

גרוזוקט וין חיו בייא רטן חערן אילו נאט סחוק

Cir. Benjamin.

T.E.B.

2. (*Left*) Title page of *Ir binyamin* by R. Benjamin Ze'ev Wolf Romaner (Frankfurt am Oder, 1698). The scene (*enlarged above*) which appears at the bottom right of the title page shows Jacob's dream (Gen. 18) with God looking down from the top right, above the ladder. Courtesy of the Jewish Theological Seminary of America

והשתערלו
פתחו
שערים
ויבא גוי צדיק
שומר אמנים

צלל כעופרת במים אדירים

וירד מנגן בידו

וירד משה אל העם

ויושט המלך לאסתר

וידם השמש וירח עמד

העצמות היבשות

ורמי לגבא דיאריתא

In Mantova
Con Licenza
De
Svperiori

וזרח אה הילד הזה

3. (*Left*) Title page of *Minḥat shai* by R. Yedidyah Solomon Norzi (Mantua, 1742).
The scene (*enlarged above from a clearer copy*) which appears at the bottom left of the
title page shows Ezekiel's vision of the Valley of Dry Bones (Ezek. 37); God appears
above, in the clouds. Courtesy of the Jewish Theological Seminary of America

Bibliography

Works by Maimonides

Commentary on the Mishnah [Mishnah im perush rabenu mosheh ben maimon], ed. and trans. Joseph Kafih, 6 vols. (Jerusalem, 1989).

The Guide of the Perplexed, trans. Shlomo Pines (Chicago, 1963).

Maimonides' Introductions to the Mishnah [Hakdamot harambam lamishnah], ed. Yitshak Shailat (Jerusalem, 1992).

Maimonides' Letters [Igerot harambam], ed. Yitshak Shailat, 2 vols. (Jerusalem, 1987).

Maimonides' Letters [Igerot harambam], ed. Joseph Kafih (Jerusalem, 1994).

Maimonides' Novellae on the Talmud [Ḥidushei harambam latalmud], ed. Mordechai Zaks (Jerusalem, 1963).

Maimonides' Responsa [Teshuvot harambam], ed. Joshua Blau, 4 vols. (Jerusalem, 1989).

Mishneh torah, ed. with commentary by Joseph Kafih, 23 vols. (Jerusalem, 1984–96).

Pirkei Moshe, ed. Sussmann Muntner (Jerusalem, 1959).

Shemot kodesh veḥol, ed. Yitshak Ratsaby (Benei Berak, 1987); of questionable authenticity.

Other Works

AARON BEN ELIJAH, *Ets ḥayim* (Leipzig, 1841).

AARON SAMUEL OF KREMENETS, *Nishmat adam* (Jerusalem, 1989).

AARON, DAVID, 'Shedding Light on God's Body in Rabbinic Midrashim: Reflections on the Theory of a Luminous Adam', *HTR* 90 (1997), 299–314.

ABARBANEL, ISAAC, *Commentary on the Torah* [Perush al hatorah] (Jerusalem, 1994).

—— *Mifalot elokim* (Jerusalem, 1993).

—— *Principles of Faith*, trans. Menachem Kellner (London, 1982).

—— *Rosh amanah*, ed. Menachem Kellner (Ramat Gan, 1993).

ABBA MARI ASTRUC OF LUNEL, *Minḥat kenaot*, in Solomon ben Adret, *Teshuvot harashba*, ed. H. Dimitrovsky (Jerusalem, 1990).

—— *Minḥat kenaot*, ed. M. J. Bislikhis (New York, 1958).

Abhandlungen zur Erinnerung an Hirsch Perez Chajes (Vienna, 1933).

ABOAB, SAMUEL, *Devar shemuel* (Jerusalem, 1983).

ABRAHAM BEN AZRIEL, *Arugat habosem*, ed. E. E. Urbach, 4 vols. (Jerusalem, 1963).

ABRAHAM IBN DAUD, *Ha'emunah haramah* (Frankfurt, 1853).

ABRAHAM BEN ELIEZER HALEVI, 'A Ruling Concerning Requests from Angels' (Heb.), *Kerem ḥemed*, 9 (1856), 141–8.

ABRAHAM BEN MORDEKHAI HALEVI, *Ginat veradim* (Constantinople, 1706).

ABRAMS, DANIEL, 'The Boundaries of Divine Ontology: The Inclusion and Exclusion of Metatron in the Godhead', *HTR* 87 (1994), 291–321.

ABRAMS, DANIEL, 'From Divine Shape to Angelic Being: The Career of Akatriel in Jewish Literature', *Journal of Religion*, 76 (1996), 43–63.

—— 'The Evolution of the Intention of Prayer to the "Special Cherub": From the Earliest Works to a Late Unknown Treatise', *Frankfurter Jüdaistische Beitrage*, 22 (1995), 1–26.

ABRAMSON, SHRAGA, 'Some Teachings of Rabbi Samuel Hanagid of Spain' (Heb.), *Sinai*, 100 [1987], 7–73.

Abudarham, David, *Abudarham hashalem*, ed. S. A. Wertheimer (Jerusalem, 1957).

ABULAFIA, ABRAHAM, *Razei ḥayei olam haba* (Jerusalem, 1998).

—— *Sefer haḥeshek* (Jerusalem, 1999).

—— *Sitrei torah* (Jerusalem, 2002).

ABULAFIA, MEIR, *Kitab al-rasa'il* (Paris, 1871).

—— *Masoret seyag latorah* (Berlin, 1760).

—— *Yad ramah: Sanhedrin* (Jerusalem, 2000).

ADANG, CAMILLA, *Muslim Writers on Judaism and the Hebrew Bible: From Ibn Rabban to Ibn Hazm* (Leiden, 1996).

ADLER, NATHAN, *Netinah lager* (Jerusalem, 1979).

ALASHKAR, MOSES, *She'elot uteshuvot maharam alashkar* (Jerusalem, 1988).

ALBALAG, ISAAC, *Tikun hade'ot*, ed. G. Vajda (Jerusalem, 1973).

ALBECK, HANOKH, *Mishnah: Nezikin* (Jerusalem, 1959).

ALBO, JOSEPH, *Sefer ha'ikarim*, ed. and trans. Isaac Husik, 5 vols. (Philadelphia, Pa., 1929–30).

ALDABI, MEIR, *Shevilei emunah* (Jerusalem, 1990).

ALTMANN, ALEXANDER, 'Beatitude', *Encyclopedia Judaica* (Jerusalem, 1971), iv, cols. 35–63.

—— *Essays in Jewish Intellectual History* (Hanover, Pa., 1981).

—— *Moses Mendelssohn* (London, 1998).

—— *Studies in Religious Philosophy and Mysticism* (Plainview, NY, 1969).

—— 'Das Verhältnis Maimunis zur jüdischen Mystik', *MGWJ* 80 (1936), 305–30.

—— *Von der mittelalterlichen zur modernen Aufklärung* (Tübingen, 1987).

ANAV, ZEDEKIAH BEN ABRAHAM, *Shibolei haleket* (Vilna, 1887).

ANKAWA, EPHRAIM, *Sha'ar kevod hashem* (Jerusalem, 1986).

ANON., *Hadar zekenim* (Livorno, 1840).

ANON., *Ḥemdat yamim* (Livorno, 1759).

ANON., *Ma'amar hasekhel* (Vienna, 1815).

ANON., *Ma'ayanot ha'emunah* (Benei Berak, 1997).

ANON., 'Notes on the Book *Mitpaḥat sefarim*' (Heb.), *Zion*, 1 (1841), 155–8.

ANON., *Okhlah ve'okhlah*, ed. S. Frensdorff (New York, 1972).

ANON., *Otsar harishonim* ([Brooklyn, NY], 2001).

ANON., *Pitron torah*, ed. E. Urbach (Jerusalem, 1978).

ANON., *Sefer hapardes*, ed. H. Ehrenreich (Budapest, 1924).

ANON., *Sefer harazim*, ed. M. Margulies (Jerusalem, 1967).

ANON., *Sefer hasidim*, ed. Reuven Margaliyot (Jerusalem, 1989).

ANON., *Sidur helkat yehoshua limot hahol* (Jerusalem, 1997).

ANON., *Sidur rashi*, ed. S. Buber and J. Freimann (Berlin, 1911).

ANON., *Tsava'at harivash* (Jerusalem, 1965).

ANUSHISKI, SHNEUR ZALMAN DOV, *Matsav hayosher*, 2 vols. (Vilna, 1887).

APTOWITZER, VICTOR, 'Zur Kosmologie der Agada: Licht als Urstoff', *MGWJ* 72 (1928), 363–70.

—— *Parteipolitik der Hasmonärzeit im Rabbinischen und Pseudoepigraphischen Schriftum* (Vienna, 1927).

—— 'The Rewarding and Punishing of Animals and Inanimate Objects', *HUCA* 3 (1926), 117–55.

—— *Das Schriftwort in der rabbinischen Literatur* (New York, 1970).

ARAKI, HAYIM BEN SHELOMOH, et al., *Emunat hashem* (Jerusalem, 1938).

ARAMA, DAVID, *Perush al harambam* (Amsterdam, 1706).

ARAMA, ISAAC, *Akedat yitshak*, ed. H. Pollak (Jerusalem, 1961).

ARISTOTLE, *Nicomachean Ethics*, trans. and ed. Roger Crisp (Cambridge, 2000).

ASHER BEN JEHIEL, *Orhot hayim* (London, 2000).

ASHKENAZI, ELEAZER BEN NATHAN HABAVLI, *Tsofnat pane'ah*, ed. S. Rappaport (Johannesburg, 1965).

ASHKENAZI, ELIEZER, *Ma'asei hashem*, 2 vols. (Jerusalem, 1987).

ASHKENAZI, SAMUEL JAFFE BEN ISAAC, *Yefeh to'ar* [commentary on *Midrash rabah*] (Jerusalem, 1999).

ASHKENAZI, SHMUEL, *Alfa beita kadmita* (Jerusalem, 2001).

ASHKENAZI, TSEVI HIRSCH, *Hakham tsevi* (Lemberg, 1900).

ASZOD, JUDAH, *Yehudah ya'aleh* (Lemberg, 1873).

AUERBACH, MENAHEM NATHAN, *Orah ne'eman* (Jerusalem, 1924).

AVERROES, *Tahafut al-tahafut*, trans. S. Van Den Bergh (London, 1954).

AVIEZER, NATHAN, *Fossils and Faith* (Hoboken, NJ, 2001).

AVINER, SHELOMOH, 'Sacrifices in the Future' (Heb.), *Iturei kohanim*, 183 (Adar I 5760 [Feb. 2000]), 6–13.

—— *She'elat shelomoh*, 8 vols. (Jerusalem, 2001).

Avot derabi natan, ed. S. Schechter (New York, 1945).

AZRAD, MICHAEL, *Torat imekha* (Ma'alot, 2000).

AZULAI, ABRAHAM, *Ba'alei berit avram* (Vilna, 1874).

AZULAI, HAYIM JOSEPH DAVID, *Midbar kedemot* (Jerusalem, 1962).

—— *Penei david* (Jerusalem, 1965).

—— *Shem hagedolim* (Jerusalem, 1992).

BAHYA BEN ASHER, *Commentary on the Torah*, ed. C. Chavel, 3 vols. (Jerusalem, 1994).

BAHYA IBN PAKUDA, *Hovot halevavot*, ed. and trans. J. Kafih (Jerusalem, 1973).

BAMBERGER, BERNARD J., *Fallen Angels* (Philadelphia, Pa., 1952).

BAMBERGER, SELIGMANN BAER, 'Open Letter', in Samson Raphael Hirsch, *Collected Writings* (New York, 1990), vi. 226–53.

BANET, MORDECHAI, *Parashat mordekhai* (Sighet, 1889).

BARDA, DAVID, *Revid hazahav* (Tiberias, 1996).

BARDA, YITSHAK, *Yitshak yeranen*, vol. iv (Benei Berak, 1991).

BAR-ILAN, MEIR, 'The Hand of God: A Chapter in Rabbinic Anthropomorphism', in *Rashi 1040–1990: Hommage à Ephraim E. Urbach* (Paris, 1993), 321–35.

BARNES, W. E., 'Ancient Corrections in the Text of the Old Testament (*Tikkun Sopherim*)', *Journal of Theological Studies*, 1 (1900), 387–414.

BARON, SALO, *History and Jewish Historians* (Philadelphia, Pa., 1964).

—— *A Social and Religious History of the Jews*, 2nd edn., 18 vols. (New York, 1952–83).

—— 'An Unusual Excommunication Formula' (Heb.), in E. E. Urbach et al. (eds.), *Mehkarim bekabalah uvetoledot hadatot mugashim legershom sholem* (Jerusalem, 1968), 29–34.

BARR, JAMES, *The Variable Spellings of the Hebrew Bible* (Oxford, 1989).

BARZILAY, ISAAC, *Yoseph Shlomo Delmedigo* (Leiden, 1974).

BASILEA, AVIAD SAR-SHALOM, *Emunat hakhamim* (Warsaw, 1885).

BEKHOR SHOR, JOSEPH, *Commentaries of Rabbi Joseph Bekhor Shor* [Perushei rabi yosef bekhor shor], ed. Y. Navo (Jerusalem, 1994).

BENAMOZEGH, ELIJAH, *Introduction to the Oral Torah* [Mavo letorah shebe'al peh], ed. E. Zeini (Jerusalem, 2002).

BENAYAHU, ME'IR, 'Letter of the Scribe Rabbi Abraham Hasan of Salonika' (Heb.), *Sefunot*, 11 (1971–8), 189–229.

—— 'Revolutionary Opinions in Halakhic Rules in R. Samuel Messer Leon's Glosses on the *Beit yosef*' (Heb.), *Asupot*, 3 (1989), 141–264.

BEN-DAVID, YEHUDAH LAVI, *Shevet miyehudah* (Jerusalem, 2002).

BENJAMIN ZE'EV BEN SOLOMON, *Ben yemini* [supercommentary on Ibn Ezra] (Vienna, 1823).

BEN-MENAHEM, NAFTALI, 'An Additional Explanation to R. Abraham ibn Ezra by R. Moses Almosnino' (Heb.), *Sinai*, 10 (1946), 136–71.

—— *Inyanei ibn ezra* (Jerusalem, 1978).

—— *Jewish Treasures of the Vatican* [Miginzei yisra'el bavatikan] (Jerusalem, 1954).

BEN-SASSON, YONAH, *The Philosophical System of the Author of* Meshekh hokhmah [Mishnato ha'iyunit shel ba'al *Meshekh hokhmah*] (Jerusalem, 1996).

BEN-SHAMAI, HAGAI, 'Sa'adiah Gaon's Ten Principles of Faith' (Heb.), *Da'at*, 37 (1996), 11–26.

BEN-SHELOMOH, YOSEF, *The Mystical Theology of R. Moses Cordovero* [Torat ha'elohut shel r. moshe kordovero] (Jerusalem, 1965).

BEN-YERUHAM, H., and H. A. KOLITZ (eds.), *Shelilah lishemah* (Jerusalem, 1983).

BEN-YITSHAK, MENAHEM, 'Keri ukhetiv', *Hama'ayan*, 34 (Nisan 5753 [Apr. 1993]), 49–55.

BEN-ZE'EV, JUDAH LEIB, *Yesodei hadat* (Vienna, 1811).

BERDUGO, RAPHAEL, *Mei menuḥot* (Jerusalem, 1900).

—— *Rav peninim* (Casablanca, 1969).

Bereshit rabati, ed. H. Albeck (Jerusalem, 1967).

BERGER, DAVID, *The Rebbe, the Messiah, and the Scandal of Orthodox Indifference* (London, 2001).

BERKOVITZ, BEN ZION, *Ḥalifot simlot* (Vilna, 1874).

BERLIN, HAYIM, *Nishmat ḥayim* (Jerusalem, 2002)

BERLIN, NAFTALI TSEVI JUDAH, *Meromei sadeh* (Jerusalem, 1973).

BERLIN, SAUL, *Besamim rosh*, ed. R. Amar (Jerusalem, 1984).

BERLINER, ABRAHAM, *Selected Writings* [Ketavim nivḥarim], 2 vols. (Jerusalem, 1969).

BERMAN, LAWRENCE, 'Ibn Bajah and Maimonides' [Ibn bajah veharambam] (Ph.D. diss., Hebrew University of Jerusalem, 1959).

BERNFELD, SIMON, *Da'at elokim* (Jerusalem, 1971).

BIBAGO, ABRAHAM, *Derekh emunah* (Jerusalem, 1970).

BILLER, AVIAD, 'God Will Not Change or Revoke His Law' (Heb.), *Alon shevut*, 137 (1992), 80–103; 138 (1993), 60–82.

BIRNBAUM, PALTIEL, *Peletat soferim* (Jerusalem, 1971).

BLAND, KALMAN P., *The Artless Jew* (Princeton, NJ, 2000).

—— 'Moses and the Law According to Maimonides', in Jehuda Reinharz and Daniel Swetschinski (eds.), *Mystics, Philosophers and Politicians: Essays in Jewish Intellectual History in Honor of Alexander Altmann* (Durham, NC, 1982), 49–66.

BLEICH, J. DAVID, *Contemporary Halakhic Problems*, vol. ii (New York, 1989).

—— *With Perfect Faith: The Foundation of Jewish Belief* (New York, 1983).

BLEICH, MOSHE, 'The Role of Manuscripts in Halakhic Decision-Making: Hazon Ish, his Precursors and Contemporaries', *Tradition*, 27 (Winter 1993), 22–55.

BLIDSTEIN, GERALD J., 'Oral Law as Institution in Maimonides', in Ira Robinson et al. (eds.), *The Thought of Moses Maimonides* (Lewiston, Maine, 1990), 167–82.

BLOCH, P., 'Der Streit um den Moreh des Maimonides in der Gemeinde Posen um die Mitte des 16 Jahrh.', *MGWJ* 47 (1903), 153–69, 263–79, 346–56.

BLUMBERG, TSEVI, 'The Separate Intelligences in Maimonides' Philosophy' (Heb.), *Tarbiz*, 40 (1971), 216–25.

BLUMENTHAL, DAVID, *The Commentary of R. Ḥoter ben Shelomoh to the Thirteen Principles of Maimonides* (Leiden, 1974).

BODOFF, LIPPMAN, 'The Real Test of the *Akedah*', *Judaism*, 42 (Winter 1993), 71–92.

BONFIL, REUVEN, 'The Evidence of Agobard of Lyons for the Spiritual World of the Jews of his City in the Ninth Century' (Heb.), in Joseph Dan and Yosef Hacker (eds.), *Meḥkarim bekabalah mugashim leyishayah tishbi* (Jerusalem, 1984), 327–48.

——*The Rabbinate in Renaissance Italy* [Harabanut be'italiyah bitekufat harenesans] (Jerusalem, 1979).

BONFILS, JOSEPH BEN ELIEZER, *Tsofnat pane'aḥ*, ed. D. Herzog, 2 vols. (vol. i: Heidelberg, 1911; vol. ii: Berlin, 1930).

BREUER, EDWARD, *The Limits of Enlightenment: Jews, Germans, and the Eighteenth-Century Study of Scripture* (Cambridge, Mass., 1996).

BREUER, ISAAC, *Concepts of Judaism*, ed. Jacob S. Levinger (Jerusalem, 1974).

BREUER, MORDECHAI, *The Aleppo Codex and the Accepted Text of the Bible* [Keter aram tsovah vehanusaḥ hamekubal shel hamikra] (Jerusalem, 1976).

——'The Divine Origin of the Torah and Biblical Criticism' (Heb.), *Megadim*, 33 (Shevat 5761 [Feb. 2001]), 127–33.

BREUER, MORDECHAI, 'Changes in the Attitude of German Orthodox Jewry towards the National Movement during the First World War' (Heb.), in *Proceedings of the Seventh World Congress of Jewish Studies: History of the Jews in Europe* (Jerusalem, 1981), 167–79.

——*Jüdische Orthodoxie im Deutschen Reich 1871–1918* (Frankfurt, 1986).

BRIN, GERSHON, 'The Question of the Composition and Editing of the Bible in the Commentary of Rabbi Abraham ibn Ezra' (Heb.), in Yisrael Levin (ed.), *Meḥkarim bayetsirato shel avraham ibn ezra* (Tel Aviv, 1992), 121–35.

——'Studies in R. Judah the Pious' Exegesis to the Pentateuch' (Heb.), *Te'udah*, 3 (1983), 215–26.

BRODY, HAYIM, 'Poems of Meshulam ben Solomon da Piera' (Heb.), *Yediot hamakhon leḥeker hashirah ha'ivrit*, 4 (1938), 1–117.

BROIDE, HAYIM TSEVI HIRSCH, *Shir ḥadash* (St Louis, Mo., 1922).

BRUNA, ISRAEL, *She'elot uteshuvot mahari bruna* (Jerusalem, 1960).

BUBER, MARTIN, *Tales of the Hasidim*, 2 vols. (New York, 1948).

CHADWICK, O. (ed.), *Western Asceticism* (Philadelphia, Pa., 1958).

CHAJES, TSEVI HIRSCH, *Kol sifrei maharats ḥayot*, 2 vols. (Jerusalem, 1958).

CHILTON, MICHAEL, *The Christian Effect on Jewish Life* (London, 1994).

CHRISTFELS, PHILIPP ERNST, *Gespräch in dem Reiche der Todten über die Bibel und Talmud* (Schwabach, 1739).

CLARK, ELIZABETH A., *The Origenist Controversy: The Cultural Construction of an Early Christian Debate* (Princeton, NJ, 1992).

COHEN, DAVID, *Masat kapai*, vol. iii (Brooklyn, NY, 1990).

COHEN, JEFFREY M. (ed.), *Dear Chief Rabbi* (Hoboken, NJ, 1995).

COHEN, JOSEPH, *The Philosophical Thought of Rabbi Abraham ibn Ezra* [Haguto hafilosofit shel r. avraham ibn ezra] (Rishon Letsiyon, 1996).

COHEN, MARTIN, *The Shiur Qomah: Liturgy and Theurgy in Pre-Kabbalistic Jewish Mysticism* (Lanham, Md., 1983).

COHEN, MENACHEM, 'The Consonantal Character of First Biblical Printings' (Heb.), *Bar-Ilan Yearbook*, 18–19 (1981), 47–67.

—— 'Some Basic Features of the Consonantal Text in Medieval Manuscripts of the Hebrew Bible' (Heb.), in Uriel Simon and Moshe Goshen-Gottstein (eds.), *Iyunei mikra ufarshanut* (Ramat Gan, 1980), 123–82.

—— 'The Idea of the Sanctity of the Biblical Text and the Science of Textual Criticism' (Heb.), in U. Simon (ed.), *Hamikra ve'anahnu* (Ramat Gan, 1988), 42–79.

—— 'Introduction to the Haketer Edition', *Mikraot gedolot 'haketer': Yehoshua–Shofetim* (Ramat Gan, 1992), 1*-100*.

—— 'The 'Masoretic Text' and the Extent of its Influence on the Transmission of the Biblical Text in the Middle Ages' (Heb.), in Uriel Simon (ed.), *Iyunei mikra ufarshanut*, ii (Ramat Gan, 1986), 229–56.

COHEN, SAUL, *Karnei re'em* (Benei Berak, 1981).

COHN, TOBIAS BEN MOSES, *Ma'aseh tuviyah* (Benei Berak, 1978).

COLON, JOSEPH, *She'elot uteshuvot maharik* (Jerusalem, 1988).

CORDOVERO, MOSES, *Elimah rabati* (Jerusalem, 1999).

—— *Pardes rimonim* (Lvov, 1863).

COSMAN, ADMIEL, 'Maimonides' Thirteen Principles in his *Commentary on the Mishnah*, in *Yigdal*, and in *Ani ma'amin*' (Heb.), in Itamar Warhaftig (ed.), *Minhah le'ish* (Jerusalem, 1991), 337–48.

CRESCAS, HASDAI, *Or hashem* (Vienna, 1859).

DA FANO, MENAHEM AZARIAH, *Ma'amar me'ah kesitah* (Munkacs, 1892).

DAICHES, SALIS, 'Dogma in Judaism', in Leo Jung (ed.), *The Jewish Library*, 2nd ser. (New York, 1930), 243–66.

DAN, JOSEPH, *Early Jewish Mysticism* [Hamistikah ha'ivrit hakedumah] (Tel Aviv, 1989).

—— *The Esoteric Theology of Ashkenazi Hasidism* [Torat hasod shel hasidut ashkenaz] (Jerusalem, 1968).

—— *Jewish Mysticism*, 4 vols. (Northvale, NJ, 1998).

—— *The 'Unique Cherub' Circle* (Tübingen, 1999).

DANIN, D., *Sha'ar emunah* (Netivot, 1990).

DANZIG, ABRAHAM, *Hokhmat adam* (Jerusalem, 1966).

DANZIGER, SHELOMO E., 'Modern Orthodoxy or Orthodox Modernism', *Jewish Observer* (Oct. 1966), 3–9.

DAVIDSON, HERBERT, 'Maimonides' Secret Position on Creation', in Isadore Twersky (ed.), *Studies in Medieval Jewish History and Literature*, vol. i (Cambridge, Mass., 1979), 16–40.

DAVIDSON, ISRAEL, *Otsar hashirah vehapiyut*, 4 vols. (New York, 1970).

DAVIES, W. D., *The Setting of the Sermon on the Mount* (Cambridge, 1964).

DAVIS, JOSEPH M, 'Philosophy, Dogma, and Exegesis in Medieval Ashkenazic Judaism: The Evidence of *Sefer Hadrat Qodesh*', *AJS Review*, 18 (1993), 195–222.

—— 'R. Yom Tov Lipman Heller, Joseph b. Isaac ha-Levi, and Rationalism and Ashkenazic Jewish Culture 1550–1650' (Ph.D. diss., Harvard University, 1990).

DE FES, ISAAC, *Hoda'at emunat yisra'el* (Livorno, 1764).

DEI ROSSI, AZARIAH, *Me'or einayim* (Jerusalem, 1970).

DELITZSCH, FRANZ, *Bikurei te'enah* (*Documente der national-jüdischen christglaübigen Bewegung in Südrussland*) (Erlangen, 1884).

DELMEDIGO, ELIJAH, *Beḥinat hadat*, ed. J. Ross (Tel Aviv, 1984).

DELMEDIGO, JOSEPH SOLOMON, *Matsref leḥokhmah* (Odessa, 1865).

—— *Novelot ḥokhmah* (Basilea, 1631).

DEUTSCH, NATHANIEL, *Guardians of the Gate: Angelic Vice Regency in Late Antiquity* (Leiden, 1999).

DI BOTON, ABRAHAM, *Leḥem mishneh* [commentary on Maimonides, *Mishneh torah*, printed in standard edns.].

DI ILLESCOS, JACOB, *Imrei no'am* (Jerusalem, 1970).

DISKIN, JOSHUA LEIB, *She'elot uteshuvot maharil diskin* (Jerusalem, 1971).

DOMB, YERAHMIEL YISRAEL YITSHAK, *Ha'atakot* (Jerusalem, 1990).

DROSNIN, MICHAEL, *The Bible Code* (New York, 1997).

DUENNER, JOSEPH TSEVI, *Ḥidushei harav yosef tsevi duener* (Jerusalem, 1999).

DURAN, PROFIAT, *Ma'aseh efod* (Vienna, 1865).

DURAN, SIMEON BEN TSEMAH, *Magen avot* (Leipzig, 1855).

—— *Ohev mishpat* (Tel Aviv, 1971).

DURAN, SOLOMON BEN SIMEON, *She'elot uteshuvot harashbash* (Jerusalem, 1998).

EHRENREICH, HAYIM JUDAH, 'On the Variations in Biblical Verses between the Jerusalem Talmud and the Masoretic Text' (Heb.), *Otsar haḥayim*, 14 (1938), 4–6, 29–30, 40–9.

EISENSTADT, AVRAHAM ZVI HIRSCH, *Pitḥei teshuvah* [commentary on the *Shulḥan arukh*, printed in standard edns.].

EISENSTEIN, JUDAH DAVID, 'Between Two Opinions', trans. Robert L. Samuels, *American Jewish Archives*, 12 (1960), 123–42.

ELBOGEN, ISMAR, *Jewish Liturgy: A Comprehensive History*, trans. Raymond P. Scheindlin (New York, 1993).

ELIAV, MORDECHAI, *Jewish Education in Germany during the Haskalah and Emancipation* [Haḥinukh hayehudi begermanyah bimei hahaskalah veha'emanzipatsiyah] (Jerusalem, 1960).

ELIEZER BEN NATHAN, *Even ha'ezer* (Jerusalem, 1975).

ELIEZER BEN SAMUEL OF METZ, *Yere'im* (Vilna, 1881).

ELIJAH BEN SOLOMON ZALMAN (the Vilna Gaon), commentary on *Tikunei zohar* (Vilna, 1867).

—— *Tosefet ma'aseh rav* (Jerusalem, 1896).

ELYASHAR, HAYIM MOSES, *Sha'al ha'ish* (Jerusalem, 1909).

ELYASHAR, JACOB SAUL, *Yisa ish* (Jerusalem, 1896).

EMDEN, JACOB, *Amudei shamayim* (Altona, 1745).

—— *Migdal oz* (Zhitomir, 1874).

—— *Mitpaḥat sefarim* (Jerusalem, 1995).

—— *Mor uketsiah* (Jerusalem, 1996).

—— *She'elat ya'avets*, 2 vols. (Lvov, 1884).

—— (attrib.), *Sidur beit ya'akov* (Lvov, 1804).

Encyclopaedia Judaica, 16 vols., ed. C. Roth (Jerusalem, 1971–2).

EPSTEIN, ABRAHAM, *Kitvei avraham epstein*, 2 vols. (Jerusalem, 1965).

EPSTEIN, ISIDORE, *The Faith of Judaism* (London, 1980).

EPSTEIN, J. N., 'The Commentaries of Rabbi Judah ben Nathan and the Commentaries of Worms' (Heb.), *Tarbiz*, 4 (1933), 11–34.

—— 'On Rashi's Commentary on *Nedarim*' (Heb.), *Tarbiz*, 4 (supplemental issue, 1933), 180–1; 5 (1934), 110.

EPSTEIN, KALONYMUS KALMAN, *Maor vashemesh* (Jerusalem, 1992).

EPSTEIN, YEHIEL MIKHEL, *Arukh hashulḥan*, 8 vols. (Jerusalem, 1950).

ERGAS, JOSEPH, *Shomer emunim* (Jerusalem, 1965).

ESH, SHAUL, 'Variant Readings in Mediaeval Hebrew Commentaries: R. Samuel Ben Meir (Rashbam)', *Textus*, 5 (1966), 84–92.

'EVEN SHAYISH' (pseud.), 'On the Reform of Judaism' (Heb.), *Hashilo'aḥ*, 25 (1911), 193–7.

EYBESCHUETZ, JONATHAN, *Tiferet yisra'el* (Warsaw, 1878).

—— *Ya'arot devash*, 2 vols. (Jerusalem, n.d.).

EYLENBURG, ISSACHAR BAER, *Tsedah laderekh* (Jerusalem, 1998).

FAIERSTEIN, MORRIS M., *The Libes Briv of Isaac Wetzlar* (Atlanta, Ga., 1996).

Faksimile-Ausgabe des Mischnacodex Kaufmann (Jerusalem, 1967).

FALAQUERA, SHEM TOV BEN JOSEPH, *Moreh hamoreh*, ed. Y. Shiffman (Jerusalem, 2001).

FALK, JOSHUA, *Binyan yehoshua* [commentary on *Avot derabi natan*, printed in the Vilna edn. of the Talmud].

FARBER-GINAT, ASI, 'Studies in *Sefer shiur komah*' (Heb.), in Michal Oron and Amos Goldreich (eds.), *Masuot: Meḥkarim besifrut hakabalah uvemaḥshevat yisra'el mukdashim lezikhro shel profesor efrayim gotlieb* (Jerusalem, 1994), 361–94.

FEINSTEIN, MOSES, *Igerot Moshe*, 8 vols. (New York, Benei Berak, and Jerusalem, 1959–96).

FELDMAN, SEYMOUR, 'The Theory of Eternal Creation in Hasdai Crescas and Some of his Predecessors', *Viator*, 11 (1980), 289–320.

FENDEL, ZECHARIAH, *Torah Faith: The Thirteen Principles* (New York, 1985).

FLECKELES, ELEAZAR, *Teshuvah me'ahavah*, 3 vols. (Kassa, 1912).

FLEISCHER, EZRA, et al. (eds.), *Me'ah she'arim: Studies in Medieval Jewish Spiritual Life in Memory of Isadore Twersky* (Jerusalem, 2001).

FLEISCHER, JUDAH, 'Supercommentaries on Rabbi Abraham ibn Ezra's Commentary on the Bible' (Heb.). The article appears in *Otsar haḥayim* (*OH*), vol. 14, and *Binoti basefarim* (*BB*), a series of supplements to *OH*, as follows: *OH* 14/3 (1937 [Kislev 5698]), 54–6; 14/5 (1938 [Shevat 5698]), 71–2; 14/11–12 (1938 [Av/Elul 5698]), 182–5; *BB* to *OH* 14/1–2 (1937 [Tishrei/Marheshvan 5698]), 18–19; *BB* to *OH* 14/3 (1937 [Kislev 5698]), 54–6; *BB* to *OH* 14/5 (1938 [Shevat 5698]), 71–2.

FOX, MARVIN, 'The Holiness of the Holy Land', in Jonathan Sacks (ed.), *Tradition and Transition* (London, 1986), 155–70.

—— *Interpreting Maimonides* (Chicago, Ill., 1990).

FRANK, DANIEL, 'The Religious Philosophy of the Karaite Aaron ben Elijah: The Problem of Divine Justice' (Ph.D. diss., Harvard University, 1991).

FRANK, R. M., *Al-Ghazali and the Ash'arite School* (Durham, NC, 1994).

FREUDENTHAL, GAD, '"The Air, Blessed Be It and Blessed Be Its Name" in *Sefer hamaskil* by R. Solomon Simhah of Troyes—Towards a Portrait of a Midrashic-Scientific Cosmology of Stoic Inspiration from the Thirteenth Century' (Heb.), *Da'at*, 32–3 (1994), 187–233; 34 (1995), 87–129.

FRIEDLAENDER, MICHAEL, *Essays on the Writings of Ibn Ezra* (London, 1877).

—— *The Jewish Religion* (London, 1891).

FRIEDMAN, MENAHEM, *Ḥevrah vedat* (Jerusalem, 1988).

FRIEDMAN, SHAMMA, 'Graven Images', *Graven Images*, 1 (1994), 233–8.

FRIEDMAN, ZALMAN JACOB, *Emet ve'emunah* (New York, 1895).

FRIMER, NAHMAN, and DOV SCHWARTZ, *The Life and Thought of Shem Tov ibn Shaprut* [Hagut betsel ha'emah] (Jerusalem, 1992).

FRISH, DANIEL, *Matok midevash* (Jerusalem, 1989).

GAGUINE, SHEM TOV, *Keter shem tov*, vol. i (Kedainiai, 1934).

GAON, M. D., 'Recitation of the Thirteen Principles' (Heb.), *Yeda am*, 3 (1955), 39–41.

GARTIG, WILLIAM G., 'A Critical Edition with English Translation of the Genesis Portion of *Avvat Nefesh*, a Medieval Supercommentary to Abraham Ibn Ezra's Commentary on the Pentateuch' (Ph.D. diss., Hebrew Union College–Jewish Institute of Religion, 1994).

GASTER, MOSES, *The Sword of Moses: An Ancient Jewish Book of Magic* (Edmonds, Wash., 1992).

GATIGNO, EZRA, 'Philosophical Supercommentaries on the Commentaries of R. Abraham ibn Ezra' (Heb.), ed. Dov Schwartz, *Alei sefer*, 18 (1995–6), 71–114.

GEDALIAH IBN YAHYA, *Shalshelet hakabalah* (Jerusalem, 1962).

GELLMAN, JEROME, 'Freedom and Determinism in Maimonides' Philosophy', in Eric L. Ormsby (ed.), *Moses Maimonides and his Time* (Washington, DC, 1989), 139–50.

—— 'The Philosophical *Hassagot* of Rabad on Maimonides' Mishneh Torah', *The New Scholasticism*, 58 (1984).

GENACK, MENACHEM, 'Ambiguity as Theology', *Tradition*, 25 (Fall 1989), 70–80.

GERLITS, M. M. (ed.), *Hagadah shel pesaḥ mibeit halevi* (Jerusalem, 1982).

GERONDI, NISSIM, *Derashot haran*, ed. L. Feldman (Jerusalem, 1977).

GERSHENSON, SHOSHANNA, 'The View of Maimonides as a Determinist in *Sefer Minhat Qenaot* by Abner of Burgos', *Proceedings of the Ninth World Congress of Jewish Studies* (Jerusalem, 1986), iii. 93–100.

GERSONIDES (LEVI BEN GERSHOM) , *Commentary on the Torah* [Perushei ralbag al hatorah], ed. Y. Levy, 5 vols. (Jerusalem, 1992–2000).

—— *Milḥamot hashem* (Leipzig, 1866).

—— *The Wars of the Lord*, trans. Seymour Feldman, 3 vols. (Philadelphia, Pa., 1984–99).

GIKATILLA, JOSEPH BEN ABRAHAM, *Sha'arei orah* [with the commentary of Mattathias Delacrut] (Jerusalem, 1960).

GINSBURG, C. D., *Introduction to the Massoretico-Critical Edition of the Hebrew Bible* (New York, 1966).

—— *The Masorah*, 4 vols. (New York, 1975).

—— *The Twenty-Four Books of the Scriptures* [Esrim ve'arba'ah sifrei hakodesh] (London, 1908).

GINZBERG, LOUIS, 'Anthropomorphism', *Jewish Encyclopedia* (New York, 1906–7), i. 621–5.

—— *Legends of the Jews*, 7 vols. (Baltimore, 1998).

GOITEIN, BARUKH BENDIT, *Zikhron avot* (Benei Berak, 1971).

GOLDMAN, S., 'The Halachic Foundation of Maimonides' Thirteen Principles', in H. J. Zimmels et al. (eds.), *Essays Presented to Chief Rabbi Israel Brodie on the Occasion of his Seventieth Birthday* (London, 1967), 111–17.

GOLDWURM, HERSH, *The Rishonim* (Brooklyn, NY, 1986).

GOODENOUGH, E. R., *Jewish Symbols in the Greco-Roman Period*, 13 vols. (New York, 1953).

GORDON, MARTIN L., 'The Rationalism of Jacob Anatoli' (Ph.D. diss., Yeshiva University, New York, 1974).

GOREN, SHELOMOH, 'Building the Temple in Modern Times' (Heb.), in *Neshemah shel shabat: Ma'amarim toraniyim lezikhro shel harav eliyahu shelomoh ra'anan* (Hebron, 1999), 226–57.

—— *Torat hashabat vehamo'ed* (Jerusalem, 1982).

GOSHEN-GOTTSTEIN, ALON, 'The Body as Image of God in Rabbinic Literature', *HTR* 87 (1994), 171–95.

GOSHEN-GOTTSTEIN, MOSHE, 'The Authenticity of the Aleppo Codex', *Textus*, 1 (1960), 7–73.

—— 'Editions of the Hebrew Bible—Past and Future', in Michael Fishbane and Emanuel Tov (eds.), *Sha'arei talmon* (Winona Lake, Ind., 1992), 221–42.

—— 'The Hebrew Bible in the Light of the Qumran Scrolls and the Hebrew University Bible', *Vetus Testamentum Congress Volume* (Jerusalem, 1988), 42–53.

—— 'Introduction', *Biblia Rabbinica* (Jerusalem, 1972).

—— 'The "Keter Aram Tzovah" and the Maimonidean Laws Concerning a Torah Scroll' (Heb.), in Shaul Yisra'eli et al. (eds.), *Sefer yovel likhvod morenu hagaon rabi yosef dov halevi soloveitchik* (Jerusalem, 1984), 871–88.

—— 'The Rise of the Tiberian Bible Text', in Alexander Altmann (ed.), *Biblical and Other Studies* (Cambridge, Mass., 1963), 79–122.

GOTTESMAN, ABRAHAM JOSEPH, *Emunah shelemah* (Brooklyn, NY, 1940).

GOTTLIEB, EFRAYIM, 'Ma'arekhet ha-Elohut', *Encyclopaedia Judaica* (Jerusalem, 1971), xi, cols. 637–9.

GOTTLIEB, EFRAYIM, *Studies in Kabbalistic Literature* [Meḥkarim besifrut ha-kabalah] (Tel Aviv, 1976).

GRAETZ, HEINRICH, *Geschichte der Juden*, 11 vols. (Leipzig, 1863).

—— *The Structure of Jewish History*, trans. Ismar Schorsch (New York, 1975).

GREEN, ARTHUR, *Tormented Master: A Life of Rabbi Nahman of Bratslav* (Wood-stock, NY, 1981).

GREENBAUM, AARON, 'R. Shmuel Hofni Gaon's Commentary on "Ha'azinu"' (Heb.), *Sinai*, 100 (1987), 273–90.

GREIVE, HERMANN, *Studien zum jüdischen Neuplatonismus. Die Religionsphilosophie des Abraham Ibn Ezra* (Berlin, 1973).

GRIES, ZEV, *Sifrut hahanhagot* (Jerusalem, 1989).

GRODZINSKI, TSEVI HIRSCH, *Mikra'ei kodesh*, 3 vols. (Brooklyn, NY, 1936–41).

GROSSMAN, AVRAHAM, *The Early Sages of France* [Ḥakhmei tsarfat harishonim] (Jerusalem, 1995).

GUENZBERG, ARYEH LOEB, *Sha'agat aryeh* (Brooklyn, NY, 1989).

GURARY, NOSON, *The Thirteen Principles of Faith: A Chasidic Viewpoint* (Northvale, NJ, 1996).

GUTTMANN, JULIUS, *Philosophies of Judaism*, trans. David W. Silverman (New York, 1964).

HABERMAN, JACOB, *Maimonides and Aquinas: A Contemporary Appraisal* (New York, 1979).

HADAS-LEBEL, MIREILLE, 'Il n'y a pas de messie pour Israël car on l'a déjà con-sommé au temps d'Ézéchias (TB *Sanhédrin* 99a)', *REJ* 159 (2000), 357–67.

HAGIZ, MOSES, *Halakhot ketanot*, 2 vols. (Jerusalem, 1974).

—— *Mishnat ḥakhamim* (Lvov, 1866).

HAHN, JOSEPH YUZPA, *Yosif omets* (Frankfurt, 1928).

HAKOHEN, ABRAHAM ISAAC, *Zekhor le'avraham*, ed. S. Rosenfeld (Jerusalem, 2000).

HAKOHEN, ALEXANDER SUSLEIN, *Sefer ha'agudah: Nidah* (Kraków, 1571).

—— *Sefer ha'agudah: Pesaḥim* (Jerusalem, 1968).

HAKOHEN, ISRAEL MEIR, *Mikhtevei ḥafets ḥayim* (New York, n.d.).

—— *Mishnah berurah* [numerous edns.].

HAKOHEN, ISSACHAR BERMAN B. NAFTALI, *Matnot kehunah* [commentary on *Midrash rabah*, printed in standard edns.].

HAKOHEN, ISSACHAR DOV BERISH, *Ohel yisakhar* (Jerusalem, 1962).

HAKOHEN, KALFON MOSES, *Berit kehunah*, 2 vols. (Benei Berak, 1990).

HAKOHEN, MOSES, *Veheshiv mosheh* (Jerusalem, 1968).

HAKOHEN, RAHAMIM, *Zikhrei kehunah*, bound with K. M. Hakohen, *Berit kehunah* (Benei Berak, 1990).

HAKOHEN, TSADOK, *Divrei soferim: Sefer hazikhronot* (Benei Berak, 1967).

HAKOKHAVI, DAVID BEN SAMUEL, *Sefer habatim*, ed. M. Herschler, 3 vols. (Jeru-salem, 1983).

HALAMISH, MOSHE, *Kabbalah in Prayer, Halakhah, and Custom* [Hakabalah bitefilah, behalakhah, uveminhag] (Ramat Gan, 2000).

HALAVEH, MOSES, *Teshuvot maharam halaveh* (Jerusalem, 1987).

HALBERSTAM, HAYIM, *Divrei ḥayim al hatorah umo'adim*, 2 vols. (Jerusalem, 2000).

HALBERSTAMM, S. Z. H. (ed.), *Letters about the Controversy over Maimonides'* Guide *and* Sefer hamada [Kevutsat mikhtavim be'inyanei hamaḥloket al devar sefer hamoreh vehamada] (Bamberg, 1875).

HALBERTAL, MOSHE, *Between Torah and Wisdom: Rabbi Menahem Hame'iri and the Maimonidean Halakhists of Provence* [Bein torah leḥokhmah: Rabi menaḥem hame'iri uva'alei hahalakhah hamaimonim beprovans] (Jerusalem, 2000).

HALEVI, HAYIM DAVID, *Aseh lekha rav*, 9 vols. (Tel Aviv, 1976–89).

—— *Torat ḥayim*, 2 vols. (Tel Aviv, 1993).

HALEVI, JUDAH, *Kuzari*, ed. J. Kafih (Kiryat Ono, 1997).

HALIVNI, DAVID WEISS, *Peshat and Derash* (Oxford, 1991).

HALKIN, ABRAHAM, and DAVID HARTMAN, *Crisis and Leadership: Epistles of Maimonides* (Philadelphia, Pa., 1985).

HALPERIN, DAVID J., *Abraham Miguel Cardozo* (Mahwah, NJ, 2001).

HALPERIN, DOV MOSHE, *Ḥemdah genuzah* (Lakewood, NJ, 2001).

HALUTSKI, SIMHAH ISAAC BEN MOSES, *Kevod elokim* (Ramleh, 2000).

HANANEL BEN HUSHIEL, *Commentary on the Torah* [Perush rabenu ḥananel al hatorah], ed. C. D. Chavel (Jerusalem, 1972).

Ḥarba demosheh, ed. Yuval Harari (Jerusalem, 1997).

HARRIS, JAY M., *Nachman Krochmal: Guiding the Perplexed of the Modern Age* (New York, 1991).

HARRIS, MONFORD, 'The Theologico-Historical Thinking of Samuel David Luzzatto', *JQR* 52 (1962), 216–44, 309–34.

HARTMAN, DAVID, *A Living Covenant: The Innovative Spirit in Traditional Judaism* (New York, 1985).

—— *Maimonides: Torah and Philosophic Quest* (Philadelphia, Pa., 1976).

HARVEY, STEVEN, *Falaquera's Epistle of the Debate: An Introduction to Jewish Philosophy* (Cambridge, Mass., 1987).

HARVEY, WARREN ZEV, 'Hasdai Crescas's Critique of the Theory of the Acquired Intellect' (Ph.D. diss., Columbia University, New York, 1973).

—— 'The Incorporeality of God in Maimonides, Rabad, and Spinoza' (Heb.), in Sarah O. Heller-Wilensky and Moshe Idel (eds.), *Meḥkarim behagut yehudit* (Jerusalem, 1989), 69–74.

—— 'Maimonides' Interpretation of Genesis 3: 22' (Heb.), *Da'at*, 12 (1984), 15–18.

—— 'The *Mishneh Torah* as a Key to the Secrets of the *Guide*', in Ezra Fleischer et al. (eds.), *Me'ah she'arim: Studies in Medieval Jewish Spiritual Life in Memory of Isadore Twersky* (Jerusalem, 2001), 11–28.

—— *Physics and Metaphysics in Hasdai Crescas* (Amsterdam, 1998).

HARVEY, WARREN ZEV, 'A Third Approach to Maimonides' Cosmogony-Prophetology Puzzle', in Joseph A. Buijs (ed.), *Maimonides: A Collection of Critical Essays* (Notre Dame, Ind., 1988), 71–88.

HAVLIN, SHELOMOH ZALMAN, 'Establishing Correct Manuscript Readings: Quantity or Quality' (Heb.), in E. Fleischer et al. (eds.), *Me'ah she'arim: Studies in Medieval Jewish Spiritual Life in Memory of Isadore Twersky* (Jerusalem, 2001), 241–65.

HAYIM BEN ATTAR, *Or haḥayim* [commentary on Torah, printed in standard edns.].

HAYIM OF VOLOZHIN, *Nefesh haḥayim* (Jerusalem, 1989).

HAYON, NEHEMIAH, *Oz le'elohim* (Berlin, 1713).

HAYOUN, MAURICE-RUBEN, *La Philosophie et la théologie de Moïse de Narbonne* (Tübingen, 1989).

HAYOUN, YEHUDAH, *Otsarot aḥarit hayamim* (Benei Berak, 1993).

HAZAN, JACOB, *Ets ḥayim*, ed. I. Brodie, 3 vols. (Jerusalem, 1962–7).

HEFETZ (GENTILI), MOSES, *Melekhet maḥshevet* (Warsaw, 1914).

HEILPRIN, JEHIEL, *Seder hadorot* (Warsaw, 1878).

HEINEMANN, ISAAK, 'Maimuni und die arabischen Einheitslehrer', *MGWJ* 79 (1935), 102–48.

HELLER-WILENSKY, SARAH O., 'The "First Created Being" in Early Kabbalah and its Philosophical Sources' (Heb.), in ead. and Moshe Idel (eds.), *Meḥkarim behagut yehudit* (Jerusalem, 1989), 261–76.

—— 'Ibn Ezra, Abraham', *Encyclopaedia Judaica* (Jerusalem, 1971), viii, cols. 1168–9.

—— *Rabbi Isaac Arama and his Teachings* [Rabi yitsḥak arama umishnato] (Jerusalem, 1956).

—— and MOSHE IDEL (eds.), *Studies in Jewish Thought* [Meḥkarim behagut yehudit] (Jerusalem, 1989).

HERTZ, JOSEPH H., *Authorized Daily Prayer Book* (New York, 1957).

—— *The Pentateuch and Haftorahs* (London, 1960).

HERZOG, ISAAC, *Decisions and Writings* [Pesakim ukhetavim], 9 vols. (Jerusalem, 1989–96).

HESCHEL, ABRAHAM JOSHUA, *Theology in Ancient Judaism* [Torah min hashamayim be'aspaklariyah shel hadorot], 3 vols. (London and Jerusalem, 1962–90).

HEZEKIAH BEN ABRAHAM, *Malki'el* (Warsaw, 1876).

HIKSHER, EPHRAIM, *Adnei faz* (Altona, 1743).

HIRSCH, SAMSON RAPHAEL, *Neunzehn Briefe über Judentum* (Frankfurt, 1911).

HIRSCHENSOHN, HAYIM, *Malki bakodesh*, 6 vols. (Hoboken, NJ, 1919–28).

—— *Musagei shav ve'emet* (Jerusalem, 1932).

—— *Nimukei rashi* (Seini, 1929).

HIRSCHFELD, BARUKH, *Mishnat rishonim* (Wickliffe, Ohio, 1992).

HOFFMANN, DAVID TSEVI, *Commentary on Genesis* [Perush al bereshit], trans. Asher Wasserteil (Benei Berak, 1969).

HOROWITZ, ISAIAH, *Shenei luḥot haberit* (Jerusalem, 1960).

HOROWITZ, JACOB ISAAC, *Zikhron zot* (New York, 1966).

HUSIK, ISAAC, *A History of Mediaeval Jewish Philosophy* (New York, 1969).

HYMAN, ARTHUR, *Eschatological Themes in Medieval Jewish Philosophy* (Milwaukee, Wis., 2002).

——'Maimonides' "Thirteen Principles"', in Alexander Altmann (ed.), *Jewish Medieval and Renaissance Studies* (Cambridge, Mass., 1967), 119–44.

——'Spinoza's Dogmas of Universal Faith in the Light of their Medieval Jewish Background', in Alexander Altmann (ed.), *Biblical and Other Studies* (Cambridge, Mass., 1963), 183–95.

IBN BILIA, DAVID BEN YOM TOV, *Yesodot hamaskil*, in Eliezer Ashkenazi (ed.), *Divrei ḥakhamim* (Metz, 1849), 56–60.

IBN DAUD, ABRAHAM, *Ha'emunah haramah*, trans. Solomon ben Lavi, ed. Simson Weil (Frankfurt, 1852).

IBN EZRA, ABRAHAM, *Commentary on the Torah* [Perushei hatorah lerabenu avraham ibn ezra], ed. Asher Weiser, 3 vols. (Jerusalem, 1977).

——*Safah berurah* (Fuerth, 1839).

——*Sefer tsaḥut* (Fuerth, 1827).

IBN KASPI, JOSEPH, *Amudei kesef umaskiyot kesef* [commentary on Maimonides' *Guide*] (Frankfurt, 1848).

——*Perush hasodot shel harav avraham ibn ezra al hatorah*, in id., *Kitvei r. yosef kaspi: Asarah kelei kesef* (Jerusalem, 1970), 145–72.

IBN MIGASH, JOSEPH, *Ḥidushei hari migash* (Jerusalem, 1985).

IBN TAHIR AL-BAGHDADI, *Moslem Schisms and Sects*, trans. Kate Chambers Seelye (New York, 1920).

IBN YAHYA, GEDALIAH BEN JOSEPH, *Shalshelet hakabalah* (Jerusalem, 1962).

IBN YAHYA, DON JOSEPH BEN DON DAVID, *Torah or* (Bologna, 1538).

IBN ZIMRA, DAVID, *She'elot uteshuvot haradbaz* (Warsaw, 1882).

IDEL, MOSHE, 'Differing Conceptions of Kabbalah in the Early 17th Century', in Isadore Twersky and Bernard Septimus (eds.), *Jewish Thought in the Seventeenth Century* (Cambridge, Mass., 1987), 137–200.

——*Kabbalah: New Perspectives* (New Haven, Conn., 1988).

——'Kabbalistic Prayer in Provence' (Heb.), *Tarbiz*, 62 (1993), 265–86.

——'Solomon b. Adret and Abraham Abulafia: History of a Neglected Kabbalistic Controversy' (Heb.), in Daniel Boyarin et al. (eds.), *Atarah leḥayim: Meḥkarim basifrut hatalmudit veharabanit likhvod profesor ḥayim zalman dimitrovski* (Jerusalem, 2000), 235–51.

IRSAI, O., 'Yaakov of Kefar Niburaia: A Sage Turned Apostate' (Heb.), *Meḥkerei yerushalayim bemaḥshevet yisra'el*, 2 (1983), 153–68.

ISAAC BEN SHESHET, *She'elot uteshuvot harivash* (Jerusalem, 1975).

ISAIAH OF TRANI (the Elder), *Kuntres hare'ayot*, ed. A. Wertheimer (Jerusalem, 1994).

ISHBILI, YOM TOV, *Sefer hazikaron*, ed. K. Kahana (Jerusalem, 1982).

ISHMAEL HANINA OF VALMONTONE, *Shivah ḥakirot* (Husiatyn, 1904).

ISRAEL BEN JOSEPH AL-NAKAWA, *Menorat hamaor*, ed. H. Enelow, 4 vols. (New York, 1929–32).

ISSERLES, MOSES, *Darkhei mosheh* [in standard edns. of Jacob ben Asher, *Arba'ah turim*].

—— *She'elot uteshuvot rema*, ed. Asher Siev (Jerusalem, 1971).

IVRY, ALFRED L., 'Islamic and Greek Influences on Maimonides' Philosophy', in Shlomo Pines and Yirmiyahu Yovel (eds.), *Maimonides and Philosophy* (Dordrecht, 1986), 139–56.

—— 'Isma'ili Theology and Maimonides' Philosophy', in Daniel Frank (ed.), *The Jews of Medieval Islam* (Leiden, 1995), 271–300.

—— 'Remnants of Jewish Averroism in the Renaissance', in Bernard Dov Cooperman (ed.), *Jewish Thought in the Sixteenth Century* (Cambridge, Mass., 1983), 243–65.

JACOB JOSEPH OF POLONNOYE, *Toledot ya'akov yosef* (Brooklyn, NY, 2000).

JACOBS, LOUIS, *Beyond Reasonable Doubt* (London, 1999).

—— *Faith* (London, 1968).

—— *A Jewish Theology* (New York, 1973).

—— *Principles of the Jewish Faith* (New York, 1964).

—— *Seeker of Unity: The Life and Works of Aaron of Starosselje* (London, 1966).

JAFFE, MORDEKHAI, *Levushei or yekarot* (Jerusalem, 2000).

JAPHET, SARA (ed.), *Rabbi Samuel ben Meir's Commentary on Job* [Perush r. shemuel ben me'ir lesefer iyov] (Jerusalem, 2000).

JEHIEL MOSES OF KOMAROVKA, *Niflaot ḥadashot* (Petrokov, 1897).

JELLINEK, ADOLF, *Ginzei ḥokhmat hakabalah* (Leipzig, 1853).

JOSEPH HAYIM BEN ELIJAH AL-HAKAM, *Ben ish ḥai* (Jerusalem, 1994).

—— *Od yosef ḥai* (Jerusalem, 1950).

—— *Rav pe'alim*, 4 vols. (Jerusalem, 1980).

JOSPE, EVA (ed. and trans.), *Moses Mendelssohn: Selections from his Writings* (New York, 1975).

JOSPE, RAPHAEL, 'Maimonides and *Shiur komah*' (Heb.), in Moshe Idel et al. (eds.), *Minḥah lesarah* (Jerusalem, 1994), 195–209.

—— *Torah and Sophia: The Life and Thought of Shem Tov Ibn Falaquera* (Cincinnati, Ohio, 1988).

—— and DOV SCHWARTZ, 'Shem Tov Ibn Falaquera's Lost Bible Commentary', *HUCA* 64 (1993), 167–200.

JUDAH BEN SAMUEL HEHASID, *The Torah Commentaries of Rabbi Judah Hehasid* [Perushei hatorah lerabi yehudah heḥasid], ed. I. S. Lange (Jerusalem, 1975).

JUNG, LEO, *Fallen Angels in Jewish, Christian and Mohammedan Literature* (Philadelphia, Pa., 1926).

KAFIH, EINAT, 'The Nature of the Soul in Medieval Jewish Thought' (Heb.), in Yosef Tobi (ed.), *Lerosh yosef* (Jerusalem, 1995), 133–65.

KAFIH, JOSEPH, *Writings* [Ketavim], 3 vols. (Jerusalem, 1989–2002).

KAFIH, YIHYEH, *Milḥamot hashem* (Jerusalem, 1931).

KAHLE, PAUL, *The Cairo Geniza* (Oxford, 1959).

KAMELHAR, JEKUTHIEL ARYEH, *Dor de'ah*, 2 vols. (Petrokov, 1938).

KAMENETZKY, JACOB, *Emet leya'akov* (New York, 1991).

KANARFOGEL, EPHRAIM, *'Peering through the Lattices': Mystical, Magical, and Pietistic Dimensions in the Tosafist Period* (Detroit, Mich., 2000).

KANEVSKY, S., *Siaḥ hasadeh* (Benei Berak, 1971).

KAPLAN, ARYEH, *The Handbook of Jewish Thought* (New York, 1979).

—— *Maimonides' Principles: The Fundamentals of Jewish Faith* (New York, 1984).

—— *Meditation and Kabbalah* (York Beach, Maine, 1982).

KAPLAN, LAWRENCE, ' "I sleep, but my heart waketh": Maimonides' Conception of Human Perfection', in Ira Robinson et al. (eds.), *The Thought of Moses Maimonides* (Lewiston, NY, 1990), 131–69.

—— 'The Multi-Faceted Legacy of the Rav: A Critical Analysis of R. Herschel Schachter's *Nefesh Ha-Rav*', BaDaD [*Bekhol derakheikha da'ehu*], 7 (Summer 1998), 51–85.

KAPLAN, MORDECAI, and EUGENE KOHN (eds.), *Sabbath Prayerbook* (New York, 1945).

KARELITZ, ABRAHAM ISAIAH, *Ḥazon ish al 'Yoreh de'ah'* (Benei Berak, 1973).

—— *Kovets igerot ḥazon ish*, 3 vols. (Benei Berak, 1990).

KARO, ISAAC, *Toledot yitsḥak* (Jerusalem, 1994).

KARO, JOSEPH, *Avkat rokhel* (Leipzig, 1859).

KASHER, HANNAH, 'Ibn Caspi's Commentary to the Secrets of Ibn Ezra' (Heb.), in Moshe Halamish (ed.), *Alei shefer* (Ramat Gan, 1990), 89–108.

—— 'Joseph ibn Kaspi as a Philosophical Commentator' [Yosef ibn kaspi kefarshan filosofi] (Ph.D. diss., Bar Ilan University, 1993).

—— 'Principal and Subsidiary in Sections of the Torah: Different Approaches in Medieval Thought' (Heb.), *HUCA* 66 (1995), 1–30 (Hebrew section).

—— ' "Torah for its own sake", "Torah not for its own sake", and the Third Way', *JQR* 79 (1988–9), 153–63.

KASHER, MENAHEM M., *Hatekufah hagedolah* (Jerusalem, 1968).

—— *Mefane'aḥ tsefunot* (New York, 1960).

—— *Torah shelemah*, 44 vols. (Jerusalem, 1992–5).

KASSIN, JACOB, *Yesod ha'emunah* (Brooklyn, NY, 1981).

KATAN, YOEL, 'I Believe with Perfect Faith' (Heb.), *Hama'ayan*, 30 (Tevet 5750 [Jan. 1990]), 41–4.

KATZ, BEN ZION, 'Judah he-Hasid: Three Controversial Commentaries', *Jewish Bible Quarterly*, 25 (1997), 23–30.

KATZENELLENBOGEN, ABRAHAM TSEVI HIRSCH, *Sha'arei raḥamim* (Jerusalem, 1981).

KAUDERS, SAMUEL LEIB, *Olat shemuel* (Prague, 1823).

KAUFMANN, DAVID, *Geschichte der Attributenlehre in der jüdischen Religionsphilosophie des Mittelalters* (Gotha, 1877).

—— 'Jehuda Halewi und die Lehre von der Ewigkeit der Welt', *MGWJ* 33 (1884), 208–14.

—— *Die Sinne* (Leipzig, 1884).

—— *Studien über Salomon Ibn Gabirol* (Budapest, 1899).

KELLNER, MENACHEM, *Dogma in Medieval Jewish Thought: From Maimonides to Abravanel* (Oxford, 1986).

—— 'Gersonides on Miracles, the Messiah, and Resurrection', *Da'at*, 4 (1980), 5–34.

—— 'Gersonides, Providence and the Rabbinic Tradition', *Journal of the American Academy of Religion*, 42 (1974), 673–85.

—— 'Heresy and the Nature of Faith in Medieval Jewish Philosophy', *JQR* 76 (1987), 299–318.

—— 'Inadvertent Heresy in Medieval Jewish Thought: Maimonides and Abravanel vs. Duran and Crescas?' (Heb.), *Jerusalem Studies in Jewish Thought*, 3 (1984), 393–403.

—— 'The Literary Character of the *Mishneh Torah*: On the Art of Writing in Maimonides' Halakhic Works', in E. Fleischer et al. (eds.), *Me'ah she'arim: Studies in Medieval Jewish Spiritual Life in Memory of Isadore Twersky* (Jerusalem, 2001), 29–45.

—— *Maimonides on the 'Decline of the Generations' and the Nature of Rabbinic Authority* (Albany, NY, 1996).

—— *Must a Jew Believe Anything?* (London, 1999).

—— 'What is Heresy?', *Studies in Jewish Philosophy*, 3 (1983), 55–70.

KIENER, RONALD C., 'The Hebrew Paraphrase of Saadya Gaon', *AJS Review*, 11 (1986), 1–26.

KIMHI, DAVID, *Commentary on the Bible*, printed in standard edns. of *Mikraot gedolot*.

KIRSCHNER, ROBERT S., 'Maimonides' Fiction of Resurrection', *HUCA* 52 (1981), 163–93.

KLEIN, MENASHEH, *Mishneh halakhot*, vol. v (Brooklyn, NY, 1998).

KLEIN, MICHAEL L., *The Personification of God in the Aramaic Targums to the Torah* [Hagshamat ha'el batargumim ha'aramiyim latorah] (Jerusalem, 1982).

KNOHL, ISRAEL, 'Between Faith and Criticism' (Heb.), *Megadim*, 33 (Shevat 5761 [Feb. 2001]), 123–6.

KOCHAN, LIONEL, *Beyond the Graven Image: A Jewish View* (New York, 1997).

KOOK, ABRAHAM ISAAC, *Igerot hare'iyah*, 4 vols. (vols. i–iii: Jerusalem, 1985; vol. iv: Jerusalem, 1984).

—— *Ma'amrei hare'iyah* (Jerusalem, 1984).

—— *Olat re'iyah*, 2 vols. (Jerusalem, 1939).

—— *Orot*, trans. Bezalel Naor (Northvale, NJ, 1993).

—— *Otserot hare'iyah*, ed. Moshe Tsuriel, 4 vols. (Sha'alvim, 1988–93).

KOOK, TSEVI YEHUDAH, *Linetivot yisra'el*, 3 vols. (Jerusalem, 1989–97).

KOOPERMAN, YEHUDAH, *Peshuto shel mikra* (Jerusalem, 2000).

KORAH, AMRAM, *Se'arat teman* (Jerusalem, 1954).

KORMAN, AVRAHAM, *Hatahor vehatame* (Tel Aviv, 2000).

KRAEMER, JOEL L., 'Maimonides' Messianic Posture', in I. Twersky (ed.), *Studies in Medieval Jewish History and Literature* (Cambridge, Mass., 1979), ii. 109–42.

—— 'Naturalism and Universalism in Maimonides' Political and Religious Thought', in E. Fleischer et al. (eds.), *Me'ah she'arim: Studies in Medieval Jewish Spiritual Life in Memory of Isadore Twersky* (Jerusalem, 2001), 47–81.

KREISEL, HOWARD, 'Intellectual Perfection and the Role of the Law in the Philosophy of Maimonides', in Jacob Neusner (ed.), *From Ancient Israel*, vol. iii (Atlanta, Ga., 1989), 25–46.

—— *Prophecy: The History of an Idea in Medieval Jewish Philosophy* (Dordrecht, 2001).

—— 'The Term *Kol* in Abraham Ibn Ezra: A Reappraisal', *REJ* 153 (1994), 29–66.

KROCHMAL, NAHMAN, *Kitvei ranak*, ed. S. Rawidowicz (Berlin, 1924).

KUNITZ, MOSES, *Ben yohai* (Vienna, 1815).

KUPFER, EFRAIM, 'Concerning the Cultural Image of German Jewry and its Rabbis in the Fourteenth and Fifteenth Centuries' (Heb.), *Tarbiz*, 42 (1973), 113–47.

—— '*Sefer haberit* and Other Works by R. Lipmann Muelhausen' (Heb.), *Sinai*, 56 (1965), 330–43.

KURZWEIL, ZVI, 'Fundamentalism and Judaism', *L'eylah*, 25 (Apr. 1988), 8–10.

—— *The Modern Impulse of Traditional Judaism* (Hoboken, NJ, 1985).

KUSHELEVSKY, AVRAHAM, *Meetings between Judaism, Science, and Technology on the Basis of Maimonides' Thirteen Principles* [Mifgashim bein yahadut, mada, utekhnologyah al yesod yod gimel ha'ikarim shel harambam] (Jerusalem, 2001).

KUTNER, JOSHUA, *Ha'emunah vehahakirah* (Breslau, 1847).

LAMM, NORMAN, *Faith and Doubt* (New York, 1971).

—— 'Loving and Hating Jews as Halakhic Categories', in Jacob J. Schacter (ed.), *Jewish Tradition and the Nontraditional Jew* (Northvale, NJ, 1992), 139–76.

—— *The Shema: Spirituality and Law in Judaism as Exemplified in the Shema, the Most Important Passage in the Torah* (Philadelphia, Pa., 1998).

LAMPRONTE, ISAAC, *Pahad yitshak*, vol. vii (Lyck, 1874).

LANDAU, EZEKIEL, *Noda biyehudah* (Jerusalem, 1969).

LANGE, ISAAC, 'Moshav zekenim', *Hama'ayan*, 12 (Tamuz 5732 [June 1972]), 75–95.

LANGER, RUTH, 'Kalir was a Tanna: Rabbenu Tam's Invocation of Antiquity in Defense of the Ashkenazic Payyetanic Tradition', *HUCA* 67 (1996), 95–106.

LANGERMANN, YITSHAK TSEVI, 'Rabbi Samuel ben Eli's Letter on Resurrection' (Heb.), *Kovets al yad*, 15 (2001), 39–94.

—— *Yemenite Midrash: Philosophical Commentaries on the Torah* (New York, 1996).

LAUTERBACH, JACOB Z., *Studies in Jewish Law, Custom and Folklore* (New York, 1970).

LAWEE, ERIC, '"Israel has no Messiah" in Late Medieval Spain', *Journal of Jewish Thought and Philosophy*, 5 (1996), 245–79.

188 *Bibliography*

LAZARUS-YAFEH, HAVA, 'Ezra-Uzayr: The Metamorphosis of a Polemical Motif' (Heb.), *Tarbiz*, 55 (1986), 359–77.

—— *Intertwined Worlds: Medieval Islam and Bible Criticism* (Princeton, NJ, 1992).

LAZI, YEKUTIEL (ed.), *Margaliyot tovah* (Amsterdam, 1722).

LEIBOWITZ, ISAIAH, *Conversations on the Theory of Prophecy* [Siḥot al torat hanevuah] (Jerusalem, 1997).

—— *The Faith of Maimonides*, trans. John Glucker (Jerusalem, 1989).

—— *Judaism, Human Values and the Jewish State* (Cambridge, Mass., 1992).

—— *On the World and its Fullness: Conversations with Michael Shashar* [Al olam umelo'o: Siḥot im mikha'el shashar] (Jerusalem, 1988).

LEIMAN, SID, Z., 'Masorah and Halakhah: A Study in Conflict', in Mordechai Cogan et al. (eds.), *Tehillah le-Moshe: Biblical and Judaic Studies in Honor of Moshe Greenberg* (Winona Lake, Ind., 1997), 291–306.

LEONE DA MODENA, *Magen vaḥerev*, ed. Shelomoh Simonsohn (Jerusalem, 1960).

LEVI BEN HABIB, *She'elot uteshuvot ralbaḥ* (Venice, 1565).

LEVINGER, YA'AKOV (JACOB), 'On the Book *Be'ur shemot kodesh veḥol* Attributed to Maimonides' (Heb.), *Meḥkerei yerushalayim bemaḥshevet yisra'el*, 4 (1985), 19–30.

—— *Maimonides' Halakhic Thought* [Darkhei hamaḥashavah hahilkhatit shel harambam] (Jerusalem, 1965).

—— *Maimonides as Philosopher and Codifier* [Harambam kefilosof ukhefosek] (Jerusalem, 1989).

LEVINSON, JACOB, *Hatorah vehamada* (New York, 1932).

LEVY, B. BARRY, *Fixing God's Torah: The Accuracy of the Hebrew Bible Text in Jewish Law* (Oxford, 2001).

LEVY, ISAIAH, 'Resurrection According to Maimonides' (Heb.), *Yeshurun*, 11 (2002), 774–90.

LÉVY, L. G., 'La Philosophie d'Abraham ibn Ezra', *REJ* 89 (1930), 169–78.

LEWIN, B. M., *Otsar hage'onim*, 13 vols. (Jerusalem, 1984).

LICHTENBERG, ABRAHAM (ed.), *Anthology of Maimonides' Responsa and Letters* [Kovets teshuvot harambam ve'igerotav] (Leipzig, 1859).

LICHTMAN, BEN ZION, *Benei tsiyon* (Jerusalem, 1995).

LIEBERMAN, SAUL, *Hellenism in Jewish Palestine* (New York, 1950).

—— *Sheki'in* (Jerusalem, 1970).

LILIENBLUM, MOSES LEIB, 'Ḥatot ne'urim', in id., *Ketavim otobiyografiyim* (Jerusalem, 1970), vol. i.

LIPSCHUETZ, ISRAEL, *Tiferet yisra'el* [commentary on the Mishnah, printed in standard edns.].

LIPSHITZ, ABRAHAM, *Studies in the Thought of Rabbi Abraham ibn Ezra* [Pirkei iyun bemishnat rabi avraham ibn ezra] (Jerusalem, 1982).

—— *Studies in the Torah Commentary of Rabenu Baḥya ben Asher* [Iyunim babe'ur al hatorah lerabenu baḥya ben asher] (Jerusalem, 2000).

LOCKSHIN, MARTIN, *Rabbi Samuel Ben Meir's Commentary on Genesis* (Lewiston, NY, 1989).

—— *Rashbam's Commentary on Leviticus and Numbers* (Providence, RI, 2001).

—— '"Rashbam" on Job: A Reconsideration', *JSQ* 8 (2001), 80–104.

LOEW, JUDAH (MAHARAL), *Tiferet yisra'el* (Jerusalem, 1970).

LOEWE, H., and C. G. MONTEFIORE (eds.), *A Rabbinic Anthology* (London, 1938).

LOEWINGER, D. S., 'The Torah Scroll Hidden in the Synagogue of Severus in Rome: Its Relationship to the Scroll of Isaiah from the Dead Sea and to the "Torah of Rabbi Meir"' (Heb.), *Beth mikra*, 15 (1970), 137–63.

—— and E. KUPFER, 'R. Yom Tov Lippman Muelhausen's Correction of the Sefer Torah' (Heb.), *Sinai*, 60 (1967), 237–68.

LOPES, ISAAC, *Kur matsref ha'emunot umareh ha'emet* (Metz, 1847).

LOPEZ, ANTONIO PACIOS, *La Disputa de Tortosa*, 2 vols. (Barcelona, 1957).

LORBERBAUM, YAIR, '"The Doctrine of the Corporeality of God Did Not Occur Even for a Single Day to the Sages, May their Memory be Blessed" (*Guide of the Perplexed* I, 46): Anthropomorphism in Early Rabbinic Literature—A Critical Review of Scholarly Research' (Heb.), *Mada'ei yahadut*, 40 (2000), 3–54.

—— 'The Image of God: Rabbinic Literature, Maimonides, and Nahmanides' [Tselem elohim: Sifrut ḥazal, harambam veharamban] (Ph.D. diss., Hebrew University of Jerusalem, 1997).

LOWE, W. H., *The Mishnah on which the Palestinian Talmud Rests* (Cambridge, 1883).

LURIA, ISAAC, *Zohar harakia* (Koretz, 1785).

LURIA, SOLOMON, 'Hanhagat maharshal', ed. Y. Rafael, in Y. L. Maimon (ed.), *Sefer yovel mugash likhevod harav dr. shimon federbush* (Jerusalem, 1961), 316–29.

—— *Ḥokhmat shelomoh* [commentary on the Talmud, printed in standard edns.].

—— *She'elot uteshuvot maharshal* (Fuerth, 1768).

LUZZATTO, MOSES HAYIM, *Ginzei ramḥal*, ed. H. Friedlander (Benei Berak, 1984).

LUZZATTO, SAMUEL DAVID, *Commentary on Isaiah* [Perush shadal al sefer yeshayah], ed. P. Schlesinger and A. Hovev (Tel Aviv, 1970).

—— *Commentary on the Torah* [Perush shadal al ḥamishah ḥumshei torah] (Jerusalem, 1993).

—— *Hamishtadel* (Vienna, 1847).

—— *Letters* [Igerot shadal], ed. S. E. Graber, 9 vols. (Przemysl and Kraków, 1882–94).

—— *Ohev ger* (Kraków, 1895).

—— *Peninei shadal* (Przemysl, 1888).

—— *Studies in Judaism* [Meḥkerei hayahadut] (Warsaw, 1873).

—— *Yesodei hatorah*, ed. A. Z. Aescoly (Jerusalem, 1947).

MCCARTHY, CARMEL, *The Tiqqune Sopherim* (Freiburg, 1981).

MAGID, SHAUL, 'Modernity as Heresy: The Introvertive Piety of Faith in R. Areleh Roth's *Shomer Emunim*', *JSQ* 4 (1997), 77–104.

Maḥzor hashalem-ḥabad (Brooklyn, NY, 1955).

Maḥzor vitri (Nuremberg, 1923).

MAIMERON, ISRAEL, *Freedom of Choice in the Thought of Rabbi Abraham Azulai* [Ḥofesh habeḥirah behaguto shel r. avraham azulai] (Jerusalem, 1993).

MAIMON, JUDAH LEIB, *Maimonides* [Rabi mosheh ben maimon] (Jerusalem, 1960).

MAIMONIDES, ABRAHAM, *Milḥamot hashem*, ed. Reuven Margaliyot (Jerusalem, 1953).

—— *Teshuvot rabenu avraham ben harambam*, ed. A. Freimann and S. Goitein (Jerusalem, 1937).

MALACHI, TSEVI, 'The Yom Kippur Service' [Ha'avodah leyom hakipurim] (Ph.D. diss., Hebrew University of Jerusalem, 1973).

MALTER, HENRY, *Saadia Gaon: His Life and Works* (Philadelphia, Pa., 1942).

—— 'Shem Tob Ben Joseph Palquera: His Treatise of the Dream', *JQR* 1 (1910–11), 151–81.

MANOR, DAN, 'Rabbi Raphael Berdugo: His Relationship to Contemporary Philosophy and Rationalism' (Heb.), *Mikedem umiyam*, 4 (1991), 127–43.

MAORI, YESHAYAHU, 'Rabbinic Midrash as Evidence for Textual Variants in the Hebrew Bible: History and Practice', in Shalom Carmy (ed.), *Modern Scholarship in the Study of Torah: Contributions and Limitations* (Northvale, NJ, 1996), 101–29.

MARCUS, AARON, *Keset hasofer* (Tel Aviv, 1971).

MARGULIES, MORDEKHAI (ed.), *Hilkhot hanagid* (Jerusalem, 1962).

MARMORSTEIN, ARTHUR, 'The Discussion of the Angels with God' (Heb.), *Melilah*, 3–4 (1950), 93–102.

—— 'Eine messianische Bewegung im dritten Jahrhundert', *Jeschurun*, 13 (1926), 16–28, 171–86, 369–83.

—— *The Old Rabbinic Doctrine of God*, 2 vols. (London, 1927–37).

MARMURA, M., 'Avicenna's Theory of God's Knowledge of Particulars', *Journal of the American Oriental Society*, 82 (1969), 299–312.

MARTIN, RICHARD C., et al., *Defenders of Reason in Islam: Mutazilism from Medieval School to Modern Symbol* (Oxford, 1997).

MARX, ALEXANDER, 'A List of Poems on the Articles of the Creed', *JQR* 9 (1919), 305–36.

—— 'Texts by and about Maimonides', *JQR* 25 (1935), 371–428.

MEDINI, HAYIM HEZEKIAH, *Sedei ḥemed*, 18 vols. (New York, 1962).

MEIR SIMHAH OF DVINSK, *Meshekh ḥokhmah* [commentary on Torah] (Jerusalem, 1974).

ME'IRI, MENAHEM, *Beit habeḥirah: Avot*, ed. S. Z. Havlin (Jerusalem, 1994).

—— *Beit habeḥirah: Kidushin*, ed. A. Sofer (Jerusalem, 1963).

—— *Beit habeḥirah: Nedarim*, ed. A. Lis (Jerusalem, 1996).

—— *Beit habeḥirah: Sanhedrin*, ed. A. Sofer (Jerusalem, 1963).

—— *Beit habeḥirah: Shabat*, ed. I. Lange (Jerusalem, 1969).

—— *Ḥibur hateshuvah*, ed. A. Sofer and S. K. Mirsky (Jerusalem, 1976).

—— *Kiryat sefer* (Jerusalem, 1956).

MEKLENBURG, JACOB, *Haketav vehakabalah* (Jerusalem, 1969).

MENAHEM MENDEL OF VITEBSK, *Peri ha'arets* (Jerusalem, 1987).

MENDELSSOHN, MOSES, *Gesammelte Schriften*, vol. xiv (Breslau, 1938).

—— *Jerusalem*, ed. and trans. Alexander Altmann and Allan Arkush (Hanover, Pa., 1983).

—— *'Jerusalem' and Other Jewish Writings*, ed. and trans. Alfred Jospe (New York, 1960).

MENDES-FLOHR, PAUL, and JEHUDA REINHARZ (eds.), *The Jew in the Modern World* (Oxford, 1995).

MESCH, BARRY, 'Nissim of Marseilles' Approach to the "Iqqarim"', in *Proceedings of the Ninth World Congress of Jewish Studies*, vol. iii (Jerusalem, 1986), 85–92.

—— 'Principles of Judaism in Maimonides and Joseph ibn Caspi', in Jehuda Reinharz and Daniel Swetschinski (eds.), *Mystics, Philosophers, and Politicians: Essays in Jewish Intellectual History in Honor of Alexander Altmann* (Durham, NC, 1982), 85–98.

—— *Studies in Joseph Ibn Caspi* (Leiden, 1975).

MESSAS, JOSEPH, *Mayim ḥayim* (Jerusalem, 1967).

—— *Naḥalat avot*, vol. v (Jerusalem, 1978).

MEYUHAS BEN ELIJAH, *Commentary on Deuteronomy* [Perush al sefer devarim], ed. M. Katz (Jerusalem, 1968).

Midrash hagadol, Genesis, Exodus, ed. M. Margulies (Jerusalem, 1967).

Midrash shemot rabah: Parashot 1–14, ed. Avigdor Shinan (Jerusalem, 1984).

Midrash tana'im, ed. D. Hoffmann (Berlin, 1908).

Midrash tanḥuma, ed. S. Buber, 2 vols. (New York, 1946); standard edn. (Jerusalem, 1975).

Midrash tehilim, ed. S. Buber (Jerusalem, 1977).

Midrash vayikra rabah, ed. M. Margulies (Jerusalem, 1993).

Mikra'ot gedolot 'haketer', ed. Menahem Cohen (Ramat Gan, 1992–).

MOELIN, JACOB, *Sefer maharil*, ed. S. Spitzer (Jerusalem, 1989).

—— *She'elot uteshuvot maharil*, ed. Y. Satz (Jerusalem, 1980).

—— *She'elot uteshuvot maharil ḥadashot*, ed. Y. Satz (Jerusalem, 1977).

MONSENEGO, YEDIDYAH, *Kupat harokhlim* (Lod, 1994).

MOPSIK, CHARLES, *Lettre sur la sainteté* (Lagrasse, 1986).

MORPURGO, SAMSON, *Shemesh tsedakah* (Venice, 1743).

MORTEIRA, SAUL, *Givat sha'ul* (Brooklyn, NY, 1991).

MOSCATO, JUDAH, *Kol yehudah* [commentary on Judah Halevi, *Kuzari*, repr. in standard edns.].

MOSES OF COUCY, *Sefer mitsvot gadol* (Brooklyn, NY, 1985).

MOSES OF NARBONNE, *Pirkei mosheh*, ed. C. Sirat, *Tarbiz*, 39 (1970), 287–306.

MOTOT, SAMUEL, supercommentary on Ibn Ezra's commentary on the Torah (Venice, 1554).

NAHMANIDES, MOSES, *Commentary on the Torah* [Perush al hatorah], ed. C. D. Chavel, 2 vols. (Jerusalem, 1998).

—— *Kitvei ramban*, ed. C. D. Chavel, 2 vols. (Jerusalem, 1963).

NAOR, BEZALEL, *Kabbalah and the Holocaust* (Spring Valley, NY, 2001).

—— *Post-Sabbatian Sabbatianism* (Spring Valley, NY, 1999).

—— 'Rav Kook and Emmanuel Levinas on the "Non-Existence" of God', *Orot*, 1 (1991), 1–11.

NATHAN BEN YEHIEL, *Arukh hashalem*, ed. A. Kohut, 8 vols. (Vienna and New York, 1878–92).

NEHORAI, MICHAEL TSEVI, 'R. Solomon b. R. Judah Hanasi and his Commentary on *Moreh nevukhim*' [R. shelomoh ben rav yehudah hanasi uferusho lemoreh nevukhim] (Ph.D. diss., Hebrew University of Jerusalem, 1978).

NEMOY, LEON, 'Al-Kirkisani's Account of the Jewish Sects and Christianity', *HUCA* 7 (1930), 317–97.

NERIYAH, AVRAHAM YITSHAK, *Yod-gimel ha'ikarim* (Kefar Haro'eh, 1992).

NETANEL BEN ISAIAH, *Maor ha'afelah*, ed. J. Kafih (Jerusalem, 1957).

NETTER, SOLOMON, supercommentary on Ibn Ezra's Torah commentary (Vienna, 1859).

NEUHAUSEN, SIMON A., *Torah or leharambam* (Baltimore, Md., 1941).

NEUMARK, DAVID, *Essays in Jewish Philosophy* ([Cincinnati, Ohio], 1929).

—— *History of Jewish Dogma* [Toledot ha'ikarim beyisra'el], 2 vols. (Odessa, 1912).

—— *History of Jewish Philosophy*, 2 vols. [Toledot hafilosofiyah beyisra'el] (Philadelphia, Pa., 1922, 1929).

NEUSNER, JACOB, et al. (eds.), *From Ancient Israel to Modern Judaism*, 4 vols. (Atlanta, Ga., 1989).

NEWMAN, J., *Faith and Knowledge of God* (Jerusalem, 1977).

NISSIM BEN MOSES OF MARSEILLES, *Ma'aseh nisim*, ed. H. Kreisel (Jerusalem, 2000).

NORZI, YEDIDYAH SOLOMON, *Minhat shai* (Vienna, 1876).

NOVAK, DAVID, 'Self-Contraction of the Godhead in Kabbalistic Theology', in Lenn E. Goodman (ed.), *Neoplatonism and Jewish Thought* (Albany, NY, 1992), 299–318.

NURIEL, ABRAHAM, 'The Question of a Created or Primordial World in the Philosophy of Maimonides' (Heb.), *Tarbiz*, 33 (1964), 372–87.

—— 'Remarks on Maimonides' Epistemology', in Shlomo Pines and Yirmiyahu Yovel (eds.), *Maimonides and Philosophy* (Dordrecht, 1986), 36–51.

NUSSENBAUM, MAX SAMUEL, 'Champion of Orthodox Judaism: A Biography of the Reverend Sabato Morais' (Ph.D. diss., Yeshiva University, New York, 1964).

OFER, YOSEF, *The Babylonian Masorah of the Torah* [Hamesorah habavlit latorah] (Jerusalem, 2001).

OLITZKY, KERRY M. and RONALD H. ISAAC, *The Thirteen Principles of Faith: A Confirmation Textbook* (Hoboken, NJ, 1999).

ORENSTEIN, JACOB MESHULAM, *Yeshuot ya'akov* (Lemberg, 1863).

ORIGEN, *Contra Celsum*, trans. Henry Chadwick (Cambridge, 1980).

ORSCHANSKY, L., *Abraham ibn Esra als Philosoph* (Breslau, 1900).

OVADIAH, DAVID, *Natan david* (Jerusalem, 1996).

PALACHE, HAYIM, *Lev ḥayim* (Jerusalem, 1997).

PARNES, YEHUDAH, 'Torah u-Madda and Freedom of Inquiry', *TUMJ* 1 (1989), 68–71.

PAULSEN, DAVID L., 'Early Christian Belief in a Corporeal Deity: Origen and Augustine as Reluctant Witnesses', *HTR* 83 (1990), 105–16.

—— and CARL W. GRIFFIN, 'Augustine and the Corporeality of God', *HTR* 95 (2002), 97–118.

PEDAYA, HAVIVAH, 'Seeing, Falling, Singing: The Desire to Behold God and the Spiritual Basis of Early Jewish Mysticism' (Heb.), *Asupot*, 9 (1995), 237–77.

PELI, PINCHAS H., 'An Attempt at Formulating Contemporary Principles of Faith', in Abraham J. Karp et al. (eds.), *Threescore and Ten* (Hoboken, NJ, 1991), 235–45.

PENKOWER, JORDAN, S., 'Jacob ben Hayim and the Rise of the Rabbinic Bible' [Ya'akov ben ḥayim utsemiḥat mahadurat hamikraot hagedolot] (Ph.D. diss., Hebrew University of Jerusalem, 1982).

—— 'Maimonides and the Aleppo Codex', *Textus*, 9 (1981), 39–128.

—— *New Evidence for the Pentateuch Text in the Aleppo Codex* [Nusaḥ hatorah baketer aram tsovah: Edut ḥadashah] (Ramat Gan, 1993).

PERLMANN, M., 'Eleventh-Century Andalusian Authors on the Jews of Granada', *PAAJR* 28 (1948–9), 269–90.

Pesikta derav kahana, ed. B. Mandelbaum (New York, 1962).

PETUCHOWSKI, JACOB J., 'Manuals and Catechisms of the Jewish Religion in the Early Period of Emancipation', in Alexander Altmann (ed.), *Studies in Nineteenth-Century Jewish Intellectual History* (Cambridge, Mass., 1964), 47–64.

—— *Theology and Poetry: Studies in the Medieval* Piyyut (London, 1978).

PILITZ, ISAAC, *Zera yitshak* (Lvov, 1876).

PINES, SHLOMO, *History of Jewish Philosophy from Maimonides to Spinoza* [Toledot hafilosofiyah hayehudit meharambam ad spinoza] (Jerusalem, 1964).

—— 'Isaac Polgar and Spinoza' [Yitsḥak polgar uspinoza], in Yosef Dan and Yosef Hacker (eds.), *Meḥkarim bekabalah mugashim leyishayah tishbi* (Jerusalem, 1984), 395–457.

—— 'The Philosophic Purport of Maimonides' Halachic Works and the Purport of the *Guide of the Perplexed*', in id. and Yirmiyahu Yovel (eds.), *Maimonides and Philosophy* (Dordrecht, 1986), 1–14.

—— 'Studies in Abul-Barakat al-Baghdadi's Poetics and Metaphysics', *Scripta Hierosolymitana*, 6 (1960), 120–99.

—— and YIRMIYAHU YOVEL (eds.), *Maimonides and Philosophy* (Dordrecht, 1986).

PINHAS SHAPIRO OF KORETS, *Imrei pinḥas* (Benei Berak, 1988).

—— *Midrash pinḥas* (Ashdod, 1990).

Pirkei derabi eli'ezer, ed. D. Luria (Warsaw, 1852).

PLOTZKI, MEIR DAN, *Ḥemdat yisra'el*, 2 vols. (Petrokov, 1927).

PREIL, ELEAZAR MEIR, *Hamaor* (Jerusalem, 1929).

PREIL, JOSEPH JOSHUA, *Eglei tal* (Warsaw, 1899).

PRIJS, LEO, *Abraham ibn Ezra on Genesis 1–3* [Avraham ibn ezra livereshit 1–3] (London, 1990).

PRINS, ELIEZER LIEPMAN, *Parnas ledorot*, ed. Mayer Herskovics (Jerusalem, 1999).

PULGAR, ISAAC, *Ezer hadat*, ed. J. Levinger (Tel Aviv, 1984).

RABBINOVICZ, RAPHAEL NATHAN, *Dikdukei soferim* (Munich, 1868–97).

RABINOVITCH, NAHUM ELEAZAR, *Yad peshutah* [commentary on Maimonides, *Mishneh torah*] (Jerusalem, 1990).

RABINOWITZ, LOUIS I., 'Torah min hashamayim', *Tradition*, 7 (Spring 1965), 34–40.

RAFFEL, CHARLES, 'Maimonides' Fundamental Principles *Redivivus*', in Jacob Neusner et al. (eds.), *From Ancient Israel to Modern Judaism* (Atlanta, Ga., 1989), iii. 77–88.

RAPOPORT, CHAIM, *The Messiah Problem: Berger, the Angel, and the Scandal of Reckless Indiscrimination* (Ilford, 2002).

RASHI, *Rashi al hatorah*, ed. Abraham Berliner (Frankfurt, 1905).

RAVITZKY, AVIEZER, *Al da'at hamakom* (Jerusalem, 1991).

—— 'Aristotle's *Meteorologica* and the Maimonidean Exegesis of Creation' (Heb.), *Meḥkerei yerushalayim bemaḥshevet yisra'el*, 9 (1990), 225–50.

—— 'The Philosophy of R. Zerachiah b. Isaac b. Shelatiel Hen and Maimonidean–Tibbonite Thought in the Thirteenth Century' [Mishnato shel r. zeraḥyah ben yitsḥak ben she'alti'el ḥen vehehagut hamaimonit–tibonit bame'ah hayod-gimel] (Ph.D. diss., Hebrew University of Jerusalem, 1978).

—— 'Samuel Ibn Tibbon and the Esoteric Character of the Guide of the Perplexed', *AJS Review*, 6 (1981), 87–123.

RAWIDOWICZ, SIMON, 'Saadya's Purification of the Idea of God', in E. J. Rosenthal (ed.), *Saadya Studies* (Manchester, 1943), 139–65.

—— *Studies in Jewish Thought* [Iyunim bemaḥshevet yisra'el] (Jerusalem, 1969).

RECANATI, MENAHEM, *Commentary on the Torah* [Perush al hatorah] (Jerusalem, 1961).

REGENSBERG, HAYIM DAVID, *Mishmeret ḥayim* (Jerusalem, 1966).

REIFMAN, JACOB, *Studies in the Teaching of R. Abraham ibn Ezra* [Iyunim bemishnat harav avraham ibn ezra] (Jerusalem, 1962).

REINES, ALVIN, *Maimonides and Abrabanel on Prophecy* (Cincinnati, Ohio, 1970).

—— 'Maimonides' Concept of Mosaic Prophecy', *HUCA* 40–1 (1969–70), 325–61.

REISCHER, JACOB, *Shevut ya'akov*, 3 vols. (Lvov, 1896).

RESNICK, IRVEN M., 'The Falsification of Scripture and Medieval Christian and Jewish Polemics', *Medieval Encounters*, 2 (1996), 344–80.

RICCHI, RAPHAEL IMMANUEL HAI, *Mishnat ḥasidim* (Brooklyn, NY, 1975).

—— *Yosher levav* (Kraków, 1890).

RIVLIN, EPHRAIM, 'Shmuel ibn Tibbon' (MA diss., Tel Aviv University, 1969).

ROBERTS, ROBERT E., *The Theology of Tertullian* (London, 1924).

ROBINSON, IRA, 'Abraham ben Eliezer Halevi: Kabbalist and Messianic Visionary of the Early Sixteenth Century' (Ph.D. diss., Harvard University, 1980).

ROKE'AH, ELEAZAR, *Perush haroke'ah* (Benei Berak, 1978).

ROLLER, HAYIM MORDEKHAI, *Ma'amrei be'er hayim mordekhai* (n.p., 1978).

ROSENBERG, SHALOM, 'Biblical Research in Modern Religious Jewish Thought' (Heb.), in Uriel Simon (ed.), *Hamikra ve'anahnu* (Ramat Gan, 1988).

ROSENFELD, ABRAHAM (trans. and ed.), *Selichot for the Whole Year* (New York, 1988).

ROSENTHAL, DAVID, 'On the Rabbinic Treatment of Textual Variants in the Bible' (Heb.), in Yair Zakovitch and Alexander Rofe (eds.), *Sefer yitshak aryeh seeligman* (Jerusalem, 1983), ii. 395–416.

ROSENTHAL, JUDAH, 'The Idea of the Abrogation of the Mitsvot in Jewish Eschatology' (Heb.), *Sefer hayovel me'ir vaksman* (Jerusalem, 1967), 217–33.

ROSIN, DAVID, 'Die Religionsphilosophie Abraham Ibn Esras', *MGWJ* 42 (1898), 17–33, 58–73, 108–15, 154–61, 200–14, 241–52, 305–15, 345–62, 394–407, 444–52; 43 (1899), 22–31, 75–91, 125–33, 168–84, 231–40.

ROTH, AARON (ARELE), *Shomer emunim*, 2 vols. (Jerusalem, 1964).

ROTH, CECIL, 'Representation of God in Jewish Art', *Fourth World Congress of Jewish Studies* (Jerusalem, 1968), ii. 139–40.

ROTH, LEON, *Is There a Jewish Philosophy? Rethinking Fundamentals* (London, 1999).

——*Judaism: A Portrait* (New York, 1960).

ROTH, MESHULAM, *Kol mevaser*, 2 vols. (Jerusalem, 1972).

ROTH, NORMAN, 'Forgery and Abrogation of the Torah: A Theme in Muslim and Christian Polemic in Spain', *PAAJR* 54 (1987), 203–10.

ROTHKOFF, AARON, 'Yigdal', *Encyclopaedia Judaica* (Jerusalem, 1971), xvi, col. 835.

ROTHSCHILD, BOAZ RAPHAEL, *Oniyah belev yam* (Fuerth, 1766).

ROTTZOLL, DIRK U., *Abraham Ibn Esras Kommentar zur Urgeschichte* (Berlin, 1996).

RUDERMAN, DAVID, *Jewish Enlightenment in an English Key* (Princeton, NJ, 2000).

SA'ADIAH GAON, *Commentary on Psalms*, ed. J. Kafih (Jerusalem, 1966).

——*Emunot vede'ot* (Kraków, 1880).

SABA, ABRAHAM, *Tseror hamor*, ed. B. Wicholder (Benei Berak, 1990).

SACHS, SENIOR, 'Investigation of the Masorah Concerning the Eighteen Corrections of the Scribes' (Heb.), *Kerem hemed*, 9 (1856), 52–60.

SAFRAN, BEZALEL, 'Maimonides on Free Will, Determinism and Esotericism', in id. and Eliyahu Safran (eds.), *Porat yosef* (Hoboken, NJ, 1992), 111–28.

SAFRIN, ISAAC, *Heikhal haberakhah*, 5 vols. (Brooklyn, NY, 1960).

——*Shulhan hatahor* (Tel Aviv, 1963).

SALTMAN, ELLEN S., 'The "Forbidden Image" in Jewish Art', *Journal of Jewish Art*, 8 (1981), 42–53.

SAMUEL OF RUSHINO, *Sefer rushino*, ed. M. Weiss (Jerusalem, 1996).

SAMUELSON, NORBERT M., *Gersonides on God's Knowledge* (Toronto, 1977).

—— 'Maimonides' Doctrine of Creation', *HTR* 84 (1991), 249–71.

SAPERSTEIN, MARC, *Decoding the Rabbis* (Cambridge, Mass., 1980).

SCHACTER, J. J., 'Rabbi Jacob Emden's Iggeret Purim', in Isadore Twersky (ed.), *Studies in Medieval Jewish History and Literature*, vol. ii (Cambridge, Mass., 1984), 441–6.

SCHACHTER, TSEVI, *Nefesh harav* (Jerusalem, 1994).

SCHÄFER, PETER, *Rivalität zwischen Engeln und Menschen* (Berlin, 1975).

SCHECHTER, SOLOMON, *Aspects of Rabbinic Theology* (New York, 1961).

—— *Studies in Judaism* (Philadelphia, Pa., 1896).

SCHERMAN, NOSSON (ed.), *Chumash: Stone Edition* (New York, 1993).

—— (ed.), *Complete Artscroll Siddur* (New York, 1995).

SCHICK, MOSES, *Maharam shik al taryag mitsvot* (New York, 1964).

SCHIFFMAN, LAWRENCE, *Who Was a Jew* (Hoboken, NJ, 1985).

SCHIMMEL, H. CHAIM, *The Oral Law* (Jerusalem, 1987).

SCHMERLER, BENJAMIN, *Ahavat yehonatan* (Bilgoraj, 1933).

SCHOLEM, GERSHOM, 'Chapters from the History of Kabbalistic Literature' (Heb.), *Kiryat sefer*, 4 (1927–8), 286–302.

—— 'The Concept of Kavvanah in the Early Kabbalah', in Alfred Jospe (ed.), *Studies in Jewish Thought* (Detroit, Mich., 1981), 162–80.

—— 'From Scholar to Kabbalist' (Heb.), *Tarbiz*, 6 (1935), 90–8.

—— 'Kabbalah', *Encyclopedia Judaica* (Jerusalem, 1971), x, cols. 489–653.

—— *Major Trends in Jewish Mysticism* (New York, 1974).

—— 'New Information on R. Joseph Ashkenazi the "Tana" of Safed' (Heb.), *Tarbiz*, 28 (1959), 59–89, 201–35.

—— *On the Mystical Shape of the Godhead* (New York, 1991).

—— *Origins of the Kabbalah*, ed. R. J. Z. Werblowsky, trans. Alan Arkush (Princeton, NJ, 1987).

—— *Studies in Kabbalah* [Meḥkerei kabalah], ed. Y. Ben Shelomoh (Jerusalem, 1998).

SCHOR, ABRAHAM HAYIM, *Torat ḥayim* (Jerusalem, 1969).

[SCHORR, J. H.], 'R. Nissim bar Moses of Marseilles' (Heb.) *Heḥaluts*, 7 (1865), 89–144.

SCHUECK, SOLOMON TSEVI, *She'elot uteshuvot rashban* (Munkacz, 1900).

—— *Sidur haminhagim*, 4 vols. (Munkacs, 1888).

—— *Sidur rashban* (Vienna, 1894).

—— *Torah shelemah*, 3 vols. (Satmar, 1909).

SCHULMAN, ELIYAHU BARUKH, 'An Essay on Matters of Prophecy' (Heb.), *Beit yitsḥak*, 26 (1994), 505–43.

SCHULZ, JOSEPH P., 'Angelic Opposition to the Ascension of Moses and the Revelation of the Law', *JQR* 61 (1971), 282–307.

SCHULZINGER, MOSES MORDEKHAI, *Mishmar halevi: Ḥagigah* (Zikhron Me'ir, 1995).

SCHWADRON, SHALOM, *She'elot uteshuvot maharsham*, 5 vols. (New York, 1962).

SCHWARTZ, DOV, *Astrology and Magic in Medieval Jewish Thought* [Astrologiyah vemagiyah behagut hayehudit bimei habeinayim] (Ramat Gan, 1999).

—— 'The Creation Theory of the Neoplatonic Circle in the Fourteenth Century' (Heb.), *Tarbiz*, 60 (1991), 616–18.

—— *The Messianic Idea in Medieval Jewish Thought* [Hara'ayon hameshiḥi behagut hayehudit bimei habeinayim] (Ramat Gan, 1997).

—— *Old Wine in a New Vessel: The Philosophy of a Fourteenth-Century Jewish Neoplatonic Circle* [Yashan bekankan ḥadash: Mishnato ha'iyunit shel haḥug hane'oplatoni befilosofiyah hayehudit shel hame'ah ha-14] (Jerusalem, 1997).

—— 'Philosophical Supercommentaries on the Commentaries of Rabbi Abraham ibn Ezra' (Heb.), *Alei sefer*, 18 (1996), 71–114.

—— 'Worship of God or Worship of the Stars: The Polemics of R. Abraham Al-Tabib and R. Solomon Franco', *Kabbalah*, 1 (1996), 205–70.

SCHWARTZ, JOSEPH, *Divrei yosef*, 4 vols. (Jerusalem, 1843–61).

SCHWARZSCHILD, STEVEN, 'The Personal Messiah: Towards the Restoration of a Discarded Doctrine', in M. Kellner (ed.), *The Pursuit of the Ideal* (Albany, NY, 1990), 15–28.

SCHWEID, ELIEZER, *Demokratiyah vehalakhah* (Jerusalem 1997).

SCULT, MEL (ed.), *Communings of the Spirit: The Journals of Mordecai M. Kaplan*, vol. i (Detroit, Mich., 2001).

SEESKIN, KENNETH, *Searching for a Distant God: The Legacy of Maimonides* (Oxford, 2000).

SELIGER, JOSEPH, *Kitvei harav dr. yosef seliger* (Jerusalem, 1930).

SENDOR, MARK BRIAN, 'The Emergence of Provençal Kabbalah: Rabbi Isaac the Blind's *Commentary* on *Sefer Yezirah*' (Ph.D. diss., Harvard University, 1994).

SEPTIMUS, BERNARD, *Hispano-Jewish Culture in Transition: The Career and Controversies of Ramah* (Cambridge, Mass., 1982).

—— 'Piety and Power in Thirteenth-Century Catalonia', in I. Twersky (ed.), *Studies in Medieval Jewish History and Literature*, vol. i (Cambridge, Mass., 1979), 197–230.

SERERO, DAVID BEN BARUKH, *Mishneh kesef* [commentary on Maimonides, *Mishneh torah*] (Salonika, 1817).

SFORNO, OBADIAH, *Kitvei rabi ovadiyah seforno*, ed. Z. Gottlieb (Jerusalem, 1983).

SHAMIR, YEHUDAH, 'Allusions to Muhammad in Maimonides' Theory of Prophecy in his *Guide of the Perplexed*', *JQR* 64 (1973–4), 212–24.

SHAPIRA, HAYIM ELEAZAR, *Divrei torah*, 9 vols. (Jerusalem, 1998).

—— *Minḥat ele'azar*, 5 vols. (Brooklyn, NY, 1991).

—— *Sha'ar yisakhar* (New York, 1992).

SHAPIRA, KALONYMUS KALMAN, *Benei maḥashavah tovah* (Tel Aviv, 1973).

SHAPIRO, MARC B., *Between the Yeshiva World and Modern Orthodoxy: The Life and Works of Rabbi Jehiel Jacob Weinberg, 1884–1966* (London, 1999).

—— 'A Letter Criticizing the Eisenstadt Yeshiva' (Heb.), *Hama'ayan*, 34 (Tishrei 5754 [Sept. 1993]), 15–25.

—— 'Maimonidean Halakhah and Superstition', *Maimonidean Studies*, 4 (2000), 61–108.

—— 'Maimonides' Thirteen Principles: The Last Word in Jewish Theology?', *TUMJ* 4 (1993), 187–242.

SHEM TOV, SHEM TOV BEN, *Sefer ha'emunot* (Ferrara, 1556).

SHERIRA GAON, *Teshuvot rav sherira ben ḥanina gaon*, ed. N. Rabinowich (Jerusalem, 1999).

SHERWIN, BYRON L., 'The Human Body and the Image of God', in Dan Cohn-Sherbok (ed.), *A Traditional Quest* (Sheffield, 1991), 75–85.

SHLOUSH, DAVID HAYIM, *Ḥemdah genuzah*, 3 vols. (Netanya, 1976–2000).

SHMIDMAN, MICHAEL A., 'On Maimonides' "Conversion" to Kabbalah', in Isadore Twersky (ed.), *Studies in Medieval Jewish History and Literature*, vol. ii (Cambridge, Mass., 1984), 375–86.

SHNEUR ZALMAN OF LYADY, *Likutei amarim* (Brooklyn, NY, 1993).

SHOHET, AZRIEL, *Changing Eras: The Beginning of the Haskalah among German Jewry* [Im ḥilufei tekufot] (Jerusalem, 1960).

SHOHET, SAUL YEDIDYAH, *Ahavat sha'ul* (New York, 1915).

SIEGEL, JONATHAN PAUL, *The Severus Scroll and 1QIsᵃ* (Missoula, Mont., 1975).

Sifrei bamidbar, ed. H. Horovitz (Jerusalem, 1966).

Sifrei devarim, ed. L. Finkelstein (New York, 1969).

SILVER, DANIEL JEREMY, *Maimonidean Criticism and the Maimonidean Controversy* (Leiden, 1965).

SILMAN, YOCHANAN, *Philosopher and Prophet: Judah Halevi, the Kuzari, and the Evolution of his Thought*, trans. Lenn J. Schramm (Albany, NY, 1995).

SIMHAH BUNEM OF PRZYSUCHA, *Simḥat yisra'el* (Jerusalem, n.d.).

SIMON, A. E., 'Philanthropism and Jewish Education' (Heb.), in Moshe Davis (ed.), *Mordecai M. Kaplan Jubilee Volume* (New York, 1953), 149–87.

SIMON, URIEL (ed.), *The Bible and Us* [Hamikra ve'anaḥnu] (Ramat Gan, 1988).

—— 'Interpreting the Interpreter: Supercommentaries on Ibn Ezra's Commentaries', in Isadore Twersky and Jay M. Harris (eds.), *Rabbi Abraham Ibn Ezra: Studies in the Writings of a Twelfth-Century Jewish Polymath* (Cambridge, Mass., 1993), 86–128.

—— 'R. Abraham ibn Ezra and R. David Kimhi: Two Approaches to the Question of the Reliability of the Biblical Text' (Heb.), *Bar-Ilan*, 6 (1968), 191–237.

SINIGAGLIA, JACOB SAMSON SHABETAI, *Shabat shel mi* (Livorno, 1807).

SINZHEIM, JOSEPH DAVID, *Minḥat ani*, 2 vols. (Jerusalem, 1974).

—— *Yad david: Sanhedrin* (Jerusalem, 2002).

SIRAT, COLETTE, *A History of Jewish Philosophy in the Middle Ages* (Cambridge, 1985).

SIRKES, JOEL, *Bayit ḥadash* [commentary on Jacob ben Asher, *Arba'ah turim*, printed in standard edns.].

SMITH, JOSEPH, *The Pearl of Great Price* (Salt Lake City, Utah, 1981).

SMITH, MORTON, *Studies in the Cult of Ya-hweh* (Leiden, 1996).

SOFER, MOSES, *She'elot uteshuvot ḥatam sofer* (Jerusalem, 1970).

—— *Torat mosheh* (New York, 1967).

SOFER, SHABETAI, *Sidur shabetai sofer*, ed. Y. Satz and D. Yitshaki, vol. ii (Baltimore, Md., 1994).

SOFER, SIMEON, *Igerot soferim* (Tel Aviv, 1970).

SOFER, YA'AKOV HAYIM, *Torat ya'akov* (Jerusalem, 2001).

—— *Yeḥi yosef* (Jerusalem, 1991).

SOLOMON BEN ABRAHAM OF MONTPELLIER, 'No. 7: A Copy of the Letter Sent by the Great Scholar Rabbi Solomon bar Abraham . . . on the Controversy between them and the Sages of Bedersi' (Heb.), in J. Kobak (ed.), 'Milḥemet hadat', *Jeschurun*, 8 (1875), 98–102.

SOLOMON BEN ADRET, *She'elot uteshuvot harashba* (Jerusalem, 1997).

—— *She'elot uteshuvot harashba hameyuḥasot leramban* (Warsaw, 1883).

—— *Teshuvot harashba*, ed. H. Z. Dimitrovsky, 2 vols. (Jerusalem, 1990).

SOLOVEITCHIK, ELIJAH, *Kol kore* (Jerusalem, 1985).

SOLOVEITCHIK, HAYM, 'Maimonides' *Iggeret Ha-Shemad:* Law and Rhetoric', in Leo Landman (ed.), *Rabbi Joseph H. Lookstein Memorial Volume* (New York, 1980), 281–319.

SOLOVEITCHIK, ISAAC ZE'EV, *Hidushei hagriz al hashas* (Jerusalem, 1967).

SONNE, ISAIAH, 'A Scrutiny of the Charges of Forgery against Maimonides' "Letter on Resurrection"', *PAAJR* 21 (1952), 101–17.

SPARKA, JOEL JACOB, *Yesodei ha'emunah* (Oak Park, Ill., 1986).

SPERBER, DANIEL, *Minhagei yisra'el*, vol. ii (Jerusalem, 1991).

SPERBER, DAVID, 'Future Sacrifices in the Teachings of Rabbi Abraham Isaac Kook' (Heb.), in Samuel Sperber, *Ra'ayot hare'iyah* (Jerusalem, 1992), 97–112.

SPIEGEL, YA'AKOV SHMUEL, *Pages in the History of the Hebrew Book* [Amudim batoledot hasefer ha'ivri] (Ramat Gan, 1996).

SPRECHER, SHELOMOH, 'The Controversy over the Recital of *Makhnisei raḥamim*' (Heb.), *Yeshurun*, 3 (1997), 706–29.

STAUB, JACOB J., *The Creation of the World According to Gersonides* (Chico, Calif., 1982).

STEINER, S., 'Linguistic Features of the Commentary on Ezekiel and the Minor Prophets in the Hebrew Scrolls from Byzantium' (Heb.), *Leshonenu*, 59 (1996), 39–56.

STEINSALZ, ADIN, 'Where Do Torah and Science Clash?', *TUMJ* 5 (1994), 156–67.

STEINSCHNEIDER, MORITZ, *Jewish Literature from the Eighth to the Eighteenth Century* (London, 1857).

STERN, DAVID, '*Imitatio Hominis*: Anthropomorphism and the Character(s) of God in Rabbinic Literature', *Prooftexts*, 12 (1992), 151–74.

STERN, ELIEZER, *Ishim vekivunim* (Ramat Gan, 1987).

STERN, GREGG, 'Menahem ha-Meiri and the Second Controversy over Philosophy' (Ph.D. diss., Harvard University, 1995).

STERN, JOSEPH ZEKHARIAH, *Tahalukhot ha'agadah* (Warsaw, 1902).

STERN, SHMUEL ELIEZER (ed.), *Me'orot harishonim* (Jerusalem, 2002).

STERNBUCH, MOSES, *Teshuvot vehanhagot*, vol. iv (Jerusalem, 2002).

STRAUSS, LEO, 'How to Begin to Study the *Guide of the Perplexed*', introd. essay to Shlomo Pines, *The Guide of the Perplexed* (Chicago, 1963), pp. xi–lvi.

—— *Persecution and the Art of Writing* (Chicago, 1952).

STROUMSA, GEDALIAHU G., 'Form(s) of God: Some Notes on Metatron and Christ', *HTR* 76 (1983), 269–88.

STROUMSA, SARAH, *The Origins of the Maimonidean Controversy in the East* [Reshito shel polmos harambam bemizraḥ] (Jerusalem, 1999).

SUKENIK, E. L., *The Ancient Synagogue of Beth Alpha* (Hildesheim, 1975).

—— *The Synagogue of Dura Europos and its Wall-Paintings* [Beit hakeneset shel dura europos vetsiyurav] (Jerusalem, 1947).

SUSSMAN, LANCE J., *Isaac Leeser and the Making of American Judaism* (Detroit, Mich., 1995).

SWARTZ, MICHAEL D., *Scholastic Magic: Ritual and Revelation in Early Jewish Mysticism* (Princeton, NJ, 1996).

—— 'Scribal Magic and Rhetoric: Formal Patterns in Medieval Hebrew and Aramaic Incantation Texts from the Geniza', *HTR* 83 (1990), 163–80.

SWEETMAN, J. WINDROW, *Islam and Christian Theology* (London, 1967).

SWICHKOW, LOUIS J., and LLOYD P. GARTNER, *The History of the Jews of Milwaukee* (Philadelphia, Pa., 1963).

TAENZER, ARNOLD, *Die Religionsphilosophie Joseph Albos* (Pressburg, 1896).

TAKU, MOSES, *Ketav tamim*, ed. Joseph Dan (Jerusalem, 1984).

—— *Ketav tamim*, ed. Raphael Kirchheim, *Otsar neḥmad*, 3 (1860), 54–99.

TA-SHMA, ISRAEL M., 'Bible Criticism in Early Medieval France and Germany' (Heb.), in Sarah Japhet (ed.), *Hamikra bire'i meforshav* (Jerusalem, 1994), 453–9.

—— *Talmudic Commentary in Europe and North Africa* [Hasifrut haparshanit latalmud be'eiropah uvetsafon afrikah], 2 vols. (Jerusalem, 1999).

—— 'Open Bible Criticism in an Anonymous Commentary on the Book of Psalms' (Heb.), *Tarbiz*, 66 (1997), 417–23.

—— 'R. Isaiah of Trani's *Sefer nimukei ḥumash*' (Heb.), *Kiryat sefer*, 64 (1992–3), 751–3.

—— '*Sefer Ha-Maskil*: An Unknown Hebrew Book from the Thirteenth Century' (Heb.), *Meḥkerei yerushalayim bemaḥshevet yisra'el*, 2 (1983), 416–38.

TEDESCHI, MOSES, *Ho'il mosheh* (Livorno, 1881).

TEICHER, J. L., 'A Literary Forgery: *Ma'amar tehiyat hametim*' (Heb.), *Melilah*, 1 (1944), 81–92.

TISHBY, ISAIAH, *Wisdom of the Zohar*, trans. David Goldstein, 3 vols. (Oxford, 1989).

TOBI, YOSEF, 'Who Was the Author of *Emunat hashem?*' (Heb.), *Da'at*, 49 (2002), 87–98.

TOLEDANO, MOSES, *Hashamayim hahadashim* (Casablanca, 1939).

TOV, EMANUEL, *Textual Criticism of the Hebrew Bible* (Minneapolis, Minn., 1992).

TRACHTENBERG, JOSHUA, *Jewish Magic and Superstition* (New York, 1939).

TRANI, MOSES BEN JOSEPH, *Beit elokim* (Jerusalem, 1985).

TRITTON, A. S., *Muslim Theology* (Bristol, 1947).

TSALAH, YAHYA, *Piskei maharits*, ed. Yitshak Ratsaby, 6 vols. (Benei Berak, 1993).

TSEROR, RAFA'EL YEDIDYAH SHELOMOH, *Dinei minhagei kehilah kedoshah arjil* (Jerusalem, 1985).

TSEVI ELIMELEKH OF DYNÓW, *Benei yisakhar* (New York, 1971).

—— *Ma'ayan haganim* [commentary on Joseph Yavets, *Or hahayim*] (Lublin, 1926).

TSURIEL, MOSHE, *Masoret seyag latorah*, 3 vols. (Benei Berak, 1990).

TURNER, MASHA, 'The Patriarch Abraham in the Thought of Maimonides' (Heb.), in Moshe Halamish et al. (eds.), *Avraham avi hama'aminim* (Ramat Gan, 2002), 143–54.

TWERSKY, ISADORE, 'Did Ibn Ezra Influence Maimonides?' (Heb.), in id. and Jay M. Harris (eds.), *Rabbi Abraham Ibn Ezra: Studies in the Writings of a Twelfth-Century Jewish Polymath* (Cambridge, Mass., 1993), 21–48 (Hebrew section).

—— (ed.), *Introduction to the Code of Maimonides* (New Haven, Conn., 1980).

—— *Rabad of Posquières* (Cambridge, Mass., 1962).

—— (ed.), *Studies in Medieval Jewish History and Literature*, 2 vols. (Cambridge, Mass., 1979, 1984).

—— and JAY M. HARRIS (eds.), *Rabbi Abraham Ibn Ezra: Studies in the Writings of a Twelfth-Century Jewish Polymath* (Cambridge, Mass., 1993).

TZARTZA, SAMUEL, *Mekor hayim* (Mantua, 1559).

ULRICH, EUGENE, *The Dead Sea Scrolls and the Origins of the Bible* (Leiden, 1999).

UNTERMAN, ISSER YEHUDAH, *Shevet miyehudah*, vol. iii (Jerusalem, 1994).

URBACH, EPHRAIM E., *Ba'alei hatosafot* (Jerusalem, 1980).

—— *From the World of the Sages* [Me'olamam shel hakhamim] (Jerusalem, 1988).

—— *The Sages*, trans. Israel Abrahams (Cambridge, Mass., 1997).

VAJDA, GEORGES, 'An Analysis of the *Ma'amar Yiqqawu ha-Mayim* by Samuel b. Judah Ibn Tibbon', *JJS* 10 (1959), 137–49.

—— *Le Commentaire d'Ezra de Gérona sur le Cantique des Cantiques* (Paris, 1969).

VARGON, SHMUEL, 'The Identity and Period of the Author of Ecclesiastes according to S. D. Luzzatto', *Iyunei mikra ufarshanut*, 5 (Ramat Gan, 2000).

VILNA GAON, *see* ELIJAH BEN SOLOMON ZALMAN

VITAL, HAYIM, *Peri ets ḥayim* (Tel Aviv, 1966).

VITERBO, ABRAHAM HAYIM, *Emunat ḥakhamim*, in Eliezer Ashkenazi (ed.), *Ta'am zekenim* (Frankfurt, 1854), 19–49.

WALDENBERG, ELIEZER, *Tsits eli'ezer*, vol. xiv (Jerusalem, 1985).

WARHAFTIG, ITAMAR, 'The Messiah Son of David and Solomon' (Heb.), in id. (ed.), *Minḥah le'ish* (Jerusalem, 1991), 414–27.

—— (ed.) *Minḥah le'ish* (Jerusalem, 1991).

—— 'Notes on Maimonides' Thirteen Principles of Faith' (Heb.), *Hama'ayan*, 30 (Tishrei 5750 [Oct. 1989]), 12–18.

WASSERMAN, ELHANAN BUNEM, *Kovets ma'amarim* (Jerusalem, 1963).

WAXMAN, MEYER, 'Maimonides as Dogmatist', *CCAR Yearbook*, 45 (1935), 397–418.

—— *Selected Writings* [Ketavim nivḥarim] (New York, 1943).

WEINBERG, JEHIEL JACOB, *Seridei esh*, 4 vols. (Jerusalem, 1977).

—— 'Über Opferwesen und Opfergebete', *Die Jüdische Presse*, 21, 28 Dec. 1917; 4, 11 Jan. 1918.

WEINBERG, JOANNA, 'Azaria de' Rossi and the Forgeries of Annius of Viterbo', in David Ruderman (ed.), *Essential Papers on Jewish Culture in Renaissance and Baroque Italy* (New York, 1992), 252–79.

WEINBERG, YAAKOV, *Fundamentals and Faith* (Southfield, Mich., 1991).

WEINBERGER, BERISH (ed.), *Igerot shapirin* (Brooklyn, NY, 1983).

WENSINCK, A. J., *The Muslim Creed: Its Genesis and Historical Development* (London, 1965).

WERBLOWSKY, R. J. Z., *Joseph Karo: Lawyer and Mystic* (Oxford, 1962).

WILENSKY, MORDECHAI, *Ḥasidim umitnagdim*, 2 vols. (Jerusalem, 1970).

WILLIAMS, JOHN ALDEN, *The Word of Islam* (Austin, Tex., 1994).

WISCHNITZER-BERNSTEIN, RACHEL, 'Jewish Pictorial Art in the Classical Period', in Cecil Roth (ed.), *Jewish Art* (New York, 1961), 191–224.

WOLFSON, ELLIOT R., *Abraham Abulafia: Kabbalist and Prophet* (Los Angeles, 2000).

—— 'God, the Demiurge and the Intellect: On the Usage of the Word *Kol* in Abraham Ibn Ezra', *REJ* 149 (1990), 77–111.

—— *Through a Speculum that Shines: Vision and Imagination in Medieval Jewish Mysticism* (Princeton, NJ, 1994).

WOLFSON, HARRY A., 'Escaping Judaism', *Menorah Journal*, 7 (June, 1921), 71–83, 155–68.

—— *Philo*, 2 vols. (Cambridge, Mass., 1947).

—— *The Philosophy of the Kalam* (Cambridge, Mass., 1976).

—— *Repercussions of the Kalam in Jewish Philosophy* (Cambridge, Mass., 1979).

—— *Studies in the History of Philosophy and Religion*, 2 vols. (Cambridge, Mass., 1973, 1977).

WORMS, AARON, *Me'orei or: Kan tahor* (Metz, 1831).

YADLER, ISAAC TSEVI ZE'EV, *Tiferet tsiyon* (Jerusalem, 1962).

Yalkut hamakhiri on Zechariah, ed. A. W. Greenup (London, 1909).

Yalkut shimoni, 2 vols. (Jerusalem, 1967).

YAVETS, JOSEPH, *Or haḥayim* (Lublin, 1926).

YOLLES, ZECHARIAH ISAIAH, *Hatorah vehaḥokhmah* (Vilna, 1913).

YOSEF, OVADIAH, *Yabia omer*, 9 vols. (Jerusalem, 1986–2000).

—— *Yehaveh da'at*, 6 vols. (Jerusalem, 1977–84).

YOSHA, NISSIM, 'The Philosophical Background of Sabbatian Theology: Guidelines towards an Understanding of Abraham Miguel Cardozo' (Heb.), in A. Mirsky et al. (eds.), *Galut aḥar golah* (Jerusalem, 1988), 541–71.

—— 'The Philosophical Foundations of the Theology of Abraham Michael Cardozo' [Hayesodot hafilosofiyim batorah ha'elohut shel avraham mikha'el kardozo] (Ph.D. diss., Hebrew University, 1985).

ZACHTER, J. S., 'The Roke'ah's Responsum Concerning "Makhnisei Raḥamim"', *Yeshurun*, 3 (1997), 41–6.

ZAVIHI, PINHAS, *Ateret paz*, vol. ii (Jerusalem, 1995).

ZIMMELS, H. J., 'The Manuscript Hamburg Cod. Hebr. 45 and its Attribution to R. Avigdor Katz' (Heb.), *Abhandlungen zur Erinnerung an Hirsch Perez Chajes* (Vienna, 1933), 248–61.

ZIMMER, YITSHAK (ERIC), *Olam keminhago noheg* (Jerusalem, 1996).

ZIONI, MENAHEM, *Commentary on the Torah* [Perush al hatorah] (Jerusalem, 1964).

ZIPOR, MOSHE A., *On Transmission and Tradition* [Al mesirah vemasoret] (Tel Aviv, 2001).

Zohar, ed. R. Margaliyot (Jerusalem, 1984).

ZUNZ, LEOPOLD, *Die synagogale Poesie des Mittelalters* (Hildesheim, 1967).

Index of Biblical and Rabbinic References

General Index